Decisionmaking in a Glass House

Mass Media, Public Opinion, and American and European Foreign Policy in the 21st Century

Edited by
Brigitte L. Nacos, Robert Y. Shapiro,
and Pierangelo Isernia

ROWMAN & LITTLEFIELD PUBLISHERS, INC.
Lanham • Boulder • New York • Oxford

ROWMAN & LITTLEFIELD PUBLISHERS, INC.

Published in the United States of America
by Rowman & Littlefield Publishers, Inc.
4720 Boston Way, Lanham, Maryland 20706
http://www.rowmanlittlefield.com

12 Hid's Copse Road, Cumnor Hill, Oxford OX2 9JJ, England

British Library Cataloguing in Publication Information Available

Library of Congress Cataloging-in-Publication Data
Decisionmaking in a glass house : mass media, public opinion, and American and
European foreign policy in the 21st century / edited by Brigitte L. Nacos, Robert Y.
Shapiro, and Pierangelo Isernia.
     p. cm.
     Includes bibliographical references and index.
     ISBN 0-8476-9826-2 (cloth : alk. paper)—ISBN 0-8476-9827-0 (pbk. : alk. paper)
     1. Mass media and public opinion.   2. World politics—1989–   I. Nacos, Brigitte
Lebens.   II. Shapiro, Robert Y., 1953–   III. Isernia, Pierangelo.
P96.P83 D43   2000
302.23—dc21   00-035294

Printed in the United States of America

⊗ ™ The paper used in this publication meets the minimum requirements of American
National Standard for Information Sciences—Permanence of Paper for Printed Library
Materials, ANSI/NISO Z39.48–1992.

Contents

Preface

The objective of *Decisionmaking in a Glass House: Mass Media, Public Opinion, and Foreign Policy in the 21ˢᵗ Century* is to broaden attention and debate about the roles of public opinion and mass media in international policymaking in the post–Cold War era and beyond. Combining the research expertise of leading European and American scholars, this book examines continuity and change in mass media and public opinion in relation to foreign policymaking on both sides of the Atlantic. While there are clear differences in the foreign policy processes in the U.S. presidential system and in Western European democracies, this book is one of the first joint efforts by scholars to enhance our understanding of the new realities by explaining the interconnections between the mass media, public opinion, and foreign policymaking. Scholarly research has revealed much about the nature and formation of public opinion, predominant patterns found in the press's reporting of foreign policy issues, and the intricate relationships between and among the mass media, public opinion, and foreign policymaking in the United States and other Western democracies. Most of our knowledge on these matters at the end of the twentieth century has been based on research conducted during the Cold War period, with the primary focus on public opinion, the press, and policymaking in the United States.

ACKNOWLEDGMENTS

The origin for the book was a conference: "Public Opinion, the Mass Media, and European and American Foreign Policy," held at the Italian Academy for Advanced Studies in America at Columbia University on November 19–20, 1998. The conference brought together prominent American and European scholars who presented formal papers to the Columbia University community and other attendees. In addition to the editors, the Americans who presented papers or participated as formal discussants included Richard C. Eichenberg, Robert M. Entman, Steven Kull and Clay Ramsay, Eugene R. Wittkopf and Ronald Hinckley, Richard Sobel, John Zaller, Benjamin I. Page, Ole Holsti, and Eric Shiraev. The European participants included Wolfgang Donsbach, Philip Everts, Maurizio Cotta, Natalie La Balme, Martin Shaw, Giacomo Sani, and Richard Sinnott. The conference concluded with a roundtable that also included Dott. Piero Benedetto Francese, Permanent Representative of the Italian Mission to the United Nations; the Honorable Giangiacomo Migone, President of the Italian Senate Foreign Affairs Committee; and American scholars Bruce Russett, Joseph La Palombara, and Michael Janeway (who also served as moderator). We thank these colleagues for their participation.

We are most grateful to the sponsors of the conference for their support and assistance: The Italian Academy for Advanced Studies in America, which participates in diverse intellectual activities on the Columbia campus and in New York City, and which spearheaded the conference and provided the additional support to produce this volume; the Universita di Siena; Monte dei Paschi di Siena; the Italian Fulbright Commission; and *Political Science Quarterly* (the principal publication of the Academy of Political Science). From Columbia University in New York, support was provided by the Paul F. Lazarsfeld Center for the Social Sciences (now part of the Institute for Social and Economic Research and Policy), the School of International and Public Affairs, the Graduate School of Journalism, and the Earth Institute.

In these organizations at the time of the conference, thanks go to Richard Brilliant (Director, the Italian Academy for Advanced Studies in America, and Professor, Columbia University), Andrea Bartoli (Associate Director, the Italian Academy), Piero Tosi (Rettore, Universita di Siena), Demetrios (Jim) Caraley (Editor, *Political Science Quarterly*; President, the Academy of Political Science; and Professor, Barnard College and Columbia University), Lisa Anderson (Dean, School of International and Public Affairs), Harrison White (Director, the Paul F. Lazarsfeld Center), James Carey (Professor, Graduate School of Journalism), and Peter Eisenberger (Vice Provost/Director, the Earth Institute).

We are also grateful to the following individuals who provided support for the conferences: Michael and Charlene Prounis, James E. Nacos, Frederick P. and Sandra P. Rose, and John and Julie Nacos.

We owe special thanks for help in organizing the conference to the indispensable Kathleen Madden of the Italian Academy and to Debra Gilchrest of the Lazarsfeld Center, David Park, and Aida Llabaly.

In addition to being a contributor, Natasha Hritzuk expertly assisted in putting together the volume, as did Amitabh Dubey and, especially, Serban Iorga and Oscar Torres-Reyna. Last, we thank Brenda Hadenfeldt at Rowman & Littlefield.

Chapter 5 is reprinted with revisions from "Government's Little Helper: Press Coverage of Foreign Policy Crises, 1945–1991." *Political Communication* 13, no. 4 (1996): 385–406. Reprinted with permission.

Chapter 8 is reprinted with revisions from Richard Ullman, *The World and Yugoslavia's Wars* (New York: Council on Foreign Relations, 1996). Reprinted with permission.

1

Old or New Ball Game?

Mass Media, Public Opinion, and Foreign Policy in the Post–Cold War World

Brigitte L. Nacos, Robert Y. Shapiro, and Pierangelo Isernia

During the nearly five decades of the Cold War, the containment of Soviet power was the guiding light of American and Western European foreign policy. The Cold War provided a powerful national-interest frame of reference for political leaders, the press, and public opinion in the United States and Western Europe. Indeed, much of what we know about the predominant patterns in news reporting about foreign affairs, the nature and formation of public opinion, and the intricate relationships involving the mass media, public attitudes, and foreign policymaking is based on research conducted during the Cold War era.

The demise of the Soviet Union and the crumbling of East-West division brought about fundamental changes in national concerns for foreign policy in the United States, Europe, and elsewhere. No longer preoccupied with real or potential Cold War threats, foreign policymakers at the threshold of the twenty-first century faced a myriad of regional conflicts, the problems associated with peace-enforcing operations, humanitarian missions, the struggle against international terrorism, and the proliferation of weapons of mass destruction, as well as a host of global and regional issues such as trade, immigration, poverty, health, and the environment. These very different problems and the wide range of debatable policy options are not conducive to reaching broad consensus on overriding national interests, as occurred during critical periods of the Cold War and World War II. Thus, while for most of the twentieth century clear differences existed between the typically partisan domestic and commonly bipartisan foreign policy processes in the United States, these boundaries seem to have faded during the 1990s, when the politics of foreign policymaking became more like domestic partisan politics. The absence of a foreign policy consensus in the United States as well as in other NATO countries, most notably among foreign policy elites, was especially striking before, during, and after the 1999 Kosovo crisis and NATO's air strikes against Serbia.

Moreover, while the United States and European NATO members cooperated during several crises and wars, such as those in Kosovo, Bosnia, Somalia, and the Persian Gulf, American and Western European priorities and international interests shifted at the end of the twentieth century. Agreement on major foreign-affairs issues was no longer as common among the longtime Western allies as it was during the post–World War II years.

As the breakup of the Soviet Union and the Eastern bloc brought about new and uncertain international conditions and problems, great transformations took place in communications and in the size and reach of multinational media corporations. While cable and satellite television and the Internet had been utilized earlier, the breakthrough of both TV and Internet as truly global mass media occurred during the last dozen years of the twentieth century. Just as the growing prominence of television news beginning in the 1960s and live satellite transmission affected the international flow of information and foreign policymaking, there is reason to expect similar consequences from the increasing traffic on the ever-expanding global information superhighway.

When they cite the "Vietnam syndrome," civilian and military leaders in the United States and Europe refer to the media's—and especially television's—power to turn domestic public opinion against military conflicts by dwelling on the visual images of the victims of war. By contrast, the "CNN effect" pointed to the ability of the first truly global television network to inform the public instantly and continuously of news from anywhere in the world and thereby force national decisionmakers to deal with the reported problems and issues quickly—often without sufficient time to deliberate. From the experiences during the Kosovo crisis, we suggest the advent of the "Internet syndrome": when newspapers and radio stations in Kosovo were shut down by Serbian leaders, and Western journalists' reports were banned, information reached the rest of the world by e-mail and through numerous Internet sites, message boards, and chat rooms. The Kosovo military conflict was called the "first Internet war." Short of totally cutting off telephone lines in the province, the Belgrade regime was simply unable to stop the flow to the outside world of uncensored information from hideouts in Kosovo. This denied Serbian President Slobodan Milosevic and his government full media control for their propaganda, just as critics of NATO's air war were successful in temporarily disabling the official propaganda website at NATO headquarters.[1] In short, the Internet as a global medium denies authoritarian and democratic governments alike control over the flow of information.

In light of the new geopolitical realities and problems on the one hand and ongoing transformations in international communications on the other, this volume explores the degree to which these changes have affected, and perhaps altered, the media's behavior, public opinion, and foreign policymaking in the United States and Europe. Specifically, we ask to what extent have shifts in news reporting and global communications affected the information available to the mass public and the influence of these publics on foreign policy. How does this influence compare to the ability of national leaders and decisionmakers to mold and lead public opinion and to thereby control the policymaking process? Is the foreign policy process in the twenty-first century more transparent than in the past? Does it now require, in essence, decisionmaking in a glass house?

The dominance of government news beats and "official sources" in foreign policy coverage during the Cold War has been well documented. Robert Entman's provocative analysis (Chapter 2) suggests that the breakdown of the Cold War consensus has heightened the independent capacity of the American media to frame foreign policy news at the expense of political elites. Instead of taking a lead from the Cold War "national interest" frame expressed by policymakers, foreign-affairs reporting has appeared to increasingly offer independent judgments and interpretations. If so, this would be a fundamental shift from past reporting patterns that John Zaller and Dennis Chiu (Chapter 5) substantiate with respect to foreign policy crises from 1945 to 1991. They found that the media took a cue from congressional leaders (and presumably other governmental leaders) and "indexed" their coverage to reflect and magnify the range of views expressed within government in the face of military conflicts or the threat of war. But while these authors did not find such "indexing" characteristics when they examined media reporting on foreign policy crises after the end of the Cold War, there is also evidence that the old "indexing" patterns are alive and well in the post–Cold War news coverage of foreign crises (Mermin 1999).

According to Entman, however, the end of the Cold War consensus deprived American leaders of the compelling story line about the "evil empire" that also satisfied the media's appetite for drama and conflict. As a result, the contemporary mass media seek out dramatic, tragic, and conflict-filled stories that they can report through striking visuals, such as those of starving children in Somalia or captured GIs in Belgrade. Of course, the press—and especially television news—did not only recently discover the power of visuals. The impact of the pictures that documented the attacks on peaceful civil-rights marchers in the U.S. South in the 1960s and the pictures of American hostages held in Tehran, Beirut, and elsewhere in the 1980s attests to this. Thus, the very real increase of visuals in foreign policy news has more likely been a consequence of the proliferation of TV channels and the increase in competition in the communications industry than the result of the media's greater independence.

Entman's hypothesis that the emerging autonomy of the post–Cold War media has diminished the influence of government leaders over foreign policy news—and thus over public opinion—differs from Robert Shapiro and Larry Jacobs's conclusion (Chapter 14) that the complexities of the new world order have in fact enhanced presidents' opportunities to lead—and manipulate—public opinion. However, Martin Shaw's innovative theory about the media, the public, and governments, together with his case studies (Chapter 3) helps to bridge this discrepancy. For Shaw, the mass media are providers of global public spaces over which national governments have increasingly lost control, as well as political actors with interests and biases in both the domestic and international arenas. Entman's model of the media liberated from acting as "government's little helpers" is certainly compatible with Shaw's concept of the media as international public spaces that cannot be controlled by national governments. Nothing makes that clearer than the "Internet syndrome." But Shaw's case studies also show that during the conflicts involving Iraq and, more recently, Kosovo, television, radio, and print media also took on the roles of political actors highlighting the positions of domestic officials or those speaking for NATO or the United Nations. As the new century arrived, then, presidents, prime ministers, and other high officials have continued to receive ample media access and opportunities to lead public opinion—if only because of the press's tendency to cover official sources prominently and the fierce competition among the growing number of profit-seeking media outlets. As Shaw sees it, "The same media that figure in one context as entertainment commodities and vehicles for corporate profit, appear in another as instruments of state policy, and in yet another as representatives of an emergent global-democratic civil society."

During the Cold War and even thereafter, most research on public opinion, the media, and foreign policy has focused overwhelmingly on crises involving military actions, the threat of war, and important security and defense issues. But after the Cold War, conflicts have arisen just as often—if not more so—in areas such as trade, the environment, and the economic and political gap between rich and poor countries. In comparing American and German coverage of the global-warming issue, Brigitte Nacos, Robert Shapiro, Natasha Hritzuk, and Bruce Chadwick (Chapter 4) synthesize the approaches taken by Entman, Zaller/Chiu, and Shaw. Their expectation, however—that the global public sphere created by the media should have resulted in similar patterns of news reporting in comparable industrialized democracies such as the United States and Germany—was not borne out. In spite of the predominance of multinational news organizations, the American and German media "indexed" and framed the news about global warming before, during, and after the 1997 conference on climate change in Kyoto, Japan, according to their country's specific domestic context. While the study of this particular issue confirmed Entman's hypothesis of American officials losing influence over how foreign policy news is reported, this does not necessarily mean that the president's influence is diminished. In the case of the Kyoto conference, President Bill Clinton simply did not make a great effort to use the media to mold domestic public opinion.

Entman observes within his new theoretical framework that the media perpetuate the myth about what he calls "perceived public opinion"—"the general sense of the public's opinions that is held by most observers, including journalists and politicians, and members of the public themselves." This question of whether foreign policymakers correctly perceive the parameters of public opinion is central to Steven Kull and Clay Ramsay's research (Chapter 7). By comparing the views and perceptions of eighty-three members of the U.S. foreign policy establishment with systematic polling data, Kull and Ramsay found significant discrepancies on a host of important foreign policy issues. Natalie La Balme (Chapter 16) and Pierangelo Isernia (Chapter 17) describe how French and Italian decisionmakers also depend heavily on what amounts to "perceived opinion," relying on the mass media and information sources other than more direct measures of public opinion.

In the new order—or disorder—of the post–Cold War world, in which there may not be clear-cut national interests and foreign policy doctrines, policymakers may be especially tempted to follow such perceptions of public opinion that may not be based on the most valid and reliable sources. Fearing the consequences of military engagements, especially according to the "body-bag thesis," decisionmakers may indeed act—out of uncertainty and caution—on misperceptions of public opinion. Philip Everts (Chapter 11) sees this happening in peacekeeping and other humanitarian missions, as well as in cases of responses to aggression or other conflict. Utilizing extensive survey data, Richard Sobel (Chapter 8) examines public attitudes in the United States and Western Europe toward intervention in Bosnia and Kosovo in the 1990s. Contrasting the relatively strong public backing of multinational intervention in the United States and Europe, with the weak U.S. and European responses, Sobel explores the reasons for this discrepancy between public support for intervention in the Balkans and governments' reluctance to intervene militarily. Isernia presents data from Italy that confirm this gap between the public's interventionist attitudes and decisionmakers' greater reluctance.

These discrepancies in recent cases do not square with the American elites' generally stronger and the American public's weaker support for a prominent U.S. role in international affairs. Looking at this gap between public and elite attitudes, Eugene Wittkopf and Ronald Hinckley (Chapter 9) examine whether domestic factors generally affect the public's foreign policy attitudes more than elite opinion.

While differences between public and elite opinions exist, the notion that the end of the Cold War has fundamentally altered public attitudes toward international affairs, peace, and security, especially specific foreign and defense policies in the United States and Western Europe, is contradicted by Richard Eichenberg (Chapter 10) and Philip Everts (Chapter 11). While tracing some changes in the 1990s, they found more stability than change in Western Europeans' support for a common European security policy and NATO and, in the case of the Netherlands, for the necessity of armed forces. Richard Sinnott (Chapter 15) traced growing support for centralized European decisionmaking in matters of defense in some European countries, and he found shifts in favor of national defense policies in others. Moreover, his data reveal that public support for European integration had declined since late 1991.

Eric Shiraev and Vlad Zubok (Chapter 12) provide a groundbreaking analysis of post–Cold War Russia. They are especially concerned with events that involved the United States and Western Europe on one side and Russia on the other: the expansion of NATO and the Balkan conflicts in the last years of the twentieth century. The authors describe how the bombing of Serbia by NATO forces in 1999 at the height of the Kosovo conflict markedly strengthened anti-Western sentiments in Russia.

Students of the complex behavioral relationships involving the media, the public, and policymaking must eventually wonder whether and how decisionmakers are affected by public opinion and, specifically, to what extent political leaders follow or lead it. After examining the European public's evaluations of integration, public knowledge of European Union politics, and voter turnout in European parliamentary elections, Sinnott concludes unequivocally that since 1990 public opinion has affected the politics of European integration. Shapiro and Jacobs, Isernia, and La Balme demonstrate that this opinion-policy linkage is multifaceted. Thus, while Shapiro and Jacobs observe that American policymakers had for a time become more responsive to public opinion, the end of the Cold War and the complexities of post–Cold War foreign policy issues have in different ways enhanced presidents' opportunities to shape public opinion.

In the very different political systems found throughout Western Europe, the relationships between and among the media, public opinion, and government policies are less transparent than in the United States. In a party state like Italy, as Isernia reminds us, the media provide less of a link between the government and the people than a means of communication among party leaders and political elites. Thus, in the case of the Bosnian crisis, Italian decisionmakers reacted "to the events in Bosnia as perceived on the basis of media coverage rather than public opinion." Similarly, based on extensive interviews with foreign policy officials in France, La Balme concludes that the impact of public opinion on French foreign policy has been limited and has depended mostly on decisionmakers' inclinations to follow or not follow public preferences. Even when massive media coverage of events or developments heightens decisionmakers' attentiveness to public opinion, they tend to base their perceptions of public opinion on sources other than the results of opinion surveys.

Commenting on leading American scholarship on the media, public opinion, and the Gulf War, Bernard C. Cohen has suggested that "real advances in theoretical development with respect to the media and foreign policy will ultimately depend on our looking at more countries, rather than just at more cases."[2] This volume takes an important step in following Cohen's suggestion, looking closely at a half-dozen countries as well as developments within the European Union and NATO. Indeed, in the age of global communication, scholars and other political analysts need to pay persistent attention to developments abroad in order to better illuminate what evolves at home. Clearly, this research needs to be continued.

Conspicuously missing from this volume is a systematic examination of the Internet as it may relate to foreign policy information and public opinion. While the traditional media (newspapers, news magazines, radio, and, especially, television) remain for the time being the dominant news sources for the mass public and policymakers, future research must pay increasing attention to the content and impact of emerging types of media.

This volume is divided into three parts: "The Media and Foreign Policy" (Chapters 2–6); "Public and Elite Attitudes after the Cold War" (Chapters 7–13); and "The Public Opinion-Foreign Policy Connection" (Chapters 14–18). Benjamin Page, Ole Holsti, and Eric Shiraev review the contributions in each part, respectively.

I

THE MEDIA AND FOREIGN POLICY

2

Declarations of Independence
The Growth of Media Power after the Cold War

Robert M. Entman

The post–Cold War era in international affairs truly began not in 1989 but in 1991, with the Coalition victory in the Gulf War against Iraq. Though that military triumph was heralded as a harbinger of a "new world order," it was more likely an anomaly. It combined forces and elements that may not coalesce very often in the future: The credibility of an American president's attempt to demonize a small state; the seemingly clear national interest in preserving access to oil; the former rival superpower, the Soviet Union, actually allying with the United States; and a relatively clear path to victory. The norm in the future is more likely to resemble the cases discussed in this chapter: Bosnia, Kosovo, and Somalia. In these cases, things were *dis*orderly on the ground, in the mass media, and in the public mind. Since the Gulf War, defining and defending "national interest" has become more difficult, security threats less direct, more diffused and hypothetical. What marks the post-1991 period especially is the disappearance of the anchoring frame around the Cold War.

What exactly do we mean by breakdown of the Cold War frame,[1] and how does it affect relationships among the news media, the public, and government? The core of this chapter's argument is that the demise of the Cold War may heighten the media's power,[2] rendering previous theories of media, public opinion, and foreign policy problematic both empirically and normatively.[3]

This chapter advances six hypotheses that describe important changes in the relationships among media, "public opinion," and foreign policy. These are assumed to have arisen in current conditions; they are not presumed permanent. In the new, uncertain epoch, we should not expect permanent traits. But taken together, these hypotheses, if true, would herald an increase in independent media influence over the foreign policy process. This chapter does not "prove" or provide systematic data analysis to test the hypotheses. Instead it sketches a general picture using examples from the events in Bosnia, Kosovo, and Somalia; other cases are not assessed, nor is all potential evidence. The validity of the picture requires testing and refinement; the chapter is an initial foray based upon uncertain and mutating—if not inchoate—relationships among human participants, institutional constraints, and unforeseeable developments.

The six interrelated developments hypothesized are:

1. With the end of convincing demons and the associated difficulty of invoking patriotism, the media become more independently powerful in defining problems for American foreign policymakers.
2. Since established frames and associative thinking do not seem to apply anymore, the media seek to fill the cognitive and emotional gap with their own theories of international relations.
3. Unmoored by consensual frames, the media impose a double bind on presidents that tends to diminish the legitimacy of their power over foreign policy: a simultaneous demand for assertive interventionist leadership by "the world's only superpower," and chastisement of U.S. leaders when interventions turn costly.
4. The media reify and promote the power of a putative "public opinion" that, because it bears only imperfect resemblance to actual public sentiments and interests, does not necessarily augment the public's representation in foreign policymaking. Rather, by raising the salience of alleged public feelings as depicted by the news, this process further increases the media's influence.
5. The mixture of information processed that affects the public, politicians, and foreign policymakers has shifted toward the inclusion of more visual data. On the often powerful visual dimensions of their messages, media can sometimes make more autonomous choices than on the verbal.
6. We can no longer generalize easily about "state" power over the media, because that power depends on which party holds the White House (and thus controls application of armed force). For several reasons, including core ideological precepts (cf. Lakoff 1996) that legitimize disciplined government control and thus media management, the Republicans may be better equipped to dominate media messages than are Democrats.

A FRAMING MODEL

This study adapts theories of information processing to suggest a frame-contestation model of news, public opinion, and government policy. Framing is selecting, highlighting, and associating elements of reality to tell a coherent story (Entman 1993). To take a simple example, framing Saddam Hussein as another Hitler invokes for most Americans a series of stored impressions, identifying Hussein as an agent of evil, the cause of grave danger to American interests, and one who must be actively opposed (cf. Dorman and Livingston, 1994).

Framing implies more slack and less direct government control over media texts and over public thinking than suggested by indexing (Bennett 1989, 1990; Bennett 1996) or hegemony (e.g., Hallin 1987; Herman and Chomsky 1988; Parenti 1993; Rachlin 1988) theories, where media are subordinate to governing elites or the state. As used here, the frame-contestation model highlights the interacting influence among media, public, and government. The media messages are framed by the government's rhetorical choices, but what the media select and highlight simultaneously influences officials' rhetorical options. Meanwhile, the media and officials shape their communications in response to perceived public opinion—that is, to the dimensions of public sentiment that are selected and highlighted for them. (More on perceived public opinion below.) And for reasons described later (Entman and Herbst 2000), "public opinion" as a force in policymaking depends heavily on media frames, on what is emphasized and what is left out of the picture. The contest to dominate the frame is now more equal than ever, and we may see news coverage that reflects no single dominant frame more frequently in the new century.

To be sure, some actors in this system, in particular the White House, have more opportunity than others to shape the frames rather than have the frames shape their thinking. But we are still speaking of a system that challenges the assumptions of both the hegemony and indexing models that government "officials," or the "state," largely control the media and through the media, public opinion.

THE END OF DEMONS AND PATRIOTISM: MEDIA AS PROBLEM DEFINERS

For analytical purposes, news coverage of foreign policy is divided into three domains: *problem*, *policy*, and *leadership*. That is, the messages that are most influential politically concern the definition of a policy problem, the discussion of policy options for handling it, and the judgment of the competence, in this case, of the American president and his administration. Whether on problem, policy, or leadership, the administration faces, more than ever, competition for control of news from journalists themselves, from other political elites, and even from "public opinion." The less anchored cognitions of the international system mean that the White House enjoys less automatic ability to control the news.

With the dissolution of the worldwide communist enemy, the main themes now are a pastiche—human suffering, lack of democracy, terrorism, instability that could cause refugee problems—rather than a tightly knit core of interrelated problems whose diagnosis and labeling symbolized the moral evaluation of evil communism and the standing remedy of U.S. vigilance (cf. Entman 1993, on the nature of framing). Ordinary Americans' interests in solving or even knowing about the new problems are diminished compared with what obtained during the Cold War. Risks and potential costs become more visible, as does uncertainty about the effectiveness or logic of remedial intervention—about the very definition of the situation.

Among its many functions, the Cold War frame served to anchor the administration's control over the problem domain. The demise of the Cold War created a void, an absence of associative links to threats against the United States that communism automatically provided. If Somalia is overrun by deeply evil "warlords," Bosnia and Kosovo beset by evil Serbs, what is it to Americans? Why, exactly, should these be *problems* for the United States?

Demonization becomes more difficult when evil regimes pose no direct threats to U.S. security and cannot plausibly be linked to the communist conspiracy and all its emotionally potent associations. We might simplify U.S. history and observe that two schemas have tugged at each other within American political culture: one supporting interventionism, the other isolation. Demonization was the engine of interventionism, and it had quite a run after World War II. The lack of a demon to threaten the United States disrupts journalists' and the public's stored associative links to the *benefits* of intervention policies. Now the salience of the stored, but often dormant, costs schema has risen.

This change renders appeals to patriotism more problematic. The White House could not call intervention in Somalia or the Balkans a patriotic duty. Even when it proposes U.S. military force against weak foes unable to inflict heavy casualties, the White House cannot in this era reliably invoke patriotism to obscure the costs and risks of intervention. That does not mean that enemies cannot be constructed, or that patriotism cannot be summoned or evoked (especially for ritualistic purposes). Terrorism and drug trafficking can substitute for the communist threat, albeit far less effectively. Humanitarian mandates for intervention are even less compelling once risks and costs are factored in. Evidence for all this inheres in the virtual disappearance from American campaign rhetoric of the formerly potent and common charge that a candidate is "soft on defense."

Without the dangerous direct enemies and certainties of the Cold War, foreign policy becomes more subjected than ever to the political gaming and strategizing long dominant in domestic politics. Elites are emboldened, able to criticize problem definitions and policy options without seeming unpatriotic. In Somalia and the Balkans, the administrations under George Bush and Bill Clinton never could construct a frame that both highlighted the dangers to the United States and constricted the policy options. For these places, the cost-risk counterframes were cognitively accessible to elites who had little reason to fear an adverse public reaction if they attacked intervention.

FILLING THE VACUUM WITH FRAMING THEORIES

Absent an overarching theory of the sort provided by the Cold War, the media seem driven to fill the vacuum. Perhaps because they trade in narrative, journalists seem constantly in search of a coherent frame: problem definitions, causes, moral judgments and remedies that fall into a consistent pattern and yield consistent meaning.

News of defense policy is suffused with the assumption that there must and can be a theory of U.S. interests and actions in the new world: that skilled policymaking can render the problems of this world as predictable, categorizable, and controllable as during the Cold War.

Foreign policy narratives frequently assume that one decision, in places like Somalia or Bosnia, betokens a decisive choice of role or category for U.S. foreign policy, rather than that the 1990s commenced a period—perhaps a very long one—of testing and groping to find a role or combination of roles for American military force and diplomacy. Thus, a subheadline in the December 14, 1992, *Newsweek* reads: "Sending troops to Somalia forces America to figure out: what are the new rules of intervention? Clinton will have to decide: should America be the world's policeman?" The story (35) asserts: "As Operation Restore Hope shaped up, new rules for humanitarian intervention were beginning to emerge, often haphazardly." Among these rules are allegedly:

- "Human suffering is a reason to act";
- "America is the world's chief of police";
- "Sometimes a regional solution is better";
- "Americans can't take charge of policing every beat"; and
- "Only attempt what's feasible."

As is hardly surprising, these "rules" are internally contradictory. Along the same lines, the story argues: "Once the precedent has been set in Somalia, it's hard to see how missions of mercy can be avoided in other large-scale threats to life." Then it says, "America is the world's chief of police. Someone has to be in charge of each military intervention, and often that will have to be the world's most powerful country." Nearly a year later, writing after the unpleasant experience of American forces in Somalia, Michael Elliot wrote in "The Making of a Fiasco," (*Newsweek*, October 18, 1993, 34): "It was a military disaster . . . and it may well have a significance in the history books. For the Somali mission was meant to be a test case for the post-cold-war world. . . . It has proved a fiasco."

Such depictions neglect the possibility that there may not be a consistent, easily deployable news narrative as during the Cold War. A media theory of the U.S. government's theory would provide an overarching and cognitively comforting schema to replace the Cold War and to help restore problem definition and remedy assessment to their former, formulaic status. The thirst for rules comes, perhaps, from the media's need for stable characters and categories to shape news narratives. It is difficult to tell a story based on constantly shifting players in a game without established rules. News narration thrives on familiar, even archetypal characters and conflicts of the sort that Cold War elites repeatedly constructed and journalists usually passed along. The yearning for theory may help explain, for example, why journalists often took seriously Bush's rhetorical invention of the new world order, even though the administration had barely analyzed it.[4]

While the hunger for rules and categories makes media vulnerable in the short term to appealing slogans like "new world order," it also establishes the potential for critical distance from the government's *policy* messages and *leadership* competence. Administrations can find themselves imprisoned by the journalistic demand for rules. Journalists move readily from reifying individual policy actions as betokening "rules" to accusing the administration of breaking them, or waffling on them. Yet these are *media*-created rules, not real policy precepts; note the criticism for "haphazard," "sloppy," and incompetent policymaking in the quoted passages. Journalistic cynicism about leaders has largely displaced the Cold War era's respectful deference.

Thus, in the media's coverage of Kosovo, little but criticism of the Clinton administration appears in many news reports. Consider *Newsweek*'s initial coverage of the NATO bombing of Kosovo and the associated controversy, featured on consecutive covers of the magazine (April 5 and 12, 1999). The tone was typified by the sarcastic assessment in the magazine's "Conventional Wisdom" section for April 5: "For weeks the [Conventional Wisdom] has been saying that there is no good end game in Yugoslavia. Turns out there was no good beginning game, either. . . . This thing is smelling like a fiasco." The cover headline of this issue was "War in Kosovo: Where Will it End?" Not one full paragraph in this issue praised Clinton's leadership or accepted Clinton's definition of the problem and remedy for it. Again and again, the narrative challenged Clinton's assumptions, discussed the risks and costs of the intervention, and cast doubt on the possibility of a positive outcome. This approach reached its height in an essay by Henry Kissinger, "Doing Injury to History," which assailed the Clinton policy for two full pages.

The April 12 issue featured a picture of three beaten American servicemen who were captured in Macedonia. The headline: " 'WE'RE TRAPPED'/HORROR AND HOSTAGES: HOW AMERICA STUMBLED INTO A NO-WIN WAR." The coverage began with a photo essay, with a headline extending over four pages of pictures: "A Tragic Exodus . . . And No Exit" (ellipsis in original). Beyond focusing in great detail on the suffering of the three (ultimately released) American prisoners, the coverage again emphasized criticism of the policy and of Clinton's leadership (including a full story on "How We Stumbled into War"). The only piece in either magazine issue that defended the bombing was an essay by Holocaust novelist Elie Wiesel, like Kissinger a member of the elite outside government, chosen by the media outlet itself. Wiesel defended the idea of attacking Slobodan Milosevic's regime, although he did not provide detailed justification of Clinton's policies. And Wiesel's piece was followed by the three-page story "How We Stumbled into War," and a one-page essay devoted to slamming Clinton (as had Kissinger the previous week) for misreading history, calling his actions "foolhardy."

The point is not that Clinton's policy deserved gentler treatment. Rather, it is that *Newsweek* (and, impressionistically, much of the other national media as well) had, far from allowing the White House hegemonic control over the framing of the Kosovo intervention, failed even to provide a balanced view. It tilted decisively against the administration. Indexing theory would have predicted at least a more equal contest between the administration and its critics. What was new here is that the media, freed of the old Cold War constraints, themselves seize opportunities to evaluate the policy, choosing sources and constructing their own frames.

When Clinton's policy actually did appear to succeed at evicting the Serb army from Kosovo and returning the Kosovar refugees home to a semblance of peace, the administration received remarkably little praise for its victory. The Kosovo success did not make even *Newsweek*'s cover (which depicted "Stress" on June 14, 1999), and the lead story on Kosovo was headed "Victory, but at a Price"—not exactly a celebratory note. *Time* magazine also did not see fit to make Kosovo the cover story, choosing instead a nontimely feature about "Heroes and Icons," and the headline on its lead Kosovo story was similarly sour. Such treatment demonstrates again a far less certain White House control over the media. Having imposed their own skeptical frame on the situation, journalists who might otherwise have reveled in an emotional story of American victory instead played it down. Trumpeting the triumph would have required admitting they were wrong to say the United States was "trapped" in a "no-win war."

DOUBLE BINDS ON LEADERSHIP

Indeed, the media may fairly be assessed as imposing a double bind in their framing of policy choice. National media outlets seem to provide the most consistently interventionist elite voices in post–Cold War America, and are most likely to suggest firm U.S. action and the use of force. Facing no electoral or budget constraints and no worries about diplomatic credibility, many pundits and foreign policy reporters pressed insistently for intercession in Somalia, Bosnia, and Kosovo. Then the same media outlets that publish words and images urging that the U.S. project its power increasingly tend to approach all policies critically—including those same interventions. Even as they push an interventionist agenda, many elite journalists tend to blame administrations for any negative results. They demand immediate and coherent responses to crises and quick or instant evidence of success. For commercial, technological, and other reasons, news organizations seem more likely in particular to suffuse their coverage with the dramatic visual details of any U.S. casualties— images that trigger the isolationist, cost-emphasizing schema of ordinary Americans and create perceived pressure against involvement.

To illustrate the striking and sometimes strident interventionist strain, consider a typical set of quotations on Bosnia. In its May 10, 1993, issue, headed "Bosnia/ Clinton Gets Tough—At Last/Will Air Power Be Enough?" with the cover depicting an injured child, *Newsweek*'s lead story was headlined: "City of the Dead." Subheads read: "The accumulated horrors of the Bosnian war finally became too awful to ignore. . . . America would sit by no longer. The world's last superpower vowed to use its might to end the savagery in the Balkans." Another story (p.22) was headed: "Getting Tough at Last," and subheaded: "Why should America take a stand in

Bosnia? Because to enjoy the benefits of global leadership, we have to bear the costs, too." The text of the story describes in hortatory fashion the benefits of acting "as a force for good." It argues that the United States derives "tangible benefits from the perception that we're a country that stands for more than its own petty self-interest; it enhances our authority to call for free trade in Tokyo." It goes on to dismiss any "public squeamishness about casualties." After this comes a long story about military plans and practical problems of intervention. This material does potentially raise questions about the interventionist enthusiasm expressed in the previous stories. But reinforcing the dominant framing is a long sidebar (28) that concludes: "It's up to Clinton to show that this time around, if the Serbs don't mean business, he does."

In the new era, this is the downside of leaders' potency as media sources: if they set the agenda and try to frame the stories, they must also be *responsible* for how the stories come out. It appears nearly unthinkable for journalists that the stories have no tidy end, that no leader can unravel the contradictions and find a completely satisfying solution.

The double bind is encapsulated in these contrasting headlines from *Newsweek*: "Going In/Should America be the World's Policeman?" (December 14, 1992) and "Globocop: Does America Have the Will to Fight?" (August 23, 1993). Both questions are tendentious, and they point toward opposing conclusions. To "go in" to one country does not mean being the world's policeman; and deciding not to fight does not necessarily reveal a country's "lacking will." It appears that journalists themselves, as indeed we might expect, are as ambivalent, inconsistent, and theoretically rudderless as governing elites. Yet the media have the power and incentive to attack government officials, whom they often view as barely competent, for failing to solve the conundrums.

The double binds arise out of the filling of the schematic void not by a conscious theory of international relations as theory is usually understood but by a logic emerging from the media's own needs, norms, and limitations. By normal logical standards, it is absurd to demand both vigorous interventionism and instant, cost-free success. But the media need narrative, and they shape it through the filter of standing biases that drive the normative order of the profession. Applying their evaluation biases, journalists constantly search for evidence of the president's competence or incompetence, popularity or unpopularity, with the Washington elite and the ordinary folks. Combining this with such production biases as simplification and dramatization (Entman 1989), it actually makes perfect sense for journalists to impose mutually exclusive demands on the White House.

What the media must have is good stories, and they believe these by definition include drama and conflict. Media narratives cannot easily encompass nuance or irony. They cannot readily acknowledge irresolvable contradiction without blaming political authority; for example: the contradiction that the United States must intervene in Bosnia to be true to its freedom-loving, democratic principles, but that it cannot intervene without violating the same principles (and others), such as responding to American "public opinion."

Having said all this, it remains true that scholars should not themse\
impose too much orderly categorization or reify traits of the media text. ĵ
be expected in this cognitively and politically unsettled period, contrac   ...s
abound in media coverage. Thus, the December 14, 1992, *Newsweek* magazine
quoted earlier contains an essay by the president of the Carnegie Endowment for
Peace. It says: "With the end of the Cold War, there's no longer agreement on what
the national interest is—especially when it comes to the use of force." It lists Russia,
Somalia, Iraq, Bosnia, and Haiti as "five totally different problems" that Clinton
will have to deal with "moving at different speeds," and it notes that these situations
are "ambiguous." But although this essay contradicts the dominant framing of the
coverage, its potentially disruptive effect is subverted by its location after the magazine's main narrative (on subverted contradiction, see Entman 1991). Nor does it
confront the dominant frame with a point-by-point rebuttal, instead making its own
points in isolation. It therefore would not allow any but the most actively attentive
and thoughtful readers to construct a counterframe. Scattered, sporadic essays like
this do register the presence of more subtle thinking among American elites. Incompatible with the media's needs for stark and dramatic narratives, they do not encourage vigorous public deliberation that takes such perspectives into equal account with
those, as described here, that dominate the media's headlines and visual images.

THE IMPACT OF POLLING OPINION AND
PERCEIVED PUBLIC OPINION

The loosening of cognitive structures and certainties may heighten the attention of
public officials to the sentiments of the public. Lacking the stable theoretical and
normative structure once offered by the Cold War, elites can no longer count on
selling dangerous, costly policies to the public by invoking the Manichaean struggle
with the Reds. Nor can officials promote most interventions by repeating a few simple keywords and emotional symbols that respondents to surveys can quickly associate with a familiar schema. The absence of the shared Cold War schema makes elites
more vulnerable to negative poll results or other readings of "public opinion."

To clarify these points, it is important to probe in more detail the concept of
"public opinion" that informs, and sometimes misinforms, journalism, political discourse, and even scholarly analysis. Those invoking public opinion on issues in foreign (and domestic) policy seem usually to mean the *comprehensive preferences of the
majority of individuals on an issue.* That is, observers imply or say that a majority of
individuals would gain utility from a particular policy or candidate.

"Comprehensive" is used here because most assertions about public opinion
imply that a majority of individuals would prefer, say, increased defense spending
while taking into account all other possible policy choices. These claims thus neglect
the absence of data on preferred trade-offs, or on whether respondents even know
what the current level of defense spending is. They also pass over the issues of aggre-

gating individual opinions into a determinate majority will (e.g., Riker 1986). Individuals may have real preferences, but obtaining truly comprehensive data on the preferences of a majority of individuals toward any specific government decision at a given moment in time becomes, in practice, difficult if not impossible, especially for journalists who lack the scholarly luxuries of space, quantification, and abstraction necessary to make credible claims about public opinion.[5] Making claims in wider public discussion about the status of public opinion thus requires selecting some data on some sentiments and ignoring the rest—or framing.

An example comes from the debate on policy toward the Iraqi invasion of Kuwait in 1990. As Mueller (1994: 82) writes:

> While it is possible to argue from some data that there was something of a movement toward greater hawkishness during this period [before the war began], other data indicate something of a movement toward dovishness, and there are considerable data to suggest that there was no change at all.

Mueller's book (1994) reveals that the Iraq situation was subjected to perhaps the most intensive surveying ever among all short-term policy issues. Yet Mueller shows that all those data do not provide a definitive description of public preferences on handling Saddam Hussein, or even a stable majority opinion on whether the United States should go to war.

For short-term policy choices (as opposed to standing issues like nuclear-arms reduction or abortion)—most of those in the post–Cold War epoch of foreign policy—we have great trouble knowing public opinion as that term is typically and implicitly defined through surveys or other forms of evidence, at least as problematic and subject to framing. But this does not mean the thoughts of ordinary citizens are irrelevant to foreign policymaking, or that the media have no real influence on the public. There are at least four distinct referents of the term "public opinion." By parsing our consideration of the phenomenon more carefully, we discover that three are more consistently knowable than "public opinion" and that they are influenced by the mass media and affect government policy.

The first referent is *actual individual preferences*, which are the desires that individuals have for government action and for public officials: what they want government to do and whom they want to run the government. These are the actual sentiments that each individual possesses—the phenomena that observers apparently believe they are aggregating into majorities when they invoke public opinion.

The second referent, *polling opinion*, consists simply of the majorities revealed by the results of publicized surveys. Despite all the problems of surveys, aggregate opinion as measured by public-opinion surveys does matter to democratic politics and to policy outcomes and, increasingly, to foreign policy decisions. Polling opinion is heavily susceptible to framing and thus to media influence. Both media and pollsters frame issues for respondents, providing the cues that guide individual responses to survey questions. The framing effects come from the survey wording and experience (such as the order in which questions are asked); from recent, "top of the head" considerations that are most accessible as people ponder the question and give a very quick answer without a real chance to think (Zaller 1992); and from how ignorance and knowledge interact with those reactions.

The media affect all of these framing operations (including pollsters' questions and wording) through what they have been reporting around the time of the survey, as well as what they have not been reporting prominently and repeatedly enough to penetrate awareness. Any actual underlying individual beliefs and preferences that observers aggregate and summarize with the label "public opinion" may be much less manipulable than polling opinion. But we have little basis for deciding if this is so. What we do know is that polling opinion may be malleable, especially in the short term, on foreign policy matters. And given elite attentiveness to opinion surveys, this conveys to the media a measure of potential influence on foreign policy.

Perceived public opinion, the third referent, is related to but significantly different from polling opinion. Perceived public opinion is the general sense of the public's opinions that is held by most observers, including journalists and politicians, and members of the public themselves. This is the convenient fiction observers use to characterize the comprehensive preferences of a majority of citizens despite all the problems we have seen in coming up with such a summary label. Polling opinion and perceived public opinion may or may not be identical, because politicians and journalists frequently ignore survey results, in part because the data are so often inconclusive and in part because neglecting polls can be strategically useful. Instead, they just declaim about what the American people allegedly believe—and they can usually find a poll somewhere to support them. In fact, a major part of politics these days is precisely the struggle among contending politicians to induce the media to construct a particular perception of what public opinion is. If the media keep asserting that public opinion holds a particular view, the resulting perceptions of public desires—perceived public opinion—can shape actual behavior by government and citizens. For example, media reports consistently asserted during the 1970s, before Ronald Reagan's presidency, that the U.S. public had moved significantly to the political right. Yet if anything, surveys provided stronger evidence of a slight leftward shift on some issues, a rightward shift on just a couple, and stability on the rest (Entman and Paletz 1980; Ferguson and Rogers 1986). Strategic public-relations efforts by elites and selective misreadings of election results trumped survey data. This and other episodes of disjunction between *perceived* and *polling* opinion seemed to have had a critical impact on the actual policy successes of President Reagan. Such effects provide examples of real media power in the policy process. Even if the media do not affect the actual sentiments of individual citizens about the president, or if those sentiments are far more complicated and potentially volatile than indicated by media reports of public opinion, media reports affect the actions of politicians and officials by shaping *perceived* public opinion.

Priorities, the fourth referent, embody the trade-offs that people would prefer among different, incompatible preferences when making such summary political choices as a vote or response to a survey on "approval" of a president or other leader. In other words, priorities determine whether a hypothetical voter will vote for a candidate she does not like on global warming and foreign aid because she strongly favors abortion rights. She has placed abortion as a priority over the other two in making that choice. By what they report and how they report (sometimes called "priming"; Iyengar 1991), the media can significantly influence the priority weights people attach to their various preferences and considerations. *For most political purposes, reducing a policy to low priority—that is, irrelevance to most Americans' voting decisions or responses to performance evaluation surveys—is as effective as generating actual individual preferences supportive of the policy.*

Consider the first Reagan administration (1981–1985). Its political success inhered in its ability to manipulate priorities and perceived public opinion, not a majority of individuals' actual policy preferences or even polling opinion. If we believe the polls on issue preferences, majorities in polling opinion persistently disagreed with most of the foreign policies Reagan pursued, including aid to the Nicaraguan contras and refusal to negotiate strategic-arms limitations with the Russians and, after 1982, his insistence on continuing to increase defense budgets. But Reagan seemed to succeed in using the media to shape priorities. From his 1984 re-election, we must conclude that the majority of the voting public did not weigh Nicaragua, arms control, and defense spending heavily at the ballot box, polling opinion notwithstanding.

So how does this discussion help us understand the roles of public opinion and mass media in foreign policy since the Cold War? It reveals more precisely the sources and nature of the media's greater power in the foreign policy process—power rooted in the media's demonstrable (although, to be sure, not yet demonstrated) impact on *polling* opinion, *perceived* public opinion, and *priorities*. Scholars would profit by moving beyond their near-exclusive, frustrating focus on proving that the media affect actual individual preferences, to pay more attention to how the media influence the other three facets of public opinion and, through those effects, foreign policy.

The end of the Cold War frame means elites do not fully understand manifestations of public opinion any better than they do world politics. The absence of the old certainties seems to have made the public more fickle and contradictory than ever, less trusting, more hostile (Fried 1997). In these conditions, many elites seem to believe they must respond in some way to what might be called the imagined public, a slippery pastiche of polling opinion and other sources of perceived public opinion. The media keep measuring and highlighting something journalists call "public opinion," and that opens the way for more powerful media impacts on policy. Thus, a 1998 survey of eighty-one members of Congress, ninety-eight presidential appointees, and 151 members of the Senior Executive Service (Pew 1998; cf. Herbst 1998), found evidence that media reports are the most important source of executive-branch elites' perceptions of public sentiments, more important than polls (although the standard survey tapping presidential approval is closely monitored):

Leaders rely heavily on the media. Three-in-four presidential appointees and fully 84% of senior executives list the media as their main source of information about public opinion. Members of Congress are more likely to cite personal contacts and communication from constituents, although those on the Hill also say the media is a major source of information. Few government leaders say they rely on public opinion polls, but as many as 80% could recall Clinton's approval ratings with reasonable accuracy at the time of the interview.

This argument for media influence and for heightened salience of public opinion does not claim unilateral media causality or determination. In two noteworthy instances, President Clinton violated widely perceived public opinion that opposed American intervention: in Haiti and then Bosnia. Even if media reports and polls suggest to elites a particular public sentiment, other forces may motivate decisions. Sometimes projections that future political costs could outweigh current ones, hidden diplomatic motives, political courage, and rational calculation of national self-interest combine to outweigh the influence of media, polling opinion, and perceived public opinion.

THE SHIFT TO THE VISUAL

Visual images are widely credited by journalists and by officials themselves with moving public opinion and, through this, government policy. Since these elites actually respond to polling opinion and perceived public opinion, this means visual messages often chosen independently by the media can directly affect elite decisionmaking. Observers seem to draw many fallacious inferences about public sentiments from the assumed impact of visuals (and other dimensions of media coverage).[6] Nonetheless, the ability to transmit powerful visual messages, heightened by technical advances in satellites, photography, and color reproduction, coupled with elite tendencies to overinterpret, hands more influence over to news organizations.

The absence of tightly wound verbal core elements potentially elevates the signifying power of visuals. A picture of a dead American soldier dragged through Mogadishu carried as much rhetorical energy as any words could. The picture, like words, could activate the public's association with the anti-interventionist strain and bring it into working memory, where polls will pick it up. But words still exert defining power. Thus, that image of a desecrated American body *could* have set off intensely angry retributive responses—*fight* rather than *flight*—with the proper verbal frame. But that framing was absent because there was no way to attach it to the Cold War conflict or any compelling substitute.

It is not that the media are unaware of the power of visuals. They just cannot help themselves, given their production and commercial needs and practices. Indeed, this helps cement the contradictory pressures on leadership. For example, a *Time* cover story headed "In Feeding Somalia and Backing Yeltsin, America Discovers the Limits of Idealism," writes (37–39) that emotions and "generous feelings" have been driving American foreign policy. This emotionalism has arisen, it says, "from pictures, either still photographs or television clips, that are mainlined directly into the democracy's emotional bloodstream without the mediation of conscious thought." Perhaps so, but just to the left of this assertion is a one-and-a-half-page picture of a young Somali boy holding the pants of a presumably dead U.S. soldier. And a large caption says, "Images like this one are mainlined directly into the democracy's emotional bloodstream."

Whether pictures are less "informative" than words—whether *Time*'s critics are right to worry about foreign policy driven by simplistic emotional responses to pictures—is less clear than it may seem on the surface. The implication is that a public relying on verbal texts alone will be more informed, more thoughtful. Yet to take one counterexample, the public's polling support for the 1986 foreign policy decision to bomb Libya relied only secondarily on pictures. It was based on a months-long campaign to stoke fear of terrorism, packed with false verbal details about the villainy of an attack in Berlin that killed some American servicemen, allegedly on the orders of Libyan leader Muammar Qaddafi. Later, the government admitted it had no evidence of Libya's role. The words here were powerful—and powerfully misleading (cf. Althaus, Edy, Entman, and Phalen 1996).

REPUBLICANS' MEDIA ADVANTAGE

Having suggested an apparent growth in the media's power to frame national defense policy, and in the imagined public's influence, we now raise an important caveat: the party that controls the White House may make a difference. Republican presidents predictably exert more framing power over the text and over public opinion than do Democratic chief executives.

The Democrats and Republicans differ in ability to execute unified media strategies. Part of the reason for the Clinton administration's failure to control polling opinion and, thus, for the media's impact and polling opinion's influence, lies in the way elite discourse structurally differs when Democrats control the White House. The Republicans, and many Democrats in Congress, freely contested the White House's shifting problem definitions in Bosnia and Somalia (and Haiti as well). These clashes helped shape the polling response even as they also reflected elites' readings of Clinton's shaky standing in the polls.

For an oppositional frame to pervade the media, there must be an opposition party that understands its function as precisely producing a counterframe. That means asserting and repeating mutually reinforcing associational linkages. It means creating slogans and shorthand symbols the media can pick up and reiterate. Republicans, ideologically more unified on foreign policy, can supply counterframes more effectively than can Democrats, who represent a more philosophically diverse coalition. This could change, however, if the Democrats become an institutionalized minority appealing to a more homogeneously liberal base, or if isolationist tendencies grow beyond the GOP fringe.

Public opinion itself may take on a different shape, then, depending on which party holds the White House. Democratic presidents may have less success manipulating the public's surveyed preferences—polling opinion—or priorities against the GOP opposition than vice versa. The imagined public would thus pose less of a constraint on Republican than Democratic administrations. The comparison between coverage of Panama under Bush and Haiti under Clinton is illuminating. Although real differences between the two events help explain the media's different emphases, fear of bogging down in a quagmire and enduring unacceptable costs formed a minor part of the discourse on President Bush's Panama policy, whereas they suffused coverage of Clinton's Haiti engagement.

A final explanation of party differences may be a change in the media's standard operating procedures. The cognitive and operational habit of accepting the government's problem definition was still engrained in journalists through to the end of the Cold War. Even during Vietnam, the media maintained allegiance to the government's core problem definitions—even when magnifying dissent on its policy choices and critiques of official leadership (Hallin 1986). The demise of the Soviet empire shook the foundations of automatic acceptance, threatening the habit of thought and tightness of a core schema. The habit was challenged in a major way during the debate on going to war with Iraq, but the government won out not only during (Entman and Page 1994) but certainly after the debate, when war came (Bennett and Paletz 1994). Yet the problematic end to the Iraq war and the series of publicized, unsolved problems that began with Bosnia seem since then to have dislodged journalists' habit of deference, replacing it with the kind of skeptical questioning more common in domestic policy. It was Bill Clinton's misfortune that this shift took firm root on his watch.

CONCLUSION

The frame-contestation model suggested here may offer greater purchase on the more visually oriented media text than earlier approaches developed for print. It accommodates the move in cognitive psychology toward understanding information processing as both a cognitive and affective matter (Fiske and Taylor 1991). It provides a theoretical basis for the long-standing disputes throughout the fields of cultural and media studies on audience reception and effects. And framing theory encourages more complete content analyses that illuminate the way media move audiences and officials' perceptions of public opinion. However, the conventional caveats apply with more force than usual here: the hypothesized traits of the post–Cold War media–opinion–foreign policy system are just that. Systematic analysis of media content and public opinion data is necessary to generate a precise and full understanding of that system.

Beyond the empirical matters, the framing perspective suggests an equally pressing obligation to think through the normative issues: Just what do we want the media, governing elites, and the public to do now that the Cold War is over and we have an international system that nobody really understands? How do we judge media performance: Do we want pictures like those of Somalia or Kosovo to frame public thinking and elites' rhetorical and policy options? If not, what *do* we want?

Consider the 1980s U.S. military operations against Grenada, Libya, and Panama. Each time, Congress accepted polling opinion, which seemed to support administration policy. Few Washington elites criticized administration policies in Grenada, Libya, and Panama because the media and polls claimed they were very popular. Yet perhaps they were so popular because the public knew so little—and their knowledge was so limited because their representatives responded so slavishly to their constituents' presumed sentiments that they apparently feared engaging in critical discussion of the policies. Our notion of democratic responsiveness and our understanding of the media's role in bringing it about become troublesome. And we see the normative irony: government responsiveness may not be desirable when it is responsiveness to an underinformed public—underinformed in large part because Washington politicians were so exquisitely sensitive to polling opinion and perceived public opinion.[7]

What Americans obtained in those cases was representation without deliberation. So it seems a misnomer to consider all instances where polling opinion matches government policy as democracy in action. For the notion of responsiveness to have meaning, it is not enough for survey results to correlate with policy decisions. Such congruence could be the product of the governing elites' manipulation, misinformation, and, perhaps as in Grenada, Libya, and Panama, failures to engage in public debate. Page and Shapiro (1992, chap. 9), Dahl (1989), and others suggest that the information on which citizens' views and survey responses rest must enjoy a degree of independence from government control and distortion to make representation truly democratic. Yet there may be no practical way for news media as currently configured to consistently channel democracy-enhancing information about foreign affairs to the public. The interlaced and shifting power relationships among the media, government, and public may call for a new normative standard, one that recognizes structural limitations on the citizenry's ability to obtain the information they need to hold government to genuine account. Here the early insights of Walter Lippmann on the limits of public opinion might profitably combine with more precise definitions of U.S. goals in national defense and foreign policy to yield more realistic normative prescriptions.

3

Media and Public Sphere without Borders?
News Coverage and Power from Kurdistan to Kosovo

Martin Shaw

Questions about mass media and foreign policy sit uneasily on the edge of contemporary international relations. Practitioners and academics alike agree that something has changed (hence this book). Nevertheless, it is too easy to conceptually limit the significance of the changes to the interpolation of new variables, the mass media and public opinion, into the relations of states and statesmen. This chapter argues that this is not enough: the expanded role of the mass media should be seen instead as part of a sea change in world politics, in which old ways of understanding are brought into question. Indeed, the problem of the media is a litmus test of the adequacy, not merely of the old realist international relations of interstate relations, but of the newer critical international relations of nonstate actors. So far, the latter seems almost as incapable as the former of conceptualizing the media. Yet in so far as international relations fails to understand the media, it also fails to grasp the new shape of world politics.

In this chapter I try to address this problem from two directions. First, I explore, somewhat schematically, the limitations of current international understanding, proposing key elements of an approach to world politics that explains mass media's structural centrality. Second, I elaborate upon empirical research on the role of the media in two important and related moments in the emerging global era of international politics—the Gulf War and the Kurdish refugee crisis of 1991. In conclusion, I use the 1999 conflict in Kosovo to help demonstrate how my approach can help illuminate specific issues of war and peace in this new context of state relations.

UNDERSTANDING MEDIA IN THE HISTORIC
TRANSITION OF OUR TIMES

Historically, the discourse of international relations has distinguished "international" and "world" politics; while the latter has been recognized as more inclusive, the former has been seen as a stronger reality. And even though an international society based on states has been seen as maturing since the 1648 Treaty of Westphalia, a "world society" has been seen as, at most, weakly emergent.[1]

The academic field of international relations matured in the shadow of the Cold War, which had contradictory significance for the relations of international and world orders. On the one hand, processes of transatlantic and European integration rendered many old international military divisions redundant and provided a framework for the emergence of a much freer, fuller world market system. On the other hand, integration took place in the framework of new interbloc military rivalries of states and depended very much on specifically international, interstate cooperation within the Western bloc. In addition, integration took place with the clear dominance of one nation-state—the United States—so that concepts of "national" interests remained strong even as policy was internationalized.

Up to and during the Cold War, the mass media also appeared primarily national in form, and international communication across borders remained secondary. From the point of view of international relations, then, media could be seen as components of the domestic order, relating to national politics and public opinion. The mass media were not seen as significant components of the international order, except to the extent that the domestic affected the international. Increasingly, international theory stressed interdependence between national economies and the emergence of nonstate actors—such as multinational corporations—in international relations.[2] By the end of the Cold War, such processes were seen as breaking down the divisions of domestic and international world politics and leading to so-called postinternational world politics.[3]

Economic and cultural integration, moreover, was seen as taking the form of globalization, in which borders were undermined. In radical versions of this argument, the proliferation of nonstate actors included social movements—for example, women's, peace, and environmental movements—and was leading toward the formation of a global civil society.[4] This was itself seen as part of a wider movement toward a fully global society.[5]

Curiously, the media figured very little in these transformations of the international-relations debate. International media groups were recognized as one variety of the increasingly important multinational corporation, and media were criticized in radical accounts as part of the dominant American hegemony.[6]

But the significance of media was often restricted to the interface of foreign policy with domestic public opinion in conflicts, which themselves were often conservatively theorized, since war remained mostly a topic in the realist end of international relations. Because domestic politics was also seen as only an inconsistent, intermittent influence on international relations, it also figured fairly marginally in the field. Even the growing recognition of cultural phenomena in general in the newer international relations debates, and the more radical, postmodernist attention to the fusion of cultural forms, brought little attention to the media through which many of these phenomena appear.

Specific media phenomena (e.g., CNN, the Internet) have achieved totemic status—the former in discussions of foreign policy, the latter in globalization debates. However, no systematic, general rethinking of the media has appeared in the critical debates over international relations. Media studies retain a Cinderella status in all main theoretical schools. A survey of six leading American and British international-relations journals shows that less than 2 percent of all articles concerned any aspect of the media.[7] There was little difference in the level of attention between the journals, despite other differences of orientation among them. These data confirm a fundamental neglect, the alteration of which requires a radical reorientation, and the scope of which can only be suggested in broad terms here.

What is at stake is more than adding media as a significant category of "actor" alongside states and other nonstate actors. The idea of the media as a single, powerful agent—whether a faithful servant of state and corporate interests (as radicals allege) or an intruder into their realms (as statesmen sometimes complain)—is the bane of serious discussion, indicating that we have not even started a meaningful analysis. What is needed is a complex conception of media as both structure and agency. To that end, we should consider the conceptualization of the state by historical sociologist Michael Mann. He sees the state as a space in which a variety of actors operate; but he also sees it, under certain conditions, as an actor. Mann's approach does not adopt the taken-for-granted concept of state as unified actor, nor does it collapse the possible unity of the state into the multiplicity of interests battling within it. Contrary to these one-sided views, we should examine the processes through which, for some purposes and in some situations, states—for all the complexity of their component institutions and actors within—may become constituted as relatively unified agents, as well as the obstacles to such processes. Michael Mann also suggests that the same state may crystallize in different ways in different situations—so that the American state appears

> as conservative-patriarchal one week when restricting abortion rights, as capitalist the next when regulating the savings and loans banking scandal, as a superpower the next when sending troops abroad for other than national economic interests. These varied crystallizations are rarely in harmony or in dialectical opposition to one another; usually they just differ. They mobilize differing, if overlapping and intersecting, power networks.[8]

We might adopt a similar approach to the understanding of media—even if the media as social constructs are rather different from states in important respects. The media in general can be seen as social spaces within which individual and institutional actors of all kinds produce representations and communicate to audiences. Journalists and editors both help to reproduce the self-representations of other social actors and produce their own individual and institutional representations. In this sense, the media are spaces in which many social actors act (including journalists) and can become themselves collective actors, as when a newspaper takes an editorial position or TV news and current-affairs coverage consistently focus on certain issues.

Media are thus *both* constitutive spaces of society *and* distinctive kinds of actor. We need first to consider that many individual and virtually all collective and institutional actors relate with each other in important ways through representations in the media. To take the example of states, relations of different centers of state power are represented simultaneously to each other and to mass audiences—both within their societies and worldwide—through media. Through these representations—and the ways in which they are consumed, processed, and re-represented by institutions and individuals—states, like all other actors, are surveyed by others.

We can further the question of media centrality through the concept of surveillance. Anthony Giddens—following Foucault—suggests this is a fundamental aspect of modern social relations, and the institutions concerned with it represent one of the four key "institutional clusters" of modernity.[9] However, as an international critic of Giddens maintains, surveillance is not confined to the internal relations of the nation-state, nor is it a one-way process.[10] States survey each other; they also survey society and are surveyed by it. Although residues of the old geopolitical privacy of states remain (in diplomacy, for example), such activity coexists with the surveillance of states themselves by many other social institutions as well as of millions or even hundreds of millions of individuals.

Mass media are clearly central institutions of surveillance in modern society. Their centrality is not merely a product of the quantity of information they produce. Their crucial importance is that they are at the heart of the *public* character of surveillance. As John Thompson explains, "The development of the media has created new forms of publicness which are quite different from the traditional publicness of co-presence."[11] Because of media, then, states, social institutions, and individuals do not simply carry out discrete mutual surveillance through their own independent data collection, monitoring, and analysis. Instead, they all have access to a common sphere in which the surveillance function is concentrated and celebrated. The media produce publicly constituted surveillance processes. Through their consumption of and input to media surveillance, everyone's and every institution's surveillance is related to everyone else's.

All actors in the public sphere must necessarily be aware of the most intensive and extensive monitoring of their behavior, reaching even into previously private arenas. Established institutions—state and nonstate—that wish to reproduce or extend their public roles must maintain and manage media attention; and individuals within them who wish to be recognized must adopt strategies for their own media visibility. Conversely, new institutions and individuals increasingly become recognized as public figures and actors by being picked up in media surveillance. This process applies in such diverse cases as when marginal political groups become "international terrorists" or when specialist entertainers become "celebrities." The means used to attract media attention may vary—from kidnapping and bombs to sex and drugs—but the nature of the process is the same.

The contemporary forms of the relations of surveillance reflect fundamental changes compared to earlier periods of modern society. The early phases of the emergence of modern mass media coincided with the high point of nation-states' control over society and the era of acute international conflict between major states. In this era, surveillance was both more national (confined within the state) and one-way (of state over society) than it has subsequently become. In that period, because the media were primarily national (or subnational) in scope, international relations between states were much less complexly mediated. States were often able to exert direct control over mass media and fashion their relationships with audiences according to state priorities. We can understand much about the roles of the media in World War II in terms of propaganda—even in democratic states—and indeed some scholars still see this as the dominant motif of international communications.[12] States were largely able to monopolize media spaces: individual and institutional actions within and by media were largely structured by state strategies. Relations between states involved mutual surveillance of a much less public kind. Although different national media monitored each other and were monitored by states, there was little sense of a publicly mediated sphere beyond the nation-state, and the mutual surveillance of states was less dependent upon it.

Not only has this particular balance of state-media relationships largely disappeared (exceptions like North Korea increasingly prove the rule) but it is no longer helpful to think of mass media primarily in the national context. National structuring is only one, even if still a very powerful, context of the media. Within an increasingly integrated Western-defined world society, there is a more or less integrated global media space within which states, like other institutions, operate. National media spaces exist as national segmentations of this increasingly common space, overlapping with other elements of structure. Within these mediated spaces, representations are contested by social actors of all kinds. States are the most powerful contesting institutions, but civil society actors—including journalists themselves—often challenge the kinds of representations state leaders and institutions promote. Indeed, while it is helpful to consider the media as constitutive spaces of the public sphere in which all public actors—state and civil society—interact, there is also a sense in which the media belong to civil society. With this in mind, state institutions' self-representations increasingly take the character of interventions in the civil realm.

The distinction of state and civil society is a vexing issue. Clearly, states and civil societies have developed historically in intimate relationships with each other, initially very much as nation-states and national civil spheres. Civil society, in modern history, can be seen as the realm in which the nation, as opposed to the state, was constituted and thus was the necessary complement of the nation-state; this is only now changing.[13] The public sphere was classically constituted through a range of social institutions changing through time. Mass media, such as newspapers, were part of this process from the eighteenth century onward, but the national civil society of the mid–twentieth century was already a mass society constituted by the media in the modern sense—the mass-circulation newspaper, cinema, radio, and, increasingly, television.

Although the mass media initially consolidated the national form of the public sphere, it is widely considered that the transnationalization of the media has speeded the development of transnational forms of society and politics. "Nation shall speak truth unto nation," proclaims the motto of the British Broadcasting Corporation (BBC), in an enlightened, internationalist crystallization of the classic mid-century broadcasting ideal. As media markets have become not only international but transnational and global, the public spaces that they embody are no longer national in the same sense that they once were. Broadcasters like the BBC still project national visions, but they do so in a much more complex worldwide market and public sphere.

Moreover, it is wrong to counterpose, as so many do, a globalized media—or civil society—to states that yet remain national states. Press and civil society were already partially internationalized in the nineteenth century. Just as the accentuation of their national character in the early twentieth century reflected political developments, so did the renewal of international discourse at mid-century. Clearly, the developing media and civil-society internationalization of recent decades has depended on the internationalization of Western states and civil societies. This also dates at least from World War II—during which, of course, American and British media first developed strong international as well as national roles.

The degree of military and political integration of the North Atlantic region after 1945 was itself unprecedented and has been consolidated in an even more unprecedented development—the European Union—as a new kind of polity. There emerged what I have called a Western "conglomerate of state power" of increasingly interdependent, harmonized, and overlapping jurisdictions.[14] With the end of the Cold War and the collapse of the rival Soviet bloc, this conglomerate has attempted to construct a global hegemony, legitimated by United Nations (UN) institutions and partially incorporating other centers of state power.

This transformation of the state order has been a condition for the development of globalized communications and global civil society (and indeed, globalization in general). The internationalized political order has been increasingly liberal in content, facilitating transnational and, increasingly, globalized communications and culture. It is in these circumstances that press and television have become, more and more, frameworks for transnationalized and globalized information and ideas. Although many have located the emergence of a global civil society in globalist social movements—environmental, feminist, human rights, and so on—the common framework of this emerging form has been the transformed public sphere of the mass media.

The development of transnational and global public spheres has coincided with the development of new media technologies, institutions, and markets. Mass media have become less homogenous—technologies have multiplied, markets have fractured even as they have expanded overall, and interactivity has increased. However, the transformation of the public sphere does not depend solely, or even mainly, on these developments, as the totemic importance of CNN and the Internet might suggest. It is important to emphasize the extent to which historic national media and institutions, such as radio, television, and the BBC, have become primary vehicles for transnational and global trends. Just as state internationalization has depended on the integration and harmonization of nation-states' practices, so the transformation of the media and civil society has involved interlinked national media. The hugely expanded and speeded-up flow of information and images between and among media institutions means that core content is increasingly harmonized, even while its framing in public broadcasting retains many distinctly national characteristics.

The location of media within civil society is reinforced by the fundamental political transformations of our time. The movements toward democratization in Latin America, East-Central Europe and the former Soviet Union, and many parts of Asia, Africa, and even the Middle East since roughly 1980 have had deep significance for the roles of the media. However uneven the spread of formal political democracy (even more so for the substance of democratic practice), a historic shift has taken place. Although the weakness of civil society is often seen as an index of the limits of democratic change, and although the viability of autonomous civil institutions is still contested in many states, there has nevertheless been a great expansion of the possibilities for an independent public sphere. The media and journalists are often in the forefront and at the cutting edge of transformative processes.

Although democratization and media development often both take specifically national forms, they are greatly dependent on the worldwide integration of authority structures and media. The embedding of global institutions and democratic norms, however contested, and the creation of global media networks go hand in hand to transform the character of the media. Certainly, global media industries center on markets for entertainment commodities, and corporations that dominate them may try to block the kinds of news coverage that challenge their authoritarian state partners (as in the notorious case of media mogul Rupert Murdoch and China). However, the diffusion of information through the increasingly global media cannot be contained within bounds that even the most powerful state leaders would prefer.

It is argued here that there are powerful processes of change that are transforming the relations of states and societies and leading to the creation, through global media, of a global public sphere, which is a crucial part of the infrastructure of an emerging global civil society. Any analysis of these trends, however, needs to emphasize their contradictory character and the contested character of all the movements involved. In particular, this chapter draws attention to the manifold and shifting crystallizations of the roles that the mass media play. The same media that figure in one context as entertainment commodities and vehicles of corporate profit appear in another as instruments of state policy, and in yet another as representative of an emergent global-democratic civil society. The "polymorphous crystallization" that Mann identified in the state is also a characteristic of media. In order to explore this further, I turn to an emblematic case of contemporary, post–Cold War international relations: the Gulf War and its Kurdish aftermath.

MEDIA AS SITES AND ACTORS IN GLOBAL POLITICS:
CONCLUSIONS FROM THE IRAQI WARS

The 1990–1991 Iraqi wars (four phases, outlined below) present a considerable paradox in contemporary international relations. On the one hand, the Gulf War appears as something of a limiting case, the first clearly interstate conflict after the Cold War to have involved the Western powers as direct protagonists rather than as war managers. It is therefore a standard against which other "new wars" (as Mary Kaldor has called them) are measured; only the 1999 Kosovo conflict has matched it.[15] On the other hand, the Kurdish refugee crisis has been taken as a paradigm of a new form of humanitarian intervention in which states use military power for ends distinct from the classic pursuit of strategic interest. Despite the obvious links of these two emblematic episodes, they have been studied for the most part separately. Moreover, despite the contrasting media roles that were central to the two cases, no attempt has been made to theorize the linkages between these experiences.

To examine the significance of the conceptualization of the media in international relations, as proposed in the first section of this chapter, I shall now apply it to the Iraqi wars, applying some of the arguments of my recent study.[16] My labeling of the conflicts is itself indicative of a theoretical starting point. Instead of privileging, as most studies by international-relations and communications scholars have done, the Gulf War as the focus of research, I examine the pattern of the interlinked wars centered on the crisis of the Iraqi state, in its relations with both neighboring states and society within its borders. The crisis originated in the war with Iran and the genocidal repression of the Kurdish people in the 1980s. In 1990–1991, it involved four distinct phases of war: the Iraqi army's invasion of Kuwait; the U.S.-led Coalition's campaign against the Iraqi state; the Shiite insurrection in the South of Iraq and its crushing by the Iraqi state; and the Kurdish insurrection in the north and its defeat.

In these wars, there were three principal military actors: the Iraqi state; the Coalition of the United States, Kuwait, Saudi Arabia, and over thirty other states fighting under the United Nations; and the Shiite and Kurdish insurrectionists. There were, however, other nonmilitary participants—and, to a large extent, victims—within the zone of conflict, including three civilian populations. The first were the citizen and noncitizen populations of Kuwait, who were attacked and forced to flee by the Iraqi army. Second, individuals dwelling in Iraq, especially those of Baghdad, Basra, and other cities, suffered in the Coalition bombardment. Third, those in Basra and other cities in the south and Kurdistan suffered through the repression of rebellions by the Iraqi armed forces.

It was clear to all, of course, that the war was heavily mediated. The postmodern sociologist Jean Beaudrillard even opined that the Gulf War did not take place: the war was a phenomenon of the media.[17] Communications researchers briefly turned their attention to international politics, and international researchers to the media, in larger numbers than ever. In neither case, however, was attention sustained. The most important studies confirmed the success of the principal Coalition states' governments and armed forces in managing media coverage to reinforce the military campaign.[18] There was little detailed attention to even this issue as it affected the Arab world. And almost all academic media studies ceased at the point at which George Bush attempted but failed to end the wars, with the Coalition cease-fire of February 28, 1991. There was, therefore, little attention given to the role of the media in the insurrectionary wars and their aftermath—the huge and desperate exodus of refugees from the repression of Saddam Hussein's regime.

This is extremely curious given that the totemic role of CNN, which arose first from its coverage of the Coalition assault on Iraq, became identified in subsequent debates with the role of the media in the Kurdish refugee crisis and the genesis of the Anglo-American-French intervention to create safe havens in Kurdistan. The CNN effect—as emblematic of the media's role in international politics today as the Vietnam syndrome was in earlier days—means the ability of dramatic TV images of suffering to force Western governments' hands in the way they are presumed to have done in the Kurdish case.

It is all the more striking that such serious attention has been given to the CNN effect in general—if not to the original Kurdish case—and that it has come from media analysts rather than international relationists.[19] Interestingly, a recent review of this literature by a political scientist finds it wanting in its understanding of political complexity.[20] This is particularly notable given that the Kurdish case became the paradigm for the debate about humanitarian intervention that preoccupied many international scholars in the early and mid-1990s and returned at the end of that decade with the Kosovo conflict. International relations has mostly been happy to take the media's role for granted in order to concentrate on the forms of intervention it was presumed to have induced.

Below I identify five main issues in the understanding of these events, and I attempt to overcome the limitations of the literature on media in the Gulf War.

First, we need to understand *the role of increasing interlinkages of domestic and interstate politics in global politics.* These are only partially and (compared to previous periods) less distinct fields within an increasingly common world political framework.[21] The first mistake of George Bush, John Major, and other leaders, reproduced in many academic studies, was to believe that interstate and domestic politics could be separated in the Iraqi situation. In effect, they mistook the convenient fiction of national sovereignty for a description of political reality. They intervened in the conflict of Iraq and Kuwait, apparently a straightforward interstate conflict, only to find once they had succeeded in resolving this issue that behind it lurked the complex social and political conflicts inside Iraq. These internal conflicts concerned, however, ethnic and religious groups that connected across the borders into neighboring states (Iran, Turkey, and Syria) and thus involved international as well as domestic politics.

Second, we need to start from the assumption that *global politics as a whole is constantly mediated in a more or less common framework.* This qualification is important, since clearly there is no simple, unified global media represented by an institution like CNN, and national segmentations of the global media sphere remain important. Nevertheless, it is clear that all politics is fought out in media as well as in political and military spaces. States, like other actors, require sophisticated understandings of the media if they are to complement their political and military with media strategies; without successful integration of the media with other strategies, the latter may also fail. So Iraqi military-political strategy failed because it was based on an outdated version of the Vietnam syndrome—the belief that media would amplify U.S. casualties to the point of withdrawal—which the United States preempted. Coalition strategy was more successful in the short term, but the second mistake of Bush and Major was to believe that it was enough to manage successfully the media coverage of their planned military campaign. They failed to foresee how the constant mediation of political events would move the situation beyond the results of their planned campaign and would thus rebound on the initial success.

Third, we need to understand that *global media spaces are inherently contested, both by a wide range of social actors and by journalists themselves.* Access to the media is highly unequal, and states have major advantages over other institutions and actors, so they can more or less manage the mediation of some situations. But if you can manage some of the media some of the time, you can't manage all of the media all of the time. Indeed, given the tension between the goals of political and military media managers and the autonomist ideology of journalism, successful management in one phase is likely to produce a reaction. Some groups of journalists are likely to respond to successful control by states by looking for opportunities to reassert their independence.

In the increasingly unusual situation of open war, states are able to mobilize reserves of legitimacy and histories of media subordination to government. In cases where national military personnel are at risk, the media generally exercise a great deal of restraint in criticizing governments. Increasingly, however, military interventions by Western states occur in wars between two or more local actors, do not amount to all-out war by the West, and do not involve great risk to large numbers of nationals. In these circumstances, the space for critical voices, both of a range of social actors—local to the zone of conflict and transnational, mainly Western groups—and of journalists themselves, is likely to be considerable.

In the case of Iraq, the two insurrections and their repressions brought local antiregime fighters and transnational humanitarian agencies into contestation with state actors, and also transformed large parts of the civilian population into very visible victims for whom Western journalists could speak. The third mistake of Western political leaders was to underestimate the capacities of all these groups to gain voices and, especially, the extent to which many journalists, having had to toe governmental lines during the Gulf War, would take the opportunities for independent coverage that the new situation opened.

Fourth, it is crucial to grasp *the significance of media as a space of civil society, both in its national and emergent global forms.* Broadcast media, especially, function as entertainment businesses, have developed in many places under the aegis of states, are owned by corporations that are politically close to ruling parties, and often accord state institutions privileged access. Despite all this, the location of the media in civil society is very important. As purveyors of information from (in principle) all sources, and for (again in principle) all legitimate viewpoints, the media are necessarily more or less open spaces. The "more or less" is important, since there is huge variation in the extent to which the media fulfill this role. However, the media's dual-representational function, in the sense of information and advocacy, places them primarily in the sphere of civil society. This aspect of media will increase to the extent that the media's independence and the expansion of civil society worldwide are growing.

In the Iraqi wars, there was a tension between the preexisting national and emergent global civil society roles of the media. Many media outlets, especially newspapers but also to a large extent mainstream television, fell back primarily on national definitions of the conflicts—echoing older experiences of national wars. This was the case even though the involvement of the armed forces was not primarily in a national role. Thus, the British media, for example, interpreted the Gulf War as a national war, even though the United Kingdom was a secondary member of a multinational coalition acting under the auspices of the UN and the leadership of the United States.

Nevertheless, television coverage in my British study was less trapped in the older, nationally centered narratives of conflict than was newspaper coverage. It was also less national than the responses of other civil society institutions and groups, such as parties, churches, and intellectuals, including even some more transnationally oriented sectors such as the antiwar movement and the emergent Muslim community. In the Kurdish crisis, there was a clear interdependence of TV news journalism with the transnationally oriented humanitarian organizations in the advocacy of globalist concepts of responsibility for victims. Kurdish political movements were not able to represent their goals effectively in the global mass media, but when Kurdish civilians were transformed into the pure victims of the Saddam regime and, indirectly, of Western nonintervention, Western journalists engaged in powerful representation of their plight.

Finally, it is important to grasp *the dynamics of television, newspaper, and other media coverage, especially the relations among film, commentary, and text, in generating political impact.* Television news programs, no more than newspapers, are simple purveyors of information and images. What is crucial is the narrative within which these two commodities are presented. Whereas predominantly visual media construct narratives in ways different from those of textual media, the narrative is still king. The ability of news presenters to frame visual images and representations of actors is crucial to their power. Governments can enhance their ability to manage coverage only when they can more or less define the narratives within which journalists operate.

The unexamined consensus about the power of the media in the Kurdish crisis of

1991 is that television was able to show shocking visual images of refugees' suffering, the transmission of which aroused public opinion and forced the U.S. and U.K. governments to change their policies. In my study of the two main British news channels in March-April 1991, I had two sets of findings that significantly qualified this assumption.[22] The first concerned the original Shiite insurrection. I confirmed that it was weakly covered compared to the Kurdish revolt because of the failure of Western journalists to gain direct access to or virtually any film of the zone of conflict. I also established, however, that television news still reported it more consistently than all newspapers except the liberal broadsheets at a time when governments were trying to ignore it. This suggested the importance of journalistic investment in following through on the Gulf crisis, even against the political tide and even without fully reliable informational and visual sources.

The second set of findings suggested that the political impact of the coverage of the Kurdish revolt did not depend simply or mainly on striking visual images. As important as these images were, they did not work by themselves. Their impact depended on two additional factors. First, the presence on the ground of authoritative reporters, able to provide a first-hand gloss on the images that the cameras produced, was central. Second, the integration of pictures as well as first-hand commentary into a general narrative—elaborated more or less consistently over a period of weeks by news anchors and through voiceovers as well as by the reporters on the ground—completed the process. I established that this narrative, while never elaborated in the overt manner of newspaper editorials, constantly repeated certain highly charged themes. In particular, it laid the highly visible suffering of the Kurdish people squarely at the door of Western political leaders such as Bush and Major. It established and constantly underlined a connection of responsibility between the actions and inactions of these leaders—their calls to remove Saddam, on the one hand, and indifference to the revolts, on the other—in ways that challenged the political strategies of the governments.

The narrative was sufficiently clear, persistent, and strongly reinforced to constitute a campaign by the news programs. This was reinforced in the newspapers—crucially, in the tabloids—in the final weeks before first the Major and then the Bush administrations made dramatic U-turns toward intervention in northern Iraq. The power of this campaign made television the pivot of Western civil society's interventions in general, mobilizing both general public opinion and the actions of other actors, such as humanitarian organizations. However, it also left the Kurds a walk-on role in their own salvation, as they were reduced to pidgin-English sound bites calling for help, their voices dwarfed by the journalists' own, much more articulate and elaborated, arguments.

This account has been criticized for neglecting nonmedia factors, like the interest of the Turkish government in preventing refugee incursions into Turkey. Since I argue against the simple CNN view of pictures driving policy, I do not claim that the public, mediated surveillance of the crisis was the only factor in forcing policy change and intervention. Nevertheless, the timing of the British government's turn-around (which in turn appeared to influence American decisions) fitted with the crescendo of the media campaigning, and the policy change was publicly elaborated in the humanitarian terms that responded to the television news programs' narrative of the crisis. Given that governments' power depends on re-election, and that electoral politics are conducted principally in the media, it is clear that no government can afford to ignore a sustained media campaign against it on an important area of policy.

CONCLUSION

I have summarized the findings of my study in general theses relating to the theoretical argument in the first section of this chapter. Clearly, we must not expect these processes to operate in identical ways in all conflicts during the global transition. Indeed, the Kurdish crisis was an almost unique conjuncture because of the investment of Western media as well as military resources in Iraq, the reaction of journalists against their subordinate role in the managed military campaign, and the very direct nexus of responsibility that television was able to exploit. These factors have not operated in the same ways even in Palestine, Bosnia, Somalia, Rwanda, Haiti, or Chechnya, in which large-scale, global media coverage has occurred and played a political role—let alone in the dozens of wars around the world that have received minimal, episodic, and generally uninfluential coverage. Nevertheless, the dynamics of the media campaign over Kurdish refugees set precedents that have been influential in these subsequent conflicts, even if the results have been different. The anticipation of negative coverage of Bosnia, for example, in the run-up to the U.S. presidential campaign of 1996 was a highly influential pressure toward the Dayton settlement. And whatever the limitations of media coverage in the other cases listed above, it is certain that the virtual noncoverage of many wars has had a negative effect on international political attention.

The Kosovo conflict of 1999 was closer than any other conflict to the conditions of the Iraqi wars of 1991. It appeared, in its early stages at least, like a speeded-up, more concentrated version of the crises in the Persian Gulf and Kurdistan. Here the interstate conflict—that is, between NATO and Serbia—was inextricably linked from the start with the genocide of Kosovo's Albanians (whereas in Iraq, the genocidal campaign against the Kurds had followed the interstate war that began over Kuwait). Here the nexus of responsibility implicating the West in the fate of Albanian civilians was present in the causes of intervention (rather than having to be established by the media against the Western state, as in Iraq). This connection of responsibility was deepened when Serbia responded to Western military action by intensifying its war against civilians in Kosovo (similarly to how ferocious repression of Shiites and Kurds followed Western action against Iraq).

Journalists were quick to point out how NATO action had stimulated the new wave of genocidal attacks by Serbia and the Kurdish-style exodus that followed.

They also suggested, repeatedly, that airpower would not suffice: only ground troops would be able to protect the civilians in Kosovo. This media criticism did not develop into a campaign, in the manner of Kurdistan, only because NATO quickly acknowledged its responsibilities toward the refugees by rushing in supplies and organization for camps, and because it appeared to be preparing for introducing ground forces. Nevertheless, media coverage repeatedly highlighted the contradiction between NATO's professed aim of protecting civilians and the consequences of bombing—the so-called collateral damage that involved killing both Serbian civilians and Kosovar refugees. Media had helped NATO's leaders lock themselves into completing the liberation of Kosovo, just as major Western powers were forced into intervening in Kurdistan in April 1991.

The 1990s have therefore ended as they began, with highly mediated wars of the Western states against genocidal nation-states. If anything, the intensity of mediation increased, with the West in Kosovo committed from the start to humanitarianism, with Serbia more astute than Iraq in utilizing world and Western media to influence the struggle. As argued in the first section of this chapter, these experiences underline the need for an account of the mass media in conflicts as located in a larger understanding of the role of the media more generally in global politics. This requires these issues to be taken out of the context of media studies and developed within international relations—but in an international theory reconstructed to encompass them.

4

New Issues and the Media
American and German News Coverage of the Global-Warming Debate

Brigitte L. Nacos, Robert Y. Shapiro, Natasha Hritzuk, and Bruce Chadwick

As the twentieth century ended, foreign policymakers in the United States and Western Europe were no longer preoccupied with the East-West confrontations of the Cold War era. Rather, they confronted regional conflicts and, increasingly, a host of global problems and issues in areas such as trade, immigration, poverty, health, and the environment. The news media tend to report extensively on major regional conflicts such as those in the Balkans, Northern Ireland, and the Middle East, but to what extent and how does the press cover the relatively new global issues that lack the immediate drama of violent incidents and threats? We explore this question by examining how the American and German media covered the global-warming debate before, during, and after the 1997 international conference on climate change in Kyoto, Japan.

Global environmental problems can be addressed effectively only when the international community recognizes their causes and agrees on significant countermeasures. News reports on such matters may influence public and elite opinion and, in democracies, the policy positions of national governments. The extent to which press coverage of global-warming issues varies from country to country may affect international agreement or disagreement on collective efforts to solve these problems. In view of the relatively new global news networks and the increasingly international scope of news organizations, one would expect that reporting on international issues is quite similar in the United States, Italy, France, Germany, and other comparable democracies. But it is also possible that the media in different countries reflect distinct national and regional interests, policies, and politics.

DEMOCRACY, THE MEDIA, AND FOREIGN POLICY

When he was Speaker of the U.S. House of Representatives, the late Thomas P. "Tip" O'Neill steadfastly believed that "all politics is local" (O'Neill 1986, chap. 1). Clearly, providing benefits to their districts or states is still an imperative for members of Congress who want to be re-elected. But while local and regional interests were once mainly apparent in the context of domestic policymaking, many such parochial matters have become increasingly connected to global conditions and politics, especially —but not only—in the economic sphere. Thus, when Americans lose their jobs, labor unions may claim that low-wage workers abroad have taken them; when the value of their savings invested in mutual funds shrinks dramatically, they may hear from Wall Street experts that troubled economies abroad have precipitated these losses. In the era of rapidly growing international interdependence, O'Neill's maxim is as relevant as ever.

Visiting the United States of the 1830s (when the country had a population of some 12 million), Alexis de Tocqueville recognized that in a democracy of this size most citizens could no longer meet to share their thoughts and debate public matters. Instead, newspapers provided citizens with civic and political information (de Tocqueville 1969, chap. 6). One hundred and seventy years later, with a U.S. population of more than 250 million, the news media are more crucial than ever for providing citizens with comprehensive information (Lippmann 1949; Robinson and Sheehan 1983; Entman 1989; Ansolabehere et al. 1993; Bennett 1996; Graber 1997). Just as modern citizens have "virtually nowhere else to turn [but to the news media] for information about public affairs and for cues on how to frame and interpret that information" (Neumann et al. 1992, 11), public debate "is (and probably must be) largely *mediated*, with professional communicators rather than ordinary citizens talking to each other and to the public through the mass media of communication" (Page 1996, 1).

In colonial times and through the early years of the Republic, the American press had an excellent track record with foreign news, reporting extensively on events, developments, and opinions abroad. More recently, even during the Cold War era, the news media's foreign reporting was limited to "the most dramatic overseas events" (Gans 1980, 37). Once the Soviet Union crumbled and the Cold War ended, the volume of foreign news coverage declined precipitously (Norris 1997; Hickey 1998).

If the media truly fail to inform the public adequately about international affairs beyond major crises, confrontations, and scandals, this void would limit Americans' ability to understand important public policy issues at a time when the once distinct line between domestic and foreign policy has increasingly become blurred (Schneider 1994; Deese 1994, Huntington 1997). During World War II and the Cold War, collective public opinion in America reflected a considerable degree of sensitivity and even sophistication with respect to both domestic and foreign policy (Page and Shapiro 1992). But the extent to which public opinion is rational "depends in part upon the political environment in which citizens find themselves, especially upon what opportunities for political learning and what quality of political information are provided to them by what we can call the 'information system' " (Page and Shapiro 1992, 389).

The quality of the information system seems even more important during the post–Cold War era, when a broad foreign policy consensus no longer exists. While certain foreign policy areas and issues stirred up domestic conflict in the past, the United States nevertheless had overriding national interests for most of this century. When push came to shove, presidents found bipartisan support in important foreign policy matters, because the Cold War—just as World War II earlier—"fostered a common identity between American people and government" (Huntington 1997, 31). This was reflected in the way the media framed foreign policy news. As Norris has noted, "From 1945 to 1989 the Cold War frame prevailed in U.S. foreign policy, providing a cultural prism to explain complex political and military events in countries from Hungary to Vietnam, Cuba, Angola, Afghanistan, and Nicaragua. . . . [As a consequence,] the Cold War frame ran like a red thread through most coverage of international news in the past because it dominated U.S. foreign policy" (Norris 1997, 276, 277).

Cracks in the foreign policy consensus appeared during the Vietnam War and remained as a result of increased partisanship in Congress beginning in the 1980s (Deese 1994; Rohde 1994). Since the end of the Cold War, however, disagreement has become more common. Instead of dealing with the "new world order" proclaimed by President George Bush after the demise of the communist bloc, the United States (like other nations) faces what has been called a "new world disorder" (Nacos 1996b; Taylor 1997)—an international environment lacking the predictable patterns of friends and foes, cooperation and conflict, and right and wrong that characterized the bipolar world of the past.

With the possible exception of serious foreign crisis situations, such as military conflicts and troop deployments abroad, there no longer exists a clear-cut national interest in U.S. foreign policy shared by most elites and most of the public (Deese 1994; Huntington 1997). With the new realities of international interdependence affecting ever more domestic conditions and groups of citizens, special interests at home have tended to diminish any notion of a shared national stake. According to one expert,

> The greater the international penetration of U.S. society, economy, and politics, the greater the demand by different sets of opinion leaders, groups, and even regions for the government to mitigate or offset perceived harmful effects on values or interests or to encourage foreign trade and investment and avoid protectionist policies. (Deese 1994, 4)

As complex global issues arise from international trade and capital flows, migration patterns, matters of public health, and the environment, the government must often deal with issues that have both international and domestic implications. Since such issues occur more often and in more policy areas than before, they are increasingly scrutinized by domestic interest groups that often communicate with similar-minded groups abroad. Thus, contemporary foreign affairs are guided "by complex policy issues and changing alliances of domestic and foreign interests" (Schneider 1994, x).

Under these circumstances, informative and accurate media reporting on international affairs is just as important as the coverage of purely domestic matters. In some cases, this connection between international and domestic issues is part and parcel of comprehensive news reporting and therefore obvious to the public. For example, the terrorist attacks on U.S. embassies in Kenya and Tanzania in the Summer of 1998 and the ensuing American air strikes on targets in Sudan and Afghanistan were extensively covered by the media, as were heightened antiterrorist security measures at home. Just as in the aftermath of earlier terrorist and counterterrorist actions abroad (Nacos 1996), the American public was exposed to a great deal of press coverage focusing on the international and domestic implications of anti-American actions in Kenya and Tanzania. But the media tend to be far less generous and transparent when global problems and issues seemingly lack the immediate drama that war or warlike threats provide.

We know a great deal about the way the media cover war, international terrorism, other foreign crises, and national security issues (Hallin 1986; Kern, Levering, and Levering 1983; Nacos 1990; Kellner 1992; MacArthur 1993; Bennett and Paletz 1994; Nacos 1996; Taylor 1997). We are far less informed, however, about patterns in news reporting on relatively new global issues, such as trade, international monetary policies, international health problems, and the global environment, that lack the drama and powerful visual images the news media prefer. More important, these issues are neither framed by political elites nor reported by the media in the context of compelling national interests, because they often mobilize different domestic interests on different sides. Pointing to recent changes in geopolitics and in international news reporting, one expert in political communications suggests that post–Cold War news may "provide viewers with a more confusing, disjointed, and violent image of the world, rather than an informed and balanced understanding of international events"(Norris 1997: 288). Pointing out that media professionals assume their "customers" are not interested in day-to-day foreign news, another media scholar calls contemporary foreign-affairs coverage "erratic, ill-informed, and spasmodic" (Taylor 1997, 73).

If the transformations in international politics have in fact resulted in reporting that is more likely to confuse than enlighten, one would expect news about relatively new and complex global conditions and issues to be just as affected, if not more so, than the coverage of dramatic foreign crises. It is precisely for this reason that we examine news coverage of an issue area outside traditional national security and defense matters, an area reflective of the new problems and issues affecting both the global and the domestic realms: the international politics of environmental protection and, specifically, the preparation and actual forging of an international accord at the 1997 Kyoto conference on global warming.

THE GLOBAL-WARMING ISSUE

On the early morning of December 11, 1997, shortly after the scheduled end of the Kyoto conference on global warming (officially, The Third Conference of the Parties to the United Nations Framework Convention on Climate Change), 1,500 delegates from 150 countries reached a compromise accord to limit the emission of greenhouse gases. The United States agreed to reduce its emissions 7 percent below the 1990 level by 2010, the European Union (EU) pledged to cut emissions by 8 percent, and Japan by 6 percent. As a group, the industrialized nations pledged a reduction of 5 percent. Some participants and observers characterized the agreement as a step in the right direction; others criticized the prescribed reductions as either too weak or too strong.

Six years before the Kyoto meeting, at the 1992 Earth Summit in Rio de Janeiro, the industrialized nations agreed to limit their output of greenhouse gases on a voluntary basis. The United States and most other developed countries failed to keep their promise. The political battles before and during the climate summit in Kyoto were especially caustic, because this time around the negotiated reduction targets were understood to be binding.

The Bill Clinton administration's pre-Kyoto position stipulated a cutback of greenhouse emissions to 1990 levels by 2010 and the inclusion of the developing nations in a meaningful reduction regime. The EU proposed a cut of 15 percent below 1990 levels by 2010 and an exemption of the developing world from reductions negotiated in Kyoto. Thus, instead of developed and developing countries being pitted against each other, a major fault line emerged between the U.S. administration and the EU. In fact, at a meeting before the Kyoto conference, the EU and a large group of developing countries (the G77) agreed to a joint position for Kyoto.

Finally, the Americans and Europeans had another major disagreement over so-called emissions trading: The fifteen EU members agreed among themselves on different reduction levels to achieve the collective EU goal. In other words, a country reducing its output of greenhouse gases beyond established targets would be able to share these reductions with fellow EU members. In spite of this "European bubble" arrangement, the EU opposed the American "umbrella" proposal for a global trading solution to allow all industrialized nations to swap emission credits. Canada, Japan, and some other developed countries supported the U.S. position.

Germany demanded the steepest reductions in greenhouse gases and promised to set an example with a 25 percent cut. Thus, the gap that separated the industrialized world was especially pronounced with respect to the positions held by Washington and Bonn.

FROM TRADITIONAL FOREIGN POLICY NEWS TO NEW GLOBAL ISSUES

Many communication scholars, former and current government officials, and media insiders believe that the communications revolution fundamentally changed the processes and methods by which foreign policy is formulated, debated, and adopted (Cutler 1984; Serfaty 1991; Gergen 1991). In the global village of the early twenty-first century, a vast and powerful multidimensional communications net is said to circumvent "the control of any national government" (Serfaty 1991, 2). By instantly and indiscriminately transmitting information from virtually any place and any person on the globe to any location, the news media have ostensibly opened up the foreign policy process to a diversity of actors at home and abroad. With respect to American foreign policy, it has been argued that the growth of this new medialism has diminished the traditional dominance of presidents, White House advisers, and a relatively small foreign policy establishment in public foreign policy debates and, ultimately, in the timing and the range of the decisions these leaders make.

But communications research does not support the notion of a foreign policy process driven and influenced by a wide-open teledemocracy (Strobel 1997). On the contrary, the traditional symbiotic relationship between reporters and government officials observed during the Cold War era (Cohen 1963; Gans 1980, Hallin 1986; Nacos 1990) has continued, as confirmed by recent research (Bennett 1994a, 1994b; Cook 1994; Entman and Page 1994). This cooperative relationship between members of the media and government officials has remained especially strong at the leading foreign policy news beats in Washington—that is, the White House and the Departments of Defense and State—especially in times of foreign crises.

Even when the media cite a relatively wide range of sources and views in foreign policy debates, administration officials still tend to receive preferential treatment, if only in terms of the frequency in which they are selected as sources, the prominence of their placement in reports, and their overall allotment of space or time (Nacos 1990; Entman and Page 1994). Moreover, the press still determines the range of different viewpoints that are presented to the public (Entman and Page 1994). Perhaps most important, the media tend to pay special attention to presidents—especially when they address major foreign policy issues.

There are a few documented exceptions to these patterns of news coverage. When terrorists strike American targets abroad, for example, the U.S. media report more from foreign beats than from the traditional Washington beats. In these cases, the press does not rely on U.S. officials—who may themselves depend on the media for information—as excessively as they usually do. Rather, the press turns to individuals who have compelling personal interests, such as the families and friends of victims (Nacos 1996).

We wondered at the outset, then, whether press coverage of new global issues follows the dominant past patterns or the few exceptions. The new global issues concern policies and politics with foreign, international, and domestic components.

Thus, our examination of the media and the conference on global warming—as well as the coverage of other global issues—must consider prominent reporting patterns or characteristics that have been found in both domestic and foreign news. Two important characteristics are the power and the tendency of the media to index and frame the news.

Indexing the News

While reasonable people can differ on the worthiness of covering particular events, developments, and policies, there is little disagreement that certain matters simply must be reported regardless of whether they concern domestic or foreign affairs. Still, the media are gatekeepers, allowing sources to participate in policy debates both in print and in news broadcasts. According to Bennett (1996, 377), "sources and viewpoints are 'indexed' (admitted through the news gates) according to the magnitude and content of conflicts among key government decision makers or other players with the power (as perceived by journalistic insiders) to affect the development of a story." Whether the press covers the critical voices and viewpoints of more or less established interests depends on the particular stance of authoritative sources, especially government insiders. This occurs far more often in domestic affairs than in foreign policy matters. In one expert's words, "The bottom line remains that the news gates tend to open or close depending on the levels of conflict among powerful players on the situation on Capitol Hill, the White House, the State Department, the Defense Department, and other relevant institutions" (Bennett 1994b, 180).

In addition to "source indexing," communications researchers have found "power indexing" patterns as well, especially in the coverage of major foreign crises (Entman and Page 1994; Zaller and Chiu 1996). Zaller and Chiu (see Chapter 5 in this volume) did not find evidence for this reporting bias in the case of foreign policy crises in the post–Cold War era, but another study confirmed the entrenched reporting pattern (Mermin 1999). In power indexing, reporters pay special attention to the views of authoritative sources who are, in the media's judgment, most likely to project and influence the outcome of particular policy issues. Thus, with respect to the coverage of environmental issues in the leading U.S. media in the 1970s and 1980s, some researchers found a strong tilt in favor of liberal, proenvironment sources (Lichter, Rothman, and Lichter 1986). But a systematic content analysis of the American press's global-warming coverage from January 1985 through August 1992 concluded that "although proponents have dominated the global warming debate, the level of support [for the view that global warming is real] has declined over time" (Media Monitor 1992). This decline took place when members of the Bush administration became very active in publicly questioning the global-warming theory. Such special attention to administration sources is a compelling example of power indexing: the media apparently concluded that President Bush and administration officials were in the best position to forecast the eventual outcome of that stage of the global warming policy debate.

Framing the News

News frames provide readers, viewers, and listeners with reference points, or cues, that influence how news consumers understand, make sense of, and evaluate the received information. According to Gitlin, "Media frames are persistent patterns of cognition, interpretation, of selection, emphasis, and exclusion, by which symbol handlers routinely organize discourse whether verbal or visual" (Gitlin 1980, 7). Journalists, photographers, editors, producers, and others in the media can and do make choices when it comes to framing the news. In Entman's view, "A frame operates to select and highlight some features of reality and obscure others in a way that tells a consistent story about problems, their causes, moral implications, and remedies" (Entman 1996, 77, 78).

In contemporary news coverage, several predominant framing patterns have been identified. Most of these frames can be collapsed into two categories: strategy and substance (Patterson 1993; Fallows 1996; Cappella and Jamieson 1997; Lawrence 1998). The strategic frame, emphasizing politics of the day, political strategies, winners and losers, horse-race updates, political bickering and conflict, and the like is also characterized by a preference for simplicity, emotions, and personalities. Strategic framing, or what Patterson calls "game schema," results in news coverage that paints "public life as a contest between scheming political leaders" (Fallows 1996, 7). Consequently, when citizens are exposed to this type of coverage, their cynicism toward politicians and politics increases measurably (Cappella and Jamison 1997) as does their alienation from civic life (Fallows 1996). In contrast, the use of substantive frames concentrates on the debate of facts, issues, context, policies, and institutional policymaking processes. While not necessarily decreasing public cynicism, as Cappella and Jamieson found with health-reform coverage in 1993–1994, substantive framing in the news provides the public with information on important policy issues. Even aspects of the episodic/event-oriented and thematic/contextual frames identified by Shanto Iyengar (1991), especially in television news, can have elements of strategic or substantive frames.[1]

While we concentrate on the game/politics/event-oriented and the substance/policy/context-oriented frames, even a cursory reading of the news on global trade, financial markets, and global-warming issues suggests a number of additional themes with competing frames. These include the following:

- *The environmental politics theme* that contains domestic and international aspects of framing. As pointed out earlier, since global warming and the efforts of the international community to deal with it affect domestic and international politics and policies, we need to wonder how the media deal with domestic and international actors, issues, and politics.

- *The science theme* involves framing global warming as a real problem versus emphasizing the lack of clear evidence for, and ambiguous attitudes toward, the reality of climate change. The questions of whether scientific evidence exists for global warming and of the harmful consequences of climate change seem fundamental to an informed public debate. Since the media can find sources and arguments emphasizing either frame, we should consider the choices made and possible biases here.
- *The economic theme* involves the framing of benefits versus the costs. Here, the issues of global warming and, more important, the policies to slow down and perhaps reverse the trend can be boiled down to one main question: Who pays, and how much, for the indivisible benefit of effective policies to combat climate change? In the industrialized countries, the critical question concerns whether drastic reductions in greenhouse-gas emissions harm the economy or offer new opportunities for the business sector now or in the foreseeable future.

COMPARATIVE PERSPECTIVE:
THE UNITED STATES AND GERMANY

Thus far, we have considered mostly the media's role in American democracy and in the American foreign policy process. However, the roles of the news media and public opinion are quite different in German government and politics (Edinger and Nacos 1998; Risse-Kappen 1994). These distinctions are the result of different institutional structures, processes, and powers (i.e., power sharing between the executive and legislature in American foreign policy versus strong executive control over foreign policy in Germany; and weak parties in the American presidential system versus strong parties that permeate all political institutions in the German parliamentary system). Moreover, according to one comparison of American and German foreign policymaking,

> The society-dominated United States provides domestic actors and public opinion with multiple access points into the political system. [In contrast,] the Federal Republic of Germany comes closest to the corporatist type of domestic structure, in which the policy networks with strong intermediate organizations linking state and society play a significant role in the decision making process. (Risse-Kappen 1994, 255)

Unlike their American counterparts, German decisionmakers do not have to worry excessively about public opinion and the media's potential effect on public attitudes. One recent example illustrates this point: although opinion surveys over the years revealed that a majority of Germans consistently opposed giving up the German mark as the national currency, decisionmakers ignored the public and decided in favor of a common European currency.

Nevertheless, declining societal milieus, changing lifestyles, waning party membership and loyalty, and the consequences of German reunification are among the factors that have weakened the traditional role of political parties as linkages between citizens and state, populace and government. As a result, the print media, radio, and television have become increasingly important as channels of political communication and as sources of information—not simply during election campaigns but between elections as well. Thus, as the Federal Republic of Germany has shown signs of moving toward a "media democracy," decisionmakers have become more concerned than ever with news content and public opinion (Edinger and Nacos 1998, chap. 3).

Finally, Germans, Americans, and people in other countries have access to some of the same news media, namely, networks, such as CNN and CNBC, and nightly television programs, such as the ABC's *World News Tonight*. Even if ordinary citizens do not have the time or inclination to watch international news shows, newsroom personnel everywhere monitor and take their clues from these sources, perhaps CNN most of all.[2] As the operations of the large and most influential media corporations are increasingly guided by profit imperatives, international news services, such as Reuters and the Associated Press, provide an increasing number of news organizations not simply with text but with video as well. More important, all American TV networks work closely with networks in other nations. CNN alone has partnership agreements "with more than 200 foreign networks, ranging from the BBC to Iranian state television" (Mifflin 1998). But when news organizations in the United States rely increasingly on international news services and on two-way partnerships with affiliates in countries around the globe, one would expect news content to become more uniform—not only in the United States but in countries with news-network affiliates, such as Germany, the United Kingdom, and Japan. In comparing the United States and Germany, then, we must consider whether the likely results of the international news-sharing schemes are offset by each country's particular circumstances, such as journalistic political partisanship, which is stronger among German than American journalists (Patterson and Donsbach 1996).

Summary: Research Questions

To what extent, then, has worldwide access to the same international media meant that reporting on new global problems has become similar in Western democracies? To explore this, we examined how American and German media covered the global-warming debate before, during, and after the 1997 Kyoto conference in terms of news indexing and framing. The questions we posed earlier with respect to customary and extraordinary patterns in news coverage of global warming informed our research design.

For content analysis, we chose two daily newspapers in the United States (the *New York Times* and the *Wall Street Journal*) and three German daily newspapers (*Die Welt, Handelsblatt,* and *Berliner Morgenpost*). Just as the *New York Times* is one of the most influential newspapers in the United States, *Die Welt* is among the most influential dailies in Germany. The *Wall Street Journal* in the United States and *Handelsblatt* in Germany are the leading newspapers for finance and business. We also examined the *Berliner Morgenpost* as an example of one of Germany's many fine regional newspapers. Finally, we studied the early evening news programs of the three American broadcast TV networks ABC, CBS, and NBC, and of CNN, the leading cable news network.[3] From September 1, 1997, through February 28, 1998, we coded all articles (news stories, commentaries, news analyses, and opinion pieces) about the global-warming issue and debate in the context of the Kyoto conference. We distinguished between the following categories of information: sources/actors and their countries of origin; viewpoints on the environment, science, and economic themes; positions on global-warming proposals, especially with respect to the Kyoto conference; and domestic and international politics surrounding the issue of how to deal with climate change.

Differences and Similarities in American and German Reporting

During the six-month period, the American press covered global warming and its related issues far more extensively than did the German press.[4] The reason was obvious: in the United States the prospect of a binding international agreement on measures to fight climate change energized the vastly different domestic interests in the area of environmental protection. By contrast, in Germany the position of the German government (and of the European Union) was backed by a broad consensus on the need to drastically reduce greenhouse gases at home and abroad. But there is another explanation for the sparse coverage in Germany and the more comprehensive reporting in American newspapers: on the heels of a strong Green movement in the 1970s and the electoral successes of the Green Party in the 1980s and 1990s, the German media regularly informed the public on environmental issues. With respect to Kyoto, therefore, the German press limited its coverage mostly to *new* developments. In the United States, where the Green movement did not have a comparable impact on policymakers, the press, and the public, the print press—especially the *New York Times*—published in-depth articles with background information and discussions on global warming to inform the public about the issues raised before, and at, the Kyoto meeting.

Broad Range of Domestic Sources

Table 4.1 reveals that administration officials and members of Congress in the U.S. and German government officials and members of the federal legislature in the German press were more frequently covered by the press than any other group of domestic actors. But contrary to the American media's more common coverage of foreign policy issues, government officials did not dominate that press coverage. Taken together, policy and scientific experts, a variety of organized interests (busi-

Table 4.1   Domestic Source Indexing

	U.S. media (N = 846)	German media (N = 85)
Executive Branch	36%	39%
Legislative Branch	7	15
Interest/Pressure Groups	28	26
Experts	20	19
Public/Public Opinion	9	1

ness, labor unions, environmentalists), as well as the public, were more frequently covered than officials at Washington's major news beats.

In the face of extreme and freely expressed differences of opinion inside the U.S. government, the news media granted generous access to a broad range of sources and views outside the government. As a result, the media—especially newspapers—reflected the kind of robust debate that is especially essential in the American system of government, where decisionmakers pay considerable attention to public opinion.

In Germany, the views of federal officials in both the executive and legislative branches combined received more media attention than those of experts and various interests (especially environmental groups and business; see Table 4.1). Contrary to the fundamentally different views about the content of an international global warming agreement in the United States, there were no elementary disagreements in Germany, where the Green Party, with its strict environmental protection platform, was an established political force and the large catch-all parties, namely, the Christlich Demokratische Union (CDU) and the Sozialdemokratische Partei Deutschlands (SPD), have also embraced strong pro-ecology programs. The only domestic issue that was raised a few times by political actors and by journalists themselves concerned the government's claims about substantial greenhouse-gas reductions in the 1990s. While not disputing those numbers, critics pointed out that the dismantling of most of East Germany's obsolete industrial plants, not actual cutbacks, was responsible for emissions declines.

In contrast to the United States, where the Clinton administration's original and altered proposals for Kyoto were attacked by friends and foes of a global-warming agreement, there was no opposition at home to the official German position on the Kyoto global-warming proposals. And unlike President Clinton, Chancellor Helmut Kohl had no reason to communicate his views on climate-change issues during this period. Thus, while indexing the news in favor of authoritative sources in governing and opposition parties, the German media did not ignore other voices, with the exception of domestic public opinion (compared to the United States). This coverage was hardly surprising in Germany's democratic-corporatist arrangement, where political parties permeate and mediate virtually all political and societal interests for the sake of consensus-building. And since the public's long-term sentiments are far more influential on policies than public opinion polls, open public deliberation is less important in Germany than in the United States.

A Different Kind of Power Indexing

Neither domestic government officials nor nongovernmental actors dominated the global-warming coverage in the United States, because there were simply no actors and institutions influential enough to foreshadow the eventual outcome of the politics of the global-warming issue. Members of Congress, business groups, and labor unions sharply opposed President Clinton for going too far with his proposals to reduce greenhouse emissions. Environmentalists opposed Clinton for not going far enough. Indeed, months before the Kyoto meeting, the U.S. Senate had signaled (through a 95–0 vote) that a global-warming agreement would not be ratified unless the developing world joined the United States and other First and Second World nations in agreeing to substantial emission reductions. Thus, uncertainty as to the policy outcome and the inability of the media to power-index the news was based on the unresolved state of affairs in domestic politics. In Germany, in contrast, there was simply no disagreement over the government's far-reaching Kyoto position and therefore no rationale for the media to index domestic voices and viewpoints according to their political weight. But while either absent (in the United States) or irrelevant (in Germany) with respect to domestic actors and viewpoints, strong power indexing can be found in the way the media in both countries framed what we earlier called the "environmental politics theme." The leading American newspaper and television networks framed global climate-change issues predominantly in terms of the domestic environment and domestic politics, whereas the German media focused overwhelmingly on international problems, competing policy proposals, and global politics. This profound difference manifested itself in the proportion of domestic and foreign voices and viewpoints reported in the news. As Table 4.2 shows, the two American newspapers and all four TV networks devoted far more of their coverage to domestic than foreign sources and actors; in contrast, the three German

Table 4.2 Frequency of Environment Frames

Sources/Actors	New York Times (N= 711)	Wall Street Journal (N= 302)	Television Networks (N= 136)
Domestic	71%	75%	83%
Foreign	29	25	17

	Die Welt (N= 140)	Handelsblatt (N= 46)	Berliner Morgenpost (N= 59)
Domestic	36%	30%	36%
Foreign	64	70	64

newspapers cited foreign sources and political players far more often than domestic ones.[5]

For the American media, the likely rationale for this focus was simply to acknowledge that the conflictual domestic debate and its outcome would influence—if not determine—the fates of the Kyoto conference and any other international initiatives on climate change. In this respect, the ethnocentrism that Herbert Gans (1980) recognized in foreign-news reporting during the Cold War remained alive and well during the late 1990s. The dominance of the domestic frame was not unreasonable, since the United States, as the only surviving superpower and the largest contributor to global greenhouse emissions, was the key to any global-warming agreement.

In the absence of a substantial domestic public debate, the German press turned its attention to foreign actors in the international debate on the Kyoto meeting. Even when domestic actors were mentioned and cited, they reacted mostly to initiatives, reactions, and controversies abroad, especially when these involved President Clinton, Vice President Al Gore, or other individuals or groups in the United States. German newspapers, too, looked upon the United States as the power to make or break an agreement at Kyoto. One-third of all articles on global warming published by the three German newspapers mentioned President Clinton, Vice President Gore, or the United States in their headlines, 29 percent reported mostly or exclusively about American voices and viewpoints, and an additional 33 percent mentioned U.S. policies and/or politics in the text. American domestic politics and conflict were far more frequently mentioned than were the marginal differences of opinion at home.

Moreover, as shown in Table 4.3, when major policy positions taken during the Kyoto conference were mentioned or described, the American media—with the exception of the *Wall Street Journal*—referred to and discussed most of all the important and most controversial U.S. positions. Conversely, the German media paid far less attention to the German government's and the EU's positions than to the policy views of international players outside Germany and the EU—most of all the United States.

Table 4.3   Frequency of Policy Positions

Policy Positions	New York Times (N=127)	Wall Street Journal (N=103)	Television Networks (N=42)
American	68%	45%	69%
International	32	55	31

	Die Welt (N=96)	Handelsblatt (N=32)	Berliner Morgenpost (N=47)
German/EU	27%	28%	24%
International	73	72	76

The unmistakable thrust of the German coverage was that in the struggle for an equitable and effective global-warming agreement the United States (interchangeable with President Clinton, Vice President Gore, business lobbies, or the U.S. Senate) was the eight-hundred-pound gorilla taking on the rest of the world. This was not a theme in the American coverage.

Strategy Versus Substance Coverage: A Mixed Bag

Cappella and Jamieson (1997) found that the news coverage of the 1993–1994 health-care reform debate was overwhelmingly framed in terms of political strategy (67 percent) at the expense of policy substance (25 percent). As Table 4.4 indicates, we did not find this one-sided framing mode in the global-warming news. However, the coverage in the *New York Times* and the *Wall Street Journal* contained slightly more frequent references to domestic and international politics than to major policy positions at home or abroad.

Television newscasts, however, referred more often to policy issues than to politics. We can only surmise that the networks' strong tilt in favor of substantive frames was the result of their more limited coverage of the Kyoto conference. In the absence of dramatic visuals about clashing interests, TV reporters and newscasters were left with summarizing positions and policy statements by prominent leaders, such as President Clinton and Vice President Gore. The three German newspapers paid more attention to policy positions and substantive differences concerning global environmental policy than to political maneuvers and calculations.

Our results correspond more closely to Lawrence's (1998) than to Cappella and Jamieson's findings. Lawrence established that the coverage of policy issues is more substantive than strategic when they are reported outside the context of election campaigns. Neither the United States nor Germany had ongoing federal election campaigns during the period we examined, potentially explaining the near balance between strategic and substantive frames in American newspapers and the dominance of issue coverage in television newscasts. Still, considering the possible effect of strategic framing on cynical public attitudes, the great emphasis on this framing mode in newspapers is reason for concern. Not surprisingly, overall we found few

Table 4.4 Strategic versus Substantive Frames

	Strategy	Substance	N
New York Times	54%	46%	276
Wall Street Journal	52	48	226
Television Networks	35	65	65
Die Welt	27	73	102
Handelsblatt	43	57	56
Berliner Morgenpost	25	75	63

strategic frames in the German press's domestic coverage, but there was considerable reporting of this sort with respect to foreign politics.

Interestingly enough, German newspapers resorted most explicitly to emphasizing strategy and conflict when they reported on Gore's weakening commitment to environmental protection because of his aspirations for the 2000 presidential nomination. As the German press saw it, the onetime "Mister Green" had his eyes on the Oval Office and was therefore willing to give in to pressure from influential business interests.

Scientific Knowledge

The extent to which one believes that scientific evidence proves or disproves global warming (or is inconclusive), and the extent to which one considers the likely consequences of global warming to be bad or good for the planet, can influence one's policy preferences. For this reason, we appraised how the American and German media framed the theme of scientific knowledge. In one respect, as shown in Table 4.5, the American and German media were alike: all news outlets that we examined framed global warming far more often as a real threat to humankind than as something unproven, or undetermined, or beneficial.

However, while German press coverage reflected mostly, or even exclusively, the view that climate change was real and dangerous, the American media differed noticeably in their attention to the various arguments in the scientific debate. To an even greater extent than the three German newspapers, the American TV networks were one-sided in their attention to what we would call the "real-threat scenario" of global warming. The Wall *Street Journal* presented the most balanced framing with respect to the various scientific arguments, and reporting in the *New York Times* emphasized a more ambiguous or uncertain position.

Table 4.5   Frequency of Science Frames

	New York Times (N=83)	Wall Street Journal (N=64)	Television Networks (N=26)
Real Threat and bad	62%	51%	92%
No Real Threat and if—good	8	22	8
Inconclusive/ambiguous	30	17	—
	Die Welt (N=25)	Handelsblatt (N=22)	Berliner Morgenpost (N=26)
Real Threat and bad	84%	100%	85%
No Real Threat and if—good	4	—	—
Inconclusive/ambiguous	12	—	15

Economic Consequences: Optimism

Table 4.6 shows that none of the print and electronic media examined paid a great deal of attention (based on the small total number found) to the very specific views expressed in the debate about the economic consequences of binding reductions in greenhouse-gas emissions—especially in industrialized countries like the United States and Germany. However, while the American media covered this debate more extensively than did the German press, the framing patterns regarding the economy were quite similar in that the media reflected optimistic and cautiously optimistic frames more often than pessimistic ones. The exception was *Handelsblatt*, a business newspaper, reflecting a more pessimistic than optimistic viewpoint.

In the United States, the *Wall Street Journal*, too, paid more attention to the pessimistic arguments than did networks and the *New York Times*, but it was nevertheless more reflective of the optimistic or cautiously optimistic business outlook as well.

CONCLUSION

Leading up to and during the Gulf War in the early 1990s, the American media domesticated the news by focusing heavily on domestic newsbeats and sources (Cook 1994) at a time when even the Bush administration characterized the conflict as completely international, pitting Saddam Hussein against the rest of the world. In 1997, the American media also domesticated the news of the global-warming debate and the international conference in Kyoto. But in contrast to the Gulf War, when official government newsbeats and their sources dominated domestic debate in the media (Cook 1994), political actors other than the U.S. government—interest groups, experts, and the public—eclipsed officials at the leading Washington newsbeats in the case of Kyoto. To some extent, these variations reflected the prevailing realities during these two different periods. During the crisis in the Persian Gulf, when the U.S. military was deployed abroad, domestic actors were more reluctant to criticize the administration than during the global-warming debate, when no such comparable and immediate threat was felt. Still, as in almost all situations, the media had leeway in how they reported the news in both cases. While the news media

Table 4.6 Frequency of Economic Frames

	U.S. media (N= 82)	German media (N= 17)
Optimistic	32%	35%
Cautiously optimistic	47	41
Pessimistic	21	24

overcovered Washington's official newsbeats and sources during the Gulf crisis at the expense of different domestic sources and viewpoints external to government, during the global-warming debate they reached out more frequently to nongovernmental voices than to public officials.

In the case of global warming, news reports in the American media were more compatible with the traditional coverage patterns of domestic policies than of foreign affairs. The domestic flavor in the global-warming news provided citizens with the rich marketplace of ideas and the mediated public deliberation thought to be essential in a strong democracy (Barber 1984; Page 1996). Lance Bennett (1994a, 172) suggests that this sort of coverage might stimulate "more interest in foreign policy among the general public." But as such mediated foreign policy debates become more like acrimonious domestic policy deliberations, the corresponding decisionmaking processes may become even more complicated and the president's foreign policy prerogatives more contested.

Because Germany lacks the superpower status of the United States, the German press is not as inclined as the American media to domesticate foreign policy news. This distinction and the consensus on Germany's global-warming position explains the German media's international focus—especially on the United States. But both countries' presses behaved very differently in framing the environment theme. The German and the American news reflected the unique power position of the United States and the American hold on the outcome of the global-warming debate. Unlike the American media, the German press emphasized voices and views criticizing the United States as the main obstacle to a tough and effective global-warming treaty. Not surprisingly, Clinton and Gore were the recipients of much of this criticism. Since chancellors and their governments are firmly in control of German foreign policy, many Germans—media insiders included—assume incorrectly that American presidents and their administrations have the same, or similar, foreign policy powers.

In covering officials in the governing and opposition parties far more generously than other political actors, the German press—unlike the U.S. media—engaged in domestic power indexing. This did not simply reflect the existing consensus on global-warming positions for the Kyoto conference. Given the intertwining of political parties, interest groups, and the public in Germany's governmental process, mediated public policy debates are not perceived to be as important in Germany as they are in the United States. While changes in the electorate, in the party landscape, and in the media seem to move Germany toward a media democracy, the lack of domestic disagreement on global warming excludes this particular coverage as a test case for possible changes in Germany's approach to mediated policy deliberations.

As we report above, the German press, far more than the American media, portrayed global warming as a definite threat to humankind.

In sum, the American and German news coverage of global warming before, during, and after the Kyoto conference was quite similar in some respects and quite different in others. In spite of the growing reach of international media organizations across national borders, the media in both countries indexed and framed the news according to the different domestic political contexts in the United States and the Federal Republic of Germany. The optimistic expectation that the internationalization of the news would be a unifying force across national borders and with respect to the new global issues seems, at least at this time, premature.

5

Government's Little Helper

U.S. Press Coverage of Foreign Policy Crises, 1946–1999

John Zaller and Dennis Chiu

It is a truism that journalists find it difficult to report critically on government activity during foreign policy crises. They must contend not only with officials who strain to control the news but also with the fear that tough reporting will undermine the government's ability to deal with the crisis. As a result, journalists often simply "rally 'round the flag" and whatever policy the government favors.

Yet journalists do not invariably support government foreign policy in times of crisis. Perhaps the most notable case of a journalistic failure to rally occurred during the Tet offensive of the Vietnam War, when reporters quickly concluded and began to report that Vietcong attacks represented a failure of American policy. In several other cases—for example, the Angola crisis during the Gerald Ford administration—media support for government policy has been notably restrained.

The aim of this chapter is to explain the general tendency of the media to support the government during foreign policy crises as well as exceptions to this tendency. The inquiry is organized around Lance Bennett's (1990) theory of press indexing, which holds that reporters index the slant of their coverage to reflect the range of opinion that exists within the government. On the basis of a study of forty-two foreign policy crises from the Soviet takeover of Poland in 1945 to the Kosovo conflict in 1999, we find strong evidence that reporters do, as Bennett suggests, appear to wax hawkish and wane dovish as official sources lead them to do.

Initially published in 1995, this chapter covered crises through the Gulf War; this update adds data from seven crisis points in the 1990s. The new data suggest that the dynamics of media politics, despite a strong indexing effect over the entire post–World War II period, have changed since the end of the Cold War. In particular, the media tend to be more independent of Congress and the president, though not necessarily more independent of government officials generally.

THEORETICAL BACKGROUND

A standard finding in studies of mass media is that reporters regard as newsworthy that which their legitimate or official sources say is newsworthy (Cohen 1963). The dependence of reporters on official sources is so great that, as Leon Sigal (1973) put it, "Even when the journalist is in a position to observe an event directly, he remains reluctant to offer interpretations of his own, preferring instead to rely on his news sources. For the reporter, in short, most news is not what has happened, but what someone says has happened" (69). An editor of one of the national newsweeklies was even more blunt: "We don't deal in facts," he said, "but in attributed opinions" (cited in Gans 1980, 130). David Halberstam explained the dependency of foreign policy reporters on their sources during the Vietnam War as follows:

> They had come to journalism through the traditional routes, they had written the requisite police stories and chased fire engines and they had done all that a bit better than their peers, moving ahead in their profession, and they had finally come to Washington. If after their arrival in Washington they wrote stories about foreign policy, they did not dare inject their own viewpoints, of which they had none, or their own expertise, of which they also had none. Rather they relied almost exclusively on what some American or possibly British official told them at a briefing or at lunch. The closer journalists came to great issues, the more vulnerable they felt. (Halberstam 1979, 517–518)

As this and other evidence suggests, dependence on sources goes beyond the need to have someone to quote; it is one of the most ingrained features of modern journalism (Hallin 1984; Althaus et al., 1996; Mermin 1999).

On both theoretical and empirical grounds, one of the most important studies of press dependence on sources is Bennett's (1990) study of coverage of U.S. policy toward Nicaragua. Taking as a given that journalists are heavily dependent on sources, he deduces that variation in coverage across time should depend on variations in the opinions of "prominent officials and institutional power blocs" (106–107). This theoretical deduction, though long implicit in the scholarly literature on the press and foreign policy, had never been explicitly drawn or systematically tested. Nor was it obvious that it could survive testing. Journalists might, for example, use officials as sources but distort or choose selectively from their views so as to produce results that journalists rather than sources want.

To test what he called the "indexing hypothesis," Bennett used stories in the *New York Times* on U.S. policymaking in Nicaragua from 1983 to 1986, as abstracted in the *Times Index*. Coders rated the degree to which articles appearing on the op-ed page agreed or disagreed with the administration's polices on Nicaragua, which were generally hawkish throughout the period examined. The coders also rated the extent to which, according to information contained in the abstracts, members of Congress agreed or disagreed with the administration's hawkish policies. Dividing coder ratings of article content and congressional opinion into seventeen discrete time periods, Bennett found that the correlations between the two sets of ratings were between .63 and .76. Thus, the *New York Times* did, as hypothesized, appear to index its editorial coverage of this issue to the range of opinion within the government.

Bennett's study is not above criticism. One concern is that it failed to develop a measure of congressional opinion that was independent of what the *New York Times* claimed it was. Thus if the newspaper gave a distorted impression of congressional opinion so as to make it seem consistent with its own editorial slant, it would create the impression that the paper was following the views of Congress even though it was not.

Another insidious possibility is that members of Congress follow the editorial line of the *New York Times*, or the media more generally, rather than vice versa. If members of Congress regarded media opinion as a rough proxy for public opinion, and if, as is often suggested, members are more concerned about re-election than promoting their own views of public policy, they might find it safest simply to follow press opinion. The possibility that public officials rather than reporters are the real followers cannot be ruled out from the correlation Bennett reports. Finally, Bennett's study is limited to a single, possibly idiosyncratic issue. The study was thus unable to investigate other factors that might either disrupt press indexing or independently affect the slant of press coverage, such as the nature of the crisis, the type of foreign adversary, and the time period.

This study, then, takes a fresh look at the relationship between press slant and government opinion.

RESEARCH DESIGN

Overview

This study is an effort to explain variations in the hawkishness or dovishness of coverage of foreign policy crises. Following Bennett, we hypothesize that the degree of press hawkishness will depend on the degree of hawkishness in the government.

What exactly constitutes "hawkishness" or "dovishness" is relative to each crisis. In one crisis, doves may want to rely on diplomacy while hawks favor military aid; in another crisis the doves may favor military aid and the hawks may favor the introduction of U.S. troops. Thus, we will be examining positions that are, within the context of each foreign policy crisis, more or less supportive of military assertiveness.

Selection of Cases

For purposes of this study, a "U.S. foreign policy crisis" is defined as an emergency situation in which the United States uses, threatens to use, or considers using military force or aid as a means to pursue foreign policy objectives. Major escalations of force within an ongoing conflict are also considered foreign policy crises.

U.S. foreign policy crises are sufficiently rare that it is feasible to examine the entire universe of them. For an unbiased compendium of events that might qualify as such crises, we turned to John Spanier's *American Foreign Policy Since World War II* (12th ed.), which contains a list of "Selected Principal Events" in U.S. foreign policy from 1945 to 1991. Some of Spanier's events have nothing to do with crises, as, for example, "Reagan denounces Soviet Union as 'Evil Empire.' " Others, however, fall within our definition of crisis, such as "Soviets blockade . . . West Berlin and the Western airlift starts" or "the United States attacks Libya for terrorist attacks." From Spanier's list, we selected thirty-nine cases that met our definition of a foreign policy crisis. They include not only historically important events, such as the Korean and Vietnam Wars, but also many smaller-scale incidents, such as the invasion of Grenada and the U.S. peacekeeping operations in Lebanon. The cases also include multiple references to some ongoing crises, especially the Korean and Vietnam Wars. Despite some unavoidable arbitrariness, we believe that these crises are a fair representation of all U.S. foreign policy crises in the period 1945 to 1991.[1]

Since Spanier did not provide specific dates for events, and since some developed over a period of weeks or months rather than on a single day, we had to assign plausible dates to each event.

"Official" Opinion

Like Bennett, we use congressional opinion as the primary indicator of the official views that reporters are hypothesized to reflect in their coverage. In so doing, we do not assume that Congress is the only, or the most important, source of official views that reporters attempt to reflect. We assume only that congressional opinion, owing to the openness and ideological diversity of Congress, is likely to be roughly representative of official opinion more generally. The great advantage of congressional opinion for this study is that, thanks to the *Congressional Record*, it is far easier to measure than other forms of official opinion, making it possible to test the indexing hypothesis across a range of cases.

To ensure unbiased measurement, we measured congressional opinion independently of media coverage of it. In eleven of the crises, we were able to find votes in which members of Congress expressed themselves on the issue at hand. Congressional votes on the Vandenberg resolution during the Czechoslovakia crisis of 1948, on the Gulf of Tonkin resolution in 1964, and on the Gulf War resolution in 1991 are good examples. In twenty-two other cases, we used speeches made on the floor of the House or Senate as indicators of congressional opinion. As shown below, the two indicators of congressional opinion produced almost identical empirical results.

In three cases, Congress was out of session during the crisis, leaving no way to gauge its opinion except through the media, which we declined to do. These cases were lost from the analysis. A fourth case, a reference by Spanier to several terrorist incidents in 1985, was also dropped because it was not sufficiently distinct from the Libya bombing of 1986, which we included in the sample.[2] In two final cases, Congress was in session and capable of expressing an opinion but did not do so. Not a single speech was given. These two cases, as it happened, were among the most important in the whole set—the Soviet takeover of Eastern Europe after World War II, and President John Kennedy's decision to send U.S. military advisers to Vietnam in 1961—and we were determined to keep them in the analysis.

Spanier lists the Soviet occupation of several Eastern Europe states as one event. Occupation occurred in the closing year of World War II, when American diplomats were struggling behind the scenes to maintain Soviet cooperation with U.S. plans for the postwar period. We focused on the Polish case, for which there was some activity in Congress. Two resolutions objecting to the Soviet takeover were introduced by Polish-American members of Congress; for reasons impossible for us to ascertain, the resolutions never came to a vote (Lukas 1978, 204).

There was even less overt congressional reaction to President Kennedy's decision to send military advisers to Vietnam. The decision, taken in the context of the Berlin Wall crisis of 1961, was not officially announced. Nonetheless, press reports at the time indicate that an American commitment of military personnel was an open secret on the streets of Saigon, where U.S. military forces were moving in and U.S. warships were taking up positions offshore. As other evidence indicates, Congress was not kept in the dark about the U.S. troop buildup in Vietnam (*Newsweek,* November 27, 1961, 40).

In view of the fact that Congress was aware of events in each case but chose not to react, it seems appropriate to regard its nonaction as tacit support for administration policy. Hence, in the analysis that follows, we code Congress as supporting a dovish policy in 1945 and a hawkish policy in 1961 (Goldberg 1979, 118–119). (These coding decisions, as we show below, do not greatly affect the results.)

Altogether, then, we were able to measure congressional opinion for thirty-five cases—eleven through roll call votes, twenty-two by floor speeches, and two by imputing opinions to Congress when it acquiesced to major executive decisions.

For the twenty-two cases in which speeches were coded, the coding was done by Dennis Chiu from the *Congressional Record.* He tried to code as many as twenty-five speeches per case but often was unable to find that many within close temporal proximity to the crisis. On average, he coded fifteen speeches per case, with a standard deviation (SD) of seven. No reliability analysis was performed on Chiu's codes, since he found that identifying individual congressional speeches as hawkish or dovish in overall thrust seemed straightforward.

Media Coverage

Our analysis is based on stories appearing in *Time* and *Newsweek.* The advantage of using news magazines is that, although all media slant the news, magazines are self-consciously interpretive and hence make less effort to disguise their slant. Even so, their stories contained few explicit statements of opinion; in most cases they conveyed opinion implicitly by what they chose to cover or ignore and by the tone of coverage.

Three students rated the news-magazine data. Two of the students had extensive prior coding experience and the third had none. All three specialized in American politics and were familiar with American history in the postwar period. To avoid biasing the coders, we provided them no "training" in their coding task, choosing instead to instruct them by written communication. Except for some verbal instruction in the innocuous details of record-keeping and progress checks, the one-page written communication was the only instruction the coders received. We include the written instructions as Appendix A.[3]

As in the case of congressional opinion, we wished to capture the extent to which newsmagazine coverage was hawkish or dovish. The unit of analysis was the paragraph, which could be rated hawkish, dovish, neutral, or (rarely) both hawkish and dovish. We based the content analysis on twenty-five paragraphs per crisis, where the paragraphs were taken from the beginning of each magazine's main story and were divided as evenly as possible between the two magazines.

Following is a sample paragraph that was rated hawkish:

> Led by tanks with 90-mm. cannon and armored troop carriers, the 2nd Battalion of the 6th U.S. Marines . . . moved cautiously into the war-torn capital of the Dominican Republic. As the columns churned down Avenida Independencia . . . people suddenly appeared in the windows and doorways. Some waved. Others stared. A few spoke. "I wish the Americans would take us over," muttered a woman. A man near by sighed and nodded. (*Time*, May 7, 1965, 28)

As the example makes clear, the media slant we seek to capture may have little to do with official sources or direct statements of opinion. In some cases, the slant consists of specific hawkish or dovish arguments that are linked to a particular source, but in other cases (including this example) it consists of images, as they cumulate in a story, that induce a reader to feel more or less supportive of military policies. Thus, for example, paragraphs suggesting that a military action is going well or badly, or that civilians in the battle zone do or do not support the American effort, are counted as hawkish or dovish, even if there is no source cited and no explicit evaluation.

Each story has been rated by three coders. For each crisis and coder, we computed the following measure of media hawkishness:

$$\frac{\#\ \text{hawkish paragraphs} - \#\ \text{dovish paragraphs}}{\#\ \text{hawkish paragraphs} + \#\ \text{dovish paragraphs} + \#\ \text{neutral paragraphs}}$$

Each coder's scores correlated with the scores of the other coders at the level of .75, with none of the coders standing out from the others as especially good or bad.[4] When combined, the three sets of ratings produced a scale with an alpha reliability of 0.87. The theoretical range of the media scale is from -1.0 to $+1.0$, with 0 as the midpoint. To facilitate interpretation of the results, the scale was recoded to a theoretical range of 0 to 1, with .50 as the neutral point. The actual range of ratings on the recoded scale was from .15 to .92, with a mean of .60 and a standard deviation of .21.[5]

FINDINGS

Congressional Opinion and Media Coverage

In Bennett's test of the indexing hypothesis, the correlation between opinions expressed on the op-ed page of the *New York Times* and congressional opinion was found to be 0.63 in one test and .76 in a related one. In our study, the correlation between thrust of news content and congressional opinion was 0.63 p < .0001. If we restrict the analysis to the subset of cases for which we have the best measures of congressional opinion—either roll call votes or ten or more floor speeches—the correlation rises slightly to .65. Corrected for the reliability of the media scale, this correlation is about .70.

What this correlation means is that an increase of one standard deviation in the hawkishness of Congress is associated with an increase of .70 SDs in the hawkishness of media coverage. This is obviously a strong relationship—and, even so, it may still understate the real strength of the relationship. This is because twenty-five paragraphs per crisis, even if coded with perfect reliability, would still be an imperfect indicator of overall news coverage, which consists of thousands of paragraphs and electronic sound bites. Floor speeches and even votes, no matter how accurately measured, are likewise imperfect indicators of congressional opinion. For example, the percent of members of Congress who support a floor resolution will depend, *independently of the actual degree of hawkishness of congressional opinion,* on how toughly worded the resolution is.

Altogether, then, our results strongly corroborate Bennett's notion of press indexing. The considerable range of cases in our study, however, raises an obvious question: Does the relationship between congressional opinion and press slant hold as well in all time periods and types of situations? Or does it hold in only certain kinds of cases?

To answer these questions, we have broken the data into subsets, exploring the press-Congress relation within each. Since for this type of investigation the correlation coefficient is unreliable, we report the unstandardized coefficients for regressions in which the independent variable is congressional hawkishness and the dependent variable is press hawkishness. Typical results are shown in Table 5.1.[6]

Given the very small sample sizes, one should pay little attention to particular coefficients. The point is the overall pattern of results, which indicates that the relationship between congressional opinion and media slant reflects a broad tendency within the dataset as a whole.

Table 5.1 The Effect of Congressional Opinion on Media Slant in Selected Subsets of Cases

	Regression coefficient
Whole sample (n = 35)	.47
Time period	
Pre-Tet Offensive (n = 17)	.40
Post-Tet Offensive (n = 18)	.44
Area of world	
Americas (n = 6)	.22
Asia[a] (n = 14)	.62
Europe (n = 5)	.37
Middle East (n = 9)	.38
Type of adversary	
Communist (n = 26)	.52
Non-communist (n = 9)	.20

Note: Cell entries are unstandardized regression coefficients, where dependent variable is media slant and independent variable is congressional opinion. Coefficients are calculated within various subsets of cases, as indicated.

[a] We include Afghanistan in Asia but exclude all Middle Eastern States.

Who Is Leading Whom?

Our interpretation of the covariation between press and congressional opinion is that reporters, in Bennett's terms, index coverage to the range of opinion that exists in the government. This interpretation comes from outside the data—from prior studies that stress, on the basis of qualitative observation, the dependence of reporters on sources.

As far as the data alone are concerned, there is nothing that either supports or refutes this interpretation. The empirical results are equally consistent with the thesis of press dependence on Congress, with a thesis of congressional dependence on the press, and with a thesis that some "third factor" causes both press slant and congressional opinion, thereby inducing a spurious correlation between them.

The data we collected have only limited value for assessing causal issues of this kind.[7] They do, however, permit some exploration. First, we have the hypothesis of reverse indexing, that is, that congressional opinion follows press slant rather than vice versa. According to this argument, the tone of press coverage frames foreign policy crises for both the public and politicians. Members of Congress have no strong reason to dispute these frames, and since many care only about re-election, they may seek safety in going along with the press slant.

Although this argument imputes a great deal of power to the press, it has an element of plausibility. Risk avoidance is, according to literature on congressional behavior, a constant feature of legislative life (Jacobson 1993). In an analysis of how members of Congress decided to vote on the Gulf War resolution, Zaller (1994: 260–261) found that many wanted to avoid voting on the issue altogether:

Some legislators . . . were eager to play the role of partisan gladiators. But the majority of members were more hesitant. They would get little credit no matter how the war turned out, but might face retribution if they either opposed a successful war or supported a disastrous one. In this situation, many members saw no reason to commit themselves to a position any sooner than necessary, and a few wanted to avoid taking a position even at the very end.

One would expect risk-averse members of Congress to maintain low profiles in foreign crises, waiting for the dust to settle before going on record. They would make few speeches and would reveal their positions only when forced to do so on a vote. Hence, if there is any inflation of the Congress-press association arising from a tendency of members of Congress to echo press opinion, it should be at its maximum on votes, where the risk averse are most heavily represented. By parallel reasoning, we would expect representatives who volunteer public positions in floor speeches to be among the more risk-accepting members of Congress—"partisan gladiators" with respect to the issue at hand. When they speak out, one would expect to find them expressing personal ideologies and convictions. Hence, whatever press-Congress association exists in such cases would be hard to explain on the grounds that members of Congress were simply following the media.

To test this line of argument, we divided the data according to whether congressional opinion was measured by speeches or votes (excluding the two cases in which it was measured by imputation). We found that the strength of the press-Congress association was slightly stronger when opinion was measured by means of floor speeches ($b = .52$) than by means of votes ($b = .41$). This difference, though far from statistically significant, is the opposite of what we should have found if the press-Congress association were driven by risk-averse members of Congress who simply echoed the media line.

A recent paper by Althaus et al. (1996) suggests an additional test. In a study of the 1986 bombing of Libya, these authors found that, particularly in the Senate, floor speeches bore little relation to a legislator's electoral vulnerability but a strong relation to the member's ideological orientation. As the authors concluded with evident surprise, many Senators seemed to be "genuine iconoclasts who said what they thought regardless of the consequences" (31).

In light of this conclusion, we examined indexing for twenty-six cases in which we could measure congressional opinion from the speeches or votes of Senators alone. The press-Congress correlation for these cases was .68, or slightly higher than in the dataset as a whole. If we accept that senators are more independent-minded than members of the House, this constitutes another reason for believing that the association between congressional opinion and press slant is not due to the followership of risk-averse politicians.

Neither of these tests is definitive, but together they complement the qualitative literature and its emphasis on the dependency of the press on official opinion.

Indexing Coverage to a Common Culture?

Thus far we have assumed that if any two actors take the same slant on a crisis, it must be because one has influenced the other. But there is another possibility: because members of Congress, presidents, and reporters are all members of the same political culture, they tend to have the same culturally conditioned response to events.

This view is hard to dismiss outright. Consider, on one hand, the fall of Saigon in 1975. After more than ten years of struggle in Vietnam, it seems unlikely that many reporters would need cues from Congress to conclude that this was _not_ the time for a renewal of American hawkishness in South Vietnam. On the other hand, consider the Soviet downing of Korean Airlines Flight 007 in 1983. How could anyone be other than outraged by this event? If reporters, presidents, and members of Congress had the same internally generated reactions—dovish to the first event and hawkish to the second—it could produce the pattern of associations we have found even if there were no indexing at all.

The contention that all members of a culture have the same culturally conditioned response to events is difficult to defeat, since it posits a universal factor that is fully capable, at least in principle, of explaining whatever associations might exist. Even the most ardent exponent of culture would, however, have to concede that there are some aspects of the international situation for which culture does not provide clear cues. Within our dataset, we have identified the following cases for which, we believe, the influence of common U.S. culture would be minimal: The firing of General Douglas MacArthur by President Truman; the decision on whether to intervene in Indochina in 1954; the marine peacekeeping missions to Lebanon in 1958 and 1982; the takeover of Cuba by the forces of Fidel Castro; the question of U.S. intervention in Angola; the Soviet invasion of its former satellite nation, Afghanistan; the question of U.S. involvement in Nicaragua; the decision to put oil tankers under U.S. protection during the Iran-Iraq War; and the decision to launch the Gulf War (i.e., before fighting began).

The effect of congressional opinion on press slant in these cases is, as it turns out, almost identical to that in the dataset as a whole. Also, the elimination of any one of the nine cases leaves the results substantially unchanged. Finally, the pattern holds when the nine cases are split into groups according to whether communism was involved.

Other Press Rules

Up to this point, we have focused on Bennett's indexing rule. We turn now to an entirely different subject, namely, whether the press has values or prejudices of its own that affect coverage independently of officialdom. We devised several hypotheses concerning the effects of press prejudices, as follows:

- The press will be _less_ hawkish in situations when the United States uses forces against a militarily weak foe than in other cases. Our reasoning was that weaker foes will induce less martial excitement and hence less hawkishness. Cases so classified are the Bay of Pigs, Dominican Republic, Mayaguez, Grenada, Libya, and Panama.

- The press will be *less* hawkish, all else being equal, in reporting military setbacks or defeats than in other cases. Our reasoning was that military setbacks encourage critical rethinking of military commitments and hence less hawkishness. Cases classified as setbacks are the Chinese entry into Korean War, Bay of Pigs, Tet, fall of Saigon, failed Iranian hostage rescue attempt, and terrorist bombing of Marine barracks in Lebanon.

- The press will be *less* hawkish, all else being equal, in situations of continuing crisis, that is, situations like the Tet offensive, in which one or more crisis points have already occurred. Our reasoning was that continuing crises indicate lack of policy success, which is likely to engender rethinking of the commitment to force.

- The press will be *more* hawkish, all else being equal, when the U.S. foe is associated with communism. Our reasoning was that the press tends to be reflexively anticommunist.

- The press will be *more* hawkish, all else being equal, at the onset of military conflict. Our reasoning was that the press tends to depict the onset of fighting in sensationalist terms, which may tend to give coverage a hawkish tone. These cases are the start of the Korean War, Gulf of Tonkin incident, Dominican Republic invasion in 1965, Mayaguez incident in 1975, failed Iranian hostage rescue attempt, Grenada invasion, Libya bombing, invasion of Panama, and Gulf War.

- The press will be *more* hawkish, all being else equal, in major wars (Korea, Vietnam, Gulf) than in other types of crises. Our reasoning was that it is more difficult to be critical when large-scale fighting is under way than in lesser crises.

- Media patience will wear thin in drawn-out crises. But what should be counted as cases of "drawn-out crisis" requires judgment. For example, was the Berlin Wall crisis of 1961 a continuation of the 1948 crisis or a separate event? Were the 1954 and 1961 crises associated with Vietnam the first and second crises in a series that included the Vietnam War, or were they separate events? We judged these as separate events. The crises that we judged as continuation crises, then, were the Chinese entry into Korea and the firing of MacArthur; the Vietnam escalations of 1965 and 1972, the Tet offensive, the Cambodian invasion, and the fall of Saigon; the failed Iranian hostage rescue; the bombing of the marine barracks in Lebanon; and the start of the Gulf War.

- To the extent that Congress and the president take different stands, both will affect media coverage. It is no accident that the president is hawkish in the vast majority of cases. If the president were dovish, there might be no question of using military force and hence no foreign policy crisis, by our definition of the term. There were, however, five cases in which we considered that a crisis existed even though the president was dovish: the Soviet takeover of Poland and

Eastern Europe, which the administration might have contested but did not; Truman's firing of the hawkish General MacArthur in 1951; the fall of Dienbienphu in 1954, when serious consideration was given to U.S. intervention; Castro's takeover of Cuba in 1959, which, contrary to the view of the administration, some in Congress wanted to resist; and the fall of South Vietnam, where the president ordered U.S. personnel to clear out of harm's way.[8] We created a dummy to capture these five cases.

Four tests of these hypotheses are shown in Table 5.2. In Column 1, the dependent variable is the average of the media scores of all three coders, which is the measure used in the paper so far. In columns 2–4, the dependent variables are the ratings of each coder alone. Thus, we have three independent tests and one that is depen-

Table 5.2 Models of Media Hawkishness

	All coders	Coder 1	Coder 2	Coder 3
Congress' opinion	0.3	0.22	0.14	0.54
(range 0 to 1)	−0.09	−0.09	−0.13	−0.12
Executive branch	0.16	0.02	0.25	0.21
(0–1)	−0.07	−0.07	−0.1	−0.09
Full War	0.03	0.01	0	0.09
(0–1)	−0.09	−0.09	−0.12	−0.11
Start fighting	0.07	0.1	0.07	0.04
(0–1)	−0.06	−0.06	−0.08	−0.08
Communist foe	0.11	0.12	0.1	0.1
(0–1)	−0.06	−0.06	−0.08	−0.08
Setback or defeat	−0.17	−0.13	−0.22	−0.16
(0–1)	−0.06	−0.06	−0.09	−0.09
Continuation crisis	−0.16	−0.1	−0.16	−0.23
(0–1)	−0.09	−0.1	−0.13	−0.12
Minor use of force	−0.16	−0.18	−0.11	−0.21
(0–1)	−0.07	−0.07	−0.1	−0.09
Year	−0.07	−0.01	−0.17	−0.02
(scaled to 0–1 range)	−0.09	−0.1	−0.14	−0.13
Intercept	0.27	0.39	0.35	0.08
Adjusted R²	0.72	0.47	0.55	0.72
N of cases	35	35	35	35

Note: Dependent variable, which has a range of .15 to .92 when averaged across all coders, is hawkishness of newsmagazine coverage; standard errors are shown in parentheses.

dent on the other three. The purpose of multiple tests is to assess the stability of the overall results.

Let us look first at the effects of congressional and presidential opinion. In the overall results, congressional and presidential opinion has impacts that easily achieve statistical significance (t-ratios are 3.40 and 2.34). However, these impacts look a bit ragged when examined separately by the coder: When Coder #1's media scores are used as the dependent variable, Congress has a big impact on the press but the president does not; when Coder #2's scores are used, Congress has a small impact and the president a big one; and when Coder #3's scores are used, both have significant impacts.

Although these results are more variable than one might wish, they appear to be within the range of chance instability that lurks in small datasets and, as such, no threat to our analysis. So long as the overall results are reflected to some degree in all subsets of the data, the overall results can be accepted as the best single estimate of actual effects.[9]

The primary purpose of the multiple tests was to assess the stability of the situational dummy variables, which were created after preliminary exploration of the data and could therefore represent "overfitting" of the data. Here the results are, happily, more consistent across coders. Communist foe, Continuation crisis, Setback, and Minor force all have comparable effects in all four estimates. The effects, moreover, are fairly large, running from about .5 SDs on the media scale to about .75 SDs. Thus the press is not wholly a creature of officialdom. In a variety of situations—most notably, those in which there was a communist foe, a continuing crisis, or a setback—it can strike out in its own direction.

The combined effect of all variables in the model can be quite large. Consider the difference between press coverage of the Gulf of Tonkin incident, which was overwhelmingly hawkish, and coverage of the Tet offensive, which ran in a dovish direction. (The raw media scores were .88 and .31 on a 0–1 scale having an SD of .21.) The House vote on the Gulf of Tonkin resolution in 1964 was 388–0, or 100 percent hawkish, while congressional speeches made at the time of the Tet offensive were only 16 percent hawkish. Given this shift in congressional opinion, press coverage of Tet is expected to be about 1.2 SDs less hawkish than it had been during the Tonkin crisis.[10] Several situational factors also come into play: In contrast to the Tonkin incident, the Tet offensive was a "setback," a "continuation crisis," and part of a war; also the Tonkin incident, but not Tet, was an instance of Start of fighting. From the coefficients in Table 5.2, it can be calculated that the net effect of these factors should be to make coverage of Tet an additional 1.75 SDs less hawkish than it had been at the time of the Tonkin crisis.[11] Thus, our expectation is that press coverage will become 2.95 SDs more dovish at the time of the Tet offensive, which is fairly close to the actual swing (2.70 SDs). The swing could, moreover, have been greater, except that the president remained hawkish and the foe remained communist, both of which lead to more hawkish coverage.

These results show that the dramatic swing toward dovishness in press coverage of Tet—a swing that has been widely noted and is often considered anomalous (e.g., Braestrup 1979)—was not anomalous at all but rather typical of the way the press behaves in situations of ebbing congressional hawkishness, military setback, and continuing crisis. The results show further that situational factors, when they occur in combination, can be an even more important determinant of press slant than indexing.

Amount of Press Coverage

We did not measure variation in overall amount of media coverage of crises because we had no reason to believe it would be important. All crises, we assumed, would be heavily covered. This assumption turned out to be wrong. Although most were, two were hardly covered at all. These were the Soviet takeover of Poland in 1945 and the American buildup in Vietnam in 1961, for which the best we could do were pairs of magazine issues containing a total of six paragraphs and ten paragraphs, respectively. Because of its intrinsic interest, we reprint a part of this coverage, a *Time* report that the Soviet Union had unilaterally taken a major province from Germany and annexed it to Poland. We show the whole story, including headline:

POLAND
Major Development
Tass, the official Soviet news agency, last week noted a major development: Major General Alexander Zawadzki, former political commissar of the Soviet-trained Polish Army, has been appointed Governor General of Silesia, thus officially expanding the new Poland as far as the Oder River. (*Time*, March 19, 1945, 38)

This case vindicates our determination, as noted earlier, not to drop cases because of the difficulty of measuring congressional opinion. For as it appears from this case, the press may downplay crises that congressional elites are unwilling to address—even when, as *Time* admitted by its headline on the bulletin on the latest partition of Poland, the story was a "major development." The press, in other words, may index not only the slant but the amount of its coverage to the balance of opinion within the government.

NEW CASES FROM THE 1990s

The data for the original version of this article were gathered in a period that coincided almost exactly with the Cold War between the United States and the Soviet Union. With the Cold War now ended, an obvious question is whether the dynamics of media politics have remained the same.

It is readily possible to find out. From the end of the Gulf War in 1991 through the Kosovo conflict of 1999, the following events qualify as foreign policy crisis points: emergency aid to the Kurds, 1991; humanitarian aid to Somalia, 1992; U.S. military losses in Somalia, 1993; invasion of Haiti, 1994; American peacekeeping troops to Bosnia, 1995; bombing campaign in Iraq, 1998; launch of war in Kosovo, 1999; apparent stalemate in Kosovo, 1999.

To examine data on these cases, the same procedures were followed as in the original study, with this exception: rather than relying on three coders to code the media coverage, we were constrained to use only Coder #3 from the original study, who also gathered the data on congressional opinion. One of the eight cases, the initial intervention into Somalia, had to be dropped from the analysis because Congress was out of session at the time.

The new data provide only slight support for indexing. The slope summarizing the relationship between congressional opinion and media slant is only about a fifth (.14) as large for the seven new cases as in the original thirty-five cases.[12] The overall relationship between congressional and media opinion remains highly statistically significant when all cases are combined into a single test ($P < .01$), but the new cases from the 1990s undermine the strength of the originally reported relationship.

The reason for this change turns out to be quite clear. In the original analysis, we examined the relationship between congressional opinion and media opinion within several subsets, as shown in Table 5.1. One of these tests distinguished cases that involve communist foes from cases that do not. The relationship between congressional and media opinion was weaker within the subset of noncommunist cases than in any other subset. But the relationship was bound to exhibit chance variation, and since we were examining several small subsets in an atheoretical manner, we felt it would be a mistake to pay much attention to results from any particular subset.

Now, however, the accumulation of seven additional noncommunist cases makes it clear that crises involving noncommunist foes really are different. Figure 5.1 summarizes the evidence. The figure presents data from Coder #3 alone, since his are the only data that are comparable across the full set of crises. The figure distinguishes crises involving communist and noncommunist foes (solid dots versus clear ones); it shows separate regression lines for the two kinds of crises; and it labels some of the most interesting cases.

The main point of the figure is the difference in slopes for communist and noncommunist cases. The slope for crises involving communist foes is .79—a magnitude that implies a nearly 1:1 relationship between congressional and media opinion—but the slope for crises involving noncommunist foes is only .17. This difference in slopes is statistically significant at the .01 level, two-tailed.[13]

If, then, we want to know why the relationship between congressional and media opinion is weaker in the 1990s, the answer is clear: foreign policy crises in the current period have involved noncommunist foes, and the press-Congress relationship has always been weak for such cases.

What is not so clear is what this implies for the indexing hypothesis. Should we conclude, for example, that indexing occurs only for cases in which there is a communist foe?

Figure 5.1 Congressional and Media Hawkishness for Communist and Noncommunist Foes

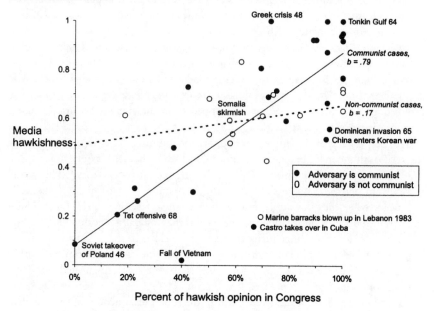

There is no straightforward answer to this question. We can, however, approach an answer by returning to Figure 5.1. There we see that the media are not, as might have been expected, more likely to be hawkish when communism is involved. In fact, the mean level of hawkishness is almost exactly the same in communist and noncommunist cases. A more subtle but equally important point in Figure 5.1 is that the media are less prone to extreme slants in cases that do not involve communism. That is, there are fewer cases in which the media are either extremely hawkish or extremely dovish when the foe is noncommunist. Rather, the media take more balanced positions. Both of these tendencies are demonstrated quantitatively in Table 5.3, which shows that the mean level of hawkishness is nearly the same for communist and noncommunist cases and that the standard deviation across cases is greater when communism is involved. The higher standard deviation indicates that the news magazines are more prone to vacillate between extreme positions when communism is involved (p < .001).[14]

Table 5.3 makes one other important point. Journalists are not the only group more prone to extreme slants in cases involving communism; members of Congress are, too. Congress is more prone to views that are either one-sidedly hawkish or one-sidedly dovish when communism is involved than when it is not. This shows up, once again, as a higher SD across cases in which communism is involved. (The p-values for equality of variance within columns two and three of Table 5.3 are both

Table 5.3   The Effect of Communist Adversaries on Media and Congressional Opinion

	Media coverage (coder #3)	Congressional opinion (speeches + votes)	Congressional opinion (votes only)
Non-Communist foe			
Mean hawkishness:	0.61	.70	.65
SD across cases:	0.15	.23	.16
N of cases:	16	16	7
Communist foe			
Mean hawkishness:	0.63	.70	.78
SD across cases:	0.31	.31	.30
N of cases:	26	26	8

.09.)[15] Note also that Congress, as in the case of media slant, is *not* more hawkish when communism is involved; legislators are merely more prone to one-sided-positions, whether prointervention or anti-intervention.

There seem, then, to be three patterns when communism is involved compared to when it is not: news coverage is more extreme (whether hawkish or dovish); congressional politicians are more prone to unity of opinion; and journalists are more inclined to index their coverage to congressional opinion. To put it another way, news is more balanced, politicians are more fractious, and the slant of the news is more independent of Congress when the nation's adversary is noncommunist.

We emphasize that none of these findings is entailed, in any direct statistical sense, by any other. For example, it is possible that Congress might become more fractious but that journalists might continue to follow such congressional cues as remained.[16] Yet this has not been the case. Even when congressional opinion has been one-sided in a crisis involving a noncommunist foe, as in the case of Haiti (see Figure 5.1), the news magazines have gone their own way.

None of this means that indexing is dead. It only means that journalists are now less tied to congressional—and, we would guess, presidential—opinion than during the Cold War. But they might have other kinds of ties. We can best investigate the nature of these ties by examining qualitative evidence.

We begin with the case of humanitarian aid to Somalia in 1992. Following a several-month period in which U.S. media highlighted starvation and anarchy in Somalia, President Bush ordered U.S. troops to the country to restore order and organize the distribution of food. The media response, however, was negative. After months of generally prointervention coverage—coverage that was, as Mermin (1999) reports, orchestrated by various government officials—*Time* and *Newsweek* turned decidedly dovish. In fact, the slant of their coverage was more dovish than for any other foreign policy crisis in the 1990s.[17]

This coverage was, in retrospect, prescient. Its basic point was, as *Newsweek* put it, that "Operation Restore Hope is more a generous impulse than a thought-out

policy." Both magazines vividly described the problems that would eventually lead
to a humiliating defeat for the United States, notably the difficulty of carrying out
food relief in the presence of well-armed militias and the question of whether any
lasting good could be done without a long-term and expensive commitment to na-
tion-building. And both magazines relied on expert sources to tell their story, as in
the following example:

> If hostility does develop between the clans and the international force, relief workers
> worry that their efforts—the point of the humanitarian exercise—may suffer. "We have
> people out there in the bush saving lives, "says Ben Foot, a field representative of the
> Save the Children Fund. "We would like someone to explain what is going to happen,
> because we're in the middle of it."
> Somalia is a country with no working economy, no police force, no government. . . .
> Many experts doubt that military steps to guard food convoys can, or should, be sepa-
> rated from rebuilding the nation. The use of troops initially is a good idea, say Howard
> Bell, acting director of CARE-Somalia, "but only if it is put within a well thought-out
> program of national recovery. . . ." A Western diplomat in Somalia agrees. "The troops
> will be able to achieve their objective of securing relief shipments," he says, "But the
> bigger question is, Then what?"[18]

Here or elsewhere, this is little evidence that reporters are indexing their Somalia
coverage to the views of American government or, still less, to the views of Congress
or the president. The views of the president are certainly reported in the story
(though we have not excerpted them), but they do not frame or dominate the account. Rather, the bulk of the coverage seems to reflect the opinions of a range of
expert sources, many of them non-Americans.

This is not to say, however, that American national interest gets short shrift in
the cases we have examined. To the contrary, U.S. interest is often the touchstone
for evaluating the soundness of policy. What does get short shrift—much shorter
shrift, we suspect, than in the Cold War period—is the interest of politicians qua
politicians, particularly when those interests appear partisan or self-serving. Thus,
when Senate Majority Leader Trent Lott expressed suspicion that President Clinton
had provoked a crisis with Saddam Hussein in order to divert attention from im-
peachment proceedings in Congress, _Newsweek_ pointedly took issue, juxtaposing
Lott's remarks with what it took to be national interest.

> When the majority leader of the Senate disavows in advance an armed American
> exercise, as Trent Lott did last week, what incentive is there for wavering votes in the
> United Nations to support Washington's actions?
> This is the true connection between the impeachment of Clinton and the crisis in
> Iraq. There is not the slightest evidence that Desert Fox was launched to divert attention
> from the impeachment vote.[19]

In reprimanding Lott for allowing partisanship to interfere with the national interest, and yet exonerating Clinton of the same criticism, _Newsweek_ sets itself up as

the guardian of national interest against partisan interests, whether in Congress or the White House. This, we suspect, may be a common posture of the elite media in the post–Cold War era.

The largest disjuncture between media slant and political authority occurred at the time of the Haiti invasion in 1994. Although 81 percent of congressional speeches opposed military action against Haiti, the news magazines took a moderate but firm prointervention stance. They acknowledged that democracy would be difficult to achieve in Haiti but felt that the existing regime was an abomination. Insofar as the magazines were critical of Clinton's policy, it was mainly for failing to make a public case that invasion was necessary. As *Newsweek* concluded its main article:

> This intervention is not like the one in 1915, which was designed to expand American hegemony and protect U.S. bank loans. The 1994 version has more respectable motives: to protect life, to build democracy and to head off a new wave of boat people. As long as the goals remain modest, the endgame can be within reach. Most Americans, however, are still not convinced that their country should be in the game at all.[20]

Again, we see a stance that is both assertive of national interest and independent of political authority.

The contrast with reporting of the Gulf of Tonkin incident at the beginning of the Vietnam War could scarcely be more stark. The incident centered on what the Johnson administration said was the second unprovoked attack on U.S. Navy vessels in a week. Yet as official information later showed, only one attack occurred, and it was not unprovoked. Stanley Karnow gives the following overview of media accounts of the second, nonexistent attack:

> The American press published vivid eyewitness accounts of the incident, dramatized by news editors with inspiration from Pentagon officials. As "the night glowed eerily," wrote *Times*, the Communist "intruders boldly sped" toward the destroyers, firing with "automatic weapons," while *Life* had the American ships "under continuous torpedo attack" as they "weaved through the night sea, evading more torpedoes." Not to be outdone, *Newsweek* described "U.S. jets diving, strafing, flattening out . . . and diving again" at the enemy boats, one of which "burst into flames and sank." Now, having won the battle, *Newsweek* concluded, "it was time for American might to strike back."[21]

This is the kind of coverage that helped propel the nation into the Vietnam War. Halberstam provided the following description of the mindsets of the reporters who produced similar coverage for CBS News:

> A few [reporters] were made uneasy by the rush to decisions, the haunting lack of information. Among them was Ed Murrow [the legendary CBS newsman]. . . . he called up his one-time protégé Fred Friendly, by then the head of CBS News, and tore into him. . . . "By what God-given right did you treat it this way? What do we really know

about what happened out there? Why did it happen? How could you not have [Dan] Rather and the boys do some sort of special analysis?" Friendly was shocked by his anger, and felt a certain guilt because he had that day been on the phone with Dan Rather, and Rather had said that it all smelled a bit tricky, and Friendly had told Rather for God's sake not to say anything like that line on the air. Friendly simply did not know how to cover something as elusive as this, how to raise questions. He was still, like the country, more hawk than dove, and the whole thing scared him. And he was also in quite close contact with the Johnson administration. There was some talk about coming back on the air later that night—perhaps a midnight special—but that too was dropped.[22]

It seems unfair to argue, as Murrow did, that reporters should have developed independent information about a naval engagement that had occurred halfway around the world. But it was well within the capacity of reporters for *Time* and *Newsweek*, who had several days to prepare their stories, to analyze the likely effects of U.S. retaliatory action against North Vietnam, as authorized by the open-ended Gulf of Tonkin resolution. The government sources necessary for such forward-looking analysis were surely available since, by many accounts, officials within the State Department and Pentagon were divided at the time about the wisdom of escalation in Vietnam. Yet nowhere in the crisis coverage in *Time* and *Newsweek* was there any such analysis. Reporters contented themselves with digging out colorful details about the alleged battle.

The reason that Halberstam adduces for this spiritless coverage—that reporters were scared and uncertain—may go a long way toward explaining why, as Figure 5.1 shows, crisis coverage in the Cold War was indexed to opinion in the political branches of government. Reporters were afraid to go it alone, at least in the heat of crisis.

Today, by contrast, reporters are surely less scared and hence less reflexive in their support for official policy. This does not mean, as Table 5.3 shows, that journalists have turned dovish. Nor does it imply that reporters no longer index stories to what sources tell them. Insofar as we can tell, reporters now index stories to a wider range of sources, using a conception of national interest—rather than fear of opposing the president—as the basis for choosing among them.

MERMIN'S STUDY OF MEDIA INDEXING

In a recent study, Jonathan Mermin (1999) reports evidence that media indexing continues to structure the coverage of foreign policy crises in the period since the Vietnam War, including crises in which communism is not involved. Although there are several differences between our methodology and his, the different conclusions we reach appear to reflect differences in coding schemes. While we tallied all negative coverage about a policy, whether it concerned basic policy premises, execution, costs, or political support, Mermin tallied only negative coverage that fairly directly challenges the premise of a policy. Our philosophy is that anything that would tend to lower public support for a policy should be tallied as negative coverage (see Appendix A); his is that only coverage that attacks the policy itself, often by recommending a wholly different policy, should be counted as evidence concerning the indexing hypothesis.

The fact that Mermin finds support for the indexing hypothesis in cases in which we don't recommends his method. He also gets consistent results across several different media, which further recommends his approach. Yet we remain doubtful. As Mermin makes plain, his coding scheme excludes much negative coverage, especially as regards execution of policies, on the grounds that coverage that does not question the premise or basic wisdom of the policy is outside the domain of the indexing theory. But how meaningful is it to say that the media have not challenged a policy if they challenge everything about it except its explicit premises? Mermin, for his part, would retort: "How meaningful is it to say that the media have challenged a policy if they offer no grounds for opposition beyond 'it's not working on its own terms'?"

The most pertinent evidence for resolving this difference in coding philosophies could be evidence concerning effects on public opinion. If the only coverage that undermines public support for a policy is coverage that directly challenges the premise of a policy, Mermin's coding scheme is more useful for understanding the dynamics of public opinion in foreign policy crises—which is, as it seems to us, the ultimate question in this sort of research. If, however, many kinds of negative coverage have essentially the same effect on opinion, our coding approach would seem more useful.

At this point, then, the evidence is unclear about indexing in the post–Cold War period. From our data, however, it does seem clear that something has changed: the slant of overall coverage, as measured across all types of media negativity, is strongly linked to congressional opinion in cases in which communism is involved and otherwise has little relationship.

CONCLUSION: ALTERNATIVE MODES OF INDEXING

If, as Halberstam colorfully puts it, many journalists came to foreign policy reporting as the culmination of a successful career of chasing fire engines, what else can journalists do besides index their stories to the sources they encounter? Even if most have undergraduate degrees in international relations or history, there is little choice but to rely on sources.

The question for any notion of indexing, then, is how exactly reporters use their sources. There are at least three possibilities that seem worthy of elaboration and testing. One possibility is that enterprising reporters simply make the rounds among persons familiar with an issue—aid workers, foreign diplomats, State Department officials, whoever—and write stories that summarize what they have been told. Reflecting this ethos, the Alsop brothers wrote that "his feet are a more important part of a reporter's body than his head."[23] As Cohen writes, "It is hard to avoid the implication that . . . the production of news is less an act of limited creativity . . . than a process of accidental discovery as he stumbles across something that looks good to him and has not been published before" (1963, 86). What drives indexing, then, is the pervasive and direct dependence of journalists on sources for everything they report.

Another, more sophisticated possibility is that journalists may consider information newsworthy in proportion to its capacity to foretell or affect future events. This idea was first proposed by Robert Entman and Ben Page (1995), who found that in Senate hearings on the Gulf War, reporters paid disproportionate attention to the statements of Bush administration officials, apparently because, far more than other witnesses at the hearings, these officials were in a position to determine whether the United States went to war or not. A tendency by reporters to highlight information that they thought would foretell future events could have broad implications for how they do their job. If, for example, government decisionmakers were convinced that Vietnam must be saved from communism, journalists might report everything they could find about whether Vietnam was likely to fall to communism, since this information would affect whether U.S. intervention occurred. By the same token, they might ignore information that policymakers regarded as irrelevant, such as whether Vietnam was embroiled in a civil war, since this information would not affect what policymakers would do. If one half of officialdom were concerned about a communist takeover and the other half believed that South Vietnam was embroiled in a civil war, journalists would report information relevant to both frames, since both may affect U.S. willingness to continue its military commitment.

The first of these mechanisms might be called "source indexing," the second "power indexing." A study by Althaus et al. (1996) tends to support the notion of power indexing. From the more fine-grained analysis that is possible in a single case study, these authors found that during the Libya crisis in 1986, reporters for the *New York Times* did a poor job of reflecting the political thrust and specific content of congressional opinion. Among other things, the newspaper neglected to report on esoteric policy options favored by members of Congress but not taken seriously by the administration, and gave disproportionate attention to any congressional discussion of the War Powers Act, which might become the basis for congressional action if Congress were to act. Also, the newspaper gave much more attention to the pronouncements of foreign governments, which constrained the administration's capacity to act against Libya, than to pronouncements by members of Congress, which had little capacity to constrain administration action. In short, the *New York Times* reporters seemed to engage in power indexing rather than source indexing.

A third form of indexing is suggested by the earlier discussion of why reporters seem to be more independent of political authorities when communism is not at issue. It might be called "political indexing." Whether from fear or uncertainty, reporters report the story that political authorities want to have reported. This is what seems to have happened in the Gulf of Tonkin incident, and it no doubt happened in other Cold War crises. We suspect, therefore, that political indexing is the form of indexing that underlies the relationship that existed between congressional opinion and media slant during the Cold War period. Now that the Cold War is ended, some combination of source and power indexing, tempered by reporters' suspicion of self-serving motivations on the part of politicians, probably structures the process by which reporters choose among sources within the mainstream.

Systematic study of indexing in any of its forms will be impeded by a subtle issue of reverse causation. Suppose that President X faces two issues, either of which he may escalate into a crisis. Fearing that the media and Congress would oppose hawkish initiatives on Issue 1, President X chooses to escalate on Issue 2 instead, where he correctly anticipates greater media and congressional support. By this action, President X assures that later observers (like us) will both fail to study Issue 1 (because it never became a crisis) and misleadingly conclude from study of Issue 2 that the media and Congress reflexively follow the president's lead in foreign policy crises.

The problem is that the process by which potential crises are converted to actual crises may lead to biased conclusions about the relationship between media and government. This endogeneity problem occurred several times in our research. One case was the seizure of the USS *Pueblo* and its crew by North Korea in 1968, which President Lyndon Johnson chose to de-emphasize, perhaps because he feared that, in the midst of the Vietnam War, the press or Congress would not follow him into another crisis. Reflecting this de-emphasis, Spanier failed to include the *Pueblo* incident on his list of principal U.S. foreign policy events, thus preventing us from counting it as a crisis (despite our inclination to do so). Thus, a potential crisis in which other elites might have failed to follow presidential leadership failed to become an actual crisis. In contrast, the Gulf War was a crisis that could easily have been a noncrisis, except that President Bush chose to make it one. Although we have no evidence on this point—and, in the nature of things, are unlikely ever to uncover such evidence—it seems likely that Bush would not have chosen to go to war against Iraq unless he had anticipated that he could mobilize adequate congressional and press support for doing so. From these two, obviously speculative, accounts, it seems plausible that the likelihood of mobilizing press support may be a positive factor in whether crises occur.

It is hard to say exactly how serious this endogeneity problem is. The pressures of realpolitik may be so strong that presidents and other government decisionmakers typically ignore the media in deciding what to do. And yet there may be media-conscious decisionmakers who shy away from commitments that afford the press too many opportunities for potshots and second-guessing.

This study has only scratched the surface of a difficult problem. Its central finding—an association between government opinion and the slant of press coverage of foreign policy crises during the Cold War but not afterward—is nonetheless a tantalizing empirical generalization.

APPENDIX A: INSTRUCTIONS TO CODERS

For each assigned paragraph of each news story, your task is to answer this question: WOULD AN ORDINARY MIDDLE-OF-THE ROAD AMERICAN READING THIS PARAGRAPH IN ITS ORIGINAL CONTEXT HAVE BEEN INDUCED TO TAKE A MORE HAWKISH OR A MORE DOVISH VIEW OF THE FOREIGN CRISIS DESCRIBED IN THE STORY.

Hawkish and dovish should be understood in their colloquial senses, that is, more inclined or less inclined to use some form of military force (including military aid to an ally), rather than purely diplomatic means, to resolve a given crisis.

Throughout the content coding, you should allow for the possibility that the same information or facts could have different actual meanings in different contexts. Reports of U.S. deaths or battlefield defeats, for example, could be framed so as to indicate that U.S. honor or national security require a military threat or response; but they could also be framed so as to suggest that threats or further fighting would be hopeless. Detailed descriptions of military operations or troop movements could contain an element of ridicule, in which case they should be coded dovish, or they could be imbued with a tone of martial expectancy, in which case they would be hawkish. The description of an enemy's skill or strength, or the weakness of the U.S., might suggest the senselessness of military action, or it might excite greater resolve or a more vigorous military response by the U.S. In all such cases, ratings should depend on your judgment of how an ordinary reader, in the context of his or her times, would tend to read the paragraph.

Try to rate each paragraph for a predominant message. In some cases, however, a paragraph may contain sharp inducements toward both hawkishness and dovishness; such paragraphs should be rated as having both hawkish and dovish content. In other cases, a paragraph may have no implications for either hawkishness or dovishness, in which case it should be rated as neutral. Some paragraphs, however, might be neutral if rated as stand-alone units, but yet contribute to the development of a point that, in its eventual implication, is hawkish or dovish; such paragraphs should be rated for the larger theme to which they contribute. (This implies that some paragraphs may have to be coded in light of the paragraphs that follow them.)

Among the contextual factors to which you may pay attention are the photographs, illustrations, and headlines that accompany the story. Do *not* code these contextual factors as such; *nor* should you consider them as "biases" that invariably color all associated verbiage. But when the meaning of an otherwise ambiguous passage takes on a reasonably distinct coloration when viewed in light of the associated pictures or headlines, your coding should aim to capture the actual effect of the communication.

In sum, your task is to capture, on a paragraph by paragraph basis, the hawkish or dovish slant of each story as it would tend to effect an ordinary, contemporaneous reader.

6

Toward General Theories of the Media, Public Opinion, and Foreign Policy

Benjamin I. Page

Taken together, the preceding chapters are quite helpful in advancing us toward a general theory—or general theories—of relationships among the media, public opinion, and the state in the realm of foreign policy. Certain contrasts and tensions among the chapters point toward fruitful directions for future theoretical and empirical work.

A pillar of political-communications research—built up over the years by many scholars—is the finding that foreign policy news coverage by the media depends heavily upon official government sources. It follows, in W. Lance Bennett's formulation, that media content should "index" official debates: the central tendency of media content should reflect the general thrust of officials' opinions. Over time, media content should track changes in officials' positions.

In this volume, Chapter 5 by John Zaller and Dennis Chiu advances our knowledge in at least two significant respects. First, it puts the indexing proposition to an initial systematic test. Using thirty-five cases during the Cold War era that are generally accepted as representing "crises" in U.S. foreign policy, in which force was considered or used, it finds that the hawkishness of public officials' stands (as measured mainly by debates and votes in Congress) does indeed correlate positively and substantially—at around the .63 to .70 level—with the hawkishness of media content (as measured by *Time* and *Newsweek* stories). This is important both for what it says and for what it does not say. A large portion of the variation in media content remains unexplained by indexing—in part, no doubt, because of imperfections in measurement (especially of executive-branch positions), but also because other things besides officials' stands very likely affect the media.

The second contribution of Zaller and Chiu's work, reinforced by their analysis of additional post–Cold War cases, is to begin to suggest what some of those other things may be. They may include such situational factors as the involvement or noninvolvement of a powerful and much-disliked antagonist (especially, a communist-bloc country during the Cold War), the duration of conflict, and the extent of U.S. losses or failure. The authors quite properly do not consider these findings definitive, and it would be too much to claim at this point that the situational factors have had as much effect upon press slant as does indexing. The power of the findings is limited by the small number of cases, imperfect measurement, an inductive methodology, and the acknowledged endogeneity of case definition: what officials choose to turn into a crisis may partly reflect how they anticipate the media will react. Zaller and Chiu raise questions about alternative models of indexing and what aspects of policy debates the media tend to index. Still, this work makes an important start. We now need research that uses additional cases, including cases not involving force, to spell out situational variables further and to see whether processes are similar or different in different contexts.

Chapter 4 (by Nacos, Shapiro, Hritzuk and Chadwick) makes an important move in this direction by closely examining a noncrisis issue—the global-warming debate surrounding the Kyoto conference—and by bringing in a crossnational comparison between the United States and Germany. Among the chapter's many rich and interesting findings (which include intriguing variations among particular media), perhaps the most striking is that in the U.S. media official sources did *not* dominate. Interest-group and expert sources outweighed them. (The indexing hypothesis fared a bit better, though it hardly scored a resounding success, in Germany. In that country, the issue was framed largely in foreign/international terms, whereas the U.S. media "domesticated" it, relying chiefly upon U.S. voices and sources.)

If this diminished frequency of official sources holds up for other domestically framed foreign policy issues, it will constitute a major qualification to the indexing hypothesis. It should also help direct inquiry into the question of when, how, and by whom some foreign policy issues but not others come to be framed in domestic terms. Robert Entman's distinction between source indexing and power indexing, touched upon by both Zaller and Chiu and Nacos et al., also deserves further exploration.

The sharp contrasts among particular media reported in Chapter 4 (the alarming scientific views about global warming reported on American TV, for example, in contrast to the more complacent views in the *Wall Street Journal*; the greater economic pessimism about emission restrictions in *Handelsblatt* and the *Wall Street Journal*, in contrast to others' cautious optimism) remind us that "the media" are not monolithic. It can be important to explain variations among media as well as general tendencies. Popular versus business versus general elite audiences, visual versus print technologies, family versus corporate control, and other distinctions may make a difference that should be explored.

Again in reference to the chapters by Zaller and Chiu and Nacos et al., the distinctions they draw among countries, types of issues, situational contexts, and types of media all constitute challenges to the kind of general theorizing offered in the chapters by Robert Entman and Martin Shaw (Chapters 1 and 2, respectively). It is by taking seriously this kind of tension and interplay between the general and the particular, I think, that we can expect to make further progress in understanding the media and foreign policy.

Martin Shaw's theorizing is firmly rooted in the Iraq war cases but he goes well beyond them. Operating in the tradition of grand social theory, it draws upon macrohistorical sociology and ideas about the general process of globalization to argue that the media now have an expanded role in world politics: they have created a globally integrated media space—a global public sphere—within which many diverse actors increasingly contest representations, interpretations, frames, and narratives. This means that the previously pervasive, state-dominated "surveillance" and consent-engineering functions of media (presumably implemented partly through Bennett's indexing or Edward Herman and Noam Chomsky's "hegemony"), are increasingly challenged by other actors, including journalists themselves, nongovernmental groups, and even ordinary citizens. It means that there are new opportunities for an independent public sphere, for democratic control of states, and for what Robert Shapiro and I have called "collective deliberation."

Robert Entman, though speaking in different theoretical language from Shaw's, draws upon the Bosnia and Somalia cases to make a similar main point: that the media have gained power vis-à-vis the state. Entman's explanation is that the demise of the Cold War, by depriving governments (particularly the U.S. government) of a powerful patriotic frame once used to squash dissent, has opened space for the media (and presumably for other elements of civil society as well) to fill the gap with their own frames and narratives. Zaller and Chiu's analysis of post–Cold War crises suggests changes in the political space opened to government officials as well as the media. In my view, Entman's explanation, though different in emphasis from Shaw's, is perfectly compatible with it. *Both* the demise of the Cold War *and* the not unconnected emergence of a global public sphere using global electronic technology have contributed to a resurgence of the media and civil society vis-à-vis the state. Both Shaw and Entman suggest that the indexing hypothesis reflected a particular configuration of the world system; it must be modified to fit a system that has been transformed.

Entman offers several new wrinkles within this general picture. He suggests, for example, that the newly powerful and independent media may voice demands for assertive interventionist policies but then chastise leaders when things go wrong, creating a leadership dilemma; that the media often tout a fabricated public opinion that increases their own influence; that the broadened availability of visual images in foreign affairs can also increase media power; and that U.S. government influence upon the media may be greater under Republican than Democratic administrations.

At some points, Entman seems to flirt with the provocative proposition that public opinion does not exist—a proposition that I reject, partly on predictable "rational public" grounds and partly because it ignores the crucial role in foreign policy of latent opinion, retrospective judgments, and their anticipation by officials. That is, even when (in some foreign policy crises, for example) citizens' policy preferences are uncertain and subject to change depending upon events and results, citizens' underlying *values* and criteria for judgment are usually quite firm. Underlying values are even more stable and strongly held than what Entman calls "polling opinion"—measured collective policy preferences. Latent opinion is ignored at politicians' peril.

Still, Entman is certainly right to alert us to the many attempts by officials, journalists, pundits, and others to manipulate and wield *perceptions* of public opinion. In many cases, perceived opinion may be an important variable that deserves a place in our theoretical and empirical work that is somewhat independent of more usually conceptualized public opinion.

So where does this leave us in terms of trying to formulate and test a general theory, or alternative theories, of the media and foreign policy?

To me, the preceding chapters highlight the inevitable tension between theoretical parsimony and generality on one hand, and complexity, differentiation, and explanatory completeness on the other. The social and political world is plenty complicated, but any theory that aspires to coherence and elegance has got to limit severely the number of concepts and relationships it deals with. The trick for achieving both parsimony and explanatory power at once is to use great care in picking precisely *which* concepts and relationships are dealt with. This requires what Brian Barry used to call "good taste in assumptions," as well as a clear eye for which concepts and relationships are most central to what actually goes on in the world.

In order to explore conflicts between parsimony and explanatory power in concrete terms, suppose that we set aside for the moment Shaw's insistence on a single global public sphere and concentrate, within a single state, on Entman's triangle of three actors: public officials (and their foreign policy statements and actions), the media (and their foreign policy content), and public opinion (concerning foreign policy). If you are visually oriented, imagine or jot down—as Wolfgang Donsbach has done (Donsbach 1998)—labels designating each of the three actors, one at each apex of an equilateral triangle, and imagine or draw two causal arrows—one pointing in each direction—between each pair of actors.

This picture schematizes a family of very simple and parsimonious theories of the media and foreign policy. Each theory in the family specifies the existence of the three actors and says something about the existence and/or the magnitude of some subset of the six possible bilateral relationships among them. Such a theory might, for example, assert (à la indexing) that public officials have substantial impact on the foreign policy content of the mass media; that the reciprocal impact of the media upon foreign policy is slight; that the media heavily drive public opinion (engineering consent or establishing hegemony); that the contrary influence, of public opinion upon media, rarely operates; that public opinion rarely influences officials (democratic control is slight); and that officials do not directly influence public opinion (they do so only indirectly, and very effectively, through the media). Or a quite different theory within this family might postulate a high degree of democratic control, with the arrow from public opinion to public officials being the most important one, and with public opinion perhaps arising on its own, quite autonomous from media content. Many other sorts of theories in this family can be imagined.

Within this context, the chief task for empirical research would be to test alternative theories (all nested in the same family) against each other, by estimating the magnitude of each of the six possible relationships among the three actors. Ideally, empirical research (presumably based on a simultaneous equation or time-series design) would yield six regression coefficients or path coefficients quantifying the magnitude of the six relationships. Some of my own work and that of other contributors to this volume can be characterized as striving toward (though falling well short of) just those sorts of results.

The preceding chapters, however, make quite evident that no theory within the simple "triangle" family can be accepted as fully adequate. No single set of six path coefficients between pairs of the three actors can possibly account for all of the empirical variation that we are likely to consider important.

For starters, Shaw and Entman persuasively argue that there has been an important system change. A satisfactory theory, therefore, must specify the *type of world system* to which it applies. At minimum, we need *two* theories of the simple triangle type, applying before and after the end of the Cold War. (Presumably other variants would also be required to deal with earlier historical periods involving different world systems, governmental forms, and media technologies.)

So far, this is still reasonably parsimonious. But—despite the appeal of Shaw's important insight into trends toward a single global public sphere—it seems clear that nation-states do still matter and that there exist some important differences dependent upon the *type of state* involved. It is not just a matter of the United States idiosyncratically differing from Germany. Crossnational research is beginning to suggest some systematic variations in state-media-public relationships according to the type of state and its institutional and societal arrangements: superpower or not, democracy or not, two-party or multiparty system, state-run or independent media, control of or subjection to global media, and so forth. Sorting out these variations with precision is a key task of ongoing research.

Things also become a bit messier if we begin to specify different relationships among officials, media, and public opinion according to the *type of issue*. It is easy enough to distinguish between domestic and foreign policy issues, even between crisis and noncrisis issues, or domestically framed and internationally framed foreign policy issues; we might get by with just two types of theories (predicting substantially different path coefficients) corresponding to two types of foreign policy issues. Even Zaller and Chiu's situational issue types (involving duration of conflict, involvement of a hostile superpower, occurrence of losses or setbacks, and so forth) might be accommodated simply by adding a few arrows to our triangle representing exogenous influences upon officials' foreign policy actions, rather than modifications of any of the six basic relationships. (That is to say: one-way, linear additive influences from additional outside factors—as opposed to statistical interactions—require only supplementation rather than fundamental modification of a basic theory.) If many different issue types require substantially different specification of relationships within a triangle-type theory, however, parsimony is in serious trouble.

Even so, we remain so far within the more or less manageable and more or less visualizable realm of a three-dimensional matrix, in which somewhat different triangle-theory relationships could be arrayed along the three dimensions of world system type, state type, and issue type. Complex, but manageable.

Parsimony and theoretical coherence threaten to break down altogether, however, once we question the unity or completeness of any of the three actors that these triangle theories postulate. And the preceding (as well as subsequent) chapters in this volume offer some very vigorous challenges to the three-actor approach.

Take the public-opinion apex of our triangle: we may need to distinguish between or among *types of public opinion*. Entman makes a plausible case that we need to distinguish polling opinion from perceived opinion. Perhaps this complication could be finessed by refusing to expand the triangle (particularly since we are unlikely, without a major effort, to get good systematic measures of perceived opinion), instead just taking account of how manipulation of perceived opinion may attenuate or modify relationships involving actual, poll-measured public opinion. But what can we do about *anticipation* of values-based and retrospectively oriented future opinion?. To me, "latent" or "anticipated" public opinion seems to play a crucial part in public opinion–media–foreign policy relationships. Perhaps it should be included as a key concept or actor, but that would require major modification of triangle-type theories.

Worse yet, there are abundant reasons to think that public opinion, even when differentiated into two or three types, still inadequately represents the diverse set of important nonmedia actors that might more properly be summed up within the rubric of civil society. Merely to substitute civil society for public opinion at the apex of the triangle is not likely to do the job. Surely, for many purposes we will have to introduce distinctions among *types of actors within civil society*, such as *interest groups* (especially corporations and trade associations, but also trade unions and broad social movements), which themselves have complicated reciprocal relationships with public opinion, the media, and government officials. Likewise *experts* and other information providers may have to be included explicitly. Any such move will produce theories with considerably more complicated structures than the simple official-media-public triangle.

Again, at least for some countries it may prove necessary to account for differentiation within the public-officials actor. In the United States, for example, particularly during periods of divided party government, it may be important to distinguish among *types of government officials*—for example, those in the executive branch versus the legislative branch.

Finally, the unitary concept of "the media" may be inadequate if there are important distinctions among *types of media*—between, say, print and electronic media, let alone differences between categories of media based on ownership type, audience, and the like. This is true even if theoretical power can be achieved without going inside the black box of media and theorizing about relationships among journalists, sources, editors, and owners. And, of course, different *aspects of media content* may be relevant for different purposes: policy-related directional thrust; narrative frame; extent of emphasis; judgments of performance or competence; and so forth. Different *aspects of public opinion* (collective preferences, beliefs, salience, evaluations, etc.) might be addressed to correspond to the relevant aspect of media content. Any distinctions of these sorts would further complicate the simple triangular type of theory.

Where does this leave us? With hard choices. Good empirical work needs to explore many of these and other distinctions in order to ascertain which make the most important differences. Good theoretical work needs to focus on the concepts and relationships that capture the largest and most important parts of reality, without abandoning parsimony or trying to account for everything. The work included in this book, in both the preceding and the subsequent chapters, makes substantial progress in those directions.

One final observation, from the perspective of an intellectual pluralist. We are well served, I believe, by a substantial division of labor, in which some empiricists explore one finite part of the picture and others explore other parts, and in which some theorists stay at a grand general level while others make finer distinctions and embrace more complexity. But each of these kinds of work can be improved by paying close attention to the other kinds.

II

PUBLIC AND ELITE ATTITUDES AFTER THE COLD WAR

7

Elite Misperceptions of U.S. Public Opinion and Foreign Policy

Steven Kull and Clay Ramsay

A central question in the study of U.S. foreign policy and public opinion is the nature of the linkage between them: how and even whether public opinion has an impact on foreign policy. In his book *Public Opinion and American Foreign Policy*, Ole R. Holsti declares that "by far the least well developed of the areas of public opinion research has been the opinion-policy link" (Holsti 1996a, 196). Holsti also offers a useful summary of real if modest scholarly progress on this topic in the concluding chapter of his book. There appears to be some consensus that public opinion has some impact on foreign policy; based on a recent review of the existing literature, Philip Powlick and Andrew Katz summarize how "few now question that American public opinion has an effect on foreign policymakers" (Powlick and Katz 1998). However, as James Stimson notes, public opinion exists largely in a latent form and becomes activated only when policies stray outside a range of public acceptability. Thus, policymakers are constrained by what they perceive as the parameters of public acceptability.

The issue addressed in this chapter is whether foreign policymakers correctly perceive the parameters of public opinion. To put it in the form of a question: Is there an intervening variable between public opinion and foreign policy, namely, the potential misperception of public opinion by the policy elite? A substantial body of research has demonstrated that policy decisions can be greatly influenced by misperceptions, just as much as by objective factors such as the distribution of resources or equations of costs and benefits (Jervis 1976). Presumably, if there is a link between public opinion and foreign policy, elite misperceptions of public opinion can play a significant role in determining policy outcomes. Indeed, in the event that there is a discrepancy between public opinion and policy decisions, one possible factor (though probably not the only one) may be these misperceptions of public opinion.

To address this question, we draw on the findings of an extensive research project that examined the relationship between public opinion and a significant trend in U.S. foreign policy in the 1990s, most prominently following the 1994 midterm elections. This was a trend away from U.S. international engagement: reducing the international-affairs budget, closing U.S. embassies, cutting foreign aid, failing to pay United Nations (UN) dues, and resisting the commitment of U.S. troops to UN peacekeeping operations.[1] A major exception, though, was defense spending; while reduced from its high point in the 1980s, it was maintained at levels close to those of the Cold War.

So what was the role of public opinion in this? Within the policy discourse, there were frequent references to this trend as not only consistent with public opinion but also prompted by it. Policymakers and media pundits asserted that U.S. policy was responding to a new wave of isolationism among the U.S. public, spawned by the end of the Cold War (Kull and Destler, forthcoming). In particular, it was believed that cooperative forms of engagement were unpopular. Thus, it was also assumed that the public dislikes the United Nations, opposes contributing troops to international peacekeeping operations, and intrinsically opposes foreign aid. (Defense spending, on the other hand, was assumed to be popular because it is seen as directly protecting U.S. interests and asserting U.S. international leadership.)

But was the public really going through such an isolationist trend? Whether or not the public's attitudes were prompting policy, was the policy community correctly perceiving the public? Existing polling data did not show such a trend. But maybe the policymakers were discerning something that the polls had not yet detected. Perhaps the polls were not asking the right questions. Then again, maybe the policy community was misperceiving the public.

Our research project sought to answer several key questions. First, did policy practitioners perceive a change in public opinion and did they relate the trend to a change in U.S. foreign policy? Second, and most important, if such a trend in public opinion was perceived to be the case, was it a correct perception? Third, if policymakers were given some control over the opinion-polling process, would they be good at predicting the public's response to foreign policy questions? Finally, if there was evidence of a misperception, how or why did it occur? To answer these questions, we undertook a multipart research project.

THE GAP BETWEEN ELITE PERCEPTIONS AND PUBLIC OPINION

The first stage of the project was a series of interviews with eighty-three members of the policy community, including members of Congress, congressional staffers, executive-branch officials dealing with foreign policy, foreign policy journalists, and members of nongovernmental organizations that dealt with foreign policy. These policy practitioners were asked about their perceptions of public attitudes on the question of America's role in the world, U.S. relations with the United Nations, the U.S. role in UN peacekeeping, U.S. foreign aid policy, and U.S. defense spending.

We also asked about their perception of the impact of these public opinions on U.S. foreign policy.

The second stage was a comprehensive review of the existing polling data. Analyzing data from all publicly available sources, we sought to determine whether policymakers were perceiving the public correctly and—to the extent that there was a gap between elite perception and public attitudes—whether there were any dynamics in public attitudes that could help account for elite perceptions.

The net result of the elite interviews and the analysis of public attitudes did indeed reveal a substantial gap in all areas. What follows is a brief synopsis of this gap. A more complete analysis can be found in the book *Misreading the Public: The Myth of a New Isolationism* (Kull and Destler, 1999).

America's Role in the World

Asked what they thought the majority of Americans felt about the U.S. role in the world in the wake of the Cold War, approximately three out of four respondents said that most Americans want the U.S. to disengage from the world. The recurring theme was that this is a result of a resurgence of isolationism in the wake of the Cold War and a renewed parochialism in American thinking. This view was especially strong among members of Congress and their staffs. It was less strong among executive-branch officials, though still a majority.

Polling data, however, indicate clearly that the majority of Americans do not want to disengage—nor has the proportion who do increased significantly since the end of the Cold War. Trend data based on responses to questions that have been asked for decades show no substantial change since the fall of the Berlin Wall. At least two out of three Americans still say the United States should take an active part in world affairs, and in response to some questions the majority supporting this general view rises to 90 percent.

There are some features of American public opinion that may contribute to the perception that the public wants to disengage from the world. Americans do want their nation to move away from the role of dominant world leader—or "world policeman." They also believe that the United States does more than its fair share in international efforts. But on further questioning, it becomes clear that these sentiments do not reflect a fundamental desire to disengage. To move away from the role of dominant world leader, most Americans want the United States not to withdraw but to put more emphasis on working together with other countries, especially through the UN. And the view that the United States does more than its fair share is founded on extreme overestimation of how much the United States actually does. Asked to specify how much the United States should do, most Americans specify an amount greater than the actual amount. When told how much the United States does do, most do not find it objectionable.

The United Nations

A substantial majority of practitioners believed that the American public is either negative or ambivalent about the United Nations. Less than a quarter of those interviewed said that the majority of Americans have positive feelings toward the UN. Less than a fifth believed that Americans would like to see a stronger UN. Only one in ten thought that the majority of Americans want the United States to pay its UN dues in full. An overwhelming majority of practitioners thought that Americans, in a situation requiring the use of military force, would prefer acting together with NATO over acting together with the UN. The negative view of public attitudes toward the UN was markedly stronger among congressional members and staff.

Public attitudes diverge sharply from these perceptions. A strong majority report positive feelings about the UN, while an overwhelming majority support U.S. participation in the UN as an active member. An overwhelming majority would also like to see the UN strengthened. The worry that this could threaten U.S. sovereignty is only a minority concern. A majority support full payment of U.S. dues to the UN. Majorities even support some forms of international taxation to bring revenue to the UN and creating a standing UN peacekeeping force made up of volunteers.

Support for the UN is especially strong when it comes to the use of military force. When offered a choice of using U.S. military force unilaterally or as part of a UN operation, the public opts overwhelmingly for the latter. In some cases, the public would even prefer the UN to NATO. Concurrent with this strong support for the UN, however, is significant public criticism of the UN's performance, especially the passivity shown by some UN peacekeeping operations. However, this frustration tends to evoke majority support for strengthening these operations rather than discontinuing them.

UN Peacekeeping

Only about one in ten of the practitioners interviewed thought that a majority had positive feelings about UN peacekeeping. Half thought that most Americans take a negative view of UN peacekeeping in general. Another quarter thought that Americans could support a specific UN operation only if certain conditions were met—such as high potential for success, no use of American personnel, or a direct connection to U.S. national interests.

On the question of contributing U.S. troops to UN peacekeeping, the majority of practitioners thought most Americans were opposed: members and staff on Capitol Hill were nearly unanimous on this point. Almost three-quarters also felt that the majority of the public was opposed to placing U.S. troops under a non-American commander in a UN operation. Finally, a plurality of policy practitioners thought that any U.S. casualties would generate strong public pressure for immediate withdrawal from a UN peacekeeping operation. Almost three-quarters, including all those from the media, said a majority of the public had favored immediate withdrawal from Somalia after the death of eighteen U.S. Rangers in October 1993.

In fact, UN peacekeeping in principle garners strong majority support from the public, while counterarguments (based on cost or lack of connection to U.S. national security) do poorly in polls. Support derives both from peacekeeping's potential for burden-sharing and from humanitarian and moral concerns, especially in cases in which genocide is a factor. At the same time, very large majorities had reservations about UN peacekeeping performance, most notably in Bosnia, where the operation was perceived as too passive.

The majority have consistently favored contributing U.S. troops to peacekeeping operations in principle. Support for contributing to specific operations varies, however, according to a number of questions, including whether the operation is clearly perceived as multilateral, whether the U.S. is perceived as contributing its fair share, whether the operation is perceived as likely to succeed, whether U.S. leadership is acting coherently and decisively, and whether the operation could mitigate widespread civilian suffering. Another concern is whether the U.S. soldiers want to be part of the operation.

The public divides over the question of putting U.S. troops under a non-American UN commander, with neither side gaining a strong majority. However, a very strong majority find a foreign commander acceptable if the United States is contributing only a minority of the troops.

Finally, on the question of U.S. casualties, in response to a variety of hypothetical scenarios, only a small minority say they would favor withdrawing U.S. troops in response to a significant number of U.S. fatalities. In response to the actual fatalities in Somalia in October 1993, numerous polls showed that only about four in ten responded by favoring immediate withdrawal. Indeed, in the short run a majority of Americans favored *more* involvement to reinforce U.S. troops. A majority did want to withdraw eventually, but this was true before the fatalities. In retrospect, strong majorities have continued to approve of the United States having undertaken the humanitarian operation in Somalia. Finally, a poll conducted in the Spring of 1998 revealed that nearly two out of three Americans mistakenly believed that the United States had suffered substantial fatalities as part of the NATO operation in Bosnia over the last year, but this did not lead to calls for withdrawal.

Foreign Aid

A very strong majority of practitioners believed that Americans have a negative attitude toward foreign aid in principle, feeling the money should be spent on domestic priorities. A substantial minority—and a large majority of those members of Congress interviewed—said that most Americans would like to eliminate foreign aid completely. Nearly every respondent said that the public overestimated the amount spent on foreign aid, but less than a tenth cited this misperception as a primary source of opposition. Only a small minority cited dissatisfaction with the performance of U.S. foreign-aid programs as a major reason for the public's negative attitude.

In fact, polling data show that an overwhelming majority of Americans embrace the broad principle of giving foreign aid to the needy. Only a tiny minority wants foreign aid eliminated. When asked to prioritize, Americans rank domestic needs higher; but when asked to distribute resources, most Americans assign more to foreign aid than is currently allocated. Support derives from both altruism and self-interest. Majorities embrace the ideas that giving foreign aid helps the United States to develop trading partners, preserve the environment, limit population growth, and promote democracy. But overwhelming majorities reject the idea that the United States should give aid only when it serves the national interest.

A strong majority feel that the United States gives too much foreign aid. But contrary to practitioners' perceptions that this occurs because Americans prefer to spend the money at home, polls suggest that this feeling is largely due to extreme overestimation of the amount of foreign aid given by the United States, both as a percentage of the federal budget and relative to other countries. When Americans are asked what percentage of the federal budget would be appropriate, they set an amount far higher than the actual level. Only a small minority find objectionable the actual amount—1 percent. A very strong majority said that the United States should give the same amount as other countries as a percentage of gross national product—considerably more than the United States gives in reality.

Defense Spending

A slight majority of policy practitioners thought that Americans support current levels of defense spending. Within this group, most said that the public was comfortable with the status quo, with a small minority saying that the public wanted increases. Only about a fifth thought that most Americans want to see cuts in U.S. defense spending. Likewise, only a fifth said that the public would be supportive if the president and Congress were to decide on a 10–20 percent cut in defense spending, while a plurality said that the public would not be supportive of such cuts. Most significant, practitioners interviewed thought that support for the current level of spending was derived from concerns that cuts would impair homeland defense, a desire to preserve jobs, and a desire to maintain the dominant U.S. role in the world. A desire for burden-sharing through greater multilateralism was rarely mentioned.

In this case, the gap between the public and policy practitioners is more subtle. Most Americans support a strong defense, and polls that simply ask for feelings about the current level of defense spending show majority comfort. However, polls that probe more deeply show support for substantial cuts, including polls that ask respondents to:

- specify their preferred spending level;
- consider defense spending in the context of the need to balance the budget or, in a budgetary context, inform respondents of the actual amount of defense spending;

- propose defense spending levels relative to potential enemies;
- make trade-offs between defense spending and nonmilitary international spending; and
- evaluate the requirement for the United States to be prepared to fight two major regional wars.

If the president and Congress were to agree to cut defense spending 10–20 percent, strong majorities say they would be supportive. If these funds were to be explicitly redirected into popular domestic programs, overwhelming majorities say they would approve.

But where the gap is most apparent is in policy practitioners' perceptions of why the public supports defense spending. Contrary to policy practitioners' perceptions, the majority do not express fears that defense cuts will make the United States vulnerable and do not favor maintaining defense spending so as to preserve jobs. Most centrally, the majority of Americans strongly reject a level of U.S. defense spending perceived as being consistent with the role of the United States as dominant world leader. Rather, the public calls for a much greater emphasis on burden sharing through multilateral approaches to security.

LETTING THE POLICY PRACTITIONERS ASK THE QUESTIONS

Although the evidence for a gap between elite perceptions and public attitudes was derived from a comprehensive review of polling data, there was still the possibility that policy practitioners have a unique insight into the public not yet revealed in the polls. The third stage of the project was to give policy practitioners the opportunity to propose poll questions and to predict what they thought the outcome would be.

In a series of workshops, policy practitioners were presented the findings from the interviews of policy practitioners and the contrasting polling data. We then asked them to challenge the notion that policymakers are misreading the American public by proposing ideas for poll questions that might reveal underlying trends toward disengagement and to predict the outcomes. These proposals were then developed into a questionnaire that was reviewed by workshop participants, as well as one Democrat and one Republican pollster. The questionnaire was then used in a poll with a random sample of 2,400 Americans. As the poll was conducted in two waves, the group was also reconvened and presented the preliminary findings to see if this prompted any new ideas for poll questions.

Overall, what was most striking was that the policy practitioners were not good at predicting public responses. Essentially, all of the predictions they made as part of their challenges to the finding of a gap were not sustained by the polling data. The challenges, and the subsequent tests, can be divided into four broad areas.

Challenges Based on Dynamics of the Electoral Process

One challenge, frequently repeated, was that even if most Americans say in a poll that they support engagement, they actually prefer candidates who support disengagement. To test this notion, different samples were asked about a position in terms of their own opinion, and then in terms of a hypothetical candidate's position. In fact, there was little difference in results between the two samples. Even on a question with a complex design that sought to factor out social-desirability effects in favor of proengagement candidates, the proengagement candidate did better.

Another frequent challenge was that an incumbent who voted in favor of proengagement policies would be highly vulnerable to attacks from an electoral challenger, especially if the policies involved spending taxpayer money. With the help of political consultants, we created political ads in which hypothetical challengers attacked hypothetical incumbents for supporting foreign aid and paying UN dues, as well as rebuttal ads from the incumbents. Responding specifically to these ads, the majority of respondents preferred the proengagement incumbents over the challengers by robust margins.

Among other challenges, one held that even if the majority say they favors engagement, they do not like to see elected officials spending a significant portion of their time on foreign policy. However, when asked in a poll how much time was appropriate for the president or a member of Congress to spend on foreign affairs, the median respondent allotted a substantial portion—30 percent for the president and 25 percent for a member of Congress.

Challenges Based on Assumptions about the Effective Public

Numerous workshop participants declared that support for engagement is weak and fragile, while opposition is intense and resilient; thus, opposition is more relevant politically. But responses to survey questions indicated that in general, supporters of engagement held their views as strongly as opponents. And when presented with strong counterarguments, proengagement respondents proved slightly less likely to change their positions than antiengagement respondents.

It was also argued in the workshops that the public that matters on foreign policy is an attentive, active minority and that this group wants to reduce U.S. involvement in the world. But among those who declared themselves attentive and those who said they are active, support for international engagement was found to be, if anything, a bit higher than in the general population. These groups were somewhat less enthusiastic toward the UN, however, and more critical of government performance.

Challenges Based on How the Public Makes Trade-offs with Domestic Programs

A key challenge from practitioners stated that even if the majority of Americans embrace an internationally engaged U.S. foreign policy in principle, in practice they are not ready to spend the necessary money when faced with making trade-offs against domestic priorities. Thus, when members of Congress cut international spending in favor of domestic items, they are doing what members of the public *would do* if they were voting on the federal budget. The prevailing view was that members of Congress were also reflecting their constituents' wishes by maintaining the current level of defense spending.

To test this assumption, a budget exercise was developed in which respondents were asked to allocate money among major items in the discretionary federal budget: four international-spending categories—the State Department, the UN and UN peacekeeping, military aid, and humanitarian and economic aid—and seven purely domestic items. Contrary to the predictions, the majority chose to maintain or increase every category of international spending. Instead, respondents cut defense severely. On average, international spending was dramatically increased and fared better than many domestic items. Thus, the view expressed in the workshops—that respondents would cut international spending in favor of domestic items while also sparing defense—turned out to be the exact reverse of the majority's actual choices.

Challenges Based on Confidence That Members of Congress Reflect Their Constituents

It was frequently stated in the workshops (and in interviews) that individual members of Congress are good mirrors of attitudes in their districts and, thus, that the aggregate legislative behavior of Congress forms a good mirror of national attitudes, more reliable than national polls. The fact that Congress has taken legislative steps limiting U.S. international engagement was seen as clear evidence that the public must support these steps.

To test this challenge, we set out to determine if the constituents of strongly anti-engagement members of Congress were indeed also opposed to engagement. We began with the fifteen cosponsors of the 1995 legislation calling for the United States to withdraw from the UN (H.R. 2535), examined their voting records for consistent opposition to international engagement, and interviewed their aides over the telephone about how calls and letters were running on international issues and how they perceived majority views on these issues in the district. Through this process, we selected four geographically dispersed districts, in each of which the congressional aide had taken the unequivocal position that the majority of constituents would favor withdrawing from the UN and eliminating foreign aid.

We polled 500 randomly selected adults in each district (2,000 total). In all districts, only one in five respondents favored withdrawing from the UN and only one in twelve favored eliminating foreign aid. Strong majorities favored strengthening the UN. Overall, these four districts were not only supportive of U.S. international engagement but, on most questions, indistinguishable from the national sample.

Why Do Policy Practitioners Misperceive the Public?

Why have U.S. policy practitioners come to believe Americans want to withdraw from the world? Why have they persisted in believing this despite a substantial survey evidence to the contrary? We have explored possible explanations in two ways: first, in terms of the subjective processes of policy practitioners as individuals, drawing heavily upon our interviews with them; and second, as policy players within the broader systems in which they operate: Washington policymaking, executive and congressional; and national politics.

Within the first approach—analyzing practitioners as individuals—we have isolated four possible explanations: (1) the failure of policy practitioners to seek out information about public attitudes; (2) policy practitioners' tendency to respond to the vocal public as if it were the majority; (3) their assumption that Congress and the media reflect the public; and (4) their tendency to underestimate the public. While the first three factors will be treated briefly, the last will receive the most attention here, because there is strong evidence that the public also underestimates itself, and this evidence can be linked to an earlier body of research that deserves fresh consideration.

1. Failure to Seek Information about Public Attitudes

In virtually every case, members of Congress said they did not do polling on international issues; nor did they show much interest in it. A congressional staffer, speaking of his boss, said, "I'm trying to think, the last time—I can't remember the last time he's asked for a poll, and I can't remember the last time I've actually seen one." Explaining this low level of interest, another member said, "Foreign affairs just doesn't win elections or lose elections."

This pattern of giving little attention to polls was also reflected in a recent Pew study ("Washington Leaders Wary of Public Opinion") that interviewed eighty-one members of Congress, ninety-eight presidential appointees, and 151 senior civil servants. Asked "What is your principal source of information about the way the public feels about issues?" only 24 percent of the members of Congress, 21 percent of presidential appointees, and 6 percent of senior civil servants mentioned public opinion polls (Kohut 1998).

2. Responding to the Vocal Public as if It Were the Majority

Consistent with their widespread negative attitudes toward polls, most policy practitioners, especially in Congress, explained that their primary means of getting information about public attitudes is through informal contacts with self-selected and outspoken citizens—the vocal public. A high-level congressional staffer explained how he got his understanding of public opinion:

> You get it from constituencies. You get it from public interest groups. You get it from tons of junk that comes in your in-box every day from half the interest groups in the

country. You get it from talking to people . . . [who] come in here all the time [and say] they need this, they need that, do this for me, do that for me. So you get a constant feel for this stuff.

This orientation was also reflected in the above-mentioned Pew study: when members of Congress were asked about their "principal source of information about how the public feels," by far the most frequently mentioned (59 percent) was "personal contacts," while the second most common (cited by 36 percent) was "telephone or mail from citizens."

While some respondents described an active constituency that initiates contacts specifically to denounce international engagement efforts, others implied, quite plausibly, that more contacts were initiated by concern about some other domestic program that the constituent was concerned would be underfunded. Attacking spending on international efforts was a way to rationalize increasing spending on the domestic program. For example, a congressional staffer said, "Usually people are saying . . . 'Medicare is going bankrupt. Why don't we just cut foreign aid and give all the money to Medicare?' "

When we probed about whether there were some contacts that were supportive of engagement, these were recognized but brushed off as being unrepresentative of the general population with comments like, "Those are just your World-Affairs-Council types."

3. Viewing Congress and the Media as Mirrors of the Public

Numerous comments from policy practitioners suggested that they base much of their thinking about the public on the assumption that Congress and the media are reliable mirrors of public opinion. In particular, journalists and Congress appear to each take cues from each other and build a shared image of the public that others in the policy elite tend to accept. Taken far enough, this tendency can generate a closed information system immune to disconfirming input from the public itself.

A key element of this system is the belief that the behavior of Congress is a reliable reflection of public attitudes. A reporter-columnist explained why he relied on Congress rather than polls to get his understanding of public attitudes, saying: "Congress is the best reflection of the American public's views. There is a good chemistry of mixing up ideas that goes on." A longtime congressional staffer said, "I think the Congress perfectly reflects public attitudes. . . . I do think they're good bellwethers."

At the same time, members of Congress and their staffs, as well as other members of the policy community, say that they get their cues about the public from the media.[2]

Most commonly, policy practitioners seemed to feel that they could get a sense of public attitudes by reading standard news reporting. A prominent policy analyst described how he gets his ideas about the public:

Mostly, I think, by talking to the press who are soaking in the public, they are reflecting public attitudes. . . . I can't readily explain how it works but daily press coverage does reflect what people are interested in, and does reflect their attitudes. . . . There is an underlying understanding of what people are thinking, and what people are willing to hear, and the press coverage is reflecting that.

4. Underestimating the Public

A fourth possible source of policymakers' misperception of the public is a tendency to view the public in a more negative light than is warranted. In the interviews, when policy practitioners characterized the public, they did so very frequently with a disparaging, if not exasperated, tone. In a content analysis of the interviews, negative characterizations of the public (e.g., "uneducated," "self-contradictory") outweighed positive ones (e.g., "sensible," "responsive to argument") by more than four to one. Implicitly, and in many cases explicitly, policy practitioners were suggesting that the public was inadequate to the task of addressing significant foreign policy issues.

Apparently this view is not uncommon among the American elite. In a 1996 survey of 2,141 American opinion leaders conducted by the Foreign Policy Leadership Project of Duke University and George Washington University, 71 percent agreed that "public opinion is too shortsighted and emotional to provide sound guidance on foreign policy." On a more general note, in the Pew study cited earlier, when asked "Do you think the American public knows enough about the issues you face to form wise opinions about what should be done about these issues, or not?" only 31 percent of the members of Congress, 13 percent of the presidential appointees, and 14 percent of the senior civil servants endorsed the public's ability.

The image of the public as lacking depth and sophistication in many cases was part and parcel of the image of the public as resisting international engagement. The public was widely viewed as so narrow, parochial, and emotional that it was unable to think about foreign policy issues within a long-term framework.

So what is it that sustains this view in the policymaking community? There is indeed evidence that the public is notoriously uninformed on many international issues. But as we have seen, this does not necessarily reflect a preference for a parochial foreign policy or an unwillingness to support long-term efforts in the international arena.

Perhaps the dynamic here may be a general human tendency to underestimate the public—a tendency that appears to exist in the public as well as the policymaking elite. Numerous polls by the Program on International Policy Attitudes (PIPA) have found that the public as a whole itself tends to underestimate the public's support for international engagement. For example, a February 1994 PIPA poll asked respondents whether they thought they were more or less supportive of spending on UN peacekeeping than the average American. Given that this sample is representative of the general public, if the sample as a whole was perceiving the public correctly, the ratio of those who said "more" would be approximately equal to those who said "less." But in fact, 70 percent said they thought they were more supportive than average and only 17 percent thought they were less—more than a 4:1 ratio. Thus, it appears the public as a whole grossly underestimates the public's support for UN peacekeeping.

This tendency to misperceive the public has been studied in the social sciences for some decades now. Floyd Allport is generally credited with coining the phrase "pluralistic ignorance" in the 1920s to describe a situation in which individuals make mistaken judgments about themselves relative to the majority (O'Gorman 1986). For example, studies have found that people tend to perceive others as more racist, more conservative, more sexist, and less willing to engage in socially desirable behaviors such as donating blood (Fields and Schuman 1976; Shami and Shamir 1997; Goethals 1986).

Perhaps most significant, it has been demonstrated that pluralistic ignorance can lead groups to take collective action inconsistent with the values and preferences of the individuals. Particularly relevant to this study is the phenomenon of "group-think" studied by Irving Janis (1982). His analysis of disastrous foreign policy decisions found that a key dynamic was that individual decisionmakers believed that others did not share their doubts. Similarly, Elisabeth Noelle-Neumann describes what she calls the "spiral of silence," whereby individuals who believe that their views are different from the majority remain silent, thus emboldening those who hold contrary views and potentially creating a momentum in favor of political outcomes inconsistent with the original views of the majority (Noelle-Neumann 1993).

Closely related is research on what has been termed the "third person effect." This refers to the demonstrated tendency for people to assume that other people, especially ones who are unfamiliar, are more reactive to media stimuli than they themselves are (Davison 1983). This may help explain the fact that policy practitioners assume that Americans are highly subject (more so than the policy elite) to the so-called CNN effect—the tendency to overreact to emotional media images. More specifically, this may help explain why policy practitioners assumed, incorrectly, that the American public reacted to the image of dead American soldiers in Mogadishu in 1993 by wanting to immediately withdraw U.S. troops.

Social scientists have argued that much of the tendency to misperceive others serves the enhancement of self-esteem (Kennamer 1990). We might call this the "inferior public effect" to describe the tendency to view the public as inferior to the self. Or perhaps we might call it the "Lake Wobegon effect," after the town described by Garrison Keillor, where "all the children are above average." In the case of policy practitioners, the perception of the public as tending toward isolationism may sustain a gratifying belief that one is more farsighted, is more broadly humanitarian, and has a more sophisticated sense of American national interests than the average American—a belief implicit in many comments made in the interviews. But again, as we have seen, this dynamic appears to be operating not only among the policy elite but among the public as well. Many members of the public may also find it gratifying to believe that they, unlike their brethren, are members of a superior group who can think in a larger framework and thus understand the need for international engagement and be less reactive than the average television viewer to emotional media images.

In addition, the belief that one is more supportive of international engagement than average may relieve policy practitioners, as well as members of the public, from a potential conflict. Many issues related to international engagement pose trade-offs between short-term costs (such as money or risked lives) and long-term gains (such as a more stable international regime). Addressing these trade-offs can be stressful. However, if one believes that one is more oriented to the long term than average, this relieves one from having to confront the difficult trade-offs because one believes that the short-term reactivity of the public requires that policy be based on a short-term framework. As discussed, the dominant theme in most interviews was that the public constrains policymakers from pursuing a more active international agenda. If in fact the majority is supportive of an active long-term agenda, this removes an excuse for not making difficult long-term decisions.

Naturally, the fact that the belief that one is more supportive of international engagement than the average can be gratifying raises a question: whether respondents in polls may in fact be fooling themselves or simply trying to fool the interviewer. Perhaps the dynamic may not be that policy practitioners and members of the public underestimate the public but that the members of the public overestimate themselves. Perhaps their estimation of the public reveals the truth about themselves, a truth they would just as soon deny, but it will nonetheless condition their behavior when, for example, they vote.

This is a crucial question, one that has been addressed in the social-science literature. Overall, the evidence suggests that when people underestimate the public they are not, in fact, simply revealing their true selves. For example, one study found that the percentage of students who predicted that they were going to contribute to a blood drive was larger than the average estimate of the percentage of their classmates who would contribute. However, the students' estimates of their own behavior turned out to be a more reliable predictor of the actual incidence of contributing blood than the students' estimates of their classmates. Another found that while respondents perceived others as less willing to behave in a nonracist fashion, their estimates of their own behavior were confirmed by behavioral indices (Fields and Schuman 1976; Shami and Shamir 1997; Goethals 1986).

CONCLUSION

One large question remains: Why do the forces of the political market not correct elite misperceptions about American foreign policy preferences? Elected officials and those who advise them have an incentive to know how their constituents think. Journalists, presumably, are motivated to understand the public correctly and to report accordingly.

While it is beyond the scope of this analysis to answer the question in depth, a few observations may be useful. First, it is important to note that the American public does not pay a great deal of attention to foreign policy. When Americans select candidates, foreign policy positions are a low-priority consideration. Thus, candidates have little incentive to understand the public's foreign policy positions, and they are unlikely to be punished for getting them wrong. Thus, once a belief about the public becomes established, there is no reliable corrective mechanism. It may be that areas of public policy that receive a higher level of public attention and that more directly influence voting behavior are less subject to such perceptual distortions.

The possibility of imperfect political markets has a counterpart in economic markets. Economists have regularly found cases where markets operate suboptimally. For example, Douglass C. North and other scholars in the emerging field of the "new institutional economics" have described what they call "path-dependent behavior." This concept has been developed to explain situations of collective irrationality: a society (or portion thereof) pursuing a historically determined behavior pattern that is suboptimal in terms of the collective interest, but is logical in terms of the trade-offs each individual faces at the time, once a particular "path" is launched. The keyboard configuration of typewriters, and now computers, is a commonly cited example: producers manufacture the format most in demand, and users learn and acquire the format most available, resulting in domination by a QWERTY pattern that is demonstrably less efficient than alternatives (David 1985). An individual could learn and acquire alternatives, but only at considerable cost: the burdens of the individual path-breaker are heavy. It is far easier to work within the established parameters. North observes that even complex societal relationships and patterns of evolution seem to owe much to historical accident, persisting even in the face of visibly superior systems because they reward individuals who operate within their incentive systems.

It is not hard to understand how American policymakers might begin to believe that the American public is going through a phase of isolationism. After all, there is reason to believe that the public did so after World War I and that it would have after World War II were it not for the Soviet threat. It seems plausible that the public would again turn to isolationism with the end of the Cold War. As Richard Neustadt and Ernest May observe, historical analogies exert a strong influence on the thinking of policymakers. Once such an image of the public is established, as discussed, media reporting and congressional behavior can then become self-reinforcing. And because of the low public salience regarding international issues, the political market does not supply a dependable corrective.

But just because the political market is imperfect such that policymakers may have inadequate information about the public, this does not mean that there is really no link between the public and foreign policy. As our study and others have found, policymakers believe that there is a link, that they are influenced by public opinion. However, the link may in fact be between policymakers' *image of the public* and foreign policy. This image is something that the media play a key role in forming through their reporting; Congress also plays a key role through its behavior. Presumably, it is possible for the public itself to have some impact on this image of the public. After all, some policymakers do show interest in polls, and some have even shown considerable interest in the findings of this study. Thus, if policymakers seek out information, their image of the public can become more accurate, and the link between the actual public and foreign policy can really be made. But it is not a given that this will ever occur.

8

To Intervene or Not to Intervene in Bosnia
That Was the Question for the United States and Europe

Richard Sobel

During the 1990s the United States and Europe faced dilemmas about intervention in Bosnia. These dilemmas were tied to questions of how democratic governments respond to citizens' opinions regarding the conduct of foreign affairs. In looking at the attitudes about Bosnia intervention held by the American public and several European publics, this analysis contrasts relatively strong popular preferences, especially for multilateral action, with relatively weak government policies about employing allied forces. It suggests why the discrepancy between supportive publics and reluctant governments persisted from the start of the fighting, in the Spring of 1992, until the Fall of 1995. Finally, it considers the implications of comparatively supportive public attitudes for the continuation of allied involvement in the former Yugoslavia.

While public opinion surveys about possible intervention began to appear in the United States in mid-1992, surveys of Western European public opinion began to be published only at the end of that year. The American data came largely from national polls conducted by the news media (ABC/*Washington Post*, CBS/*New York Times*, and NBC/*Wall Street Journal*) and major pollsters (Gallup, Harris, Princeton Survey Research). The data for Britain, France, Germany, and Italy came from national polls as well as the crossnational Eurobarometer series.[1] (See Appendix A for polls consulted and Appendix B for question wordings.) Because the survey organizations and question wording varied, identifying trends over time or making direct comparisons across nations is complex (Sobel 1996a). But the responses generally reveal similar attitudes in favor of allied intervention among Americans and Europeans alike and distinct contrasts between public opinions and government responses on both continents. Among the European publics in particular, there was consistent plurality-to-majority support for intervention in Bosnia, in contrast to the reluctance

of national governments and international organizations to take forceful action until
Summer 1995.

U.S. ATTITUDES TOWARD INTERVENTION IN BOSNIA

Though a wide majority of Americans began paying attention to the events in Bosnia early on (Harris 8/13/93: 84 percent), until Summer 1995 only a third to a
half followed the situation closely (see Sobel 1996b, table 6.1) Very few Americans
considered the war in Bosnia to be the most important issue the United States faced
(Harris 1/22/93–5/23/94: typically 1 percent), though a somewhat greater proportion considered it the most important U.S. foreign policy issue (Harris 4/4/94: 11
percent; PSR 6/8/95: 18 percent). The large proportions of early respondents who
did not know how to evaluate the president's handling of the Bosnia situation also
suggested that Americans had not been very knowledgeable or focused on the problem (Table 8.1).

The vast majority of Americans viewed military action as largely a European
(Sobel 1996b, table 6.3) or a multilateral responsibility (Sobel 1996b, table 6.4).
The proportion of Americans who thought the United States had a responsibility to
act militarily in Bosnia increased significantly into mid-1994, then declined (Sobel
1996b, table 6.4). If there were no other way to "get humanitarian aid to civilians"
and prevent the "practicing [of] atrocities," 58 percent felt that the United States
had an "obligation to use military force" (27 percent agreed strongly; Kull and Ramsay 1994). But only a plurality of 37 percent believed the main reason the United
States should take military action was that it had "a moral responsibility to stop
ethnic cleansing" (Gallup 1/28/93). Although the "post-Vietnam syndrome" was
still apparent in the desire of most Americans to stay out of such foreign involve-
ments as the Reagan-era interventions in Central America (Sobel 1989), 49 percent
of Americans thought intervention in Bosnia would be comparable to the quick victory in the Gulf War, compared to 43 percent who thought it would end in slow
defeat like in Vietnam (Gallup 4/6/93).

American attitudes about intervention in Bosnia could be gauged by looking at
both questions concerning the president's handling of the Bosnia crisis (Table 8.1)
and those concerning the use of U.S. air and ground forces for humanitarian or
military purposes (Tables 8.2–8.4). Since August 1992, when George Bush was in
the White House, most polls showed a plurality, majority, or relatively even split in
approval of the president's handling of the Bosnia situation (Table 8.1). During
times of inaction or vacillation, the public tended to disapprove more than approve
(e.g., Gallup 6/15/94: 31–48 percent).[2] When the president threatened or participated in direct allied action in Bosnia, a larger proportion of Americans typically
approved than disapproved of his handling of the situation. For example, the public
approved when President Bill Clinton discussed possible U.S. intervention in Spring

Table 8.1 Presidential Handling of Bosnia/Serbia/Yugoslavia Situation

			Approve	*Disapprove*	*Don't know*	*N*
1992	8/6	Gal	38	38	24	930
	8/11	CBS	32	28	40	1434
	8/13	Gal	43	33	24	946
1993	2/10	ABC	46	23	23	1004
	4/22	PSR	44	37	19	750
	4/22	Gal	43	38	19	1000
	4/26	Har	38	57	5	1252
	4/28	PSR	39	30	31	750
	4/29	CBS	35	35	30	834
	5/4	Gal	48	35	17	603
	5/20	ABC	51	36	17	1005
	5/6	PSR	39	40	21	750
	5/26	CBS	38	35	27	1184
	6/21	CBS	36	24	40	1363
	8/2	CBS	32	38	30	870
	8/6	ABC	48	39	13	1216
	8/13	Har	31	61	8	1260
	10/21	PSR	36	43	21	1200
1994	2/7	ABC	41	46	13	521
	2/15	CBS	35	35	30	1193
	2/24	ABC	48	39	13	1531
	3/3	Yan	45	36	19	600
	3/4	NBC	53	33	14	1503
	4/4	Har	39	55	5	1255
	4/21	CBS	31	40	29	1215
	4/21	Yan	35	47	18	600
	4/30	NBC	54	41	5	1002
	5/4	Yan	35	49	10	800
	6/15	Yan	34	47	19	800
	6/23	ABC	40	47	13	1531
	7/15	Gal	31	48	21	1001
	8/4	Yan	34	46	20	600
	12/10	NBC	41	43	16	1000
1995	4/19	PIPA	43	39	18	1204
	6/1	PSR	33	35	32	751
	6/2	NBC	41	43	16	1008
	6/4	CBS	33	47	20	1256
	6/5	Gal	51	47	3	1005
	6/8	PSR	39	46	15	1500
	6/21	Yan	36	46	19	1000
	4/28	ABC	37	56	7	1548
	10/18	Har	50	42	9	1005
	11/10	Yank	38	37	25	1046
	11/29	ABC	44	39	17	1005
	12/1	ABC	40	50	10	523
	12/1	ABC	42	47	11	612
	12/6	ABC	41	48	11	2007
	12/9	Yan	43	43	14	1000
	12/9	CBS	42	47	11	1111

1993 (Gallup 5/6/93: 49–35 percent) and when he issued an ultimatum following the first Sarajevo market massacre in early 1994 (ABC 2/23/94: 48–39 percent).

Distinct differences in attitudes among Americans appeared, however, depending on the type of proposed intervention in Bosnia (Sobel 1996b, table 6.12). Support was strongest for sending UN peacekeepers (Harris 7/7/92: 80 percent), airdrops of humanitarian relief (Gallup 2/26/93: 67 percent), air cover for UN peacekeeping troops (CBS 8/2/93: 61 percent), and shooting down Serb planes in the no-fly zone (Harris 4/28/93: 61 percent). Support for lifting the September 1991 arms embargo (CBS 4/21/94: 57 percent), NATO bombing to protect safe havens (CBS 4/16/94: 54 percent), and joint U.S./UN peacekeeping after a settlement (CBS 6/21/93: 54 percent) ranged at times above 50 percent. A majority of Americans thought that any military intervention in Bosnia should be a coordinated effort with Western European allies through the UN or NATO (Harris 1/22/93: 62 percent; 4/28/93: 52 percent). There was little enthusiasm for the United States acting alone. For instance, approval for unilateral American air strikes ranged from only a fifth to a quarter (Sobel 1996b, table 6.9).

Although support for allied air strikes against Serb military forces in Bosnia was initially low (Gallup 4/22/93: 30 percent), approval grew over time (Table 8.2). During the Summer of 1993, a majority approved of retaliatory strikes in response either to Serbian attacks (Yankelovich 8/4/93: 54 percent), to threats against UN peacekeepers (ABC 8/6/93: 85 percent), or to protect humanitarian aid shipments (Yankelovich 8/4/93: 69 percent). Unexpectedly, there was less sentiment at that time for air strikes to protect the Bosnian Muslims in Sarajevo (Yankelovich 8/4/93: 50 percent) or to force the Bosnian Serbs out of territory occupied earlier in the war (Yankelovich 8/4/93: 40 percent). Thus, Americans were more willing to use air-power to protect UN soldiers providing aid than to save Bosnian civilians or punish the Serb military. Later, most Americans became willing to use U.S. airpower when either UN troops (CBS 8/2/93: 61 percent) or Bosnian civilians in safe havens (CBS 4/21/94: 54 percent) were attacked.

Moreover, besides the high approval ratings for U.S. planes joining in NATO bombing, there was generally plurality-to-majority support for UN humanitarian or peacekeeping efforts (Table 8.3), even those involving some U.S. ground troops (Table 8.5). But only a minority of Americans supported the use of U.S. ground troops for combat against the Serbs (Table 8.4), though somewhat more approved of the use of allied forces for this purpose (Table 8.6). Again, there was typically more support for protecting UN soldiers than Bosnian civilians (cf. Tables 8.4 and 8.5). In short, for air drops of humanitarian aid, for which the justification was compelling, or for air strikes, where the risk to U.S. soldiers was low and expectations of success relatively high, support was fairly strong (CBS 4/16/94: 54 percent). When the risks to American forces increased, approval dropped. There was, however, some public support even for committing U.S. ground forces in allied efforts under appropriate circumstances (Table 8.5).

In sum, between 1992 and 1995 there was generally majority support for U.S.

Table 8.2   (US) Airstrikes against Bosnian Serbs

				Approve	Disapprove	Don't know	N
1992	UN	7/31	Gal	35	45	20	1001
	UN	8/6	Gal	53	33	14	930*
		8/6	Gal	50	37	13	970*
		8/13	Gal	49	39	12	946
1993		1/10	LAT	49	34	17	1733
		4/22	PSR	39	49	12	750
		4/22	Gal	30	62	8	1000
	All.	4/28	Yan	36	52	12	1000
		4/28	Har	44	48	7	1252
		4/29	PSR	40	45	15	750
		5/4	CBS	38	51	12	834
		5/5	PIPA	53	31	16	810
	All.	5/6	ABC	65	32	3	516
		5/6	Gal	36	55	9	603
	UN/PK	6/21	CBS	61	29	10	1363
	Hum.	8/2	CBS	45	43	12	870
	PK	8/2	CBS	61	28	11	870
	PK	8/4	Yan	54	35	10	1600
	Prot.	8/4	Yan	50	38	12	1600
	Hum.	8/4	Yan	69	24	7	1600
		8/4	Yan	40	45	15	1600
	All.	8/6	ABC	60	34	6	1216
	PK	8/6	ABC	85	13	2	1216
		8/6	ABC	27	70	3	1216
	NATO	8/8	Gal	51	48	9	1003
	Prot.	8/13	Har	38	50	12	1260
	PK	9/10	NBC	58	33	5	1006
	Prot.	10/18	CBS	26	60	14	893
		12/4	LAT	33	48	19	1612
1994		1/15	NBC	35	56	9	1001
		2/7	ABC	17	79	3	521
	All.	2/7	Gal	48	43	9	635
	NATO	2/9	PIPA	80	16	4	700
	NATO	2/10	Yan	50	38	12	500
	NATO	4/16	LAT	46	38	16	1682
	PK	4/16	Gal	65	28	8	1002
	NATO	4/21	CBS	54	32	14	1215
	All.	4/21	Yan	35	58	7	600
	NATO	4/30	NBC	64	26	10	1002
	All.	12/7	Yan	31	62	7	800
	All.	12/7	Yan	27	64	9	800
1995		6/1	PSR	37	49	14	751
	All.	6/2	NBC	56	33	11	1008
	UN	6/4	CBS	71	24	5	1256
	All.	7/19	Yan	35	54	11	1200
	NATO	7/23	CBS	59	30	11	1014
	All.	7/29	NBC	61	27	12	1005
	NATO	9/5	CBS	59	25	16	1069

Key: All. = with Allies, Hum. = protect Humanitarian aid, NATO = with NATO, PK = peacekeepers attacked, Prot. = protect civilians/safe havens, UN = with United Nations, *registered voters

Table 8.3   US Troop (Humanitarian/Peacekeeping)

			Approve	Disapprove	Don't know	N
HUMANITARIAN						
1992	8/11	CBS	41	45	14	1434
	8/12	LAT	54	43	13	1460
	12/3	PSR	42	45	13	602
1993	12/4	Gal	57	36	7	1005
1994	1/12	CBS	67	26	7	1179
	1/15	PSR	55	41	5	750
	1/29	PSR	57	35	8	754
	4/8	PSR	37	46	17	750
	4/22	PSR	40	51	9	750
	5/4	PIPA	66	33	2	700
PEACEKEEPING						
1993	2/10	Yan	58	32	10	1000
	3/5	NBC	41	51	8	1503
	5/4	CBS	48	45	9	834
	5/5	PIPA	76	12	11	810
	5/6	Gal	68	30	2	603
	5/27	CBS	44	49	7	1189
	6/21	CBS	54	38	8	1363
	9/10	NBC	36	59	5	1006
	9/23	Yan	57	36	7	800
	10/6	NBC	23	67	10	806
	10/8	Gall	40	52	8	1019
	12/4	LAT	46	47	7	1612
1994	2/9	PIPA	72	25	3	700
	3/4	NBC	53	40	7	1503
	4/21	Yan	39	56	5	600
	5/5	PIPA	73	25	2	700
	12/10	NBC	57	36	7	1000
1995	4/19	PIPA	52	44	5	1204
	6/1	PSR	61	32	7	751
	9/22	Gal	52	43	5	1011
	10/18	Yan	42	50	8	1046
	10/18	PSR	27	59	14	750
	10/19	Gal	50	44	6	1229
	10/22	CBS	39	58	9	1069
	10/27	NBC	30	65	5	1465
	11/6	Gal	47	49	4	931
	11/10	ABC	38	58	4	1005
	11/22	PIPA	50	47	4	722
	11/27	Gal	46	40	4	632
	11/27	CBS	33	58	9	504
	11/29	ABC	38	58	3	523
	11/30	Har	29	67	4	1004
	12/1	ABC	40	56	5	612
	12/6	Yan	36	57	7	1000
	12/6	Yan	38	55	7	1000
	12/9	CBS	40	55	5	1111
	12/15	Gal	41	54	5	1000

Table 8.4   US Troop (Active Involvement/Peacemaking)

			Approve	Disapprove	Don't know	N
1992	7/5	NBC	27	65	8	1105
	7/19	Har	30	65	5	1256
	8/10	NBC	33	54	18	810
	8/19	Yan	24	66	14	1250
	12/12	NBC	26	62	12	1004
1993	1/3	PSR	32	51	17	1216
	1/14	LAT	37	47	16	1733
	1/23	NBC	34	54	12	1009
	4/17	NBC	35	52	13	1004
	4/22	PSR	40	51	9	750
	4/29	PSR	27	60	13	750
	5/4	CBS	31	60	9	834
	5/6	ABC	40	58	2	516
1994	1/6	Gal	28	68	4	1023
	2/7	ABC	13	85	2	521
	2/7	Gal	35	7	8	635
	2/7	ABC	47	50	3	521
	2/10	Yan	40	50	10	500
	4/16	Gal	41	53	6	1002
	11/27	CBS	34	58	8	1120
	12/7	Yan	17	78	5	800
1995	6/2	Yan	40	51	9	600
	6/4	CBS	21	73	6	1256
	6/8	PSR	32	61	7	1004
	6/8	Har	36	57	7	1004
	6/8	Har	35	59	16	1004
	6/9	LAT	41	50	9	1109
	7/14	ABC	40	58	3	1548
	7/19	Yan	28	64	8	1000
	7/19	Yan	40	48	12	1000
	12/6	Yan	36	57	7	1000
	12/15	Gal	41	54	5	1000

assistance in providing humanitarian aid and protecting peacekeepers (Tables 8.3 and 8.5). Most Americans were also willing to use U.S. airpower to protect UN troops and Bosnians in safe havens. Support grew for active U.S. involvement (Table 8.4) and specifically for the use of U.S. combat troops (Gallup 12/11/93–4/16/94: 27 percent to 41 percent), though it remained in the minority (Yankelovich 6/2/95: 40 percent; cf. PIPA 4/5/94: 56 percent overall approval, 31 percent strong approval). There was somewhat more support for allied military actions in which the United States might participate (Sobel 1996b, table 6; Table 8.6 herein), and sig-

Table 8.5 US Troops Help UN Peacekeepers

				Approve	Disapprove	Don't know	N
1994	Evacuate	12/10	NBC	57	36	7	1000
1995	Relocate	6/1	PSR	66	26	8	751
	Rescue	6/1	PSR	78	18	4	751
	Withdraw	6/1	PSR	86	11	3	751
	Relocate	6/2	Yan	65	31	4	600
	Rescue	6/2	Yan	62	33	5	600
	Withdraw	6/2	Yan	59	34	7	600
	Relocate	6/2	NBC	45	46	9	1008
	Rescue	6/4	CBS	57	37	6	1256
	Protect	6/4	CBS	43	52	5	1256
	Relocate	6/5	Gal	70	28	3	1005
	Withdraw	6/5	Gal	64	31	5	1005
	Attacked	6/8	PSR	71	22	7	1500
	Relocate	6/8	PSR	65	29	6	1500
	Strengthen	6/8	Har	39	56	6	1004
	Withdraw	6/8	Har	68	27	5	1004
	Evacuate	6/9	LAT	71	21	8	1104
	Withdraw	7/14	ABC	84	15	1	1548
	Withdraw	7/19	Yan	53	41	6	1000
	Protect	7/23	CBS	31	61	8	1014

Key: Evacuate = evacuate U.N. troops, relocate = relocate U.N. troops, strengthen = strengthen, withdraw = withdraw U.N. troops.

nificant approval of U.S. soldiers protecting UN forces (Table 8.5). Yet as the risks grew, support generally dropped (Sobel 1996b, table 6.12).

A key issue for Americans was whether any intervention was to be unilateral or multilateral. Only one in four Americans (27 percent) wanted the United States to undertake air strikes alone; this contrasted sharply with the 60 percent who approved allied strikes (cf. ABC 8/6/93 and Table 8.2). Yet Americans were ambivalent about turning U.S. forces over to UN or NATO commanders. While most Americans (51 percent) thought the UN was doing a good job in general (Harris 4/28/93) and favored UN (39 percent) over NATO (25 percent) command (PIPA 4/5/94), in September 1993, a month before the Somalia disaster, over two-thirds of Americans preferred that American forces remain under U.S. (69 percent) as opposed to UN command (25 percent; PSR 9/3/93). Evidently, Americans thought that U.S. soldiers were less at risk when they were commanded by U.S. officers. The reluctance of the United Nations to call in NATO air strikes on Serbian targets both in Fall 1994 and Spring 1995, moreover, provided the basis for Americans' suspicions of the UN's military effectiveness.

Public opinion is typically volatile on issues not perceived to be of vital importance to U.S. security, as was, for most people, the case for Bosnia. American atti-

Table 8.6 UN/NATO/Allied Troops (Peacekeeping/Military)

				Approve	Disapprove	Don't know	N
PEACEKEEPING							
1992	PK	7/17	Har	80	18	3	1255
	Hum.	12/4	Gal	57	36	7	1005
1993	US	5/5	PIPA	76	12	11	810
	US	5/5	PIPA	67	21	11	810
	US/UN	5/6	Gal	68	30	2	603
	US	5/27	CBS	44	49	7	1184
	US	6/21	CBS	54	38	8	1363
	US	10/8	Gal	40	52	8	1019
1994	US	2/9	PIPA	72	25	3	700
	US	3/4	NBC	53	40	7	1503
	UN	4/5	PIPA	63	34	3	700
1995	UN	4/19	PIPA	87	9	3	1204
	UN	9/22	Gal	52	43	5	1011
	Int'l.	10/18	Yan	42	50	8	600
	NATO	10/22	CBS	37	57	6	1077
	Int'l.	11/16	Gal	47	49	4	931
	Int'l.	11/10	ABC	38	58	4	1005
MILITARY							
1992	UN	7/17	Har	50	44	6	1256
1993	UN/US	1/13	Yan	68	22	10	1000
	UN/US	1/22	Har	62	32	6	1255
	US	4/28	Har	52	42	6	1252
	UN/US	5/5	PIPA	59	26	15	810
	UN	5/6	ABC	56	40	4	516
1994	US/NATO	1/6	LAT	28	68	4	1023
	US/All	2/7	Gal	35	57	8	635
	US/NATO	2/10	Yan	40	50	10	500
	UN/US	4/5	PIPA	56	39	5	700
	US/Eur	4/16	Gal	41	53	6	1002
1995	UN	4/19	PIPA	64	26	10	1204

tudes toward Bosnia and the issue of intervention did not crystallize until late, too, because Americans were buffeted by events and changes in U.S. policy. Contradictory pronouncements from the White House, inconsistent UN policies, and multiple peace proposals, threats, and cease-fires all contributed to the inconsistency of American public opinion. Because leadership by high U.S. officials like the president is a central factor in catalyzing American public opinion (Brody 1991; Kelleher 1994), when the administration took a clear position against Serbian aggression in

May and August 1993, in February 1994, and in August 1995, public opinion typically moved toward supporting military action. For instance, during the Spring of 1993, when the Clinton administration began talking about possible American intervention, support for military action rose from 23 percent to 40 percent (Sobel 1996b, table 6.9; Morin 1993). In late Summer 1993, in fact, nearly a majority of Americans thought that Clinton had not been tough enough on the Serbs (Harris 8/13/93: 47 percent). A plurality (44 percent) supported U.S. military intervention, and another 13 percent would have supported earlier action (Yankelovich 8/4/93).

During Summer 1993, when the Serbs began attacking UN peacekeepers in Sarajevo and the Clinton administration again threatened air strikes, support for U.S. air attacks to protect UN troops grew to 61 percent (CBS 8/2/93). The American-backed NATO ultimatum on air strikes after the first Sarajevo market killings in February 1994 not only produced a breakthrough with the Serb pullback but also contributed to higher support among Americans for military action (up to 80 percent for air strikes; PIPA 2/9/94).[3] In late Summer 1995, 59 percent approved NATO air strikes (NBC 9/5/95).

In short, when the United States or NATO provided forceful leadership that countered Serb maneuvers to gain dominant military positions, the American public also responded favorably. Even though, when asked in advance, only half (48 percent) supported air strikes, two-thirds (65 percent) of Americans said they would support air strikes if the president and Congress ordered them (Gallup 2/7/94). When U.S. and UN leaders vacillated in response to Serb advances around Bihac in late 1994, and to the renewed attacks on the safe havens in Spring 1995, support for a U.S. response weakened. Interestingly, approval for lifting the arms embargo was below a majority (PIPA, PSR, ABC, Yankelovich 4–7/95: 36 to 40 percent) until July 1995; by the time the U.S. Senate voted to lift the embargo, it reached 61 percent (Sobel 1996b, table 6.11).

During the crises of mid-1995, there was also remarkably high approval of possibly sending U.S. troops to protect (61 percent), relocate (66 percent), or rescue (78 percent) UN peacekeepers under Serb attack (PSR 6/1/95). Polls conducted in June 1995 (Gallup, NBC, PSR, Yankelovich) all show similar results. Forty percent of Americans even supported sending U.S. troops to join in NATO efforts "to punish Serb aggression" (Yankelovich 6/3/95). A plurality (37 percent) supported sending U.S. troops to help the United Nations enforce an agreed-upon cease-fire, even if this meant a hundred American casualties (PIPA 4/19/95). This challenged the idea in the media and partisan rhetoric that there was absolutely no public support for sending U.S. forces to Bosnia.[4]

Because approval for U.S. intervention in Bosnia was often near to majority levels and responsive to presidential leadership, if the United States had became more directly involved militarily earlier, the public would likely have rallied around the president, at least initially (Mueller 1973; Brody 1991). If direct U.S. intervention had been quick and successful, support would have remained strong. But if costs and casualties had risen, leadership weakened, intervention dragged on, and a way out became elusive, support would have dropped and opposition would have increased in both public opinion and the partisan Congress (Sobel 1990). While more was at stake if U.S. soldiers were in combat, similar dynamics showed here applied to sending U.S. forces for peacekeeping. Yet at the time of the peace agreement at the end of 1995, public support reached a bare majority only for the most general question of sending peacekeepers (Gallup 9/22/95: 52 percent). Approval stayed in the minority when the public faced the realities of deploying 20,000 Americans to Bosnia for over a year following the actual deployment of troops (Kull 1998: 39–42).

Support dropped significantly, moreover, when the American public faced the possibility of U.S. soldiers actually dying for Bosnia: While two-thirds (67 percent) supported a U.S. deployment if no American soldiers were killed, only a third (31 percent) approved if a hundred died (Gallup 9/19/95). Yet the perceived success of the action to some extent compensated for the potential sacrifice of lives. A majority felt that if the peacekeeping operation were successful, the United States would have done "the right thing in contributing troops," even if fifty American soldiers were killed (PIPA 11/22/95: 60 percent). Only a quarter (27 percent) of the public thought the NATO force would be "successful in establishing a long-term" peace (Yankelovich 12/6/95). Yet potential support lay in substantial majorities of Americans who thought that both the realistic concerns for keeping the war from spreading (63 percent) and the humanitarian desire to stop more killing (64 percent) justified the sending of U.S. forces (CBS 12/9/95).

An awareness of potentially declining public support as a legacy of Vietnam underlay the demand of those like Senator Sam Nunn, who called for an exit strategy before U.S. troops were committed (Sciolino 1993). In the face of both relatively supportive public attitudes for air strikes and continuing evidence of Serb misdeeds, the reluctance of the Clinton administration and the Republican congressional majority to act suggested that the American leadership was more mired in the Vietnam syndrome than was the public (Times-Mirror Center 1993; Rielly 1995). While the U.S. administration's earlier willingness to commit troops to withdraw UN peacekeepers but not to protect Bosnian Muslims reflected to a degree the public's greater concern for protecting soldiers rather than saving civilians, it also provided a confusing message to the American people (Morin 1995). The actual deployment of U.S. peacekeepers after a settlement provided a focus for raising public support (Sobel 1995; Morin 1995). After the settlement but before most of the soldiers reached Bosnia, approval of the deployment rose slightly (CBS 11/27/95: 33 percent; 12/9/95: 40 percent) but remained a minority sentiment for the next year. In short, the American public retained an open, but skeptical, mind about the wisdom of sending American forces to enforce the Dayton peace accord.

EUROPEAN ATTITUDES TOWARD INTERVENTION IN BOSNIA

European governments generally had stronger bases of support for potential action among a citizenry aware of the perils of appeasement and even willing to undertake unilateral action to counter Serb aggression. Since late 1992 the French, British, Italian, and (usually) German publics typically supported intervention in Bosnia. But the reluctance of European governments and the United Nations to engage in military action other than peacekeeping restricted the direct action against the Bosnian Serbs. Only after the Serbs attacked British and French UN peacekeeping forces in August 1993 were the British and French governments willing to respond forcefully. The first Sarajevo market massacre in February 1994 led to NATO air strikes against Serb positions around Sarajevo and Gorazde and reduced the leaders' reluctance to intervene. Yet the allied countries and the UN vacillated after Serb attacks on Bihac, at the end of 1994, and on Srebrenica and Zepa in mid-1995. Nor did British and French threats to pull out the beleaguered peacekeepers deter further Serb aggression. Only the Croatian offensive and robust allied air strikes in Summer 1995 pushed the weakened Serbs toward a willingness in Belgrade to agree to a peace settlement.

European publics were generally more willing than their governments to act against Serb misconduct. A plurality (47 percent) across Western Europe held very negative images of the Serbs (Eurobarometer May 1993), and a majority approved the use of force against them (ORM 1/27/93). Like the American public, Europeans also preferred multilateral action and leadership. Majorities in each European country thought "the United Nations should authorize a multinational force to intervene militarily in the former Yugoslavia" (ORM 1/18/93). While Americans preferred to look to Europe or the United Nations for leadership (CBS 11/29/94: 73 percent), Europeans looked to the United States or the UN. An early 1993 European poll revealed that a plurality said that "the United States should take the lead" in UN-authorized military action (ORM 1/27/93). But European citizens were also more supportive of direct intervention than were U.S. or European leaders.

Citizens of Western Europe expressed strong support for the use of force (Tables 8.7 and 8.8). In late 1992 and early 1993, pluralities to majorities in France, Britain, Italy, and western Germany[5] supported authorizing multilateral UN intervention in the crisis. Large majorities supported humanitarian intervention, particularly by a multilateral force (Table 8.7, Q9a: 64 percent to 92 percent). But majorities supported unilateral humanitarian intervention by their own governments (Table 8.8, Q10a: 64 percent to 79 percent). And one-third to two-thirds thought their countries had demonstrated too little involvement in Yugoslavia. Majorities supported multilateral intervention to enforce a cease-fire (Table 8.7, Q9b: 51 percent to 87 percent), and the French, British, and Italian publics supported enforcing a cease-fire by their own troops (Table 8.8, Q10b: 63 percent to 66 percent), though only a minority of western Germans initially concurred (42 percent to 52 percent). Majorities also supported using multilateral force to separate the warring parties (Table 8.7, Q9c: 52 percent to 78 percent), similar to the support for unilateral action (Table 8.8, Q10c: 53 percent to 60 percent; except western Germany, 40 percent).

Even support for imposing a military solution on Bosnia multilaterally was significant (Table 8.7, Q9d: 52 percent to 79 percent). Moreover, near majorities in

Table 8.7   Use of Multilateral Military Force to . . . (Q9)

	United Kingdom		France			Western Germany			Italy
	1/93	*3/93*	*11/92*	*1/93*	*3/93*	*1/93*	*3/93*	*11/93*	*3/93*
9a) Protect humanitarian aid									
Favor	83	84	76	84	86	77	64		92
Oppose	11	10	16	11	10	21	27		4
DK	5	6	8	4	4	3	9		4
9b) Enforce cease fire									
Favor	69	73	70	81	85	60	51		87
Oppose	24	19	21	15	11	36	39		9
DK	7	8	9	4	5	4	10		5
9c) Separate warring parties									
Favor	67	66	61	72	70	56	52		78
Oppose	24	22	27	21	19	39	37		14
DK	10	12	12	7	12	6	11		9
9d) Impose solution									
Favor	58	58	52	61	65	57	52		79
Oppose	32	32	38	34	27	39	38		13
DK	10	10	10	5	8	4	10		7
E) all (a–d)	47		54			45			

See Appendix B for question wordings
Sources: USIA ORM, 1/6/93, 1/18/93, 1/27/93, 12/7/93 and Tables (4/8/93, 8/19/94)

Britain and France supported imposing a military solution unilaterally (Table 8.8, Q10d: 48 percent to 56 percent), but only a minority in western Germany (40 percent). Overall, "roughly half of the French (54 percent), British (47 percent), and western German (45 percent) publics supported the use of multinational forces for *all* [proposed] actions" from protecting aid shipments to imposing a solution (ORM 1/27/93, emphasis in original).

At the end of 1993, support remained high for intervention even by individual countries. In March 1993, a majority in each of the four nations surveyed approved of NATO enforcing a cease-fire (Table 8.7, Q9b: 51 percent to 85 percent), and a majority in the United Kingdom and France approved of their own troops participating (Table 8.8, Q10b: 63 percent to 66 percent). Early-1993 majorities in Britain and France also approved sending NATO troops to help impose a peace settlement (52 percent to 79 percent), including their own troops (52 to 56 percent), though only a minority in western Germany approved (40 percent).[6]

Table 8.8   Use of Military Force to . . . (own country) Q10

	United Kingdom	France		Western Germany
	1/93	11/92	1/93	1/93
10a) Protect humanitarian aid				
Favor	79	71	73	64
Oppose	18	22	33	34
DK	3	7	4	3
10b) Enforce cease fire				
Favor	63	64	66	42
Oppose	32	27	31	56
DK	5	9	4	3
10c) Separate warring parties				
Favor	60	53	57	40
Oppose	35	27	37	57
DK	6	10	6	3
10d) Impose solution				
Favor	56	48	52	40
Oppose	38	42	43	58
DK	6	10	6	3

Sources: USIA ORM, 1/6/93, 1/18/93, 1/27/93, 12/17/93, and Tables (4/8/93, 8/15/94)
N = 900+

British public support for Bosnian intervention grew over time. From June 1993 to February 1994, approval of British troops protecting humanitarian aid grew from 67 percent to 74 percent, though it declined to 72 percent in October 1995 (Table 8.9). From June 1993 to February 1994, support for sending British troops as a part of an international contingent to enforce a peace settlement grew from 67 percent to 75 percent, though it dropped to 62 percent in June 1995 (Table 8.9). Nearly half (47 percent) of those surveyed thought that Britain should help to impose a peace settlement if an agreement were not reached (Gallup Political and Economic Index Report 402, February 1994).[7]

In fact, support for allied European military intervention to establish peace grew from 1993 into 1994 in all four nations (Sobel 1996b, table 6.16): Britain, 60 percent to 65 percent, France, 59 percent to 75 percent, Italy, 64 percent to 65 percent, and Germany, 43 percent to 57 percent). There remained majority opposition to withdrawing troops (Table 8.10b: 52 percent to 71 percent), and majority support

Table 8.9   British Attitudes about Intervention in Bosnia

B1.1
Do you approve or disapprove of the use of British troops in Bosnia to protect humanitarian aid convoys?

	4/93	6/93	9/93	2/94	6/1/94	6/8/94	10/12/95
Approve	72	67	73	74	62	64	72
Disapprove	20	25	21	21	27	26	20
Don't Know	8	7	7	6	11	10	9

B1.2
If the British troops protecting the aid convoys suffered serious casualties, should we pull them out, continue to limit them to fighting back only when they are attacked or take steps to reinforce them?

	4/93	6/93	9/93	2/94	6/1/94	6/8/94	10/12/95
Pull them out	32	39	36	32	38	39	30
Limit	17	17	16	16	16	14	15
Reinforce	43	34	41	43	35	38	43
Don't Know	8	10	6	8	11	9	11

B1.3
If an international force were trying to enforce a peace settlement in Bosnia, would you personally like to see British troops forming part of that force or not?

	4/93	6/93	9/93	2/94	6/95
Yes	67	64	68	75	62
No	22	25	21	17	24
Don't Know	11	11	10	8	14

Source: Gallup Political and Economic Index, Report 402, February 1994.

for fighting to ensure that aid convoys get through (Table 8.10: 58 percent to 90 percent). Majorities in Britain, France, and western Germany supported air strikes (50 percent to 57 percent), minorities in Italy and East Germany (30 percent to 45 percent). However, opposition to lifting the arms embargo against the Bosnian Muslims ranged from 43 percent to 67 percent, except in Britain, where it remained a plurality in July 1995 (MORI 7/24/95: 46 percent to 37 percent). In early 1994, most Italians favored the participation of Italian troops (DOXA 2/9/94: 57 percent). In mid-1995, 53 percent of Italians favored allied military intervention (CIRM 7/17/95), but a plurality opposed Italian involvement (47 percent).

In short, most French, British, Italians, and western Germans generally favored the use of multinational forces for actions ranging from protecting aid shipments to imposing a solution on the warring parties. German support, especially in the east, was consistently lower than British or French. The strong approval of European publics for the use of force contrasted sharply with the reluctance of European gov-

Table 8.10   European Attitudes About Intervention in Bosnia, 1994

	Britain			France			Germany			Italy		
	2/25	3/25	6/29	2/25	3/25	6/29	2/25	3/25	6/29	2/25	3/25	6/29
A) Continue as are												
Favor	12	28	16	8	15	11	20	17	20	6	7	9
Oppose	80	66	78	89	80	85	79	77	72	91	90	86
DK	8	6	5	3	6	4	6	6	8	3	4	6
N	506	507	501	497	502	502	1576	1580	1573	505	510	502
B) Withdraw all troops												
Favor	25	27	28	24	27	31	28	25	27	34	33	37
Oppose	67	68	66	72	68	62	71	71	66	59	57	52
DK	8	5	6	5	6	7	2	4	8	7	10	11
N	506	507	501	497	502	502	1576	1580	1573	505	510	502
E) Lift Bosnia embargo												
Favor	28	26	26	32	30	36	30	30	34	41	36	37
Oppose	56	59	58	58	59	54	67	63	58	44	47	44
DK	16	15	16	10	11	11	3	7	8	15	18	19
N	506	507	501	497	502	502	1576	1580	1573	505	510	502
F) Fight to get convoys through												
Favor	84	84	78	90	89	85	59	65	58	80	76	68
Oppose	12	10	17	7	7	10	39	30	36	12	17	23
DK	4	6	5	3	4	5	1	5	6	8	8	9
N	506	507	501	497	502	502	1576	1580	1573	505	510	502
G) Launch air attack												
Favor	39	55	43	53	58	48	43	50	40	30	37	31
Oppose	52	37	47	41	33	46	56	45	50	58	49	56
DK	9	8	10	6	8	6	1	6	10	12	14	15
N	506	507	501	497	502	502	1576	1580	1573	507	510	502

Source: Flash Eurobarometers 24 (2/25/94), 25 (3/25/94), 29 (6/29/94)

ernments to intervene forcefully. Serb attacks on allied soldiers in 1993 and on civilians in the Sarajevo marketplace in early 1994 temporarily catalyzed European leaders to respond to their publics' willingness to intervene. The reluctance of the United Nations to act when Bihac was attacked reflected the unwillingness of European governments to risk the safety of their peacekeeping troops. Yet European publics were largely opposed to removing their peacekeepers despite governmental threats to do so. With France's call for action after the safe havens fell in Summer 1995, however, Europe moved more aggressively into the conflict. European publics remained supportive of military pressures for a settlement and for redeploying peace-keepers for more forceful activity (Whitney 1992).

WHAT THE POLLS REVEAL

In sum, both the American and European publics were generally supportive of out-side intervention in the Bosnia conflict for over three years. Although the American public opposed deploying U.S. troops on a unilateral basis, Americans generally approved intervention with U.S. troops as part of a UN- or NATO-led force. Europeans preferred UN- or U.S.-led intervention but also supported their own militaries acting alone. These findings contrasted with the impression of most governments and the media that American and European publics were unwilling to intervene in the Bosnia conflict. This misperception explains some of the inaction of the American and European governments, which in turn accounts for UN indecisiveness.

When U.S. Secretary of State Warren Christopher visited European capitals in February 1993 to seek support for a unified response to Serbian aggression, his arguments were ignored, as were pleas of Bosnian President Alija Izetbegovic for intervention on the side of the Muslims. Allied governments appeared unresponsive to either moral imperatives or public attitudes. The concentrated allied response to the Sarajevo-market massacres of 1994 and 1995 began to change the complexion of the problem. The strength of interventionist attitudes among European publics, combined with the perceived success of military pressures on the Bosnian Serbs, made it easier for the European governments to undertake stronger actions. This appears to have been the case particularly for France, whose early-1994 call for sending NATO troops came with the strong support of the French public. The French government switched in late 1994 from threatening to remove its peacekeepers in the face of Serb attacks and UN inaction around Bihac to urging again stronger action. The continuing desire of the French public to take action in the Bosnia crisis bolstered this approach. The earlier absence of a response by the major European governments, then, reflected unwillingness among leaders more than among the public.

The European and, to a lesser extent, American public preferences for both leadership and multilateral action continued across the crisis: they appeared in the support for deploying UN forces and for NATO air strikes. While most Americans thought that the United Nations was generally doing a good job, they questioned UN and NATO effectiveness in multilateral efforts. Though Americans were willing to have U.S. fliers carry out NATO air strikes, they feared risking U.S. casualties, especially under UN command. There was also limited sentiment among European publics or governments for lifting the arms embargo against the former Yugoslavia, despite the Clinton administration's decision to curtail U.S. enforcement and the vote in Congress to lift the ban. Disagreements between the UN and NATO in late

1994 and early 1995 over how to deal with the Serb attack on Bihac and Srebrenica also weakened the allied response; yet European publics continued to support an ongoing peacekeeping presence. The general approval among Europeans and, less clearly, the U.S. public provided a basis for accepting the greater political and military risks of more active intervention and peacekeeping.

The U.S. and European governments typically were unwilling to act militarily because they wanted to avoid taking risks in a complex and dangerous conflict. European leaders first expressed a concern lest intervention endanger their peacekeeping troops and thus avoided escalation until the peacekeepers were attacked. Their lack of response to the Serb advances near Bihac, Sarajevo, and Srebrenica, in fact, contributed to the Serbs' making hostages of UN forces. Americans, too, feared that U.S. ground troops would be captured or killed. Yet they supported using American forces to protect or remove UN peacekeepers. More focused on domestic problems, generally unpopular European and American leaders felt less risk in doing nothing than intervening.

Moreover, European leaders and the Bush administration had hoped that during "Europe's hour" (Hoffmann 1996), continental diplomacy could handle the Bosnia problem. The less direct linkages between constituent opinion and policymaking in European parliamentary systems may have led politicians to disregard public attitudes.[8] Despite public support in the polls about intervention, no government was close to falling for failure to solve the Bosnia crisis. It was surprising, however, that more opposition-party politicians than Bill Clinton in 1992 and Bob Dole in 1996 did not become more vocal advocates of intervention. Recognizing interventionist attitudes among the public and the failure of officeholders to respond to their desire, other challengers might have cultivated electoral favor through more aggressive rhetoric. Republicans' demands after the 1994 U.S. elections for stronger action may have resonated with at least part of the American public. And the readiness of French President Jacques Chirac to send troops to Bosnia and his near demand for allied air and ground action in mid-1995 may likewise have been an example of entrepreneurship in the political marketplace of the French public's willingness to take aggressive action. The vote of confidence for British Prime Minister John Major in June 1995 may also have provided a stronger basis for British action in Bosnia and for reversing British public dissatisfaction with the handling of the Bosnia situation.

A collective-action problem also occurred among the American and European governments: each government apparently hoped to be a "free rider" on someone else's willingness to take up the leadership burden. The relative preference for multilateral action among leaders paralleled the public preferences for other countries to act. The American public's support for multilateral action, despite reluctance to put U.S. forces under UN or NATO command, suggested as well a desire for others to take responsibility. No government had a special incentive to get involved, and all clearly had disincentives to take risks, so that European and American leaders delayed confronting the crisis. The inability of either the United Nations or NATO to act in the face of the Bihac crisis, in particular, reflected the limits of relying on the leadership of others in order to act together. The French calls to action were also premised on allied involvement. In the absence of allied leadership, Bosnians perished.

U.S. and European leaders may also have seen the crisis in terms of realpolitik—as self-limiting prior to an inevitable Serb victory. Continental leaders hoped to contain the crisis without direct action. The Sarajevo-market bombings, the Muslim-Croat military resurgence in mid-1994, and the Russian and Belgrade Serbian criticism of Bosnian Serbs' intransigence changed the perceptions of European leaders and the balance of military and diplomatic forces. With publics more aroused and Muslim-Croat forces more successful, government policies began to reflect the more interventionist elements of the American and European publics. It also destroyed the myth of Serb invincibility.

The quick victory in the Gulf War and some dissipation of the post-Vietnam syndrome led some Americans and Europeans to see less risk of another stalemate in Bosnia, as well as later in Kosovo in 1999. Continental citizens closer to the problems and disastrous consequences of appeasement were more willing to act than their not-very-popular leaders. Growing public pressures after continuing Serbian misconduct moved European and American leaders to embrace more assertive actions. The aggressive French rhetoric, the U.S. Senate vote to lift the embargo, Croatian recapture of lost territory, robust allied air strikes, and evidence of allied military superiority (especially in the war with Serbia over Kosovo) changed the situation considerably. This combination led first to a cease-fire, then to a political settlement, and finally to deployment of 60,000 NATO peacekeepers, including 20,000 Americans. While this was less popular after the deployment than before, its success ultimately led to public approval and perhaps to the later high, though declining, support for the U.S.-NATO bombing of Kosovo (Yemma 1999; Madigan 1999).

During much of the Bosnia conflict, then, there was unrecognized support among allied publics for more aggressive multilateral action in Bosnia. The U.S. and European publics were surprisingly predisposed and sensible about the need for cooperative action. In short, the missing element appeared to be decisive leadership. Whether allied policies and peacekeeping continue to contribute to regional stability in both Bosnia and Kosovo depends on how strongly U.S. and European publics maintain their support for the pursuit of peace and on how carefully their leaders listen to and heed them.

APPENDIX A: POLLS CONSULTED

ABC/*Washington Post* Poll (ABC/WP)
CBS/*New York Times* Poll (CBS/NYT)
NBC/*Wall Street Journal* Poll (NBC/WSJ)

CIRM (Italy)
DOXA (Italy)
The Eurobarometer (EC)
The Gallup Poll (Gal)
The Harris Poll (Har)
Los Angeles Times Poll (LAT)
Market and Opinion Research, Incorporated (MORI, Britain)
Program in International Policy Attitudes (PIPA)
Princeton Survey Research (PSR)
Opinion Research Memoranda (ORM/U.S.IA)
Yankelovich Partners Surveys (Yan)

APPENDIX B: SELECTED QUESTION WORDINGS

Presidential Approval Questions (Table 8.1)

(ABC/WP) Do you approve or disapprove of the way President Bill Clinton is handling the situation involving the former Yugoslavian Republics of Serbia and Bosnia?

(CBS/NYT) Do you approve or disapprove of the way (President) Bill Clinton is
[has been] handling the situation in what used to be Yugoslavia [Bosnia]?

(Gallup/PSR) Do you approve or disapprove of the way George Bush is handling
the situation in [the former Yugoslavian Republic of] Bosnia? (Registered voters)

(Harris) Overall, how would you rate President Clinton's handling of the situation
in Yugoslavia/the war in Bosnia? Excellent, pretty good, only fair, poor?

(NBC/WSJ) In general, do you approve or disapprove of the job (President) Bill
Clinton is doing in handling the situation in Bosnia?

(Yankelovich) Do you think President [Bill] Clinton is doing a good job or a poor
job . . . of handling the situation in Bosnia?

European opinion questions (Tables 8.7 and 8.8):

9. Concerning the situation in the former Yugoslavia, are you personally in favor or
opposed to the use of military force to . . . (Is that strongly or somewhat?) (10/92,
1/93, 3/93)
   a) Protect the delivery of humanitarian aid in the former Yugoslavia
   b) Enforce a ceasefire
   c) Separate the warring parties
   d) Impose a solution

10. Are you personally in favor or opposed to [own country] using its military forces to . . . (Is that strongly or somewhat?) (10/92, 1/93)
  a) Protect the delivery of humanitarian aid in the former Yugoslavia
  b) Enforce a ceasefire
  c) Separate the warring parties
  d) Impose a solution

9

Internationalism at Bay?

A Contextual Analysis of Americans' Post–Cold War Foreign Policy Attitudes

Eugene R. Wittkopf and Ronald H. Hinckley

It became commonplace in the years following the fall of the Berlin Wall and the stunningly quick U.S. victory in the Gulf War to assert that the American people had turned inward, shunning the burdens of leadership abroad in favor of a focus on domestic priorities. Bill Clinton's presidential victory in 1992 reinforced that viewpoint, as the electorate chose a governor from a small southern state who was inexperienced and uninterested in foreign policy over an incumbent president who only recently had scored unprecedentedly high job-approval ratings stimulated by remarkable foreign policy achievements. For the first time in more than two generations, it seemed, foreign policy had effectively been removed from the nation's psyche. Indeed, given the closeness of the vote, Bill Clinton's victory over George Bush arguably *depended* on the irrelevance of foreign policy as a campaign issue.

Later, public-opinion polls reinforced the 1992 electoral message. Although a 1994 Gallup poll sponsored by the Chicago Council on Foreign Relations found that nearly two-thirds of the American people continued to "think it will be best for the future of the country if we take an active part in world affairs," a further probe of the data revealed that they embraced an internationalism that sought to promote American economic and social interests rather than "non-self-interested" activities in global affairs (Schneider 1997, 27–28). Pursuing foreign policy objectives that seek to protect American jobs, control illegal immigration, stop illicit trafficking in drugs, and reduce the U.S. trade deficit, for example, gained wider support from the public than promoting human rights, advancing democracy, and supporting allies abroad. Thus, John Rielly, president of the Chicago Council and editor of its widely acclaimed quadrennial series *American Public Opinion and U.S. Foreign Policy*, wrote that "pragmatic internationalism" now characterized the public mood: "Americans are committed to an active role for the United States in the world, . . . but their focus has shifted toward . . . home life and feelings of personal economic vulnerability" (1995, 6).[1]

Arthur Schlesinger (1995, 7) seized on the Chicago Council findings and those of an earlier survey it had sponsored in late 1990 to castigate the American public for its readiness to "endorse euphonious generalities in support of internationalism" without a corresponding commitment of "money and lives." At about the same time Ronald Steel (1999, 23) argued that evidence from a 1993 Times Mirror survey (Times Mirror Center for the People and the Press 1993) revealed "overwhelming support for a domestic agenda in preference to an international one." Unlike Schlesinger, however, and borrowing a theme popular among "declinists" in the 1980s, Steel (1999, 31) urged that "our task today is . . . to recognize our limitations, to reject the vanity of trying to remake the world in our image, and to restore the promise of our neglected society."

Steel buttressed his prescription with an assessment of the gulf between elite and mass attitudes. "Clearly there is a chasm between a foreign-policy establishment mesmerized by notions of American leadership and 'global responsibilities' and an American public concerned by drug trafficking and addiction, jobs, illegal aliens, crime, health-care costs, and the environment," he concluded. "Not since the early days of the Cold War, when the establishment rallied the public to a policy of global activism under the banner of anticommunism, has there been such a gap between the perceptions of the foreign-policy elite and the realities of the world in which most Americans live" (1999, 23).

Important questions about Schlesinger's and Steel's interpretations of the data on which they based their bold conclusions are warranted (see Wittkopf 1996). Moreover, more recent data suggest that the American people remain "connected" to the international environment.[2] Still, the broad parameters of their arguments are not easily dismissed. The widening gulf between the internationalist preferences of elites and the seemingly more domestically circumscribed preferences of the general public that Steel notes is especially intriguing. Indeed, Ole R. Holsti and James N. Rosenau, who have conducted surveys of elites' (opinion leaders') foreign policy attitudes every four years since 1976, recently concluded that elites' greater preferences for "internationalism and multilateral cooperation" compared with the general public "may be the closest thing we have to an iron law of American public opinion" (1999a, 137).

Data supporting their bold conclusion include the quadrennial Chicago Council surveys of elite and mass attitudes and similar surveys in 1993 and 1997 by the Pew Research Center for the Public and the Press. In all of them, support for *liberal internationalism*—defined by Richard Gardner (1990, 23) as "the intellectual and political tradition that believes in the necessity of leadership by liberal democracies in the construction of a peaceful world order through multilateral cooperation and effective international organizations"—is demonstrably greater among elites than the general public. For example, the 1997 Pew surveys (Pew 1997) reveal that "the public feels the United States should be no more or less active than any other country, restrained in its commitment of troops and resources to foreign adventures. In contrast, a majority of influential Americans ranging from union leaders to national security experts believes the U.S. role should be prominent and forceful" (Kohut and Toth 1998, 22). Analysts Andrew Kohut and Robert Toth (1998, 22) conclude that "never before has the difference on such a fundamental issue as America's place in the world been so wide."[3]

Studies conducted under the direction of Steven Kull at the Center for International Security Studies at the University of Maryland give a somewhat different spin to the "iron law of American public opinion." Based on an extensive two-year study, Kull and his associates (Kull, Destler, and Ramsay 1997) conclude that the majority of Americans do not seek disengagement from the post–Cold War world. On the contrary, they "support international engagement as much as before the end of the Cold War" (1997, iii). From this perspective, the gap between elite and mass attitudes is a product of elites' failure to understand what most Americans really think. Still, it is noteworthy that the "broad global engagement" that Kull and his associates say is supported by the American people carries notable caveats: one being that "the [United States] is not playing the role of dominant world leader (or 'world policeman') and is contributing its 'fair share' to multilateral efforts to resolve international problems" (1997, iii). Furthermore, "even if the majority embraces engagement in principle, Americans will not support spending the necessary money when faced with making trade-offs against domestic priorities" (1997, v).[4] That conclusion smacks of Schlesinger's "return to the womb" argument.

In this chapter we seek to explain the gulf between elite and mass preferences regarding the U.S. global role through a contextual analysis that assesses the impact of domestic factors on foreign policy attitudes. Drawing on research traditions outside the normal public opinion/foreign policy domain, we hypothesize that elites' post–Cold War foreign policy preferences are more responsive to the tenets of liberal internationalism than the general public's because elites are less attuned to conditions in the domestic environment in which they live than are other Americans. Put somewhat differently, we hypothesize that domestic environmental factors better explain mass than elite preferences, since partisan, ideological, and socialization experiences are more pertinent among the elite. We find, however, that that is not true. Instead, elites and masses seem to march to the beat of the same drummer. Thus, we conclude by raising some of the same questions about the factors that shape Americans' foreign policy attitudes that have long intrigued scholars of foreign policy opinion, most of which predate the "quiet cataclysm" (Mueller 1995) marked by the collapse of the Berlin Wall.

ON PRIORITIES

The list of domestic ills presumed to have shaped Americans' domestic and foreign policy priorities and their introspection in recent years is quite long. The "declinist" literature popular in the waning days of the Cold War and the early post–Cold War era helped to identify the core issues. Paul Kennedy's best-selling book *The Rise and Fall of the Great Powers* (1987) stands out.

Kennedy advanced the theory of "imperial overstretch" to explain how hegemonic powers eventually fall from the pinnacle of power. Simply stated, the theory asserts that a state's overseas commitments eventually outstrip the ability of its domestic base to support them. As Kennedy (1992, 345) wrote at the time of the Gulf War, "A power that wants to remain number one for generation after generation requires not just military capability, not just national will, but also a flourishing and efficient economic base, strong finances and a healthy social fabric, for it is upon such foundations that the country's military strength rests in the long term."

Conservative critics argued "imperial overstretch" was a ruse designed to depreciate the defense-spending initiatives of the Reagan administration, but the relationship between the health of the economy and American foreign policy was not easily dismissed, even as the Cold War waned. In the afterglow of victory in the Gulf War, for example, syndicated columnist Charles Krauthammer (1991, 26) concurred that "an American collapse to second-rank status will be not for foreign but for domestic reasons. . . . America's low savings rate, poor educational system, stagnant productivity, declining work habits, rising demand for welfare-state entitlements and new taste for ecological luxuries have nothing at all to do with engagement in Europe, Central America or the Middle East." A bipartisan report issued in 1992 by the prestigious Center for Strategic and International Studies reinforced that theme, concluding that "some of America's biggest trouble spots are not abroad but here at home. They are in manufacturing, capital formation, education, the federal budget, science and technology" (Nunn and Domenici 1992). Defense strategist Edward Luttwak (1993) echoed that sentiment in a controversial book, *The Endangered American Dream*, suggesting that conservatives as well as liberals now viewed the state of the economy as critical to the ability of the United States to pursue not Cold War military conflict with the Soviet Union but post–Cold War economic competition with Japan and Europe.

The revival of the U.S. economy and growing productivity among its workers have muted the prominence of the declinists' message in more recent years. Still, domestic concerns remain. Especially prominent are ones growing out of the changing demographic composition of the American melting pot fueled by recent patterns of immigration (both legal and illegal). During the 1980s, more immigrants came to the United States than at any time since the early twentieth century. But whereas 90 percent of the immigrants in the early part of the century came from Europe, in the 1980s more than 80 percent came from Asia and Latin America. The influx of immigrants, many of whom wish to retain their cultural identities and ties to homelands, has been a source of domestic discord and promises to remain so, as Hispanics are today the most rapidly growing ethnic group in America. California's Proposition 187, passed in 1994 in an attempt to exclude illegal immigrants from such publicly funded services as education and health care, is illustrative of what by mid-decade looked to be a rising xenophobic tide. To other Americans, immigrants not only threaten to swell the welfare rolls; they also threaten to take away jobs. Concern about the rising tide of immigrant groups thus takes on a distinctly self-interested cast. Furthermore, the strains of multiculturalism (which imply that people should be treated not on the basis of individual achievement but group identity) that often surround immigration issues pose potential threats to the ethos of liberal internationalism that has provided the domestic bedrock of American foreign policy for half a century (Citrin et al. 1994).

Domestic contextual factors have long been regarded as sources of political attitudes and behavior on racial and ethnic issues. In his classic study of southern politics, for example, V.O. Key (1949) argued that variations in the concentration of African Americans in southern communities explained conservative voting behavior, as proximity to large concentrations of minorities was thought to stimulate perceptions of threat and competition (and thus whites' self-interest in maintaining their political control). The veracity of Key's hypothesis continues to stimulate research (see, e.g., Giles and Evans 1985; Giles and Buckner 1993; Huckfeldt and Kohfeld 1989; and Wright 1977; but cf. Voss 1996) and is not easily dismissed. Other researchers (Citrin, Reingold, and Green 1990; Hood and Morris 1997) have found that high concentrations of Hispanics and Asians have a negative impact on whites' attitudes on immigration issues involving them.

Our research strategy (discussed in more detail below) draws on these traditions as we seek to relate variations in environmental conditions across U.S. states to Americans' foreign policy attitudes.[5] We also pattern our inquiry on the model of sociotropic voting articulated by Donald R. Kinder and D. Roderick Kiewiet (1981). They present two contrasting viewpoints: One suggests that citizens' own *individual* (that is, *egocentric*) economic predicaments predict their voting behavior; the other says that the *nation's* (that is, *sociotropic*) situation predicts vote choice. In much the same vein, we argue that variations in the environmental conditions composing the domestic (state and local) contexts in which Americans live shape their foreign policy preferences, especially those often regarded as self-interested.

The symbolic-politics model also informs our conceptual design and empirical analyses. Similar to the sociotropic model, the symbolic-politics perspective suggests that individuals' policy preferences are explained either by self-interest (egocentrism) or by symbolism. Political symbols are those affective preferences that individuals acquire "through conditioning in their preadult years, with little calculation of the future costs and benefits of those attitudes" (Sears et al. 1980, 671). As political psychologist David Sears and his colleagues explain, "Political attitudes . . . are formed mainly in congruence with long-standing values about society and the polity [such as party identification, liberal or conservative ideology, nationalism, or racial prejudice], rather than short-term instrumentalities for satisfaction of one's current private needs. In the world of 'symbolic politics,' one's political and personal lives exist largely isolated from one another" (Sears et al. 1980, 671).

Consistent with the symbolic-politics hypothesis, research on foreign policy attitudes shows that partisanship and ideology are powerful determinants of Americans' foreign policy preferences (Holsti 1996, 131–156). That research shows that socio-demographic variables may also be important. In particular, generation, gender, education, region of the country, and race sometimes explain differences among Americans' foreign policy opinions and beliefs (Holsti 1996, 156–183; Wittkopf 1990). Advocates of the symbolic-politics model argue that policy preferences driven by either ideological predispositions or self-interest are distinct from the variables that measure social background characteristics (Sears et al. 1980). We chose not to draw that distinction here, arguing instead that the symbolic-politics model, broadly defined, enables us to contrast individuals' personal political preferences and life experiences with contextual factors as we seek to explain the presumed inward-looking, self-interested, post–Cold War preferences of those Americans outside opinion-making circles.

ON MEASUREMENTS AND METHODS

We hypothesize that elite and mass foreign policy preferences differ because people composing the mass public are more sensitive to their domestic social and economic environments than are elites, among whom preferences are driven by political symbols and the life experiences related to their individual sociodemographic characteristics. To test the hypothesis, we map the characteristics of the state environments in which respondents in two elite and three mass surveys live (and, in one instance, of counties as tracked by their zip codes) onto their corresponding survey responses. This permits us to relate foreign policy preferences to respondents' contextual circumstances. Our hypothesis states that environmental conditions will not impact elites' foreign policy opinions but that variations among environmental conditions experienced by the mass public will explain why, in the post–Cold War world, some Americans are prone to support the tenets of liberal internationalism while others are more disposed toward a self-interested foreign policy agenda.

Our dependent variables are items from the 1992 and 1996 surveys of opinion leaders conducted by Holsti and Rosenau as part of their ongoing Foreign Policy Leadership Project (FPLP); the 1994 survey of the mass public sponsored by the Chicago Council on Foreign Relations; a 1994 postelection survey of the mass public conducted by Ronald H. Hinckley as part of a continuing *Defense Monitor* series; and a 1997 mass survey of foreign policy opinions conducted by the Pew Research Center. We seek to explain Americans' general internationalist-isolationist orientations and their attitudes toward specific issues with a distinctly self-interested content. The foreign policy orientation variables include single items and composite scales created by Holsti and Rosenau (1990; 1999b) and Wittkopf (1990; 1996) that measure dispositions toward cooperative and militant internationalism. Self-interested items include American foreign policy goal questions popular in elite and mass surveys taken over the past two decades, plus others that deal with perceived threats to U.S. security and interests. Skewed distributions in several other items potentially germane to our analyses and a lack of comparability across the surveys limited our analytical terrain. Still, we believe the items we examine speak to our theoretical concerns.

Our symbolic and individual-level sociodemographic variables are those in the original surveys. As in the choice of survey items, variations in coverage limited our ability to ensure comparability across the variables. To the extent possible, we control for sex (0 = female, 1 = male); generation (in the mass samples: 1 = 18–24 years old; 2 = 25–49; 3 = 50–65; 4 = 66 and over; in the leader samples 1 = 24–49, 2 = 50–65, 3 = 66 and over); education (1 = 8th grade or less; 2 = high school through technical school; 3 = some college through postgraduate education); Hispanic origin (0 = no, 1 = yes); and African American (0 = no, 1 = yes). Partisanship is coded 1 for Republicans, 2 for independents, and 3 for Democrats. In the mass samples, ideology is a five-point scale ranging from very conservative (coded 1) to very liberal (coded 5); in the leader samples, ideology is a seven-point scale ranging from far right (coded 1) to far left (coded 7). We also control for attentiveness in the general public using measures of how interested in or how much respondents follow the news (from little at the low end of the scale to much at the high end).

We use nine contextual variables that draw on standard U.S. government statistical sources (described in the Appendix at the end of this chapter), as follows:

1. *Crime:* the FBI index of violent and property crimes[6] per unit of population for each state[7] and, for use with the 1994 Chicago Council survey, for each county in which survey respondents live. State-level crime data used in the analysis of the 1992 and 1996 leader surveys correspond to the years of the surveys; 1996 state data are used in the analysis of the 1997 Pew survey; and 1993 country data are used for the 1994 Chicago Council survey.

2. *Social malaise:* a composite index derived from a principal components analysis of state-level poverty and infant mortality data. "Poverty" is defined as the percent of state population below the federally defined poverty level. "Infant mortality" is the number of deaths of infants under one year old per unit of population. Data are contemporaneous with the year of the foreign policy surveys analyzed except for the 1997 Pew survey, for which 1996 data are used. The higher the index, the greater the level of social malaise.

3. *Unemployment rate:* the total rate of unemployment (male and female) among persons sixteen years old and over. Data are contemporaneous with the year of the foreign policy surveys analyzed except for the 1997 Pew survey, for which 1996 data are used.

4. *Percent Hispanic:* the percent of states' resident population of Hispanic origin. No distinction is made between Hispanics on the basis of race (white versus black). Data are contemporaneous with the year of the foreign policy surveys analyzed except for the 1997 Pew survey, for which 1996 data are used.

5. *Percent Asian:* the percent of states' resident population of Asian origin. Asian

includes Pacific Islanders. Data are contemporaneous with the year of the foreign policy surveys analyzed except for the 1997 Pew survey, for which 1996 data are used.

6. *Educational achievement:* a composite index derived from a principal components analysis of state-level data measuring the percent of persons not enrolled in school and not a high school graduate; the percent of persons who have completed high school or achieved a higher educational level; and mean educational expenditures per pupil in public schools. Because these data are highly correlated through time, we use the same index for all of the foreign policy surveys examined. The higher the index, the greater the level of educational achievement.

7. *Rate of growth in states' gross product (GSP):* the rate of growth in gross state product between year t-1 and t, where t is the year of the foreign policy survey analyzed except for the 1997 Pew survey, for which t is 1966.

8. *Exports as a percent of states' gross product (GSP):* the value of exports to foreign countries by each U.S. state as a percent of its gross state product. Data are contemporaneous with the year of the foreign policy surveys analyzed except for the 1997 Pew survey, for which 1996 data are used.

9. *Per-capita income:* personal income per capita in current dollars. Data are contemporaneous with the year of the foreign policy surveys analyzed except for the 1997 Pew survey, for which 1996 data are used.

We can now recapitulate our hypotheses in more specific terms. Once political symbols (partisanship and ideology) and sociodemographic characteristics have been controlled, we expect that:

- Among the general public, support for internationalism will be negatively related to the incidence of crime, social malaise, the rate of unemployment, and high concentrations of Hispanics and Asians. Conversely, support for domestically oriented foreign policy goals and threats will be positively related to each of these contextual variables.

- Among the general public, support for internationalism will be positively related to high levels of educational achievement, high rates of growth in states' gross product, high levels of exports in their gross product, and high levels of per-capita income. Conversely, support for domestically oriented foreign policy goals and threats will be negatively related to each of these contextual variables.

- Among opinion leaders, there will be no relationship between contextual factors and attitudes toward internationalism generally or domestically oriented foreign policy goals and threats. Instead, political symbols and the life experiences related to leaders' sociodemographic characteristics will explain their foreign policy preferences.

ON FINDINGS

How Do American Leaders Respond to Their Domestic Environments?

In their 1992 and 1996 surveys of American opinion leaders, Holsti and Rosenau included several Likert-type items with a distinctly internationalist-isolationist cast. Taking a page from journalist and Republican presidential hopeful Pat Buchanan, for example, they asked if respondents agreed that "what we need is a new foreign policy that puts America first, and second and third as well." They also asked if "the United States should only be involved in world affairs to the extent that its military power is needed to maintain international peace and stability." Few agreed strongly with either proposition, although the number did grow somewhat between the two surveys. Still, less than a third agreed (somewhat or strongly) with either statement in either year.

In contrast, in 1992 nearly 60 percent of the respondents agreed that "our allies are perfectly capable of defending themselves and they can afford it, thus allowing the United States to focus on internal rather than external threats to its well-being." The proportion dropped to less than half in 1996 but remained a hefty 46 percent. The question is thus a useful one to test the hypothesis that symbolic politics and socialization experiences, not contextual factors, shape elites' preferences for liberal internationalism.

In Table 9.1 we use ordinary-least-squares (OLS) regression to examine the effects of the contextual and other variables on leaders' responses to the foregoing question. We also examine their effects on two internationalism dimensions described above: cooperative internationalism (CI) and militant internationalism (MI). Each scale is built from fourteen Likert items (seven each).[8] When cross-classified, responses to the two sets of scales yield four foreign policy belief systems, described by the labels "internationalist," "isolationist," "accommodationist," and "hardliner" (Wittkopf 1990; Holsti and Rosenau 1990). By themselves, the CI and MI dimensions measure dispositions toward (or opposition to) cooperation with other nations to solve global and national problems, and toward (or opposition to) unilateral approaches, which often involve military or covert intervention in the affairs of others.[9]

The results of the analyses are generally consistent with our expectations. None of the contextual variables explains (in a statistically significant way) variations in leaders' preferences for attention to internal concerns, leaving U.S. allies to themselves. Instead, partisanship and ideology are the two factors that count. Gender is also important in 1996, with women more attuned to domestic concerns than men. The only surprising result is that liberals are more willing than conservatives to support U.S. allies over domestic concerns in 1996, with the reverse (and the more expected result) true four years earlier. We suspect that the widely discussed preference among liberals for humanitarian and peace-enforcement interventions (as in Somalia and Bosnia), both more in evidence by the time of the 1996 survey, and

Table 9.1   The Impact of Contextual, Symbolic, and Individual-Level Sociodemographic Variables on Leaders' Internationalist Dispositions, 1992 and 1996 (standardized regression coefficients)

	Allies defend selves US concerns local		Cooperative internationalism		Militant internationalism	
	1992	1996	1992	1996	1992	1996
Contextual						
Crime	−0.044	0.022	0.032	0.030	−0.043	−0.019
Social malaise	0.000	0.061	0.031	−0.022	0.048	0.008
Unemployment rate	0.035	−0.025	−0.046	0.051	.058**	0.017
Percent Hispanic	−0.056	−0.039	0.007	−0.054	0.030	−0.025
Percent Asian	0.019	0.028	0.053	0.033	−0.048	−0.016
Educational achievement	−0.004	0.047	0.042	0.026	0.017	−.073**
GSP growth rate	0.029	0.006	−0.015	−0.008	0.000	0.011
Exports as % GSP	−0.044	−0.002	0.040	0.020	−0.025	−.064**
Per capita income	0.052	0.020	−0.065	−0.083	−0.033	0.006
Symbolic						
Party ID	−.072**	−.091**	0.015	.080**	−.132***	−.083**
Ideology	−.101***	.136***	.455***	.467***	−.496***	−.417***
Sociodemographic						
Sex	0.016	.094***	−0.011	−.059**	−.034*	−.043*
Generation	−0.028	−0.019	.163***	.015***	−.034*	−0.023
Intercept	1.898	2.996	7.474	−3.093	−4.152	−3.317
R²	0.03	0.03	0.26	0.31	0.35	0.19
N	1991	1615	1901	1573	1881	1542

*p < .10; ** < .05; ***p < 0.001

the changes in partisan control of the White House and Congress following the 1992 presidential and 1994 midterm elections may explain this apparent anomaly.[10]

The results for the two internationalism scales are similar. Partisanship and ideology move in tandem and track expected patterns: Democrats and liberals support CI, while Republicans and conservatives support MI. Generation also now matters in ways that parallel the changing composition of the domestic political landscape. Older members among the American elite support CI, while younger members are more prone toward MI (though less consistently so, as judged by the absence of statistical significance for the 1996 coefficient). Interestingly, however, women now appear more supportive of the dual tenets of global involvement than men.[11]

Militant internationalism also finds correlates among the contextual variables. Although there is little consistency across the two FPLP surveys,[12] the analyses do suggest that high levels of unemployment, low levels of educational achievement, and limited exposure to foreign markets (exports as percent of GSP) lead to greater support for a more militant set of foreign policy preferences. In the final analysis, however, environmental factors are less important than political symbols or sociodemographic characteristics in explaining the broad outlines of opinion leaders' internationalist-isolationist preferences.

That conclusion also holds for attitudes toward issues that emphasize the domestic content of American foreign policy. In Tables 9.2 and 9.3 we examine two of the popular-goal questions that appear in the 1992 and 1996 FPLP surveys and three that ask about threats to American national security. For purposes of these analyses,

Table 9.2 The Impact of Contextual, Symbolic, and Individual-Level Socio-demographic Variables on Leaders' Opinions About the Goals of American Foreign Policy, 1992 and 1996 (logit regression coefficients)

	Protect jobs of American workers		Protect American business abroad	
	1992	*1996*	*1992*	*1996*
Contextual				
Crime	0.000	0.017	.010*	−0.097
Social malaise	−.188*	−.251**	−.253**	0.130
Unemployment rate	0.035	.306**	0.090	−0.088
Percent Hispanic	−0.014	0.002	−0.010	0.015
Percent Asian	0.055	−.057*	−0.032	−0.018
Educational achievement	−0.006	−0.087	−0.048	−0.219
GSP growth rate	0.068	0.013	0.014	−0.067
Exports as % GSP	0.001	−0.018	−0.028	0.026
Per capita income	−0.042	0.003	0.030	.061*
Symbolic				
Party ID	.211**	.274**	−.217**	−0.103
Ideology	0.003	−0.123	−.170**	−0.086
CI	.057**	.058**	0.009	0.017
MI	.214***	.215***	.208***	.269***
Sociodemographic				
Sex	−.585***	−.660***	−.435**	−0.106
Generation	−.223**	−0.055	0.051	−0.020
Intercept	−0.788	−2.898	9.367	−2.114
Model chi-square	143.54***	140.01***	207.52***	158.10***
Nagelkerke R^2	0.11	0.13	0.16	0.16
Percent predicted	71.26	73.77	76.88	80.31
N	1820	1540	1821	1539

*p < .10; **p < .05; ***p < 0.001

Table 9.3   The Impact of Contextual, Symbolic, and Individual-Level Socio-demographic Variables on Leaders' Opinions About Threats to American National Security, 1992 and 1996 (logit regression coefficients)

	Domestic problems		Mass migrations/ immigrants/refugees		International drug trafficking	
	1992	*1996*	*1992*	*1996*	*1992*	*1996*
Contextual						
Crime	0.000	−0.012	.000*	−0.181	0.000	−.117**
Social malaise	0.104	−0.071	−0.233	−0.055	0.070	0.095
Unemployment						
rate	−0.006	.211**	−0.015	−0.008	−0.049	0.144
Percent Hispanic	0.012	0.004	0.013	0.022	.037***	−0.013
Percent Asian	0.022	−0.001	0.069	−0.071	−.137***	0.000
Educational						
achievement	.202*	0.059	.322*	−.472**	−0.137	−0.162
GSP growth rate	−0.001	.109*	0.039	−0.015	−.078**	0.088
Exports as % GSP	0.038	−0.009	−.071*	0.026	0.020	0.015
Per capita income	−0.015	−0.002	−0.130	0.077	0.025	−0.009
Symbolic						
Party ID	−.410***	.163*	−0.007	−0.089	0.066	−0.140
Ideology	0.032	−0.010	0.015	−.316**	−228**	−.234**
CI	.183***	.046**	−0.001	−.058**	.160***	.113***
MI	−0.019	.190***	.080**	.211***	.196***	.212***
Sociodemographic						
Sex	−.280*	−.510***	−.868***	−1.248***	−.093**	−.861***
Generation	.194**	−0.033	.442***	0.010	.581**	.258***
Intercept	−1.003	−2.029	−0.622	−3.093	−1.484	−1.756
Model chi-square	242.82***	153.83***	54.14***	205.66***	251.09***	224.45***
Nagelkerke R^2	0.17	0.13	0.07	0.21	0.18	0.19
Percent predicted	67	63.31	90.7	83.76	67.36	69.84
N	1819	1540	1763	1539	1814	1542

*p < .10; **p < .05; ***p < 0.001

we add the CI and MI scales as independent (symbolic-politics) variables. In this way we control for leaders' general foreign policy beliefs as we simultaneously address their attitudes toward specific policy issues. We recoded the items to create dichotomies, so we can compare those leaders who attach highest salience to the goal or security threat in question with all others. Logistic regression is now the appropriate analytic technique.

The goal questions in Table 9.2 ask whether protecting the jobs of American workers and the interests of American business abroad should be the most important

U.S. foreign policy goal(s). The questions in Table 9.3 inquire about the most serious threats to American national security in the waning days of the twentieth century: an inability to solve domestic problems ("decay of cities, homelessness, unemployment, racial conflict, and crime"); an influx of immigrants and refugees; and international drug trafficking. In both, we find that our symbolic-politics measures (partisanship, ideology, and international orientation) and sociodemographic variables are important predictors in consistent and easily explained ways. But we also find other intriguing relationships that are inconsistent with our hypotheses, pointing instead to the impact of contextual factors on elites' foreign policy attitudes—sometimes in unexpected ways.

Note that higher levels of social malaise lead to less support for protection of either American jobs or American business interests (Table 9.2). This is not easily reconciled with the long-standing argument that American elites are social-regarding. Yet there is some hint (1996) that high levels of unemployment may lead to greater support among opinion leaders for American workers.

Note also that opinion leaders from states with high concentrations of Asians appear to be less prone (in 1996) to support American workers than those from other states.[13] This is inconsistent with the xenophobic explanation of foreign policy preferences. Yet the results show that (in 1992) leaders from states with high concentrations of Hispanics find international drug trafficking a major concern (Table 9.3). In much the same vein, the relationship between educational achievement and the perceived threat posed by immigrant and refugee populations, while statistically significant, is not consistent between the two leader surveys. Our findings, then, contain evidence that American elites are more responsive to conditions in the domestic environment than we had anticipated. But while intriguing, the pattern of responses paints a rather elusive picture of the shape and pervasiveness of contextual factors in shaping their foreign policy preferences.

HOW DOES THE GENERAL PUBLIC RESPOND TO ITS DOMESTIC ENVIRONMENT?

Do "ordinary" Americans respond to their domestic environments in more predictable and understandable ways than their leaders, as our hypotheses suggest? The statistical analyses summarized in the three tables that follow suggest that they do not. As with elites, political symbols and socialization experiences are generally more pertinent.

Table 9.4 for the mass public is the analogue to Table 9.1 for opinion leaders. Here we ask if responses to the long-standing internationalism-isolationism question noted earlier ("Do you think it will be best for the future of the country if we take an active part in world affairs or if we stay out of world affairs?")[14] and if dispositions toward cooperative and militant internationalism[15] are explained by domestic factors. All three are based on the 1994 Chicago Council survey of the general public.

Table 9.4   The Impact of Contextual, Symbolic, and Individual-Level Socio-demographic Variables on the Mass Public's Internationalist Predispositions, 1994 and 1997 (standardized regression coefficients)

	Active in world affairs 1994	Involved, not involved 1994	World leader or not 1997	Cooperative internat'lsm 1994	Militant internat'lsm 1994
Contextual					
Crime (1994 = county; 1997 = state)	− 0.027	− 0.038	0.013	0.012	0.013
Social malaise	0.054	− 0.046	.092**	− 0.036	0.065
Unemployment rate	− 0.074	0.053	− 0.021	0.011	0.051
Percent Hispanic	0.028	0.033	0.024	− 0.057	0.022
Percent Asian	− 0.004	− 0.010	0.007	.139**	− 0.073
Educational achievement	0.069	− 0.013	0.049	0.088	0.017
GSP growth rate	− 0.015	0.034	0.015	0.000	− .078*
Exports as % GSP	0.024	− 0.037	0.017	0.011	− 0.003
Per capita income	− 0.065	0.071	.066*	− 0.036	− .089**
Symbolic					
Party ID	—	0.044	0.088	—	—
Ideology	− 0.019	0.004	—	.101***	− .071**
Sociodemographic					
Sex	.110***	− 0.010	− 0.029	− 0.003	.076**
Generation	.075**	− 0.051	− 0.001	0.000	− 0.001
Education	.178***	.178***	.093***	.150***	− .052*
News interest/attention	.115***	—	.119***	.128***	.170***
Hispanic origin	0.043	.068**	− 0.014	0.002	− 0.017
African-American	− 0.038	.061**	− .070**	0.036	− 0.055
Intercept	1.230	0.575	0.959	0.213	0.694
R²	0.07	0.06	0.04	0.08	0.06
N	1100	941	1709	1160	1160

*p < .10; **p < .05; ***p < 0.001
—indicates not available/applicable

We also examine one item from the 1997 Pew survey (we label it "internationalism"), which asked respondents if they thought the United States should play the role of world leader, either by itself or in combination with other countries. Although the responses are highly skewed (nearly 90 percent said yes), we use it later (Table 9.5) as a control (symbolic-politics) variable to enhance comparability with the Chicago Council survey. We use another "internationalism" control (Table 9.6) based on Hinckley's 1994 survey. Respondents were asked if the United States should pursue its security interests unilaterally or with other nations, or if its interests were better protected by avoiding involvement with others. Here the distribution more nearly tracks the long-standing "active part in world affairs" question, with 70 percent embracing the internationalist response and 30 percent the isolationist. The analyses summarized in Table 9.4 for the mass public are quite similar to those shown in Table 9.1 for opinion leaders. Only four of the coefficients for the contextual variables are statistically significant, and, according to our hypotheses, only one of the four is correctly signed (per-capita income on the 1997 world-leader variable). In contrast, political symbols and sociodemographic variables prove quite important. Ideology is not related systematically to the three broad internationalism-isolationism questions, but it is an important predictor of respondents' positions on cooperative and militant internationalism. As in the leader samples, liberals are the strongest proponents of CI, conservatives of MI. Among the sociodemographic variables, education and attentiveness stand out, with both positively related to internationalist predispositions. Gender is also positively related to MI, suggesting that among the general public, men are more hawkish than women.

Table 9.5 includes five goal questions from the 1994 Chicago Council and 1997 Pew surveys. The ones on protecting workers' jobs and American business interests parallel the questions for elites in Table 9.2. To these we add items that relate to controlling illegal immigration and combating international drug trafficking. Using logistic regression, we again compare those who attach the greatest salience to these issues (identified either as "very important" or "top priority" foreign policy goals) with all other respondents.

As with the general internationalism questions, there is little evidence in Table 9.5 to support our hypothesis that contextual factors stimulate greater support for a self-interested foreign policy program among the mass public than among leaders. There is some hint that crime, unemployment, and large concentrations of Hispanic people heighten concern for immigration issues, but the data are not conclusive. Instead, we again find that symbolic and sociodemographic factors are the more powerful predictors of public preferences.

Ideology and CI and MI are notable, showing that liberals and supporters of CI are less prone to support domestically oriented goals.[16] Conversely, supporters of MI attach comparatively greater importance to them, as we would expect. Among the sociodemographic variables, education again stands out. Predictably, those with less education are more likely to support a domestically oriented agenda. Women also attach greater importance to these goals than do men. Surprisingly, however, attentiveness matters little.

Table 9.6 (which parallels Table 9.3 on opinion leaders) completes our empirical inquiry. Here we examine four items from the 1994 Chicago Council survey that asked respondents to rate possible threats to the vital interest of the United States. We compared those who rated the threats as critical with those who deemed them either important but not critical, or simply not important. Three of the four items— economic competition from Europe and Japan[17] and the influx of refugees and immigrants—can reasonably be construed as self-interest questions in contrast with

Table 9.5 The Impact of Contextual, Symbolic, and Individual-Level Sociodemographic Variables on the Mass Public's Opinions About the Goals of American Foreign Policy, 1994 and 1997 (logit regression coefficients)

	Protect jobs of American workers		Protect American business abroad		Control/reduce illegal immigration		Stop illegal drugs	
	1994	1997	1994	1997	1994	1997	1994	1997
Contextual								
Crime (1994 = county; 1997 = state)	0.001	0.048	0.001	0.063	−.002**	0.030	0.000	0.135
Social malaise	−0.087	0.045	0.213	−0.212	−0.120	−0.173	0.041	−0.022
Unemployment rate	0.039	0.025	−0.130	0.028	.183*	−0.007	−0.091	0.071
Percent Hispanic	0.029	−0.011	−0.010	−0.002	.026*	−0.022	−0.014	0.004
Percent Asian	−0.064	−0.015	−0.004	−0.019	−.094*	0.057	0.016	−0.066
Educational achievement	−0.086	−0.042	−.222*	−.320*	−0.125	−0.105	−0.142	0.112
GSP growth rate	0.060	−0.071	−0.057	−.176*	−0.081	0.125	0.068	0.037
Exports as % GSP	−0.020	−0.005	−0.009	−0.015	−0.034	−.064**	0.010	−0.035
Per capita income	0.074	0.050	0.037	.107**	−0.028	0.012	0.052	−0.013
Symbolic								
Party ID	—	.199*	—	−.408***	—	−.193***	—	−0.096
Ideology	0.111	—	−.134**	—	−.210**	—	−0.143	—
CI	−.470***	—	−.147***	—	−.436***	—	−.389***	—
MI	.592***	—	.373***	—	.412***	—	.507***	—
Internationalism	—	−0.037	—	.774*	—	−0.315	—	−0.086
Sociodemographic								
Sex	−.386**	−0.220	−.388**	0.252	−0.168	−0.192	−.549**	−.485**
Generation	−0.068	−.179*	−.207*	0.012	0.175	.284**	.246**	.435***
Education	−.790***	−.814***	−.353**	−.453***	−.244*	−0.232	−.848***	−.342**
News interest/attention	0.095	0.001	−0.060	−.045*	−0.008	−0.021	0.032	−0.029
Hispanic origin	0.307	0.004	0.196	0.489	−1.144***	.652**	0.263	0.356
African-American	0.461	0.537	−0.071	.761**	−0.090	−0.016	0.198	0.229
Intercept	−1.485	−0.920	0.950	−3.759	1.630	−0.868	−0.332	−0.229
Model chi-square	117.29***	51.14	96.26***	55.58***	152.93***	44.93***	118.70***	60.01***
Nagelkerke R²	0.18	0.08	0.11	0.1	0.19	0.07	0.18	0.1
Percent predicted	85.62	77.36	61.43	83.46	76.17	59.84	86.26	69.83
N	1105	871	1094	866	1104	846	1105	848

*p < .10; **p < .05; ***p < 0.001
—indicates not available/applicable

Table 9.6 The Impact of Contextual, Symbolic, and Individual-Level Socio-demographic Variables on the Mass Public's Opinions About Threats to American Interests/Security, 1994 (logit regression coefficients)

	Economic competition from Japan	Economic competition from Europe	International terrorism	Influx of refugees & immigrants	Loss of jobs to Third World
Contextual					
Crime	−0.001	0.001	.001**	0.000	−0.001
Social malaise	0.101	0.148	0.232	−0.050	0.100
Unemployment rate	−0.099	−0.047	−.182**	0.095	−0.012
Percent Hispanic	−0.007	0.005	.038*	.039**	0.007
Percent Asian	0.030	−0.058	0.066	−.160***	−0.020
Educational achievement	0.008	0.028	0.200	0.072	−0.040
GSP growth rate	−0.046	−0.079	−0.061	−0.040	−0.010
Exports as % GSP	0.022	0.001	−0.041	−0.030	−0.008
Per capita income	0.024	0.042	0.022	0.010	0.019
Symbolic					
Party ID	—	—	—	—	0.163
Ideology	−.114*	−0.035	−.013**	−.181**	0.054
CI	−0.078	.132*	−0.109	−.331***	—
MI	.253***	.145**	.238***	.266***	—
Internationalism	—	—	—	—	−.330**
Sociodemographic					
Sex	−0.100	0.122	−.435**	−.314**	0.012
Generation	−.145*	0.094	0.138	0.106	0.131
Education	0.175	0.017	−.372**	−0.211	−.305**
News interest/attention	−0.012	−0.046	0.116	0.030	—
Hispanic origin	0.178	0.273	−0.394	−.849***	−0.085
African-American	0.392	0.342	−.543**	0.115	0.399
Intercept	1.741	−1.214	1.396	1.093	−2.139
Model chi-square	31.32**	29.82**	74.30***	91.81***	25.85*
Nagelkerke R^2	0.04	0.11	0.09	0.12	0.04
Percent predicted	65.85	71.19	71.61	74.12	68.24
N	1084	1062	1091	1100	910

*p < .10; **p < .05; ***p < 0.001
—indicates not available/applicable

symbolic issues, in response to which we would expect contextual factors to exert an especially powerful impact. The last question, on loss of jobs to the Third World, is also self-interested. It comes from Hinckley's 1994 postelection survey, in which respondents were asked if this constituted a critical threat (compared with important or no threat) to the security of the United States.

The results parallel our earlier findings: symbolic and sociodemographic variables are consistently better explanations of public preferences than are environmental factors. Three of the contextual variables are significant on the terrorism variable, but one them (unemployment) is incorrectly signed. Similarly, the two ethnic variables are related significantly to the refugee-immigrant question but in inconsistent ways. Arguably, this tells us something meaningful about how communities across the American states respond to these different ethnic groups. Notable in this respect is that respondents of Hispanic origin responded negatively to the question, while respondents in states with large numbers of Hispanics responded positively (i.e., refugees and immigrants constitute a security threat). Nonetheless, from the perspective of our theoretical concerns, these analytical results do not support the proposition that the foreign policy preferences of "ordinary" Americans are driven more by self-interests than those of American elites. Or to borrow phrases from John Rielly and Ronald Steel, cited in the introduction to this chapter, we find little empirical evidence to explain why "pragmatic internationalism" explains mass preferences at the same time that elites remain "mesmerized by notions of American leadership and 'global responsibilities.' "

ON REFLECTION

Academics are paid to do path-breaking research (or at least to find new acorns in the extant pen). Nonfindings are anathema to what the academy prizes most. Alas, this chapter is one of nonfindings. Our research design and particularly the absence of better contextual data may be to blame. The distance between environmental effects on self-interested foreign policy preferences, which we hypothesize to affect mass attitudes but not elite attitudes, may be so great when we measure them at the level of U.S. states as to be irrelevant. Furthermore, perceptions arguably are more important than objective facts and may account for variations in opinions across individuals who share similar environments. Ideally, then, we would like survey data that address attitudes toward domestic circumstances and foreign policy issues simultaneously so that we can directly compare the egocentric and sociotropic models of policy preferences. Absent that, linking contextual data more closely to community levels might be helpful (see Huckfeldt and Sprague 1995). Still, we are struck that our data on crime at the county level in Tables 9.4 and 9.5 produced results not notably different than those at the state level in the same tables. Could it be that attitudes toward foreign and domestic policy remain on separate tracks—even in a rapidly globalizing world in which, as President Clinton repeatedly remarked, the line between foreign and domestic has become so blurred as to be irrelevant?

What, then, accounts for Americans' foreign policy beliefs and preferences? Our analyses show that symbolic politics and socialization experiences are important, reinforcing long-standing research traditions that focus on these variables. Still, there is something unsatisfying about this conclusion. It says that we can explain constancy in Americans' foreign policy attitudes, but we cannot explain dynamic processes like the inward-turning thesis advanced in Schlesinger's and Steel's arguments noted in the beginning section of this chapter. Elsewhere (Wittkopf 1996), we show that Schlesinger and Steel may be wrong insofar as their analysis of mass attitudes is concerned.[18] But their attention to the distance between mass and elite preferences continues to demand our attention. The suspicion is that a focus on the media's role as agenda-setters, framers, and gatekeepers may be crucial in explaining the disjuncture.

Consider, for example, data from a September 1998 survey that suggest how reliant Americans are on the media for their information on international events (see Table 9.7). Those who identified an international issue (the global economy, defense and military preparedness, going to war, terrorism and bombings, and foreign instability in general) as the country's most important problem were significantly more likely to name the media as their source of truthful information or honest opinion about the issue (38 percent) compared to those concerned with domestic issues (25 percent).

The importance of education and attentiveness to public affairs documented in our empirical analyses reinforces the view that the gulf between opinion leaders and the general public is dictated by factors that can be explained only at the individual level. Still, we are struck that in the post–Cold War environment the media has taken a decidedly inward turn. Garrick Utley, longtime foreign correspondent for several major TV news networks, has documented the decline in foreign policy coverage by ABC, CBS, and NBC. Between 1988 and 1996, for example, the total minutes of nightly news coverage devoted to foreign policy by ABC dropped from roughly 600 minutes to less than 350, by NBC from nearly 700 minutes to only 320 (Utley 1997, 5). Similarly, Pippa Norris (1997, 282) shows a dramatic decline in TV network coverage of international news during the transition to the post–Cold War world and since.

These shifts arguably reflect market forces, which dictate that the media report on things that animate audience interests.[19] Understandably, those interests have

Table 9.7   Americans' Sources of Information on the Most Important Problem (percentages)

News Source	International Problem Most Important	Domestic Problem Most Important
Media	38	25
Government	22	11
Civic Organization	2	21
Other	38	43

Source: Telephone survey by Research/Strategy/Management, Inc., Ronald H. Hinckley, principal investigator for the Public Relations Society of America Foundation, September 2–11, 1998. N = 1001.

been less focused on foreign policy since the end of the Cold War. The result, however, is the classic chicken-and-egg question: If the media do not report on what is happening in the world, how are "ordinary" Americans to think about and respond to the world around them? By focusing attention on domestic rather than foreign policy issues—because this is what the agenda-setters, framers, and gatekeepers tell them is important—how are the American people to become informed about the world around them and be able to make the reasoned choices about public policy— foreign and domestic—that democratic theory demands?

Troubling in this respect is Richard Sobel's research on public attitudes toward the continuing conflict in the Balkans. Drawing on a range of public opinion data, he argues that the media failed to report high levels of public support for U.S. intervention in the former Yugoslavia. Instead, the media framed the issue in terms of opposition to involvement, which may have had the effect of misdirecting policymakers away from that option (Sobel 1998). We surmise that this also means that most Americans came to believe that American interests were not at stake there. As U.S. Secretary of State James Baker reportedly said, "We don't have a dog in that fight." Given such framing and related elite cues, is it surprising that the general public should turn its attention inward? Environmental factors thus do not explain why most Americans, compared to elites, are less concerned with issues at the core of the liberal internationalist ethos. Instead, the media's lack of attention to these issues leads Americans to believe that international affairs do not demand attention or concern. Still, the chasm between elites and masses on self-interested foreign policy issues remains an intriguing paradox.

APPENDIX: SOURCES OF CONTEXTUAL DATA

Crime

Number of offenses (murder, manslaughter, forcible rape, robbery, aggravated assault, burglary, larceny-theft, and motor vehicle theft) known to police per 1 million population, as defined and reported in Federal Bureau of Investigation, *Uniform Crime Reports for the United States*, Washington, D.C.: FBI, various years.

Social Malaise

Poverty and infant mortality (except for 1996) are from the *Statistical Abstract of the United States*, Washington, D.C.: Government Printing Office, various years. Based on U.S. Bureau of the Census data. Infant mortality for 1996 are from the *Monthly Vital Statistics Report* 45 (February 1997): table 9.4.

Unemployment

Statistical Abstract of the United States, Washington, D.C.: Government Printing Office, various years. Based on U.S. Bureau of Labor Statistics data.

Percent Hispanic and Percent Asian

Calculated using total state resident population and resident population by race from the *Statistical Abstract of the United States*, Washington, D.C.: Government Printing Office, various years. Based on U.S. Bureau of the Census data.

Educational Achievement

Data on persons not enrolled in school and not a high school graduate, and persons who have completed a high school diploma or more are for 1990 and from *We the Americans: Our Education*, Washington, D.C.: U.S. Commerce Department, Bureau of the Census, 1993, 6–7. School expenditures are the average dollars spent per pupil in public elementary and secondary day schools in 1991–1992, 1993–1994, 1995–1996 from National Education Association, *Estimates of School Statistics*, Washington, D.C.: NEA, various years.

Rates of Growth in States' Gross Product

Rates calculated using state product data for 1991–1994 from the *Statistical Abstract of the United States*, Washington, D.C.: Government Printing Office, various years. Based on U.S. Department of Commerce, Bureau of Economic Analysis data. Calculations for 1995–1996 use data from *Survey of Current Business* 78 (June 1998): table 9.6. The *Survey of Current Business* is published by the Bureau of Economic Analysis.

Exports as a Percent of States' Gross Product

GSP data sources are described above. State export data are from the U.S. Bureau of the Census, International Trade Administration, available at URL: http://www. ita.doc.gov/industry/otea/state/merchandise/world3.txt (accessed May 9, 1998).

Per-capita Income

Survey of Current Business 77 (May 1997): table 9.1.

10

NATO and European Security after the Cold War
Will European Citizens Support a Common Security Policy?

Richard C. Eichenberg

The Union and its member states shall define and implement a common foreign and security policy. . . . The Member States shall support the Union's external and security policy actively and unreservedly in a spirit of loyalty and mutual solidarity. . . . The common foreign and security policy shall include all questions related to the security of the Union, including the eventual framing of a common defence policy, which might in time lead to a common defence.

—Treaty on European Union, 1992, Article J, J.1 and J.3.

The members of the European Council are resolved that the European Union shall play its full role on the international stage. To that end, we intend to give the European Union the necessary means and capabilities to assume its responsibilities regarding a common European policy on security and defence. We therefore commit ourselves to further develop more effective European military capabilities from the basis of existing national, bi-national, multinational capabilities and to strengthen our own capabilities for that purpose.

—European Council Declaration on Strengthening the Common European Policy on Security and Defence, Annex III to Presidency Conclusions, European Council, Cologne, June 3–4, 1999.

To develop European capabilities, Member States have set themselves the headline goal: by the year 2003, cooperating together voluntarily, they will be able to deploy rapidly and then sustain forces . . . in operations up to corps level (up to 15 brigades or 50,000–60,000 persons). These forces should be militarily

self-sustaining with the necessary command, control and intelligence capabilities, logistics, other combat support services and additionally, as appropriate, air
and naval elements.

—Annex IV to Presidency Conclusions, European
Council, Helsinki, December 10–11, 1999.

The European Council asks the [Intergovernmental Council] to base its work
on the fact that the citizens are at the core of the European construction: the
Union has the imperative to respond concretely to their needs and concerns.

—Presidency Conclusions, European Council,
Turin, March 29, 1996.

These declarations of the European Council illustrate the complicated legacy that
history bequeathed Europe's leaders as they continue on the road to economic and
political union. First, the end of the Cold War and the decade-long crisis in the
former Yugoslavia once again challenged Europeans to define the institutional context in which they pursue their security. With the reduction in Russian military
power and the emergence of security crises near the borders of the European Union
(EU), Europe at the beginning of the twenty-first century is proceeding on the path
of a truly European defense and security policy, long an implicit alternative to the
NATO alliance.

Quite apart from the evolution of the security environment, that path has seemed
a natural extension of the EU's dramatic progress in policy integration since the
mid-1980s but has been complicated by the requirement of domestic consensus.
The security politics of the 1980s, together with the history since then of the integration process itself, have reinforced the requirement that Europe's policies rest on
a firm basis of citizen support. In the 1980s, it was the reaction of citizens to Cold
War tensions and NATO nuclear weapons that brought public opinion and consensus to the center of governmental deliberations (Eichenberg 1989). During the
1990s, the difficulties of ratifying the Maastricht Treaty in some member states coincided with a drastic decline in support for the EU in all member states and thus
raised the issue of public consensus to the highest priority of Europe's political leadership.[1] Finally, the war against Serbia in 1999 demonstrated once again that the
deployment and use of military force was not uniformly supported within or across
the European states.

Of course, the choice between NATO and a truly European security policy is not
really novel. It is merely a new version of a very old question: To what extent is
European dependence on the NATO alliance and the United States consistent with
the competing national interests of the Europeans, with the process of European
integration, and with the general European aspiration to "play its full role on the
international stage"? Although events in the late 1990s brought new salience to these

questions, they represent a set of choices that European governments have faced since the inception of both the European Union and the NATO alliance.

Traditionally, Europeans have favored the Atlantic connection, and we will see below that this preference rested on a fairly firm foundation of public support. Nonetheless, with new times come new complications, so it is useful to ask just how much European public opinion has changed in reaction to the fundamental transformation of the security environment and to the dramatic progress that has been achieved as Europe has moved from the market reforms of the Single European Act (SEA) to the aspiration to an "ever closer Union" codified in the Maastricht and Amsterdam Treaties.

The purpose of this chapter is to examine this question by reviewing the state of European public opinion on the subject of defense-policy integration. I proceed by comparing two historical periods. In the first section, on the Cold War period, I briefly review the origins of the NATO alliance as the dominant framework for the pursuit of European security. I then recapitulate some of the policy controversies that bedeviled the Alliance during the 1970s and 1980s, and I examine public-opinion surveys to ascertain the balance of support for the NATO and European security alternatives. The primary questions in this first section are: What was the historical level of support for a common European security policy during the Cold War? Did that level of support change in response to the transatlantic policy controversies and the relaunching of European integration in the 1980s?

In the second section, I turn to the Maastricht Era that began with the end of the Cold War, the unification of Germany, and the signature and ratification of the Treaty on European Union. Following a brief review of the security dilemmas that this period provoked, I examine the level of popular support for EU's aspiration to complete political union, which was symbolized most clearly by the Maastricht provision for a Common Foreign and Security Policy, and later accelerated by the war in Yugoslavia and by the EU's declarations in June and December 1999 on the implementation of a Common Policy on Security and Defence. In the conclusions, I return to the central question: Do Europeans now want a common security policy any more than they ever did?

EUROPE BETWEEN THE SUPERPOWERS: THE COLD WAR ERA[2]

There is something of a paradox in the fact that the European Union has achieved the *least* amount of progress in the integration of foreign and defense policy.[3] To be sure, it is these policy areas that most directly touch on national interest, national tradition, sovereignty, and territorial security. As Stanley Hoffmann (1966) long ago observed, it is precisely these issues of "high politics" that may represent the most intractable obstacles to European unification.

Nonetheless, it is also the case that European unity and European institutions were conceived in part to serve the pursuit of external political and security interests.

First and most obvious, since 1957 Europe has been a customs union, and the institutions of the EU have become thoroughly engaged in the diplomatic representation of trade and other economic interests abroad. Second, the very creation of the European Union was strongly motivated by foreign and security policy considerations. With the failure of the European Defense Community in 1954, the creation of integrated European institutions offered the only option that would bridge the U.S.-supported desire to rearm West Germany and the reservations that this step understandably provoked, especially among the French. Like American participation in NATO, the new institutions of the European Union served the dual purpose of deterring the Soviets through unity while simultaneously integrating and containing the newly rehabilitated West Germany.

Finally, a united Europe was seen as a balancer—a lever—in an external environment characterized by superpower dominance. As Anton DePorte has put it:

> Finally, on the international level, [the Schuman plan for a European Coal and Steel Community] promised not only to strengthen Western Europe in face of the Russian threat but also—though this was less talked about—to strengthen it vis-à-vis its indispensable but overpowering American ally. These Frenchmen, like many West Europeans, did not doubt that they had to rely on American strength for their security. But they did not want to rely entirely on the Americans to manage relations with the East which involved no less than war and peace, that is, the lives of the European nations. At the least a more united Europe could better influence American decisions affecting its vital interests; at the best it could break through the rigidity and risks of bipolar Europe by becoming strong enough to cease to be a stake of the superpowers in cold or hot war. (DePorte 1986, 222–223)

However, the European aspiration to be a global balancer soon fell victim to the Cold War context of alliance with the United States. Increasingly, foreign and security policies were starkly defined as a choice between the Atlantic and European options. The very real threats and tensions of the Cold War help to explain why the choice was framed this way, but it also resulted from the fact that the most energetic proponent of a European voice was General Charles de Gaulle, who nonetheless complicated matters by making it clear that Europe should be led by France, and who in any case was a strong critic of supranational solutions in the form of a federalist Europe (Lerner and Gorden 1969; Grosser 1982; DePorte 1986).

Yet the French position always contained a contradiction. Given the Soviet Union's geographic advantage, its perceived conventional dominance, and its large nuclear arsenal, European security required a nuclear deterrent, but of course the first and most emphatic principle of French security policy under de Gaulle was the insistence on *indépendence*, most particularly in the nuclear realm. In the absence of French willingness to share its nuclear deterrent, let alone integrate its defense forces, the remaining European states chose to privilege the Atlantic connection, a result that certainly slowed the evolution of a separate European position in foreign and security policy. The transatlantic solution may have been *faute de mieux,* but it did reflect power realities as well as the lack of available alternatives.

There matters rested until the end of the 1960s, when a vigorous European challenge to U.S. foreign policy began to reemerge. In fact, it is difficult to overstate the degree of tension and acrimony that colored transatlantic relations in the 1970s and 1980s. Beginning with the Vietnam War and continuing through the Afghan and Iranian crises in 1979, the European critique reached its peak in the criticism of nuclear-weapons and arms-control policy under President Ronald Reagan (the most lucid and penetrating analysis of this period remains Hoffmann 1984).[4]

Perhaps not surprisingly, it was during this period that the process of European integration, somewhat dormant since the completion of the common market, began to show signs of reawakening. The 1970s saw the creation of European Political Cooperation (EPC) and the European Monetary System, both arguably in response to U.S. policies. Moreover, calls for a stronger European voice in security as well as foreign policy became equally apparent during this period, although it was not always clear whether the desire was for a stronger European voice within NATO or a completely independent European policy. Nonetheless, among defense intellectuals, the 1980s saw a decided drift toward discussion of both the broad issue of a stronger European defense pillar and the more narrow issue of defense and weapons collaboration (Bull 1983; Wallace 1984). Speaking at Harvard in 1983, the president of the European Parliament echoed earlier talk of a "balancing" role for Europe: "A more unified approach could help Europe to act as a moderating influence in the current standoff between the superpowers" (Dankert 1986, 69).

During the 1980s, European integration did accelerate in reaction to the controversies noted above but also in reaction to a broader set of concerns that arose from perceptions of the distribution of global economic and military power. The SEA, which in 1985 liberalized and deregulated the internal market, had its origins in European concerns about its ability to compete with Japan, as well as in the concern that America's economic and military power was in decline even as its attention was turning away from Europe:

> Changes in the international structure triggered the 1992 process [SEA]. More precisely, the trigger has been a real shift in the distribution of economic power resources (crudely put, relative American decline and Japanese ascent). What is just as important is that European elites perceive that the changes in the international setting require that they rethink their roles and interests in the world. . . . American coattails, they seem to have concluded, are not a safe place when the giant falters and threatens to sit down. (Sandholtz and Zysman 1989, 95–96)

The events of the late 1980s combined to propel the European Union ahead. The collapse of the Soviet Union and its empire, together with the unification of Germany, were of course the most significant events. However much Europe yearned for an end to the costs and tensions of the Cold War, its end nonetheless posed a severe problem: the concern that the United States might withdraw given the absence of a Soviet threat, leaving Europeans to balance both a unified Germany and a potentially threatening Russia. As Robert Art persuasively argues, the end of the Cold War and the unification of Germany threatened Europe with the dual problem of influencing external actors (the United States and Russia) while erecting structures to prevent Europe from regressing into its own internal security competition (Art 1996). A speedup in the process of integration seemed the logical answer to these concerns.

European citizens were very much in tune with this sentiment. In fact, as early as the mid-1970s, majorities of Europeans had endorsed the notion that external relations should be handled by an integrated EU rather than by individual member states. For example, in 1974 and 1975, polls asked respondents if the EU or individual member states should handle certain policies, including (significantly) "making our presence felt in discussions with the US and USSR." Almost 70 percent supported the notion of integrated, Union responsibility.[5] In 1976, 55 percent favored an integrated Union policy to "defend our interests against the superpowers" and 48 percent to "strengthen military defense." It is also interesting to note that unified foreign and security policies have traditionally been *more popular* than integrated Union policies in housing, education, consumer protection, and unemployment, which attract only 15–38 percent in support.

This "Europeanist" sentiment increased during the 1980s. Figure 10.1 reports the percentage of citizens who believed that Europe should conduct "security and

Figure 10.1   Percent Favoring Joint EU Action in Security and Defense

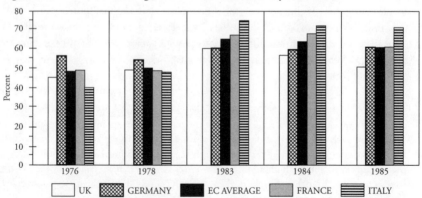

Source: Eurobarometer 22 (1984, 43).

Question Wording: The exact question wording is: "Here are a number of present day problems . . . For each one, would you tell me if it is better that decisions about it be taken by each country acting separately or by the member countries of the European Union acting together . . . security and defense?" The percentage shown here is for "acting together". In 1983 and 1984, the question referred to "Strengthening our country's military defense against possible enemies," and in 1985 to "protecting our country's security against external threats."

defense" policy together rather than separately.[6] The data show that support for a collective European defense is fairly long-standing and that the 1980s were indeed a period of growth in this sentiment. The European Community average was close to 50 percent as early as 1976, and it grew by 13 percentage points through 1985. Support for defense integration increased in each member state as well. Notice also that the largest spurt in pro-Europeanist sentiment occurred in the early Reagan years (1983), when deployment of the Euromissiles had led to substantial European disenchantment with the hard-line tone of American policy.

However, the profiles in Figure 10.1 also reflect traditional national perspectives and interests. France, traditionally motivated to question superpower dominance and concerned during this period by antinuclear protest and potential "neutralism" in Germany, reveals a particularly strong growth in Europeanist sentiment (12 percentage points through 1984). Germany and the United Kingdom, traditionally much more "Atlanticist" in orientation, evince more modest support for European defense. Nonetheless, by mid-decade, there was strong majority support for a common defense policy in all countries but the United Kingdom, where it nonetheless stood at 51 percent. Moreover, in somewhat different surveys administered in 1985 and 1987, there was never less than majority support for a common European defense. In these years, support levels were 50–60 percent in the United Kingdom and Germany and 60–70 percent in France and Italy (Dalton and Eichenberg 1998, 272).

Finally, in 1989 the Union's pollsters posed a question that represents a fairly precise test of support for the integration of security policy. Rather than ask the more general formulation of conducting policies "together or separately," the Eurobarometer began asking respondents specifically if security and defense policy should be handled at the EU level or by the separate national governments. The results mirror the patterns of the 1980s: majority support in Germany, France, Italy and other strongly pro-European states, with decidedly negative attitudes in the "Euroskeptic" countries such as Denmark and the United Kingdom.

In summary, not only is there evidence of support for a common European defense in the 1970s and 1980s, but it is difficult to find any evidence of significant resistance to it. Only in the United Kingdom is support tenuous, but even there it remains about 50 percent. In fact, although differences in question wording make it difficult to trace the exact extent of historical change, it is clear that there has been a substratum of support for a common European position since the mid-1970s, and comparable data for the 1980s suggest that it grew modestly during that decade.

As I observed in the introduction section, support for a European role in the abstract has never been controversial. In fact, the aspiration to global strength and influence that would come with European unity were motivating forces in the creation of the European Economic Community. However, that aspiration has always been complicated by security needs and competing national perspectives. In the security field, deterrence of the Soviet Union (and containment of Germany) required the participation of the United States and therefore acceptance of the primacy of

NATO. Within Europe, the unwillingness of France to share its nuclear deterrent left other states with little choice but to rely on the United States.

That pattern is evident in Table 10.1, which shows historical levels of support for the NATO alliance. Specifically, the question states: "Some people say that NATO is essential to our country's security. Others say NATO is no longer essential. Which view is closer to your own?" The responses confirm several familiar patterns. The French, of course, have always been the most skeptical of NATO, and this skepticism remained throughout the 1970s and 1980s, while Britain and Germany continued to evince strong majority support for NATO. Second, British and German support for NATO is much higher than comparable levels of support for a European defense: 70–80 percent support for NATO versus the 50–60 percent support for European defense that we saw above. The same is not true of France. Indeed, in a splendid reflection of the Gaullist vision, support for European options is generally higher than support for NATO: almost 70 percent in the mid-1980s versus the approximately 40 percent support for NATO (cf. Table 10.1 and Figure 10.1). In short, although the turbulence of the 1980s had brought American policy into question and led to an increase in abstract Europeanist sentiment in the security field, the questions on NATO suggest that only in France did this sentiment outweigh the traditional support for NATO.

However, a third pattern in Table 10.1 might suggest that this consensus choice began to break down as the 1980s came to a close. In all countries where data is available for 1989, support for NATO declined markedly from the levels of the previous few years, a result perhaps of the Reagan-Gorbachev détente and the emerging decline of Soviet military power, which reduced the perception of threat and thus perhaps the utility of alliance in NATO.

Of course, to explore this possibility requires survey questions that directly confront respondents with a choice: "Do you prefer NATO or the EU as the framework of security policy?" Unfortunately, that blunt question has rarely been asked, but there have been a series of questions that ask respondents to choose among various alliance alternatives. The questions are complicated and wording varies, but the surveys have always included two responses that help to sort out citizen preferences: "NATO as it now stands" versus "an Independent European Command."

Three important findings emerge from these questions.[7] First, in 1979 and even as late as 1987, when abstract Europeanist sentiment had grown, there remained majority or plurality support for NATO in Germany, the United Kingdom, and the Netherlands. In Italy and France, NATO has traditionally been less popular, and a Gaullist "national" option has always been attractive. However, a second pattern is also clear: by 1989, with East-West tension much reduced, the end of the Cold War at hand, and the SEA in full implementation, support for the NATO option was everywhere lower, and support for the European option had increased dramatically in virtually every country (although NATO remained the plurality choice in the traditionally Atlanticist countries). However, a third pattern is perhaps most interesting: as the Cold War context eroded and threat declined, with all the resulting uncertainty for the future role of the United States in Europe, it was the former Gaullists in France and Italy who became the most committed Europeanists.

A very similar pattern is displayed in Figure 10.2, which summarizes responses to two separate questions asked in late 1989. The first question is the familiar "NATO essential" question that was displayed in Table 10.1, shown here in the form of "net support" for NATO when the question is posed in this isolated fashion. The second question was posed in precisely the same questionnaire and asked respondents, "In your opinion, should NATO continue to be the most important forum for making decisions about the security of Western Europe in the future, or should the European Union make those decisions, or should some other organization?" (Eurobarometer 32, 1989, 41). In Figure 10.2, I subtracted the percentages who chose "European Union" and "West European Union" (WEU) from the percentage who favored NATO to yield this NATO-versus-Europe net-support measure.

Figure 10.2 shows that, queried in isolation, net support for NATO (the shaded bars) is positive and high in all but France and the Mediterranean countries that have traditionally been skeptical of the Alliance. In Northern Europe, however, NATO support has always been quite strong. However, when NATO is compared to the alternatives (NATO versus Europe), an interesting picture emerges. First, there is a decidedly Europeanist group that includes France and the Mediterranean countries. Here, support for NATO was weak to begin with, and it is even less so when compared to the European option, as revealed by the negative score on NATO versus Europe (support for the European option is larger than support for NATO). A second group is about evenly divided (Portugal, Belgium, Ireland), and a third group remains supportive of the NATO framework, although by varying margins (the Netherlands, Germany, Denmark, and the United Kingdom). However, even in the latter group, support for NATO is lower by a substantial margin in every country but Denmark when it is contrasted directly with the European alternative. At the end of the 1990s, then, the generally positive support of Europeans for a common security policy was accompanied by increased support for a European policy even in preference to NATO, a pattern that had not been present earlier. The margin of this preference varied by country, but there seems to be no question that citizens were receptive to the adoption of the Common Foreign and Security Policy that would come in the Maastricht Treaty of 1991.

EUROPE *INDÉPENDENTE?* THE MAASTRICHT ERA

If the 1980s were the decade of transatlantic discord and East-West tension on the Cold War issues of nuclear weapons and arms control, the 1990s have been marked by three principal events: the unification of Germany; the Gulf War; and the series of conflicts in the former Yugoslavia.[8] Each challenged Europe to influence events by acting in unison. Each also reopened transatlantic debates and irritations. Yet the combined effect of these events at the time of NATO's Berlin summit in 1996 was

Table 10.1 Percent Responding NATO Is "Essential"

	NATO Is Essential	NATO Is Not Essential	Net % Essential
FRANCE			
1967	34	30	4
1969	47	37	10
1971	54	35	19
1973	42	34	8
1976	42	35	7
1977	44	29	15
1978	39	35	4
1980	44	34	10
1982	34	25	9
1987	48	19	29
1989	41	28	13
Average	**43**	**31**	**12**
UNITED KINGDOM			
1967	59	15	44
1969	68	15	53
1971	81	12	69
1976	69	15	54
1977	73	8	65
1978	70	10	60
1980	79	13	66
1981	70	15	55
1982	65	25	40
1984	76	12	64
1985	76	13	63
1987	72	16	56
1989	67	17	50
Average	**71**	**14**	**57**
WEST GERMANY			
1967	67	17	50
1969	76	13	63
1971	84	11	73
1973	73	13	60
1976	85	10	75
1977	79	7	72
1978	84	5	79
1980	88	8	80
1981	62	20	42
1982	66	18	48

(Continued)

Table 10.1 (Continued)

	NATO Is Essential	*NATO Is Not Essential*	*Net % Essential*
1983	*86*	*12*	*74*
1984	*87*	*10*	*77*
1987	*70*	*15*	*55*
1989	*59*	*24*	*35*
Average	**76**	**13**	**63**
ITALY			
1976	45	23	22
1977	36	16	20
1978	42	16	26
1980	49	23	26
1981	62	27	35
1982	55	31	24
1983	61	26	35
1984	63	24	39
1987	62	26	36
Average	**53**	**24**	**29**

Source: USIA, as cited in Eichenberg (1989, 124–125) and Eurobarometer 32 (1989, 41) Data for Italy are from Szabo (1988, 69).

Question Wording:

The question on "NATO essential" asks "Some people say that NATO is still essential to our country's security. Others say NATO is no longer essential to our country's security. Which view is closer to your own?" The 1967 wording was slightly different; it says "Some people say that the Soviet Union does not pose a serious military threat that there is therefore not much need for NATO . . . others say that NATO is still essential." In 1973, the question asked if NATO was "still important" rather than "still essential."

Net Support is "NATO Essential" minus "Not Essential".

to reconcile Americans and Europeans to a security order that retained American participation and preserved NATO as the dominant institution of European security, a fact that was highlighted by the Alliance's actions in the 1999 war against Serbia.

To be sure, the EU's potential independence from NATO was strengthened through the European Defense Identity (EDI) that was adopted at the Berlin summit. This role will presumably grow even more prominent as a result of two EU decisions announced in 1999 after the war in Serbia: the Declaration on Strengthening the Common European Policy on Security and Defence, and the Helsinki summit decision to create a substantial European Defense Force. However, it is important to note that European governments continue to insist that the EU's independent profile will supplement—rather than compete with—NATO capabilities.

Figure 10.2   Two Measures of Net Support For NATO (Fall 1989)

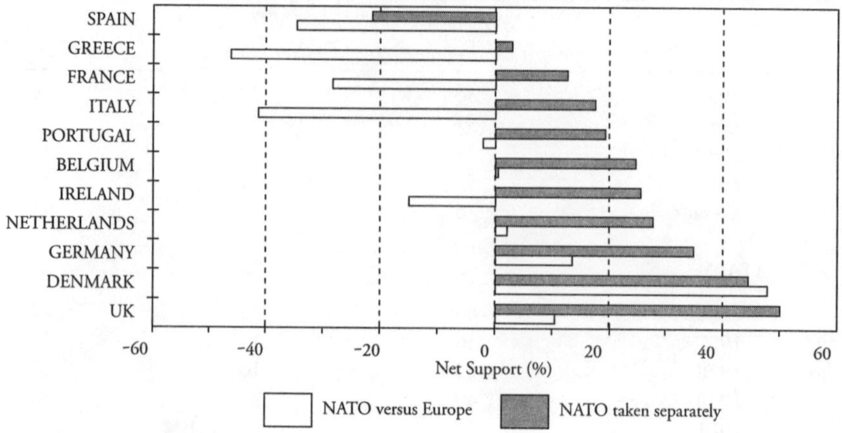

Source: Eurobarometer

This outcome contains some irony, for a fourth event—the signing of the Maastricht Treaty in 1991—had seemed to herald the beginning of a transition to a security order based on further European integration. The Common Foreign and Security Policy was merely the legalistic expression of a notion that rested both on common sense (the changing balance of power) and on a long-held European aspiration. With the end of the Soviet threat, it was not entirely clear that the United States would maintain an interest and presence in European security. First, given an isolationist tradition, budget constraints, and U.S.-European differences of interest and perspective, the opposite was feared. Second, given the potential for American distraction, European institutions offered the principal venue to continue the integration and containment of Germany. Third, the Gulf War and the conflict in Bosnia had reminded Europeans that the failure to act with a single voice reduced their ability to influence the United States. Finally, the crumbling of what the French had called the "Yalta order" offered Paris the opportunity to fulfill the leadership role that it had long sought.

Certainly, public attitudes during the 1990s remained receptive. Figure 10.3 reports the average, European-wide responses to the question of whether policy should be handled by "the national government . . . or jointly within the European Union."[9] Two policy areas are shown: "security and defense," and "foreign policy toward non-EU countries." An average of close to 70 percent of Europeans supports a common foreign policy.[10] This support is stable and long-standing, rooted perhaps in EPC and in the Union's long experience with the diplomatic representation of trade interests and the negotiation of development assistance (the Lomé conventions).

Support for a common security policy, in contrast, is both lower and more vari-

Figure 10.3   Support for Common EU Foreign and Defense Policies

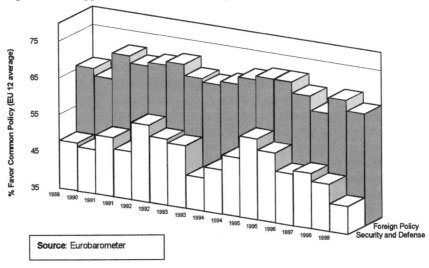

Source: Eurobarometer

able, fluctuating around an average of 47 percent. Indeed, it seems accurate to characterize the support for a common security policy as essentially constant, with the exception of two temporary peaks: the first in 1992, apparently in reaction to the signing of the Maastricht Treaty, and again in 1995, most likely in response to the situation in Bosnia and the Dayton peace accords, which led to a European peacekeeping role. However, it is important to emphasize that these surveys are probably conservative measures of Europeanist sentiments, for they literally force a consideration of the trade-off of sovereignty for integration, a fact that presumably depresses the level of support independent of security policy considerations. Interestingly, in separate polls conducted by the U.S. government in 1998 and 1999, support for a common defense policy is 15–20 points higher in all countries.[11]

However, if we study the individual national trends, a more variegated picture emerges (Table 10.2).[12] First, the overall European averages mask substantial variation among countries. In six countries (the Netherlands, Germany, Belgium, Italy, France, and Spain), there is generally majority support for an integrated defense, and support levels remained higher in the mid-to-late 1990s than they had been before the Maastricht Treaty. In the remaining countries, support is much lower, and in all but Greece and Portugal, Maastricht and the events of the 1990s did not increase support from its earlier level; in fact, generally the opposite occurred. Clearly, Europe has always been polarized on the issue of a common security policy, and the effect of the Maastricht era has been to intensify that polarization. Second, although one must exercise caution due to lack of comparability in question wording, these data on support for defense integration in the 1990s are not dramatically

Table 10.2 Percentage of Europeans Favoring EU-level Policy in Security and Defense

	1985	1989	1990	1991	1992	1993	1994	1995	1996	1997	1998	1999
NETHERLANDS	*64*	63	67	66	70	75	71	77	76	75	71	72
GERMANY	*61*	58	50	53	57	58	59	60	61	62	61	52
BELGIUM	*64*	58	53	63	57	57	56	65	61	54	61	62
ITALY	*71*	56	60	59	69	54	60	64	60	64	59	51
FRANCE	*61*	51	42	46	53	42	51	56	52	54	53	49
SPAIN	*60*	37	40	48	48	43	41	52	50	54	49	45
PORTUGAL	*46*	24	26	41	52	41	38	52	36	33	35	35
UNITED KINGDOM	*51*	39	42	42	41	39	39	42	37	35	34	27
GREECE	*51*	23	31	38	43	33	25	34	33	33	32	17
DENMARK	*55*	33	42	41	45	35	37	40	33	36	30	30
IRELAND	*53*	25	24	29	29	23	26	30	26	28	23	20
EUROBAROMETER	**24**	**32**	**33**	**35/36**	**37/38**	**39/40**	**41/42**	**43/44**	**45**	**47**	**49**	**51**

Note: where two Eurobarometers are displayed, the mean for the two bi-annual surveys is shown. The wording for 1985 is slightly different and thus the results are displayed in italic.

Source: Eurobarometer

higher than those for the 1980s presented earlier, despite a number of events that should have pushed opinion in that direction.

To understand the reason for this unexpected result requires an understanding of the policy debates that accompanied the end of the Cold War in Europe (Art 1996; Gordon 1997). Three distinct national positions emerged. Not surprising given its history and what we have seen here, France emerged as the most clear proponent of a truly European security position, motivated primarily but not exclusively by its goal of containing Germany by furthering German integration in the European Union. Britain, in contrast, continued to favor the primacy of NATO, motivated primarily but not exclusively by its antifederalist animus and by its desire to preserve the American commitment to NATO as the primary means for balancing Germany.

Germany was forced to want it both ways. It strongly supported European integration, including the common security policy, as a means to reassure its very nervous neighbors and to meet the expectations of the French. Nonetheless, perhaps for some of the very same reasons, Germany also continued to assert the importance and even primacy of NATO. Robert Art's characterization of the German situation perfectly captures the state of the European security debate in the early 1990s:

> Therefore, with the French trying to "Gulliverize" Germany, with the British trying to balance against it, with the other states of Europe warily watching it, and with its citizens having their own concerns about their future, Kohl strongly supported the creation of a meaningful European Defense Identity and the preservation of a strong NATO. The close Franco-German relationship was, after all, the core of a peaceful and prosperous Europe. But the NATO alliance was the bedrock of Germany's security and the ultimate key to the rest of Europe's reluctant acceptance of its unification. Kohl wanted to lock Germany into both institutions while he still retained power. (Art 1996, 25)

This is precisely the outcome that occurred: the Maastricht Treaty institutionalized, for the first time, a common security policy and European Defense Identity (EDI)—a victory for the French. However, in a series of negotiations that resulted in NATO'S Berlin communiqué, the relevance and primacy of NATO were also acknowledged—a victory for the British and Germans. Thus was a hybrid security structure formed: the European Defense Identity would exist, but only within the structure of NATO. The military capabilities of the EDI would also be "separable but not separate" from NATO's.[13]

This was a satisfying result for the Americans. In fact, if we are to explain why European public opinion, as well as government policy, did not emerge from the end of the Cold War in a groundswell of support for a purely European defense policy, then at least one major answer must be found in the fact that, far from becoming distracted from European security concerns, successive American governments reacted to the end of the Cold War by recommitting the United States to the preservation of the European balance of power (see Art 1996, 10–12, for an account of American considerations and deliberations). In so doing, the United States in effect continued to offer the option that had long formed the consensus opinion in Europe: a strong European policy but one anchored in partnership with the United States. As had been true throughout the trying controversies of the 1980s, in the 1990s abstract support for European initiatives (or for French aspirations to lead those initiatives) gave way to the practical need to secure American assistance both to provide additional reassurance about the unification of Germany and to contribute to a defense burden that is under budgetary pressure.

In any case, the evidence is that European public opinion fully agrees with the contours of these compromises. Table 10.3 displays the evolution of support for NATO and for a common European defense (that is, the percentage of people who think NATO is essential and the percent supporting an integrated EU security policy). The most obvious fact in the table is the nearly unchanged pattern of British opinion: in 1998, as in 1990, British opinion is overwhelmingly Atlanticist, and the effect of Maastricht has been a reaction in which the already low Europeanist sentiment declined even farther.

In France, the NATO and Europeanist trends appear almost to compete with each other. In the early aftermath of Maastricht, the Europeanists in France increased, but the pro-NATO sentiment also increased as events in Bosnia highlighted the Alliance's "essentiality." In any event, during the 1990s, French support for NATO has generally been higher than the historical average (about 43 percent), and by 1998 French opinion seemed fully compatible with the NATO compromise of an enhanced European pillar within NATO. On balance, the decade has left the

Table 10.3 Support for NATO and Common Defense Policy Compared

	France			*UK*			*Germany*	
	NATO is Essential %	*Favor EU-level Defense* %		*NATO is Essential* %	*Favor EU-level Defense* %		*NATO is Essential* %	*Favor EU-level Defense* %
1989	41	51	1989	67	39	1989	59	58
1990	50	42	1990	60	42	1990	53	50
1991	57	46	1991	71	42	1991	66	53
1992	52	53	1992	65	41	1992	65	57
1993	61	42	1993	73	39	1993	67	58
1994	58	51	1994	66	39	1994	76	59
1995	68	56	1995	78	42	1995	76	60
1996	54	52	1996	71	37	1996	69	61
1997	54	54	1997	68	35	1997	60	62
1998	50	53	1998	67	34	1998	60	61

Note: The table shows the (separate) responses to two questions: Is NATO "essential"? (see Table 10.1 above), and the percentage of respondents who respond that "security and defense" should be handled at the EU level rather than the national level (see Table 10.3 above).
Source: Eurobarometer

French more, rather than less, Atlanticist than had been the case in the 1970s and 1980s.

The opposite is true of Germany, although by 1998 its opinion profile looks very much like that of France. With the exception of the Bosnia period, German support for NATO in the 1990s is in fact much lower than its prior average (76 percent), while support for the EU's common security policy has slowly but noticeably grown to about 60 percent. In the end, however, there is approximately equal support for an essential NATO and an EU role in security. However, it may be a source of concern for the Alliance that, unlike the French, Germans arrived at this position as a result of a declining sense of support for NATO. That concern would be allayed to some extent by the strong support in Germany for the air war in Serbia, but it is also worth noting that Chancellor Gerhard Schroeder strongly endorsed the Europeanist proposals of the French.

Before turning to the implications of these surveys, it is useful to compare the patterns revealed in these questions on support for NATO versus support for the European Defense Identity to more specific polls that gauge citizens' confidence in these institutions' comparative defense capabilities. The importance of such a comparison arises out of a common finding that emerged from research on public opinion and security policy in the 1970s and 1980s: citizen support for alliance structures and international institutions contains a substantial "diffuse," or affective, element that captures their sense of common values and identification in addition to assessments of security policy choices (Eichenberg 1989; Risse-Kappen 1991). Thus, to inquire of citizen assessments of NATO's "essentiality" is in part to inquire of a sense of identification with the values and interests of the North Atlantic community. Similarly, to ask Europeans of their support for an integrated security policy is in part to inquire of their support for the process of European integration as well as their identification with the values and norms of the European Union.

There is an interesting approach in U.S. Information Agency surveys that allows us to assess citizen attitudes when this more concrete consideration is raised. Table 10.4 summarizes the results of two questions posed in U.S. government polls in Europe. Each question asks respondents: "How much confidence do you have in the following institutions to deal effectively with European problems . . . NATO . . . the EU?" The responses to the NATO question show substantial majority confidence in all three countries both before and after the crisis in Bosnia. However, if we examine net confidence, a familiar picture emerges. In Britain, net confidence in NATO is high and stable. In France, net confidence grew during the Bosnia period as doubts about NATO's effectiveness receded, confirming the trends reviewed earlier that showed an Atlanticizing France. Finally, although we must be careful because of the small number of surveys in this table, the German responses confirmed a pattern reviewed earlier: confidence in NATO appeared to be declining at this point in time.

Notice also that it is only in France that net confidence in the EU exceeds net confidence in NATO (the second question in Table 10.4), although by 1998 Ger-

Table 10.4   Confidence in the Effectiveness of NATO and of the EU

	Confidence in NATO			Confidence in EU		
	Have Confidence	*Lack Confidence*	*Net Confidence*	*Have Confidence*	*Lack Confidence*	*Net Confidence*
FRANCE						
1994	62%	35%	27%	65%	31%	34%
1996	67	29	38	78	21	57
1998	67	27	40	73	24	49
GERMANY						
1994	69	27	42	56	38	18
1996	62	36	26	55	42	13
1998	55	33	22	54	37	17
UK						
1994	74	21	53	49	41	8
1996	78	20	58	53	43	10
1998	72	14	58	52	34	18

Note: These are two separate questions. They inquire "how much confidence do you have in the following institutions to deal effectively with European problems . . . NATO? . . . the EU??"
Source: USIA (1996, 7–8; 1998, 1)

man confidence in NATO had declined to levels that more closely approximated the level of confidence in the EU. In Germany and Britain, confidence in the EU is at a majority level, but lack of confidence is almost equally high. On balance, then, the picture that emerges from public opinion represents a fairly accurate reflection of the actions taken by governments during the 1990s. In France, a surge of enthusiasm for common European positions was nonetheless accompanied by growth in the endorsement of NATO's role. The United Kingdom, in contrast, has remained committed to the primacy of NATO. And Germany remains in the middle: still committed to NATO, but with some evidence that Atlanticist sentiment is eroding as support for the Europeanist position increases. The interesting question for the future, of course, is whether the war in Yugoslavia at the end of the decade substantially altered these patterns.

SUMMARY AND CONCLUSION: THE WAR AGAINST YUGOSLAVIA AND THE FUTURE OF EUROPEAN SECURITY

It is difficult to avoid the conclusion that Europeans today want a common security policy only slightly more than they ever did. In the abstract, there is now support for the general notion of a common approach to security policy in a substantial number of EU member states, but it is not clear that these levels of support represent a dramatic increase over levels that existed in the past. In the mid-1980s (Figure 10.1) and throughout the 1990s (Table 10.2), support for the European defense pillar increased. However, with the exception of scattered evidence for the turbulent period surrounding the events of 1989, there is little evidence that this abstract support for Europe came at the expense of support for NATO. Indeed, in France, support for NATO has actually increased over earlier periods.

In fact, the compromise reached by NATO governments—a European Defense Identity that will operate in tandem with NATO—seems on the evidence to be the preferred option of Europeans. One might argue that this option differs in emphasis from NATO's long-standing structure, but it is not entirely clear that it differs in substance. As the war against Yugoslavia demonstrated, substantial military actions require the intelligence, logistics, and military assets of the United States, and with this predominance comes a primary voice in the planning and execution of military missions.[14]

Of course, this conclusion must be qualified by the substantial—even radical—change that has occurred in the institutional structure of European security. Most important, in the space of eight years since the Maastricht Treaty, the EU: institutionalized a Common Policy on Security and Defense and designated the West European Union as its agent; appointed a "High Representative," who is both the head of the WEU and a senior official in the European Council; and agreed to the creation of a substantial Common Defense Force, along with specific logistical and force goals to support it. As Philip Gordon (1997) noted, the sheer level, detail, and depth of these initiatives represent a degree of integration that would have been impossible when EPC began in 1970.

These are significant developments, mostly because Europe may now theoretically undertake separate security initiatives in the name of Europe rather than NATO. As we have seen, this hybrid structure largely mirrors the state of popular consensus over the last several decades, an important point given the attentiveness of EU elites to domestic consensus. Europeans have long supported an independent EU security policy, but its implementation foundered on the practical requirement of preserving NATO. Now the two have been reconciled in a form that meets practical realities and citizen consensus at once.

Finally, the war against forces in the former Yugoslavia clearly reinforced the movement of elite action toward the popular opinion consensus that has always existed. The major question is whether this movement will be temporary or permanent. For example, during the Persian Gulf crisis in the Fall of 1990, an overwhelming majority (70–80 percent) of Europeans in all member states except Britain and Denmark agreed that to deal effectively with such crises the EU should "form a common defense organization"—but that sentiment was not translated by governments into a strong EU commitment. As we have seen (Figure 10.3), similar sentiments were strong during the subsequent Bosnia crisis, but ultimately the latter experience seemed to reinforce elite perceptions of the need for NATO—or at least for the coexistence of NATO and the EDI. Tellingly, when asked during the first month of the air war against Serbia if "Europe should develop a new defence and peacekeeping force consisting only of European troops, to replace NATO," an average of only 36 percent in NATO countries supported the proposal; only in France (57 percent) and Italy (58 percent) did the proposal attract majority support. In March and April 1999, Europeans were again asked if "security and defense" should be conducted at the EU level or by national governments (see Table 10.2), and this time support for an EU policy declined slightly compared to the prewar level.[15] It is worth noting, however, that this poll was taken before the EU issued its Cologne and Helsinki decisions. To that point, of course, NATO had dominated public perceptions of the actions against Serbia. Should the EU in fact undertake the rationalizations and investments envisioned under the Helsinki decisions, public opinion will likely respond favorably. In short, European leaders are acting in a way that has long been consistent with domestic opinion.

Nonetheless, problems may also emerge. The ability of European governments to fund the necessary infrastructure and logistical capabilities is potentially the most intractable. For example, the Cologne declaration commits the EU to providing "the necessary means and capabilities to assume its responsibilities" and to "the capacity of autonomous action, backed up by credible military forces," including "notably the reinforcement of our capabilities in the field of intelligence, strategic transport, and command and control" (Presidency Conclusions, Cologne Summit, Annex III, paragraphs 1 and 2). Increased defense spending will be necessary.

Yet when asked during the war against Serbia how much "their country" should be spending on defense, the percentage in Europe who responded "spend more" ranged from 8 percent in Germany to 21 percent in the United Kingdom (Angus Reid Group 1999, chart 3). As in the past, then, the European aspiration to autonomous action appears unmatched by a willingness to pay for it, and this political consideration will surely be further complicated by the need for cautious budgetary policies to ensure the successful management of Economic and Monetary Union and the Euro.[16]

In addition, the ability of NATO and the EU to coordinate planning and action in the presence of conflicting national perspectives and priorities is likely to be sorely tried. In both the Gulf War and the war against former Yugoslavia, for example, there were substantial differences among Europeans on the question of just how and how much military force should be deployed. Moreover, the problems that may emerge from the expansion of both the NATO alliance and the EU present new challenges to the security architecture. Finally, the apparent change in the balance of German opinion will no doubt attract increasing attention and concern.

To judge from the historical patterns described here, however, the most likely source of disruption to the stability of public consensus will be the actions of the United States. Many of the inflection points in European opinion (as in European policy) on security issues occur in reaction to American actions. As the Cold War came to an end, several scholars predicted that a withdrawal of both the United

States and the Soviet Union from Europe could lead to a historical regression in which European peace and prosperity would be lost as its societies descended once again into balance-of-power politics (Art 1996 and Mearsheimer 1990 provide useful overviews of the arguments).

We do not know if that prediction was correct, precisely because the United States did not abandon its European commitment. However, we may yet have the occasion to evaluate the prediction. Although the United States and the EU have reached a modus vivendi as a result of the June 1996 NATO summit and the joint operations in Bosnia and Kosovo, the compromise has yet to be severely tested. It does not take a gloomy pessimist to point out that a dramatic catastrophe in the Balkans or an extended burden-sharing debate may yet test the resilience of American commitment to Europe.[17] Moreover, given the domestic climate in the United States, it seems unlikely that there will be a warm welcome to the increasingly Gaullist tone of European rhetoric.

Thus, whether the United States will maintain a robust commitment to NATO remains an open question. In any case, the crucial question—admittedly a hypothetical one—is how Europeans will react in the absence of an American commitment to provide the security structure that is most preferable to Europe. For fifty years, the crucial question has not been how Europeans react when the Americans are present in Europe; the key question is how they will react if the Americans leave.

Two theoretical views are relevant to this question. The first, represented by the analyses of Robert Art and John Mearsheimer cited above, is that Europe may very well descend into renewed security competition. In this view, the peace and prosperity provided by European unity will be no protection from the primordial fears of insecurity. Indeed, in this view, European prosperity and integration were themselves the result of a stable peace rather than its cause.

The opposite view is that European unity in the field of external relations was in fact hindered by the Cold War structure and the continued commitment of the United States. Put bluntly, the presence of the United States provided the luxury of disunity, especially in the security field. Should the United States ever truly abandon or even severely weaken its security commitment to Europe, then the incremental progress toward security integration would in fact pick up steam. The same might occur were Europe's episodic irritation with the United States to be replaced by a profound alienation.

The evidence presented here cannot, of course, provide a conclusive test of these competing notions, but a tentative assessment is that on balance it tends to favor the latter view—at least as concerns citizen attitudes. As we have seen, European public opinion has always favored the abstract notion of common security policies, but that consensus has never been rewarded with a real European alternative. Now that Europe has announced the intention to progress toward a truly common defense policy, the evidence presented here suggests that public opinion (in most of Europe) will not be an obstacle. Whether European leaders are ready for a common security policy is something we do not know, but we do know that the citizens of Europe appear somewhat more ready for it.

11

Public Opinion after the Cold War
A Paradigm Shift

Philip Everts

The end of the Cold War clearly was a watershed and had enormous, obvious benefits, including a fundamental liberation in Eastern Europe, the unification of Germany, the reduction if not the total elimination of the danger of nuclear war in Europe, as well as major reductions in armaments and military expenditures.

Another consequence of the end of the Cold War and the increased pace of European integration is that the problem of war and peace, at least in Western industrialized societies, has fundamentally changed. A basically stable, albeit inherently dangerous, bipolar situation of mutual nuclear deterrence was replaced by a much more complex and apparently unstable system. Specific dangers have been replaced by diffuse risks entailing a variety of possible uses of the military and of armed force. Conflicts have become manifold and primarily intrastate in character. Individuals were or are being killed in these conflicts, which have yet to threaten the system as a whole. In the recent past, the peace-through-deterrence system was predicated on the willingness to run enormous risks and to kill millions in revenge for an attack. Now, at least in the West, governments fearing a domestic backlash have become risk-avoiders, and they have almost totally renounced the willingness to actually use military force, except when the risks are minimal. The conflict between NATO and Serbia over Kosovo during 1998–1999 is the most recent and obvious example. Rather than counting on traditional balance-of-power arguments and acting according to realist reflexes in the pursuit of stability, governments (again, at least in Europe) are relying increasingly on the thesis of democratic peace that has received so much attention in recent years. Still groping with the processes of change, the NATO alliance is, for the first time, taking seriously its character as an alliance of democracies. Consequently, it is accompanying its shift from an organization for collective defense to one for collective security with the extension of its membership to applicants that are also democracies. Unlike in the past, when the realist argument usually prevailed (i.e., that Great Powers are potential troublemakers, whatever their domestic regimes), the emphasis today is put on the notion that Russia can also become an ally once it has become a stable democracy. However, the usefulness of the democratic-peace thesis may have outlived itself and is perhaps less relevant in a situation where interstate wars have become far less likely and less frequent compared to forms of violent intrastate conflicts erupting for reasons other than the spread of democracy.

Moreover, national interests, which traditionally have provided the justification for use of military force, usually appeared self-evident for most people in the Cold War. This seems to be much less so in the case of traditional interstate conflicts, when armed forces are used for purposes of peacekeeping or peace enforcement in an international context. In these cases, the national interest is often not at all immediately evident.

MASS-OPINION STABILITY AS AN ARTIFACT?

This chapter examines the extent to which the changes just described have been reflected in changes in peoples' attitudes, opinions, and political preferences. In this context, the end of the Cold War has brought with it other, unexpected benefits. One is that it offers an almost ideal context in which to explore the more general issue of how peoples' attitudes are affected by major changes in their environment.

It has been argued convincingly since the 1980s, contrary to earlier studies, that the public is "rational," "prudent," and meaningful in the foreign policy process (Holsti 1992, 1996; Holsti and Rosenau 1984; Oldendick and Bardes 1982; Page and Shapiro 1988, 1992; Russett 1990; Wittkopf 1990). Its stability over time has been stressed time and again (Kaase and Newton 1995; Isernia 1996; Oreglia 1997).

Contrary to earlier conclusions based primarily on the study of the opinion-policy connection in the Cold War context, these "revisionist" results stress that public opinion should be taken into account in explaining foreign policy. The stability that was found may therefore have been an artifact of a basically stable international situation and the fairly straightforward nature of the problems of war and peace at the time. Hence, it would not be surprising if opinion stability did not survive the watershed of 1989 and was instead characteristic of the opinion climate in the more uncertain circumstances of the new international situation. Yet we would be on much safer ground if the stability had survived beyond the end of the Cold War. So far, this hypothesis has not been tested thoroughly or crossnationally. An earlier effort was made to look into the changes affected by the events of 1989 (Manigart 1992), but it ended not very successfully because of the lack of distance from the events and the lack of relevant data at the time. Remarkably, since then there has not been any significant effort to fill this gap.

The new orthodoxy should, however, perhaps be considered with equal skepticism as the earlier consensus on the volatility of public opinion. Where stability has become the rule, one can be concerned in normative terms with the extent to which it presents an obstacle to desirable adaptations to changed international circumstances (as illustrated, e.g., by the cases of Israel, with its traditional reliance on the realist perspective, and Ireland, accustomed to a perhaps outdated policy of neutrality). Sometimes, one is confronted with undesirable policy consequences of too much stability for the foreign and defense policies of several countries. Stability, moreover, is but one criterion by which one should judge the quality of public opinion. It should not be confused with other characteristics, including knowledge, ability, consistency, and rationality.

CURRENT LIMITATIONS IN OUR UNDERSTANDING

There are clear limitations to our understanding of the nature, content, and impact of public opinion and its evolution over time. First, for a variety of reasons, much of the evidence (at least with respect to continuity and structure) comes from studies of American public opinion. Less abundant, even if more recent, attention has been devoted to European publics (e.g., Eichenberg 1989; Everts 1992, 1996a; Isernia 1996; Flynn and Rattinger 1985; Niedermayer and Sinnott 1995; Manigart 1992; Rattinger 1996). While European studies on this question tend to support American findings, a lack of comparability across nations and across time poses severe limitations to our understanding and the ability to generalize from our findings.

Second, theoretically, the focus on public opinion in a presidential system (as in the U.S. case) tends to overlook the more diffuse and different roles public opinion might play in European parliamentary, multiparty systems, with strong parties that shape and mediate the connection between mass opinion and foreign policy. In view of this, one shortcoming in public-opinion research, particularly research on the opinion-policy relationship, is the inadequate treatment of the various ways in which public opinion enters the political process, either actively or passively (i.e., in the form of perceptions by decisionmakers). There may be obvious reasons (including the wish to be as "objective" as possible) why public opinion is for all intents and purposes equated with "unstructured" and "nonorganized" opinion that is measured by mass surveys. Nevertheless, to understand the opinion-policy relationship one must examine and take into account a more diffuse concept of public opinion, that is, one that includes public opinion as organized and structured by and through political actors, groups, and organizations (Everts 1983, 1996a).

THE ROLE OF THE MILITARY AND THE USE OF MILITARY FORCE: STABILITY OR CHANGE?

Regardless, we need to understand more fully the impact of the end of the Cold War on international attitudes. There are strong indications of continuing stability in many areas—but also of rapid and often considerable change in other respects. This is, of course, most evident in the former communist countries, but Western democracies also seem to be heavily affected, especially in their conceptualizations of war and the conditions justifying use of military force (Isernia and Bellucci 1998; La Balme 1998; Van der Meulen and De Konink 1998).

As for changes in the role of military force and its support by the public, it is a matter of dispute with considerable implications for politicians, military professionals, and policy analysts, regardless of whether the changes in the international situation justify or even necessitate an entirely new perspective or whether traditional views still suffice.

Thus it is often argued—but not yet convincingly—that the willingness to use military force and sustain casualties has become very much constrained, especially when national interests are not immediately involved, as in the case of international peacekeeping operations. One can thus identify a growing neopacifism. In particular, the so-called casualty, or body-bag, hypothesis has become a topic of intense debate. Supporters of this hypothesis argue that while publics often force their governments to act forcefully internationally—for example, when the media report on brutal violations of human rights—they recoil at the prospect of casualties if military force is actually used. In fact, the conventional wisdom, brought forward in the media and parliaments, accepts this hypothesis as if it were an indisputable fact. This is done, however, on the basis of a particular, but often mistaken, reading of recent history (Kull and Destler 1999). Thus, we see the often paraphrased assumption that the West refrained from powerful military intervention (i.e., use of ground forces) in the former Yugoslavia because public opinion would not accept the risk of possible casualties (Everts 1996a, 1998b, 1998a; Sobel 1996b). This alleged shift in thinking also stimulated the development of the so-called zero-dead doctrine, which was applied to the Kosovo conflict. Yet with respect to the casualty hypothesis, it has also been argued that its operation is to some extent the result of a self-fulfilling prophecy; politicians use it as an alibi to avoid taking their responsibilities seriously (Everts 1996a, 1998a, 1999).

One way or another, the casualty hypothesis does have considerable impact on decisionmaking, as the case of Kosovo demonstrated most forcefully in 1999.

EVIDENCE FROM THE NETHERLANDS

The evidence analyzed in this chapter illuminates the thesis that the end of the Cold War carries fundamental implications for public opinion on international peace and security. I analyze data on mass opinion and also look at the structure of public opinion and the larger political process, which includes what I refer to as "structured public opinion" and the role of the media that express and shape the climate of opinion and the salience of issues. Evidence is drawn mainly from the case of the Netherlands, but comparisons with other countries will be included.

Apart from the regular Eurobarometer surveys and a few exceptions, public-opinion research in the Netherlands has thus far lacked the continuity and consistency necessary to test seriously the proposition that popular world images and public preferences have been strongly affected (or not at all) by the end of the Cold War. Most surveys are sponsored by private groups, particularly the media, which are interested primarily in the topicality and publicity value of particular issues and not the question of continuity. Polls are usually of the single-shot variety; little, if any, effort is made to trace the evolution of attitudes and opinions over time. Thus, for the post-1989 period, we find many clusters of data on such topics as German unification (1989–1990), the Gulf War (1990–1991), and the conflicts in the former Yugoslavia (1992–1995) (see Everts 1992, 1993a, 1994a, 1996a). Indeed, the number of polls itself could be taken as a useful indicator of societal salience. In any event, we have to make do with what is available.[1]

Looking at the available polling data on defense matters, one is struck first by the degree of continuity and stability of attitudes. To give one example: Since the early 1960s, the degree to which the armed forces are seen as either superfluous, necessary, or a necessary evil has been regularly polled; with small fluctuations, the numbers expressing one of the two latter views have always been around 70–80 percent. Over time there has been a slight decrease of some 10 percentage points (see Figure 11.1).[2] It is remarkable, though, that the change from a pattern of stability to one of apparent uncertainty, and (modestly) from very high to high levels of belief, does not coincide with the end of the Cold War but preceded it by several years, having already started in the mid-1980s.

This is noteworthy when one takes into account the factors briefly touched upon

Figure 11.1 Necessity of the Armed Forces, the Netherlands 1963–1997

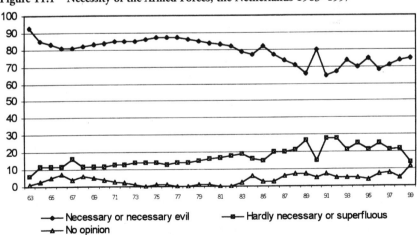

Source: Stichting Maatschappij en Krijgsmacht, The Hague

above. Testifying to the stability of defense attitudes is their correlation with the traditional left-right distinction. Although there has been a discursive shift away from the debate between pacifists and militarists toward one between neointerventionists and neopacifists—which transcends the traditional left-right distinction—it is generally true that the more leftist one is, the less likely one is to agree with the necessity of having a military.

The end of the Cold War failed to affect to any degree not only the views on the self-evident necessity of armed forces but also the images of the Dutch and their self-identity. The absolute figures are less striking here than the relative stability. Neither the belief that armies are indispensable, nor the idea that national armies should be replaced by an international, Western European force, changed in those years of shifting paradigms of international politics. In absolute terms, it is remarkable that so many still thought that armies were as necessary as ever, even if the time of national armies had perhaps gone (Table 11.1).

Likewise, during these years neither the strength of national identity ("I feel more European than Dutch"), nor the view that "Fatherland is an outdated word," changed. Another indication of stability rather than change can be found in data on preferences concerning the military budget (see Table 11.2). Respondents were asked to state whether defense expenditures should be cut much more than other government expenditures. Relative levels of support for defense were calculated by subtracting the number of supporters from opponents, then adjusting the scores to a range between 0 and 1. We see that the figure for 1989 is the only exception to an otherwise stable pattern in which proponents and opponents of more-than-average reductions (i.e., compared with other departments of government) more or less balanced each other. At each moment of time about as many wanted increased expenditure

Table 11.1   The Support for the Armed Forces (in percent)

	1)			2)			3)		
	1989	1990	1991	1989	1990	1991	1989	1990	1991
Agree completely	5	6	4	19	38	23	36	47	33
Agree	10	6	9	43	28	34			
Neither agree nor disagree	20	18	20	12	12	14	25	22	26
Disagree	48	47	48	15	14	18			
Disagree completely	15	24	27	9	8	8	36	30	36
Don't know/no answer	2	—	3	2	—	2			

Question wording:
1) "Armies are something of the past"
2) "I cannot imagine a country without armed forces"
3) "Instead of every country having its own army it would be better to have one West European army"
Source: NIPO for Stichting Maatschappij en Krijgsmacht

Table 11.2   Average Preferred Reductions in the Military Budget (the Netherlands, 1982–1998)

1982	.59
1983	.56
1985	.57
1986	.59
1988	.63
1989	.69
1998	.59

Source: Data from Stichting Maatschappij en Krijgsmacht

as preferred reductions. There was only a slight tendency for sympathy with reductions to increase somewhat over time.

These figures refer not to absolute but to relative preferences compared to other categories of government expenditures. Thus, for instance, the figure for 1998 refers to a budget which in real terms was roughly 25 percent lower than that of ten years earlier. In 1998, the argument that preference should be given to other societal goals was felt to be the strongest one for reductions, at least stronger than the ones that there are no more military threats or that the Netherlands could not afford armed forces consisting of an army, air force, and navy.[3]

Another indicator of strong continuity (as in other European countries) is the attitudes toward membership in NATO. In the Netherlands, support for NATO membership has sometimes fluctuated, especially in the years when the United States was unpopular because of the Vietnam War, but since then support has remained high and stable (see Everts 1995). NATO membership has never been opposed by more than 20 percent and—like the organization itself—support for NATO easily survived the end of the Cold War. A poll conducted in September 1998 showed almost universal support for NATO membership, with 81 percent in favor and only 3 percent opposed.[4] As puzzling as it has appeared to many in the NATO bureaucracy over the years, this has never meant that NATO policies or strategy found the same general support (Flynn and Rattinger 1985). Indeed, the opposite was the case. Throughout NATO's history—and not only during the height of protest against nuclear weapons in the early 1980s—some 40 percent consistently (with possible exceptions due to question wording) rejected not only the use but also the possession of nuclear weapons for deterrence. This did not change as the 1990s ended. While a majority (54 percent) in October 1998 still accepted a role for the possession of nuclear weapons, 46 percent wanted NATO to get rid of such weapons, whereas 43 percent felt that the Netherlands should abandon its last remaining nuclear assignment (i.e., air-delivered weapons).[5]

The situation in the Netherlands is not unique, as there is no evidence that the armed forces have become less popular or trustworthy in Great Britain, France, and Germany. Comparing data from 1981, 1990, and 1997, two patterns emerge.[6] In the Netherlands, France, and Germany, confidence declined from 1981 to 1990 but rose again by 1997 (caused, we assume, by the end of the Cold War). Between 1990 and 1997, France witnessed an increase from 55 percent to 73 percent,[7] Germany from 40 percent to 71 percent, and the Netherlands from 32 percent to 56 percent. While the Netherlands scored lowest here, none of the data supports the thesis of a general decrease in legitimacy. It is unclear whether the increased trust has been caused by attitudinal changes in society or, for instance, by the perceived performance of the armed forces in particular tasks. The restoration of confidence remained less than in Great Britain, however. Confidence in the military in Britain remained unchanged from 1981. Indeed, in all three years for which data are available, around 80 percent expressed much confidence in the British armed forces.

There is a general and positive correlation, however, between the confidence expressed in the execution of specific tasks and the priority given to that task. In this respect, the content of legitimacy has apparently changed rather smoothly. The shift in focus with respect to the functions of the armed forces has been accepted quickly by public opinion. In the Netherlands, humanitarian tasks are now seen as relatively important and as a source of confidence, while crisis management enjoys little priority and support. Similar acceptance of the "new" functions of the armed forces is evident in Italy (Isernia and Bellucci 1998). The shift is illustrated in Table 11.3.

Over the years, sizable and stable majorities in the Netherlands have supported participation in international peacekeeping, in spite of the dishonorable defeat of the Dutch contingent in 1995 in the Srebrenica enclave, where thousands of Yugoslav Muslims had to be abandoned and were killed by Serb forces (Everts 1996a). Neither the experience itself nor the very critical reports and evaluations that have appeared since 1995 have led to a more negative assessment of the extent to which the Dutch presence was useful (see Table 11.4; Van der Meulen 1998).

Similar levels of support of the new kind of military operations can be recorded in other European countries, such as Great Britain, France, Germany, and Italy.

At the end of 1997, respondents in the Netherlands, Germany, Great Britain, and France were asked a similar set of questions. There was much agreement concerning the participation in the international military actions in Bosnia. A sizable minority in each of these countries wanted to continue the operation of the NATO-led Implementation force (IFOR) in Bosnia "in any case," whereas sizable percent-

Table 11.3   What should be the most important task of the military? (in percent)

	1993	1994	1996	1998
Defense of national and allied territory	40	35	27	20
Worldwide crisis management	21	38	20	39
Humanitarian aid	35	21	43	36
Don't know/no answer	4	6	10	5

Source: NIPO for SMK, The Hague, 1993–98

Table 11.4 Was the Presence in Srebrenica Useful? (in percent)

	1995	1996	1998
Very much so	18	12	13
Somewhat	41	37	39
A little bit	11	15	15
Hardly useful	10	14	11
Not useful at all	4	10	8
Don't know/no answer	17	11	14

Source: NIPO for SMK, The Hague, 1995–1998

ages also wanted to do so only if the Americans or the British and the French continued to do so as well. This sentiment was expressed most forcefully in the Netherlands, whereas Germans were relatively skeptical (see Figure 11.2).

The fact that few rejected this mission outright shows the extent to which the legitimacy of the new tasks of the armed forces had grown and become an uncontested phenomenon.

This did not, however, imply that the legitimacy of the traditional task diminished. This was particularly the case in France and Great Britain, where most respondents felt the defense of one's own and allied territory to be the most important task of the armed forces. In the Netherlands, however, national defense came in only third place, after crisis management and humanitarian actions. The latter neverthe-

Figure 11.2 Contribute Troops for SFOR Mission in Bosnia

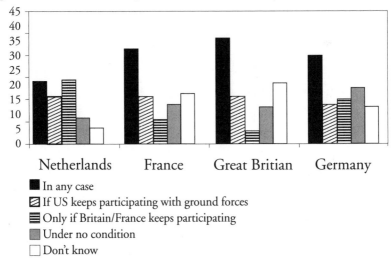

■ In any case
▨ If US keeps participating with ground forces
☰ Only if Britain/France keeps participating
▦ Under no condition
☐ Don't know

Source: Stichting Maatschappij en Krijgsmacht, The Hague

less found widespread acceptance, with around 25 percent considering it to be the most important task. The most remarkable exception was Germany, where humanitarian action was felt to be the most important task (42 percent).[8] With the exception of the Netherlands, crisis management came in third, with fewer than 20 percent citing it as most important (see Figure 11.3).[9]

These are not abstract theoretical matters and answers, as evidenced by widespread public support for the actions undertaken by NATO in the Spring of 1999 inspired by the humanitarian disaster in Kosovo.[10]

In the Netherlands, the existence of strong support for NATO air bombardment and the participation of the Netherlands, including the willingness to incur casualties in this context, had already been shown in October 1998.[11] Although many were undecided at the time, a near majority (47 percent) favored air attacks, while 54 percent favored participation by the Netherlands; 84 percent said that this should happen even if casualties among Dutch soldiers would be incurred.

When the attacks actually began, general support did in fact materialize (Everts 1999). Majority support of the actions at the beginning and after two weeks showed up in a poll that asked, "For two weeks, NATO has carried out air attacks against Yugoslav territory. When you think back two weeks ago: Did you then agree or disagree with bombing of Yugoslavia?"; and "For two days, air attacks on Yugoslavia have been intensified. How do you feel about these attacks today?"[12] With respect to the first question, 64 percent expressed support for the attacks, and 57 percent indicated support in the second. In the same poll, 47 percent expressed support for

Figure 11.3   Most Important Task for the Armed Forces

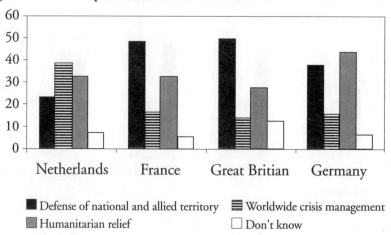

Source: Stichting Maatschappij en Krijgsmacht, The Hague

Source: Stichting Maatschappij en Krijgsmact; The Hague

ground attacks, and 58 percent supported participation by the Netherlands in such attacks. In two other polls (at the end of March and mid-April), 78 percent expressed support for the military actions against Serbia, even though (in the second poll) 51 percent feared that events in Yugoslavia increased the likelihood of world war and 43 percent felt that the war could not be won without sending in ground forces.[13]

These outcomes were confirmed in another poll held in April 1999 in which 43 percent said the decision to take military action against Yugoslavia had been "totally right" and 35 percent said "rather right." Only 10 percent opposed the action. Seventy-one percent agreed that the violation of human rights was the most important motive to take action,[14] and 68 percent again agreed that the Netherlands should continue to participate in actions even if Dutch soldiers would be killed during the operation.

THE QUESTION OF SALIENCY

For public opinion to have an impact on an issue, the issue must be salient to the people. For instance, when attitudes are latent and become activated only when pollsters ask, issues are unlikely to significantly influence political actions. It is thus a normative matter whether policymakers should give much attention to these views. In an opinion climate where the silent majority stays at home, vocal and committed minorities may come to play a major role in influencing government decisions. It is therefore vitally important not only to know what people think but also how relevant certain issues are to them. However, public opinion is a matter of perception, and so saliency is primarily a hypothetical political question and one of mobilization—changing latent opinions into manifest ones. Despite its importance, saliency has received much less attention in research than has the content of opinions. In most conventional polls, including those in the Netherlands, the question of saliency is usually overlooked entirely.

As far as the Netherlands is concerned, there is one exception. Since 1981, involvement with a number of topics has been regularly explored by way of three survey measures: (1) the degree to which people are aware of a particular problem (knowledge); (2) the degree to which an issue is perceived as being talked about (topicality); and (3) the degree to which people are prepared to take action on the basis of a problem (involvement). These data provide useful information on the degree of change or continuity in the political climate. With respect to the issue of armament and disarmament, salience has gradually declined since the height of the nuclear-weapons debate of the early 1980s. The potential willingness to act has diminished by roughly half (see Figure 11.4).

On the related issue of "likelihood of war," the picture is somewhat different. Figure 11.5 shows a declining concern in the 1980s, continuing into the post–Cold War period, but also a remarkable interruption around 1990–1991, during the Gulf

Figure 11.4   Involvement with Problems of Armament and Disarmament, 1981–1996

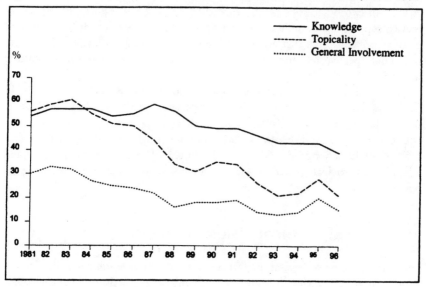

Source: NSS/MDI-marktonderzoek BV

War against Iraq. This is a general (Western European) pattern, as is shown by the results of a regular question in the Eurobarometer (1971–1990).

CHANGES IN THE FOREIGN POLICY CLIMATE

Despite all the evidence pointing to the stability and continuity of attitudes, a perception exists among elite observers that public opinion on foreign affairs has fundamentally changed in recent years. In particular, it has been argued that there have been major changes in the sense that there has been a "return to normalcy" in Dutch foreign policy and that the traditional foreign policy consensus has been restored after a period of strong divisions and contestation (e.g., Pijpers 1996; see Everts 1991 for a survey of the debate). This is said to have happened not only with respect to questions of security (nuclear weapons) but also in the realm of development cooperation and human rights, traditional darlings of the liberal left.

This has become visible already to some degree in Figures 11.4 and 11.5, but it becomes clearer yet if we look beyond the data on nonstructured opinion and focus on structured and organized public opinion, which manifests itself in the form of activities by groups, parties, and other organizations.

In the late 1960s and 1970s, the Netherlands went through a period of increased political participation as well as contestation of the established powers and authori-

Figure 11.5 Involvement with the Problem of War 1981–1996

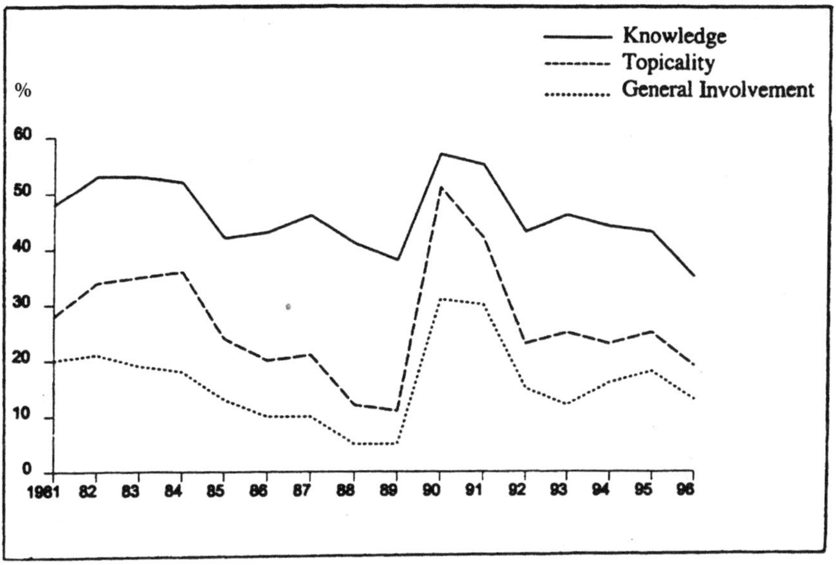

Source: NSS/MDI-marktonderzoek BV

ties. There was a general drive toward the democratization of society. After a while, this also reached foreign affairs. The debates and political struggle over nuclear weapons, largely due to a rapidly growing peace movement, were the most visible part of this general increase in salience and concern. It was, however, not the only area in which more and more people began to organize groups and activities. Involvement also increased in areas such as development assistance and human rights. One source (*Pyttersen's Almanak*) indicates that the number of organizations active in the foreign policy field increased rapidly. In 1950, 1960, 1970, and 1982 there were, respectively, twenty-four, thirty-two, sixty-four, and 174 such organizations.

This process also had political fallout in the form of an increasingly more active parliament, which forced the government—which traditionally enjoyed a permissive consensus—to the defensive. Toward the late 1970s and early 1980s, this culminated when the ruling coalition hardly survived four major crises over foreign policy issues—a very new situation for the Netherlands.

This period of contestation also stimulated new research. When, in the early 1980s, a group of researchers undertook a major study of the role of domestic factors in the foreign policy process, it had no difficulty finding many cases in which specific foreign policy issues had been highly controversial and the object of intense debate and societal activity (Everts 1985). Today, such a study of foreign policy activism would simply be impossible given the lack of such issues. Moreover, not only has this form of involvement disappeared from the political scene; the concomitant ideological debate among the traditional foreign policy elites—of which it was an expression—has also diminished to a fraction of what it used to be.

This development finds a corollary in the changes in the country's ambitions in the realm of foreign policy. In the 1960s and 1970s, governments, in line with societal confidence, tended perhaps to overestimate the degree to which the Netherlands could have international influence, and they did not feel any discomfort in stressing that the Netherlands, though small, could set shining examples for other nations. Some critics spoke condescendingly of "Hollanditis" as a contagious illness. Today, following several international disappointments and setbacks, the assessment of what the country can realize tends toward the other extreme: the Netherlands has no influence, however worthy its motives and brilliant its ideas may be. The country thus suffers from a Calimero complex, that is, a notion that the world is not fair but that the Netherlands is small and that nothing can be done about this state of affairs. Such a political climate does not stimulate societal debate; rather it reinforces apathy and unconcern. Yet there is a striking absence today of the grand debates that took place in the 1970s over such issues as armament and disarmament, changes in the world economic system to breach the gap between North and South, and possibilities of overcoming the East-West conflict.

Apart from the extended debate in the aftermath of the dramatic events in former Yugoslavia and Dutch coresponsibility for the worst massacres in Europe since 1945, there are no contemporary examples of the elite-level debates that took place two and three decades earlier. Therefore, as a result, public opinion at large is also unaffected. Neither the events of 1989 nor such profound changes as the enlargement of NATO, the impending enlargement of the European Union, the adaptation of the armed forces to a no-threat situation, and the introduction of a single currency (the Euro) have led to major debates or organized activities of opponents or supporters. Even the highly controversial aspects of war in Kosovo in 1999 failed, unlike in other countries, to stimulate an elite debate, let alone one involving society at the mass level. This is difficult to understand.

However, it may be a mistake to pose the question in this way. Yet rather than wondering about the absence of salient foreign policy issues today, we should perhaps treat the intense involvement of the 1970s as an exception to the rule of noninvolvement of the general public in distant issues upon which their influence appears minimal.

We may also be misguided by using indicators of involvement which have outlived their usefulness and are therefore no longer adequate. Memberships in international organizations like Amnesty International and Greenpeace, for instance, have remained at the same high levels as in the past. Neither has the willingness of the public to contribute money to international humanitarian actions diminished.

In this connection, also, there is the impact of the neoliberal ideology. If in the 1970s foreign policy attitudes could be neatly arranged along the traditional left-right distinction, today this is less evidently so. The pervasive influence of the neoliberal creed, with its emphasis on a society of calculating individual citizens instead of responsibility toward society as a whole and the concomitant de-emphasis on national and international solidarity, has had major consequences. Not only is politics being individualized, but neoliberalism has also tended to reduce the basis of societal action and the reservoir from which people can be mobilized for causes in which their immediate interests are not directly involved, such as issues of foreign and defense policy.

If one believes that the effectiveness of foreign policy suffers more from too little than from too much societal involvement, whether in the form of organized or unorganized public opinion, this is a cause for serious concern.

THE ROLE OF THE MEDIA

The notion that public opinion plays a role in the foreign policy process, particularly in military affairs, is now generally accepted (Russett 1990; Sinnott 1995a). The mass media are said to play a central role in forming public opinion and in communicating it to political decisionmakers.

The wars in the former Yugoslavia illustrated the principal functions of the media. Contrary to the familiar, pervasive tension of the Cold War, these conflicts were different in that the dividing lines were not easily understood and judged in general and ideological terms. It has subsequently become relatively easy to plead ignorance about new and complicated conflicts in faraway countries and to be fatalistic about them. The ideological certainties, which had drawn sharp lines between "good" and "bad," as well as the concomitant Cold War distinctions between "them" and "us," have dissipated. Yet there is also the intrusive stream of constant information in the mass media, which fosters and increases feelings of concern and heightens our sensitivity (the so-called CNN effect in action).

As conflict in Yugoslavia began to escalate in 1991 and 1992, the Dutch were fairly skeptical of the likelihood that an international peacekeeping force would be able to keep the parties apart or bring about successful negotiations. This was consistent with the way the conflict was portrayed in the media. Either because of lack of knowledge or disinterest, little was done to explain the detailed background of the conflict and the claims of the parties concerned. The emphasis was often put on violent traditions in the Balkans. Consequently, only a minority of the public felt that the Netherlands should commit itself if asked to participate in a peacekeeping force, let alone a force that would enforce a solution.[15] While initially emphasizing the value or necessity of keeping an existing state territorially intact, the media gradually began to stress the virtues of the right of self-determination, even if it gave rise to many new problems. Confusion increased when it became evident that plans for new territorial divisions (such as the Vance-Owen plan) also implied an acknowledgment, even a recognition, of the reprehensible policies of ethnic cleansing.

All these perspectives and resulting dilemmas were recognized, to some degree, in the Dutch media, though the information provided was more focused on individual events than on structures and contextual information. This was not very helpful in assisting people to make up their minds. The fact that outside the circle of a few area experts not very many were truly knowledgeable about Yugoslavia meant that politicians and the general public had to cope first with a backlog of information. This implied a major role for the media that was partially discharged by providing platforms for experts and politicians to present their views and shape the public debate.

By and large, however, the media failed to explain the conflict. What dominated were stories of brutal incidents, bloodshed, and concentration camps and images of a society in the grip of age-old rivalries, in which little or nothing could be done from the outside due to some unique Balkan viciousness.

In the course of 1992–1993, a widely shared consensus formed in the Netherlands as to the desirability of external intervention in the conflict, especially with respect to the three-sided civil war in Bosnia-Herzegovina. Hence, it was not difficult for the government to decide to take part in the United Nations Protection Force (UNPROFOR II) with considerable contingents (adding 1,000 men to some 2,200 already engaged in the former Yugoslavia), when that operation was decided upon in 1993. The government also succeeded in overriding strong reservations among military leaders who felt that the troops were sent into action with an uncertain mandate, unprepared, and under-armed for the deployment. This decision was preceded by extensive discussions in the media (de Boode 1993).

As the war in Yugoslavia dragged on and success remained ephemeral, public opinion became both more cynical and extreme (Everts 1998a; Van der Meulen and De Konink 1998). It also became more polarized, with less support for UNPROFOR and more for withdrawal, on the one hand, and increased support for strong military action on the other. Risks were increasingly felt to be unacceptable. This became even more marked after the events in the first half of 1995: the taking of hostages by the Bosnian Serbs and the humiliating forced withdrawal of Dutchbat (the Dutch contingent in Srebrenica). Even though Dutchbat had suffered only a few casualties, it seemed to be a perfect example of the thesis of diminishing support when the going gets tough. Thus one is struck by the facile way in which the body-bag argument was used by politicians and the media. There was a tendency for them to parrot one another and to anticipate situations that may, in fact, be caused by such talk. Frequent statements of politicians and observers about an expected body-bag effect on public support may turn out to be self-fulfilling prophecies.

In the aftermath of Srebrenica, the moral and political uneasiness increased after the media and some in the military unashamedly turned the reception of the withdrawn and defeated Dutchbat into a heroes' welcome. These events led to intense societal and political debates, especially between parliament and the cabinet. The discussions were drawn out, because it took time to put together a debriefing report while the media kept discovering new and often unpleasant facts.[16] All of this affected the public and undermined its confidence in the government's argument that the Netherlands and Dutchbat could not be blamed for the events (de Boode 1995). Since the parliament had been strongly in favor of dispatching Dutchbat, it largely accepted the government's defense, and the debates focused on questions of who had been politically responsible for the drama and which, if any, political consequences should be extracted. Finally, the government was forced to charge a research institute to draw up a full analysis of what happened, while the ministers who had been politically responsible stayed on.

On the basis of press reports on this national debate, it was easy to conclude that the Netherlands was suffering from a terrible hangover. This, it was said, would imply that the societal basis for participation in future military operations organized or mandated by the UN was damaged or eroded, at least for the time being and perhaps permanently. The empirical evidence at the level of mass opinion pointed in quite another direction, however. The first signs of the resilience of the public became visible in a poll conducted at the end of August 1995.[17] The downward trend in support for participation in UN military actions, which was so evident up to July, reversed again, with 62 percent supporting taking part in UNPROFOR and even more (68 percent) supporting participation in UN action in general (with only 11 percent against). This was the same high level that was previously observed. Seventy percent supported taking part in peacekeeping operations outside the Balkans. Despite repeated suggestions to the contrary in the media and by political observers, the events surrounding Srebrenica seem not to have had a strongly negative and durable impact on the degree of support for collective-security operations. To the degree that there was a dip in support, it was not very deep and only short-lived. By not acknowledging sufficiently the stamina and resilience among the public, the media helped the political elites to maintain their alibi that if the Netherlands hesitated to share the international burden—for instance, in making decisions on the commitment of NATO ground troops to Kosovo—this would occur due to the lack of public support and risk aversion among the general public.

A TENTATIVE CONCLUSION

Provisionally, we can draw some conclusions from the analysis of these events:

- The major changes in the international system in recent years did not affect general images of the necessity and legitimacy of armed forces per se, but it had important implications for the legitimacy and relative importance given to specific missions, tasks, and structures of the armed forces.
- Data from Western Europe—the Netherlands, in particular—suggest that public opinion reflected the changes in the roles of the armed forces. Although the salience of these issues remained low, the adaptation and conversion processes in the armed forces were both understood and accepted at the level of public opinion.

- The legitimacy of the armed forces, tied to the performance and accorded priority of specific tasks, did not suffer and even increased in the wake of the Cold War.
- There was a major change, however, in thinking about military matters, amounting to a shift in discourse. The traditional debate between the military and the pacifist mind-sets was replaced by a debate between neopacifists and neointerventionists.
- The shift from the use of military force for internationalist rather than nationalist goals, while morally attractive, runs the risk of losing public support. This contradiction is not easy to solve.
- One of the implications of the changes in the armed forces and the conditions under which they operate is the increase in visibility of the casualties to which they may lead. As to the relationship with perceived interests and likelihood of success, this may affect the tolerance of such casualties. The fact that such fears are immutable and present fundamental obstacles to internationalist policies is not a foregone conclusion.
- The casualty hypothesis is very likely a self-fulfilling prophecy. The alleged inconsistency of public opinion in this regard is a careful reflection of the real dilemmas in foreign policy.
- In objective terms, there is both room and the need for further reductions in the relative importance and priority of military instruments to counter security risks, which have become much more differentiated. In many instances, military power is used to no avail.
- It is to be expected that the mass public will accept the adaptations and conversion processes to which this would lead. While public opinion does not press actively in certain directions, it seems to present no obstacle to sensible conversion and adaptation policies.

12

Public Opinion and Decisionmaking in Russia
The Impact of NATO Expansion and Air Strikes on Serbia

Eric Shiraev and Vlad Zubok

On May 1, 1999, thousands of demonstrators turned out for traditional May Day marches in Moscow and Saint Petersburg, the two major Russian cities. Since the late 1980s, such political and primarily antigovernment rallies and marches have become fairly common and frequent. However—perhaps for the first time in a decade—an unusual development took place: the May Day protesters carried slogans that had nothing to do with Russia's internal issues. Moreover, what the demonstrators demanded had already been endorsed by government officials in their public statements. An anti-Western nervous outburst, caused by the air war started by the United States and its NATO allies against Yugoslavia, was sweeping Russia in the last spring of the millennium. Russian officials, referring to public opinion, began to speculate about a new "Cold War era" in the relationship with the United States and other Western countries (Lapitsky 1999).

Was such a clear congruency of Russian public opinion and the government's foreign policy rhetoric always present in the course of the ten-year development of post-Soviet Russia? Why did such anti-Western sentiment become a dominant trend in both mass opinion and foreign policy debates of the late 1990s? Can one indicate the direction of the causal relationship between Russian mass opinion and foreign policy? To answer these questions, we will bear in mind that the links between public opinion and political decisionmaking are likely to be indirect and based on a set of diverse factors. In the context of foreign policy, understanding the mediating factors between public opinion and policy requires critical examination of Russia's foreign policy itself, the dynamics of public opinion, the role of opinion leaders, the nature of political struggles in the country, and some of the basic cultural and ideological factors that shape Russia's foreign policy and the debates around it.[1]

DOMESTIC PROBLEMS

The period from 1991 to 2000, covering the time from the breakup of the U.S.S.R. to the second presidential election in independent Russia, marked a period of extreme political and social turbulence. Internal political battles and economic problems, the search for a new national ideology, and overall restructuring of the government greatly complicated the process of the country's democratization. Despite the ongoing radical reforms, the economic decline of the 1990s—with a few brief periods of robust growth—resulted in the painful financial collapse of 1998. Russia had to be remade politically in every sense: as a state, nation, federation, legitimate government, as well as a democracy. As part of the political restructuring, elites had to rebuild their relationship with a newly born civil society—one vocal and diverse in its expressed interests, unpracticed at democracy, and contending with hardship, lawlessness, and a general sense of insecurity. Property and power were changing hands in Russia, thus encouraging various groups to fight—using all available means—for power and economic opportunities (Glad and Shiraev 1999).

Foreign Policy

In the Soviet past, foreign policy was the unquestioned purview of Communist Party elites. Politburo members, in particular, exercised decisive sway over policy, especially over decisions related to security.[2] Since 1985, perestroika marked the beginning of open foreign policy debates, and Soviet officials for the first time felt political pressure on foreign policy from below (Dobrynin 1997). But most of the restructuring in the foreign policymaking machinery came after Russia gained independence in 1991, the period under review. While the new Russian constitution passed in December 1993 helped to sort out some of these problems, practical struggles over details continued into the new century.

In essence, while power over Russian foreign policymaking was more dispersed in the 1990s than it had been earlier, it still remained, according to the constitution, in presidential hands.[3] In short, the president and his appointees had decisive say over foreign affairs. The legislature (and, by extension, the citizenry represented therein) was thus left with relatively weak influence over foreign policy matters. The role of the legislature started to become more visible in 1993, when members of the Supreme Soviet passed several resolutions challenging President Boris Yeltsin's foreign policy in many areas. Between 1994 and 1996, the legislature's impact on foreign policy formation grew (see, for example, Sherman 1995, 125–128). Opposition parties had been victorious in both the December 1993 and the December 1995 legislative elections (dominated by the Communist Party of the Russian Federation and the Liberal Democratic Party of Russia, respectively) and gained a significant amount of votes in the 1999 Duma elections. Thus, the legislature—renamed the Federal Assembly—and especially its lower house, the Duma, continued to be the arena where Yeltsin's foreign and domestic policies were under continuous pressure. Gradually, for reasons to be discussed further below, Yeltsin and his executive foreign policy team began to alter their rhetoric, change foreign policy personnel, and reshape certain aspects of foreign policy in limited ways along lines more conducive to opposition legislators and, subsequently, to the voters who elected them. The fact that Foreign Minister Andrei Kozyrev, a committed supporter of a pro-Western course, was dismissed on January 5, 1996, showed that forces outside Yeltsin, especially opposition legislators, were gaining strength.

Kozyrev's fall signaled a new age in Russian foreign policy, which began to be shaped primarily by elite power struggles and the search for a new Russian post–Cold War identity. The rise of foreign ministers Yevgeny Primakov and then Igor Ivanov was a turning point in the process of weakening the "pro-Western" course of the Yeltsin administration. Primakov built bridges to communists and ultranationalists in the Duma, promising to put an end to the foreign policy of his predecessor. In his rhetoric, he indirectly renounced American world dominance and emphasized Russia's need for alliances to counterbalance U.S. power. After two and a half years in office, Primakov built his reputation among the anti-Yeltsin opposition to such an extent that the opposition enthusiastically supported his candidacy for prime minister in August 1998. The collapse of Russia's pro-American course of the early 1990s was virtually finalized by Ivanov's replacement of Primakov as foreign minister.

Foreign Policy Highlights

The goals of domestic reconstruction and stabilization pushed Moscow to end the Cold War, avoid future tensions with the West, and seek extensive economic and other aid from Western sources.[4] Two major international developments of the 1990s, namely, NATO's expansion and the Yugoslav conflict—including the war in Kosovo—became testing grounds for Russian foreign policy and the development of the post–Cold War doctrine.

The strong desire for Russia to play a central role internationally in the post-Soviet world was demonstrated by how Kremlin leaders volunteered to broker peace in the Bosnia conflict. Playing mainly a "good citizen" role (Goble 1996, 190), through the end of 1993 Russian elites generally cooperated with the Western powers and followed UN policy on Bosnia.[5] A significant political victory for the Russian government was the decision to send several thousand servicemen to Bosnia as a part of a special multinational contingent and not a part of NATO forces (*Kommersant-Daily*, October, 31, 1995).

However, Russian policy toward Bosnia—the balancing between cooperating with the West and supporting the Serbs—failed to pan out. Most important, Russia

was shown that it was not viewed as an equal partner with the West. These developments began to heighten anti-Western and anti-NATO sentiments among the Russian political elite. There were persistent calls for radical reassessment of relations
with the West (see Baker 1995; Mikulski 1995).

The 1999 war in Kosovo became a casus belli for the further strengthening of
anti-Western tendencies in Russian foreign policy. America's and NATO's unilateral
actions throughout the conflict reinforced growing fears of Russia's encirclement
and isolation. When the first missiles and bombs began to fall on Serbia in Spring
1999, Prime Minister Primakov refused to visit the United States. Alexei Arbatov,
deputy head of the Duma's defense committee, stated that the Strategic Arms Reduction Treaty (START II) has been "put back for a long time" (Johnson's Russia
List #3224, April 3, 1999).

Most important, since March 1999, the war in Yugoslavia has created for the first
time an anti-U.S. consensus cutting across the old ideological and political divisions
of Russian public opinion. During almost a ten-year period, communists and ultranationalists had not contributed to the strength of anti-Western attitudes as much
as had a few weeks of NATO's attacks against Serbia. The war catalyzed the transformation of anti-American attitudes into a high-profile social and political phenomenon. While understanding that an open break with the United States would be a
diplomatic catastrophe, foreign policy experts, meanwhile, began to talk about a significant change in Russian foreign policy.

Russian Public Opinion

Several major domestic problems and events preoccupied the average Russian citizen: the breakup of the Soviet Union in 1991; the parliamentary coup of 1993; the
war in Chechnya; the parliamentary elections of 1993, 1995, and 1999; the presidential elections of 1996 and 2000; frequent political assassinations; street violence;
and—above all—people's unpaid salaries (ITAR-TASS and Agence France Presse,
February 22, 1997; *Argumenty i Fakty*, No. 76, February 1999, 24)[6]

While interest in politics was relatively high in 1989–1990, when the first democratic elections were held, interest sharply declined thereafter.[7] According to sociologist Nuzgar Betaneli, only 10–12 percent of Russians fell into the politically active
category (*Ogonyok* No. 12, March 1998, 6; Kagarlitsky 1997, 53).[8]

This apathy was perhaps a function of a widespread feeling among many Russian
people that there was little they could do to influence the course of political events.[9]
In a comparative Times-Mirror survey in 1991, only 47 percent of Russians expressed agreement that voting gives them a chance to voice their opinion on how
government runs things.[10] In a study conducted in 1996, 56 percent of respondents
said that officials in Moscow were unable to make improvements in ordinary peoples' lives. More than 60 percent said politicians are only interested in helping themselves (Ferguson 1996, 44).

Popular disillusionment with the way things were in the country was accompanied by increasingly negative attitudes toward the Yeltsin government[11] and regrets about the breakup of the Soviet Union (*Openkin*, 1996; *Izvestia*, October 13, 1995, 6; *Ogonyok* No. 12, March 1998, 6; poll conducted by the All-Russian Center for Public Opinion Research [VTSIOM], February–March 1998).

Foreign Policy Attitudes

Russian opinion polls and survey questions focusing on foreign policy issues have been relatively scarce. While domestic politics held great public appeal in the late Soviet period when the first elections took place (1989–1990), interest sharply declined thereafter. Many surveys conducted in the 1990s and numerous analysts have also confirmed this trend (see, for example, Shiraev 1999). In *How Russia Votes*, Stephen White and colleagues suggest that "a large number of Russians take little or no interest in what other countries are doing" (White et al. 1997, 56; see also Shiraev 1999; Mikulski 1995). "The average Russian thinks about his salary and prices. He's not in a position to think about foreign policy," wrote Viktor Kremenyuk, a well-known policy expert (*Moscow Times,* February 1997, 8). According to the daily *Izvestia* (October 13, 1995, 6), 72 percent of citizens thought domestic problems were a priority, compared with only 18 percent who thought foreign problems were.

However, when opinion about foreign policy has in fact been measured, foreign policy attitudes have shown a relatively clear pattern over time: from neutral and relatively favorable opinions about the West and Western policies in the early 1990s, to suspicion and hostility by the end of the millennium (see, for example, Smirnov 1997; *Boston Globe*, February 17, 1997; *Izvestia*, October 13, 1995, 6; Kelley 1994; *News and Record* [Greensboro, NC], January 15, 1994).

Russian isolationist attitudes were manifested steadily during the 1990s (Kondrashov 1995; VTSIOM; *Moscow Times,* April 16, 1999). This trend was confirmed by a key foreign policy survey that was conducted in early 1994 by the Center for International Sociological Research when the first threats of NATO air strikes against Bosnian Serbs occurred. At that time, 77 percent of those surveyed said they opposed the threatened air strikes (*Daily Telegraph,* February 18, 1994, 14).

Yet another survey, conducted by VTSIOM in mid-1995, displays an isolationist trend in Russian opinions on Bosnia (Interfax, September 21, 1995). Nearly 28 percent said they did not support any ethnic group involved; almost 21 percent indicated they sympathized with the Serbs; 2 percent sympathized with Croats and Muslims; and the rest could not indicate their preference. The results also detract from claims by some observers that the Russian populace held strongly pro-Serb attitudes.

The 1995 survey also revealed attitudes about what form the Russian government's involvement in the conflict should take. Thirty percent of respondents favored Russia's involvement in the conflict in providing humanitarian and economic assistance. Only 8 percent said Russia should act jointly with the UN and NATO.

Another poll conducted in October 1992 by Romir Ltd. suggests an important caveat. According to this survey, 46 percent of respondents said Russia should send troops to any former Soviet republic if the security of Russians there was at stake; 40 percent said Russia's government should not take military action even in this case; and 14 percent expressed no opinion on the subject (*National Journal*, Opinion/Outlook section, "Views on National Security," Vol. 25, No. 11, 654). This suggests that while many Russians had a strong general desire to avoid war, they perhaps would have been more inclined to support military action if the lives of ethnic Russians were at stake.

Russians expressed some mixed views on how tough the government should be when dealing with some of the country's neighboring regimes. In March 1999, 34 percent of 1,600 Russians polled believed that Moscow should try to cooperate with the breakaway republic of Chechnya. Yet almost an equal number (32 percent) wanted the authorities to isolate Chechnya from the neighboring parts of Russia and tighten border control in these areas. Bomb and missile attacks against Chechen fighter bases were supported by 7 percent, as was a large-scale ground operation (VTSIOM; Interfax, April 8, 1999). In Winter 1999, 45 percent—or close to half—of Russians believed that the Federation Council should not have ratified the Russian-Ukrainian Peace, Partnership, and Mutual Aid Treaty as long as Ukraine's debts for Russian oil and gas remained unpaid, and the division of the Black Sea Fleet and the status of the city of Sevastopol (a long-disputed issue between two governments) had not been decided. The view that Russia should own Sevastopol was supported by 78 percent. Ratification of the treaty was supported by only 28 percent of respondents, with 27 percent undecided. As few as 7 percent said that Ukraine should own the city, with 15 percent undecided (Interfax, February 26, 1999; poll by All-Russian Public Opinion).

A turning point in Russian public opinion on international issues was March 1999, when a single international development—the war in Kosovo—gained so much attention from pollsters, officials, and the media. According to the Mnenie [Opinion] polling service, more than 93 percent of respondents said in March 1999 that NATO's decision to bomb Yugoslavia was wrong, and only 1 percent said the decision was right (with nearly 5 percent undecided). More than 55 percent feared that a new world war could break out (almost 29 percent said the war was out of the question, with 16 percent undecided). More than 50 percent believed Russia had to support the Serbs, while only 0.4 percent said Moscow should back Kosovar Albanians. Eighteen percent said neither of the parties should be supported, while only 9 percent suggested both parties should be backed. Almost 40 percent was convinced that NATO was supporting Kosovo's Albanians, and 41 percent said Russia should supply arms to Yugoslavia, while almost 37 percent opposed this. In a protest against the war, 41 percent wanted Russian peacekeepers to withdraw from Bosnia, while 40 percent wanted them to stay (ITAR-TASS, March 30, 1999).

Given a choice of several courses of action for Russia in the Balkan crisis, 69 percent replied that the country should concentrate on mediation. Nearly a quarter (24 percent) said that Russia should send air-defense systems to Yugoslavia. While only 9 percent wanted Russia to pressure the Yugoslav leadership into succumbing to NATO's demands and just 12 percent said that the Kremlin should make more restrained statements on the conflict, most Russians were not eager to encourage a confrontation between Russia and the West. Dispatching Russian warships to the conflict area was supported by 10 percent. Six percent backed sending volunteers to fight for Yugoslavia, and 6 percent would support none of the above, because these respondents did not clearly understand the situation (Interfax, April 6, 1999; All-Russian Public Opinion Center in Moscow only).

More than six in ten—63 percent, according to the VTSIOM—believed that NATO was to blame for the Kosovo conflict, whereas 13 percent stated that both sides were to blame; 6 percent of respondents accused Yugoslavia only. However, more than a third of all Russians did not know what caused the conflict in Yugoslavia (Radio Ekho Moskvy [Moscow], May 3, 1999). The Russian people were predominantly in favor of a peaceful settlement to the conflict in Kosovo. A total of 47 percent of those polled by the Public Opinion Foundation suggested that Russia should put pressure on the United States and other NATO countries through international organizations. Also, 44 percent of Russians responded that it was important to support the movement worldwide against the bombardment of Yugoslavia. More than 40 percent favored urgently drawing up a peace plan to resolve the Kosovo problem. The same percentage wanted to send humanitarian assistance to Yugoslavia (Radio Ekho Moskvy (Moscow), April 9, 1999).

The events in Kosovo perhaps triggered a change in the way Russians felt about the United States. According to a poll conducted in December 1998 by the VTSIOM, 13 percent of Russians had a very good attitude toward the United States, 54 percent had a good attitude, 17 percent had a bad attitude, and 6 percent very bad (10 percent of respondents didn't have an answer). The picture changed in April 1999, when only 3 percent of citizens had a very good attitude toward the United States, 30 percent good, 33 percent bad, and 20 percent very bad (13 percent didn't have an answer) (Central TV, Moscow, April 15, 1999, 7:15 p.m.). The war in Kosovo influenced concerns and fears for Russian security. Eighty percent agreed that Russian military aid to Yugoslavia could lead to a third world war (Agence France Press, May 3, 1999).

In sum, the NATO military campaign against Serbia in 1999 not only provoked an avalanche of anti-American rhetoric in Moscow but also caused a serious crisis in U.S.-Russian relations. Practically every Russian opinion leader—including most liberal reformers—denounced American involvement in the Balkans and began to use old Cold War language of warnings and threats. American policy was called "barbaric," American actions were labeled as the most dangerous since the Cuban missile crisis, and a new Cold War era was proclaimed. It seemed that Russia—at least according to its media and public-opinion surveys—was unified again in the Spring of 1999. The new tide of anti-Americanism came not only from communist sympathizers and nationalists—persistent and devoted faultfinders of the West—but also from Russian liberal intelligentsia, reformers, and vigorous supporters of democracy who had been defending what they earnestly thought to be Western values, yet they were overwhelmed with anger at American and NATO policies.

At this writing (Fall 1999), we can only ask: Does this anti-Western unity of public and government opinion represent a short-lived episode in Russia's history, or does this opinion-policy congruency rest on deeper and stronger roots that would determine Russia's public opinion–foreign policy links for years to come?

ANTI-WESTERN ATTITUDES IN HISTORIC CONTEXT

A glance at Russia's social and cultural history reveals that during the lifetime of one generation Russians passed through three stages in their attitudes toward the West: the Cold War consensus, a brief "honeymoon" during the postcommunist transition, and, recently, noticeable symptoms of suspiciousness and hostility. Long before the reforms of the 1980s led by Mikhail Gorbachev, several groups of intellectuals broke out of the isolated and xenophobic culture of Stalinism and embraced the ideas of integration and reconciliation with the West. This pro-Americanism formed a growing and vibrant alternative culture under the official Soviet façade. During the crumbling of the communist order during perestroika, pro-Western attitudes became prevalent among both reformers and the public (Glad and Shiraev 1999). Mythological foundations of perceptions of the outside world help explain why during the Gorbachev years (1985–1991) the balance of attitudes toward the West—the United States, in particular—swung from the prevalent hostility toward extreme pro-Westernism and pro-Americanism. Gorbachev and his advisers jettisoned official ideology and introduced a range of romantic social-democratic and liberal ideas to the people. In his foreign policy, Gorbachev elected to end the Cold War by reconciling with the West and integrating the Soviet Union into the "family of civilized nations" (Levesque 1997; Brown 1996; Baker 1996). Gorbachev's "revolutions from above" conducted in foreign policy, ideology, and political life went side by side with a euphoric rise of pro-Western attitudes among opinion leaders and the majority of Russians (Shlapentokh 1988). The rejection of communist ideology by the average Russian also led to the abandonment of the age-old tradition of foreign policy based on geopolitical calculations. A significant part of educated Russian society associated the United States with the West, with which it longed to reconcile and reunite. Again, in a simple logic, people who had been frustrated by the hardships of Soviet life now riveted their admiring gaze on the democratic, prosperous West. Formerly denounced as "war mongers," Ronald Reagan and Margaret Thatcher became popular figures in the Soviet Union because of their denunciation of communism (Glad and Shiraev 1999; Zubok and Pleshakov 1996). The policies of glasnost and the elections of 1989–1990 propelled Russian liberals and radical democrats—then the main carriers of pro-Western attitudes—to a position of ideological and cultural leadership.

While Gorbachev viewed Russia's integration into the international community as a long and complex process, the new crop of politicians gathering around Boris Yeltsin in the early 1990s wanted to achieve integration in one big leap. For these politicians, traditional yearning for a model abroad became a hectic search. Possible models that could fit the Soviet conditions better (from Hungary to Sweden to China) were quickly discarded in favor of the United States.

The pro-Americanism of Yeltsin's supporters was also based on specific political and material reasons. First, Yeltsin's camp regarded the West as an ally in its political struggle (at the beginning against Gorbachev, then against the Russian communists and ultranationalists). Second, it expected a massive program of economic assistance, similar to the Marshall Plan, to be provided to a new, democratic Russia. Third, it anticipated the United States and its allies to accept a postcommunist Russia as a legitimate power and equal partner in world affairs.

In retrospect, however, the pro-Western and anticommunist consensus of the early 1990s between the public and its leaders was ephemeral: it was supported by euphoria caused by a bloodless victory over the communist regime. Expectations of "becoming the West" overnight were simply unrealistic. It became obvious that radical policies of "shock therapy" introduced in 1992 only aggravated a deep systemic crisis in Russia (Melville 1999). In a time of hangover and new frustrations, attitudes toward the West were bound to change again. What factors contributed to such a change in Russian public opinion? How has such a change affected Russian foreign policy?

The oldest and most persistent of the observed features of Russian public opinion is the "chronically ambivalent" attitude in Russia toward the West that ran through Russian intellectual debates and policy for many years (Simes 1994; Carr 1958, 10). Modern Russian elites have come to live on a fault line of history between the two tectonic plates: the traditionalist and backward peasant country, isolated from the outside world, and the dynamic and ever-superior West. Vladimir Shlapentokh (1988) in his path-breaking article on the subject, pointed out that Russians have always been keen to measure themselves against the West. At the end of the twentieth century, as much as one hundred years ago, resistance to Westernization is miraculously combined with the attraction and acceptance of its symbols, both cultural and materialistic (Kliamkin and Lapkin 1996).

The second powerful tradition was the strong, self-sufficient, and domineering state that projected its power not only internally but externally, seeking influence and recognition on a European and global scale. Russian policymakers learned to look at the European situation through the prism of what came to be known as "geopolitics." In particular, any signs of European economic, social, and political integration were often seen in Russia as a violation of the balance of power and an intolerable security threat. Historical experience seemed to vindicate Russian fears: at least twice, under Napoleon and then Hitler's Third Reich, the most powerful forces in Europe invaded Russia and almost destroyed its statehood. Besides, ideologically, the Russians tend to see themselves as exceptional—just like Americans do. They treated every attempt to exclude them from international affairs as an intolerable insult. And when confronting a rival, Russia preferred to risk defeat than to compromise its status (Hosking 1997; Kissinger 1994, 142, 172–173).

All in all, some historic and cultural factors contributed to the growth of anti-Western attitudes in the 1990s. Both the elite and the masses shared an ambivalent attitude about the West and were frustrated about Russia's isolation from the world. Moreover, such a mutual influence of public attitudes and elite opinions was, in turn, moderated by many contextual factors that are necessary to identify and outline further.

How Opinions Influence Policy: Anti-Western Sentiment and Democracy

In 1995, writing for *Izvestia*, Stanislav Kondrashov suggested that even though foreign policy issues would play a subordinate role in Russian election campaigns—as a seasoning for the main dishes—international developments would be used more and with greater effectiveness by the Russian political opposition. He argued that while the Yeltsin administration was unable to offer the general public an attractive foreign policy strategy, the opposition would be scoring points in forthcoming elections by appealing directly to the electorate's concerns. He was partially right. Although foreign policy issues were not debated in great detail during the presidential elections of 1996 (Sigelman and Shiraev 1998), the opposition—by generating persistent appeals to public opinion—was able to influence Russian foreign policy in the late 1990s.

Internal political considerations can affect foreign policy decisions in any democracy. As in most democratic societies, Russian political opposition tried to use each and every occasion to apply pressure on the government and gain momentum for forthcoming elections.

In 1991–1995, the Yeltsin administration and its minister of foreign affairs, Andrei Kozyrev, were ardent and consistent advocates of policies of close cooperation and strategic partnership with the West. By contrast, domestic opposition in the Duma seized any opportunity on virtually every international policy issue to criticize or condemn the existing "pro-Western" course.[12] Because of the predominance of communists and ultranationalists in the Duma after the 1993 and, especially, the 1995 elections, nationalism and chauvinism became two key weapons used against Yeltsin and his government. This situation created an atmosphere of poorly concealed anti-Western sentiment in foreign policy rhetoric (Eggert 1995). However, this attitude cannot be ascribed only to machinations of antidemocratic forces. Significantly, the most consistent liberal reformers in Russia of the 1990s (for example, 1996 presidential candidate Grigory Yavlinsky) had long ago become critical of the Yeltsin administration and distanced themselves from its policies. Pursuing their own political goals and appealing to public opinion, the opposition leaders began to insist that Russian national interests differed from the pro-Western and faulty course of the government.

The Marshall Plan That Never Happened

Besides the political battles against the Yeltsin administration, there were other factors that contributed to the demise of pro-Western attitudes at the governmental and public levels. One was the public reaction to economic reforms and perceptions of the United States and its economic policies in Russia. Since the beginning of the 1990s, when the Russian government launched unprecedented economic transformations, this process was viewed as an integration of Russia into a civilized world. Yeltsin and other Russian reformers regarded the support of the United States and other Western countries as crucial to the success of this undertaking. In 1991–1992, there were wide expectations that Americans should undertake another Marshall Plan in Russia as a sign of recognition and gratitude for Yeltsin's role in slaying the communist dragon.[13]

However, the Yeltsin administration did not create democratic political institutions that could have supported the proposed economic reforms. There were no institutions of state support of the market economy and the social security system (Melville 1999). Painful economic reforms—not accompanied by a social contract or supported socially or politically—fell upon the socially unprotected population. Among many opposition leaders there was an emerging opinion that the West benefited not only from the collapse of the Soviet Union but also from Russia's weakness (Arbatov 1992; Lebed 1996, May 13). Another stream of criticism came from liberal politicians and opinion leaders, who consistently claimed that the American economic and social model of capitalism associated with economic prosperity should be reproduced on Russian soil (Kremenyuk 1994).

After the financial crash of August 1998, communists and ultranationalists as well as moderate Russian politicians started to blame the United States for the disaster (Arbatov 1999, 8). Some openly speculated that Washington, after the dissolution of the Soviet Union, took upon itself the arrogant role of economic and political mentor for Moscow. As a result, the United States should have shared prime responsibility for Russia's failures in the 1990s (see *Mezhdunarodnaia Zhizn* No. 10, 1998, 102).

A search for a new scapegoat satisfied both the public and the ruling elite[14] (see, e.g., Thornton 1988, *Literaturnaya Rossiya*, December 12, 1992; *Izvestia*, July 15, 1994; Rubtsov 1995). Again, public irritation over the course of economic reforms coincided with the visible defeat of the Western model of economic transformation, thus justifying a new wave of anti-Western and anti-American sentiment.

Search for a New Identity

Another substantial factor contributing to the anti-Western sentiment was a reaction to the demise of the Soviet Union. At its core was the loss of a collective Russian national identity (Barner-Berry 1999). The old Soviet identity was to a great degree based on ideas that demanded from the Soviet people enormous sacrifices in the name of global projects. The dramatic experience of the Soviet Union and its rise to the status of superpower filled the Soviet identity with additional contents. The Cold War that divided the world into two camps—one led by the Soviet Union— also gave structural support to the psychological syndrome of Great Power chauvinism in Soviet ideological thinking. All these developments, in turn, further reinforced traditional Russian messianism (Smith 1989) and the senses of moral superiority over other nations—Russian greatness and uniqueness. [15]

Unfortunately, many Russian opinion leaders chose to link a new Russian identity to the refurbished, but still antiquated, ideas of Great Powers and state grandeur. Moreover, they began to interpret the end of the Cold War and the collapse of the Soviet Union as a historic defeat of the nation. This, in turn, magnified the already pervasive perception of Russia's humiliation by the United States and the West and the painful feeling of inferiority (Umbach 1996, 478). In view of Russia's greatly diminished military and economic potential, this argument went hand in hand with popular fears of encirclement of Russia and its exclusion from the European community (see "Patterns in Russian Foreign Policy," *Swiss Review of World Affairs*, May 2, 1997; AG fuer Die Neue Zuercher Zeitung NZZ). Viacheslav Nikonov, a former Duma deputy and head of a Moscow-based political think-tank, suggested that during the transformation period the old Cold War ideology has been naturally replaced by a paradoxical combination of authoritarian beliefs, fear of inferiority, geopolitical ambitions, and nationalistic, isolationist views (Nikonov 1996, 49).

Anti-Western and anti-American assessments of Russian opinion leaders began to penetrate Russian press (see Surikov 1997; Gorbachev 1994, February 22).[16] By the end of the 1990s, even the most pragmatic Russian security experts began to link the acute feeling of collective humiliation and inferiority to the behavior of the United States. Alexei Arbatov wrote that "Washington treated Russia as a defeated country—as if it were the Soviet Union who had lost the cold war—thereby increasing the future negative reaction of the Russian side" (MEIMO (6) 1998, 8). Other writers from the same highly educated and pragmatic Moscow milieu went even farther. They based the search for a new Russian identity on various philosophical and historical postulates, thus justifying Russia's messianism, its exceptional role in history, and an anti-Western mentality (Kortunov 1998). All in all, such manifesto-like articles can be considered as a serious attempt to form what could be called a "neoconservative" trend in Russia's policy climate, with a clear aim to influence identity-building process of the nation.

NATO, the Balkans, and Anti-Americanism in Action

All these factors—Russia's search for a new identity, the perception of threat caused by NATO expansion and its engagement in Bosnia and Kosovo, economic insecurity, the frustration caused by inadequate Western help, and domestic political considerations—converge most articulately in Russia's foreign policy debates, a natural place for defining attitudes toward the outside world. Since 1992, there has been an accumulation of irritation and frustrated hopes in Russia regarding its relationship with the West. But the real turn in the debates can be attributed to two developments: the American decision to expand NATO into Central Europe, and NATO's intervention in the former Yugoslavia on the side of Bosnian and, later, Albanian Muslims.

Russian political opposition was eminently reluctant and unhappy to accept the appearance of NATO near Russia's borders. At first, the vanguard of reaction consisted of communist sympathizers and the most radical nationalists (Busuyev 1992; Volkov 1994; Bolshakov 1994; Zhirinovsky 1996, June 16). They accused the United States and NATO of threatening Russia near its borders and refused to recognize the right of the United States to play global policeman. Very soon thereafter, formerly pro-Western politicians (such as Yegor Gaidar and Grigory Yavlinsky) also had to take a more negative stand on the issue of NATO expansion. Also, since 1996, centrist and liberal groups in the Russian elite began to react negatively to NATO enlargement, suggesting that NATO expansion was the reason for the development of mistrust and hostility between Moscow and Washington (see *Nezavisimaya Gazeta*, January 15, 1997). Most strikingly, liberally inclined experts began to talk about the politics of selective resistance to America's world leadership (Bogaturov 1998, 29–39).

Long before the war started between Slobodan Milosevic's Serbia and NATO, Russia's public opinion leaders cited U.S. policies in this region, especially American diplomatic and military pressure against the Bosnian Serbs, as grounds for overwhelmingly negative assessments of American foreign policy in general (Kondrashov, April 20, 1994; Peresvet 1995).[17] Leading policy experts in Russia came to view the United States as a breaker of the geopolitical status quo in Central Europe, which duplicitously used the issues of human rights and national self-determination for projecting its power as the world's police force. In their opinion, the United States would never stop until it absorbed former Soviet bloc states and some parts of the former Soviet Union into their sphere of influence (Bogaturov 1998, 35; Kortunov 1998, 147).

This crisis had become an extremely personal and ideological issue among policymakers and opinion leaders. "To be honest, when I was working on this problem the main thing I was trying to prevent was a national humiliation for Russia," wrote Deputy Foreign Minister Vitaly Churkin on the Bosnia conflict (*Literaturnaya Gazeta*, No. 11, March 16, 1994, 14).

The clear anti-Western pattern can be seen in other situations, most notably in the case of the joint U.S.-British air strikes against Iraq in December 1998. At that time, the Duma demonstratively suspended debates on START, the Russian ambassador to the United States was theatrically recalled from Washington, and numerous politicians and policy experts publicly denounced U.S. actions in Iraq.

The 1999 war against Yugoslavia, which started with an escalated bombing campaign by NATO forces, catalyzed emerging anti-American attitudes into a high-profile social and political phenomenon. First, there were significant outbursts of violent anti-Americanism in April 1999, including attacks on the U.S. embassy in Moscow. There were reports of hostile attitudes, even open harassment, toward American citizens in Russian cities (Russia's nightly news, *Vremya*, ORT, March 28–April 12). Second, nonviolent protests united not only the communist-nationalist majority of the Russian parliament; for the first time, they involved President Yeltsin (Reuters, April 9, 1999), who issued an order to redirect Russian nuclear missiles to targets in the United States, repealing the goodwill gesture of a few years ago. A stunning 92 percent of Russians polled on this issue denounced the U.S.-led bombing of Yugoslavia. Alexei Arbatov, deputy head of the Duma's defense committee, said that START II has been "put back for a long time" (Johnson's Russia List, No. 3224, April 3, 1999). Specialists began to talk about "very dramatic" outbursts of anti-Americanism in Russia (Weir 1999; Lloyd 1999).

CHANGES IN FOREIGN POLICY

The first signs of the Russian government's bowing to public pressures in foreign policy began to appear in December 1993, when the Yeltsin administration started to adopt some elements of the opposition's rhetoric (Yushin 1994).[18]

Why did such a change in government rhetoric occur? One reason was the slipping popularity of the Yeltsin administration, including the opposition's first electoral victories in 1993. As a result, Yeltsin advisers decided to arm themselves with the opposition's slogans, that is, to follow what millions of voters wanted to hear. In the media, the beginning of 1994 was identified as a time of cooling relations between Russia and the West (Shiraev 1999). At this time, the Foreign Ministry also got involved in the internal political struggle and began to give more thought to how to outplay Yeltsin's political opponents, gain public support, and refute accusations of "pro-American" and "Western" foreign policies (Mlechin 1994). Furthermore, the responsibility for the Chechen campaign's setbacks in 1994 became solely the government's, which caused it—almost in self-defense—to further increase the tone of its nationalistic rhetoric (Simes 1994).

There is evidence that Yeltsin's advisers, being aware of the necessity to face the forthcoming parliamentary and presidential elections, convinced him to begin taking public opinion more seriously (MacKenzie 1995). Even pro-Yeltsin media accused the West of trying to shut Russia out of foreign markets and of underestimating Russian national interests (Sidorov 1994). Political pressures on the Yeltsin administration and its foreign policy mounted in the popularly elected legislature, notably after the 1993 and 1995 elections.

To cite an illustration of this political pressure, Russia began to move visibly away from a policy that was closely aligned with Western powers to one that was more assertive in supporting Serbian interests. In the Spring of 1994, Moscow leaders vigorously objected to NATO air strikes against the Serbs (Pushkov 1994).

The next stage of the transformation in rhetoric occurred in late 1995 and early

1996, in the midst of Kozyrev's being replaced by Yevgeny Primakov and the U.S.-NATO decision to send a military contingent into Bosnia. A majority of Russian lawmakers quizzed by the Mnenie [Opinion] Service hailed Kozyrev's resignation and called for immediate corrections in foreign policy. Despite a virtually hawkish position that Kozyrev adopted by the end of his tenure as foreign minister, his opposition always considered him soft on the West (Kremenyuk 1994). Moreover, as early as January 1994, the largest faction in the Duma, led by Vladimir Zhirinovsky, began to demand the foreign minister's resignation (Rodin 1993; Baturin and Gryzunov 1994).

While most of the rhetoric used by major candidates in the 1996 presidential elections did not cover foreign policy (Sigelman and Shiraev 1998), the candidates tried to distance themselves from the West and the United States (see, e.g., Zhirinovsky, June 14, 1996; Zyuganov, May 17, 1996). Such distancing and the rise of Foreign Minister Primakov were turning points in the process, a serious weakening of the pro-American course set by the Yeltsin administration. Primakov built bridges to communists and ultranationalists in the Duma (and in the electorate) by promising to end the allegedly pro-American foreign policy of his predecessor, denouncing American world dominance, and emphasizing Russia's need to counterbalance U.S. power. Most significantly, Yeltsin himself had to provide unreserved support for Primakov's search for a new foreign policy (*International Affairs*, No. 3, 1998). The collapse of Russia's pro-Western course of the early 1990s became an accepted reality in Russian politics.

There were numerous indirect indicators that public opinion did affect some aspects of foreign policy decisionmaking and rhetoric. For example, in 1997 a group of high-ranking Russian military officials visited the British defense minister and pointed out that Russian officials as well as public opinion did not support NATO expansion (ITAR-TASS, February 7, 1997). In September 1997, retired General Alexander Lebed, considered to be among the main candidates for president in 2000, said that the Russian government was delaying negotiations with Japan about a territorial dispute because Russian public opinion was strongly against making any concessions to Japan (BBC, September 20, 1997). References to "nonpermissive" public opinion regarding the dispute with Japan were also made by the Russian ambassador to Japan, Alexander Panov (Japan Economic Newswire, February 26, 1998). According to Alexei Arbatov, head of the Duma defense committee, those politicians who would compete in forthcoming Russian elections should take into account the widespread anti-NATO public sentiments (Interfax, March 26, 1999).

Even assuming that Russian officials paid careful attention to domestic public opinion, such watchfulness would not necessarily result in foreign policy changes. One should not discount the possibility that public opinion can influence symbolic diplomatic gestures and foreign policy rhetoric. Such symbolic changes can be made deliberately to accommodate public opinion within a country. To illustrate, some of Yeltsin's and Kozyrev's tough anti-NATO and anti-American pronouncements of the 1990s were primarily for domestic consumption, not for officials in Washington and Brussels (Bausin 1995). Let us assume further that anti-Western sentiments in Russian public opinion will continue to grow and have an impact on the policy climate. It is probably expected, then, that anti-Western public opinion can be used in Russia by some politicians and public officials who might try to achieve personal political goals by initiating parliamentary hearings, organizing public boycotts, and making flamboyant and provocative anti-Western and anti-American public statements.[19] And although foreign policy is the prerogative of the Russian president, he or she is not expected to take serious steps without keeping an eye on the legislators and voters (Gornovstaev 1994).

Some authors imply that a swing of Russian public opinion against the West, particularly the United States, is healthy. They argue that if postcommunist euphoria was naive, then disillusion among the nation's citizens could be a sign of maturity (Hearst 1995). In fact, such predictions assume the institutionalization of anti-Western public sentiment for a particular foreign policy.

However, the institutionalization of such attitudes should not be regarded as final and irreversible. Most Russians understand that no matter how frustrated they are about the economy and their national identity, there are grave potential consequences that attend open conflict with the West, especially in the tension between nuclear powers. One should expect that a vast majority of educated Russians are not prepared to sacrifice political liberty for the sake of xenophobic and isolationist ideas amplified by ultranationalist politicians. It is true, however, that many of these isolationist and nationalist ideas are seen in the public's frustration.

Analyzing the changed attitudes of the Russian public about the West, a reporter from the newspaper *Segodnya* suggested—with a great deal of sarcasm—that the West should thank God that Russian military planners did not base Russia's national security policy on public opinion (Smirnov 1997). In fact, the reporter was not necessarily being accurate. Russian politicians and military planners have found it increasingly useful to refer to public opinion in following an anti-Western policy. This is perhaps another paradox of opinion-policy relationships in democratic societies: one should accept the fact that the public can develop and express some contentious, belligerent, even hostile attitudes about a foreign nation or alliance. Nationalism and expansionism can find millions of eager sponsors and backers within public opinion, and the government can thus alter its policy, justifying its action as a "democratic" response to public opinion. It seems that the job of any responsible government in this situation is to do what is right for the world's peace and freedom and not only what is useful for victory in forthcoming elections. Perhaps it is not always "undemocratic" for a policymaker (see Chapter 14 in this volume, by Robert Shapiro and Lawrence Jacobs) to decide against public opinion in some cases when some basic human values are at stake. It can only be expected that Russian politicians will choose not to pursue, without further deliberation, an anti-Western course even though there is an anti-Western and anti-American force in the country's public opinion.

13

Public Attitudes after the Cold War

Ole R. Holsti

The observation is now commonplace that since roughly 1980 the world has witnessed a sea change in thinking and research about public opinion and foreign policy. The earlier consensus was that public opinion was volatile, so poorly structured as to constitute "nonattitudes," and, in the final analysis, largely irrelevant to the conduct of foreign affairs. Each of these alleged attributes of public opinion has come under significant challenge from a variety of quarters.[1] Consequently, whereas public opinion had once been viewed as a residual category that serves primarily to explain deviations from the rational pursuit of vital national interests, it has recently emerged as the subject of serious inquiry among foreign policy analysts. Perhaps the only generalization that has survived through more than sixty years of "scientific" polling is that the general public, especially in the United States, is on balance very poorly informed about foreign affairs.

Philip Everts calls the results of these challenges the "new orthodoxy," a label that should encourage us to adopt a skeptical stance. The dramatic events of the past decade—including but not limited to the end of the Cold War, disintegration of the Soviet Union, and international conflicts that have their origin within the boundaries of failing states—provide an even more compelling reason to reexamine the new orthodoxy. Not only has most of the evidence about public opinion and foreign policy come from the United States, but the bulk of it also emerged from a period dominated first by World War II and soon thereafter by the Cold War. One can plausibly argue that this period was sufficiently atypical to question any generalization derived from public-opinion research. Thus, we need to ask whether and how the end of the Cold War may have affected or even rendered obsolete much of what we have learned about public opinion and foreign policy, and to do so through comparative research that extends beyond the United States. Finally, the end of the Cold War has expanded the range of accessible research sites, opening up opportunities for surveys and analyses in areas, including Eastern Europe and the former Soviet Union, where it had previously been difficult if not impossible to conduct such studies. Chapter 12, by Eric Shiraev and Vlad Zubok, effectively illustrates the kind of analysis that would have been unthinkable a little more than a decade ago.

Before turning to some themes that emerge from the chapters contained in Part 2, it may be useful to provide an overview of the research questions, approaches, and sources of evidence that they encompass. The six chapters are characterized by a rich diversity of perspectives, collectively encompassing virtually the entire range of questions that have engaged public-opinion analysts. All of them describe and analyze some aspect of public opinion; four undertake trend analyses and explore the linkages between public opinion and policymakers; three discuss the role of the media; and Eugene Wittkopf and Ronald Hinckley (Chapter 9) compare the structure and sources of attitudes among the public and opinion leaders.

The chapters also vary in domains of inquiry. They all discuss opinions among the general public, and two chapters also undertake comparisons with policymakers and opinion leaders. Two chapters focus on the United States, three undertake comparative studies using survey data from several Western European countries, and one examines public opinion on foreign policy issues in Russia. Finally, all the authors draw upon survey data; Kull and Ramsay also include evidence from elite interviews.

This commentary will focus on three themes: *stability and change* in public opinion during a period of substantial international changes; the *impact* of public opinion; and the *sources* of public attitudes.

STABILITY AND CHANGE IN POST–COLD WAR PUBLIC OPINION

Historian and former presidential adviser Arthur Schlesinger, once a vocal critic of U.S. intervention in Vietnam, wrote in 1995 that the age of American internationalism was coming to an end. Looking back on the commitment to collective security during the Cold War, he described the hope that "Americans had made the great turning and would forever accept collective responsibilities" as "an illusion." He went on to write, "The collapse of the Soviet threat faces us today with the prospect that haunted Roosevelt half a century ago—the return to the womb in American foreign policy. . . . The isolationist impulse has risen from the grave, and it has taken the new form of unilateralism." In his view, the entire spectrum of American society—including "the housewife in Xenia, Ohio," members of the Council on Foreign Relations, and many officials in Washington—have abandoned the "magnificent dream" of collective security.[2]

Is Schlesinger's obituary for internationalism valid for the United States? Has the spirit of isolationism and unilateralism also taken root among other Western democracies since the end of the Cold War? For almost six decades since Pearl Harbor, there was a widespread belief among American leaders that vital national interests require the United States to play an active leadership role in world affairs; disagreements among elites tended to focus not on the desirability of assuming the burdens—and enjoying the benefits—of international leadership but rather on the goals, strategies, and tactics that should be employed in implementing that role. While European allies were not always persuaded about the wisdom of U.S. policies—the Suez crisis and the Vietnam War were only the most visible sources of dissension—support for cooperative internationalism and such institutions as NATO persisted.

Several chapters address a variant of the Schlesinger thesis. Has "Cold War fatigue" set in not only in the United States but also throughout Western democracies, eroding public support for multilateral internationalism, whether in the form of support of the United Nations, development assistance, or peacekeeping activities? The chapters by Richard Eichenberg (Chapter 10) and Philip Everts (Chapter 11) address most directly the question of how the end of the Cold War has affected European public attitudes toward important issues of foreign and defense policy. Although they focus on somewhat different questions and draw upon different data sets, their overall conclusions are rather similar. Neither Eichenberg nor Everts found dramatic shifts in public sentiments as the Cold War era gave way to the post–Cold War period.

Specifically, Eichenberg concludes that although there are interesting differences among the major countries, public views toward a common European defense force and NATO have remained relatively stable. Although the impact of the 1999 air war against the former Yugoslavia on the future of NATO has yet to play itself out, as of now such findings do not support the prediction by an eminent realist that "NATO's days are not numbered, but its years are."[3] In a similar vein, Everts found greater evidence of continuity than change in Dutch opinions about the necessity and legitimacy of armed forces, although international changes did have implications for specific tasks and the structure of the military. Having uncovered considerable evidence of continuity in public attitudes, he raises an interesting question: In an era of dramatic international change, does stable public opinion present a serious obstacle to sensible policies for conversion and adaptation of the armed forces? He concludes that it does not.

Richard Sobel (Chapter 8) traces the level of public support, both in the United States and in some European countries, for various policy options in the Bosnia conflict of the early and mid-1990s. His findings pose a rather direct challenge to the argument, espoused by the media and a good deal of partisan rhetoric, that these publics were adamantly opposed to taking military action against Serbian forces. They also contradict the Schlesinger thesis of an American reversion to unilateralism. To the contrary, publics on both sides of the Atlantic expressed a strong preference for multilateral action.

Turmoil in the former Yugoslavia also plays a central role in the Shiraev-Zubok analysis of Russian public opinion on international affairs since the end of the Cold War. They describe the public as focused largely on domestic rather than external issues during the early post–Cold War years—the Russian equivalent of "It's the economy, stupid!"—and as largely pro-Western in general orientation, arising in part perhaps from expectations of generous foreign aid from abroad. Those opinions have undergone rather dramatic transformation toward an "anti-U.S. consensus" since the mid-1990s, however, for both external and internal reasons. The expansion of NATO to include three former Warsaw Pact members—Poland, Hungary, and the Czech Republic—brought the NATO alliance to Russia's doorstep. Moreover, Western intervention in Bosnia and the bombing campaign to drive Serbian forces out of Kosovo were perceived as direct and unacceptable challenges to a traditional Russian ally. While ultranationalists of the Zhirinovsky faction have long argued that the West was trampling upon core Russian interests and dignity, NATO expansion and Western interventions on behalf of Muslims in the former Yugoslavia provided many other Russian leaders with ammunition to arouse the public against the United States and its allies. The 1999 attacks on Serbia were especially important, provoking an avalanche of anti-American rhetoric in Moscow.

The Kull-Ramsay and Wittkopf-Hinckley chapters (Chapters 7 and 9) also have implications, albeit less directly, for assessments of attitude changes brought on by the end of the Cold War. In brief, their central findings do not reveal striking changes, but because these studies focus primarily on the impact and sources of public opinion, respectively, they will be discussed in the next two sections.

THE IMPACT OF PUBLIC OPINION

The most difficult questions and elusive answers about public opinion concern its impact on policymakers. There is ample evidence that policymakers differ in their general sensitivity to and assessment of various indicators of public attitudes. Thus, even the most sophisticated quantitative analysis of survey data will not provide adequate answers to queries about whether, under what circumstances, and how strongly they may affect leaders. Elite interviews can be very useful for contemporary cases as well as those in the recent past, and archival research can be used to good advantage for earlier cases.[4] Whereas public opinion was once described as of little demonstrated impact in the foreign policy process, today it is often depicted as a powerful force that policymakers can disregard only at great peril.[5] For example, assertions about the constraining impact of public opinion were a prominent feature of almost every commentary on the NATO air war against Yugoslavia. According to the conventional wisdom, public opinion had created a virtually insurmountable barrier against the introduction of ground troops to protect Kosovars against ethnic cleansing by the Milosevic regime in Belgrade because a NATO troop deployment would surely entail costs—casualties—that Western publics were allegedly no longer willing to tolerate. The strategy of flying beyond the reach of Serbian air-defense systems, even if the less-precise, high-altitude bombing campaign resulted in collateral loss of life among civilian bystanders, was also linked to the public's unwillingness to countenance the loss of pilots.

Attributions of such sentiments and potency to the public have not been limited to the Kosovo conflict, to the Clinton era, or even to the United States. The body-bag syndrome is said to be a significant feature of post–Cold War politics in most, if not all, democracies. According to some observers, public aversion to casualties severely restricts the ability of democracies to pursue their interests effectively, whereas others argue that it serves as a valuable constraint against military interventions that are neither desirable nor likely to be successful.

Although this is not the place to review the cases for and against deploying ground troops in post–Cold War conflicts such as Kosovo, it is appropriate to consider whether the conventional wisdom about public aversion to casualties could possibly be a *misperception* on the part of policymakers. We will return to this point later.

Elite misperceptions of public sentiments are not without precedent. For example, throughout World War II President Franklin D. Roosevelt feared that the American public would reject international engagement as soon as Germany and Japan had been defeated, thus replaying the failures of 1919–1920. Roosevelt's concerns in this respect were amplified by a memorandum that Hadley Cantril, one of the founders of the new science of polling, gave the president just before he left for the Yalta Conference with Stalin and Churchill early in 1945. According to Cantril:

> Although the overwhelming majority of the American people now favor a strong international organization necessarily dominated by the big powers, it is unrealistic to assume that Americans are international-minded. Their policy is rather one of expediency, which, at the moment, takes the form of internationalism. The present internationalism rests on rather unstable foundations: it is recent, it is not rooted in any broad or long-range conception of self-interest, and it has little intellectual basis.[6]

Wartime survey data revealed support for postwar international engagement, but it appears that Cantril's warning was heavily influenced by the expectation that the post–World War I pattern, when the U.S. rejected membership in the League of Nations, would be repeated. Yet only a few months after Cantril's pessimistic memo, the public supported U.S. entry into the United Nations, a fact that surely contributed to the U.S. Senate's overwhelming (89–2) vote favoring membership in the new international organization. Moreover, during the half-decade that followed, the general public also accepted such unprecedented international engagements as charter membership in a "permanent entangling peacetime alliance."

The onset of the Cold War no doubt explains, in part, public support for the Truman Doctrine, the Marshall Plan, and membership in the North Atlantic Treaty Organization, three pillars of American Cold War foreign policy; but at least two other factors may also have been important. Cantril and others who feared that the United States would revert to a mindless isolationism after the war appear to have underestimated the ability of the public to learn from changed international conditions; even a public possessing very limited factual knowledge apparently understood that the international system of 1945 differed significantly from that of 1919. These analysts may also have underestimated the ability of presidents and other top leaders to persuade the public to rethink the alleged virtues of the isolationist tradition, much as Senator Arthur Vandenberg had done on learning of the Japanese attack on Pearl Harbor: "In my own mind, my convictions regarding international cooperation and collective security for peace took form on the afternoon of the Pearl Harbor attack. That day ended isolationism for any realist."[7]

The Kull-Ramsay and Everts chapters highlight the importance of elite perceptions and misperceptions. The former authors present a concise overview of a major public-opinion research undertaking, the Project on International Public Attitudes. Although the chapter summarizes but does not present the wealth of survey data that have emerged from the PIPA project, it does provide an outline of a creative, multistage research design that will serve as a model for future research on the linkages between the public and policymakers.[8] Through a combination of elite interviews and several surveys of the general public, the authors are able to explore and challenge the conventional wisdom, as represented by the Schlesinger thesis, that after five decades of active international engagement the American public has turned isolationist and unilateralist.

Kull and Ramsay provide compelling evidence that during the post–Cold War era U.S. policymakers have often misperceived the actual state of public opinion by consistently underestimating the public's willingness to accept the costs of international engagement, including foreign aid, support for the United Nations, and peacekeeping activities. Although Kull and Ramsay clearly reveal that many leaders in Congress as well as in the media are misreading the public, it should also be noted that they do not romanticize or let the general public off the hook. A thin base of factual knowledge about international affairs also leads the public to misperceive significant aspects of international affairs, including how fellow-citizens feel about such issues. More generally, Kull and Ramsay reveal that misperceptions play a strikingly potent role in all the linkages between the public and policymakers.

In his study of public opinion on defense issues in the Netherlands, Everts also emphasizes the role of elite perceptions and misperceptions in the relationship between the public and policymakers. His observations about the body-bag thesis are pertinent to the question posed earlier:

> In this connection one is struck by the facile way in which the body bag argument was used by politicians and in the media. There is a tendency to parrot one another and to anticipate situations, which may indeed be caused by such talk. Frequent statements of politicians and observers about the expected body bag effects on public support may turn out to be self-fulfilling prophecies.

The death of eighteen U.S. Rangers in Somalia is often cited as the source of the body-bag syndrome in the United States. Yet the initial public response to the horrific deaths in the streets of Mogadishu was to stay the course rather than to withdraw. Thus, it is worth pondering whether the current conventional wisdom is correct in stipulating that the public will not accept the deployment of ground troops in situations such as the conflict in Kosovo that may result in casualties. Or has this been another case of policymakers, abetted by the media, seriously misreading the public?

Several of the themes that emerge from other chapters are reinforced by Sobel's study of public opinion on the Bosnia conflict. Both American and European publics had a strong preference for multilateral rather than unilateral action. Moreover, while his data show that the American public was indeed sensitive to casualties, it was nevertheless prepared to support deployment of ground troops into Bosnia if that were required to punish Serbian misconduct. His conclusion is also strikingly congruent with those of the Everts and Kull-Ramsay chapters.

Kull and Ramsay propose a number of explanations for the tendency of leaders to misread the public: failure to seek out information about public attitudes, responding to the vocal public as if it were the majority, viewing Congress and the media as mirrors of the public, and underestimating the public. In the conclusion of his chapter, Everts suggests still another reason for the tendency of Dutch policymakers to underestimate the public's willingness to engage in peacekeeping and other defense-related activities: it provides them an excuse and a form of legitimization for their own reluctance to support such undertakings. The process described by Shiraev and Zubok is a somewhat more complex variant of the elite-public relationship. External events—NATO expansion, interventions in the former Yugoslavia, and the failure of the West to meet expectation of foreign aid on the scale of the post–World War II Marshall Plan—energized even formerly pro-Western Russian leaders to reshape public opinion about the United States and its allies. Having succeeded in that undertaking, these leaders can then point to anti-Western public opinion as a constraint upon their own policies. The recent Russian invasion of Chechnya provides an example. Western complaints about Russian human-rights violations provoked President Boris Yeltsin into a bitter denunciation of American society, military domination, and the Clinton administration. A Russian political scientist and presidential adviser asserted that had Yeltsin failed to respond in this manner "he would have been viewed as an idiot before his public, his army, his government."[9]

SOURCES OF PUBLIC OPINION

Efforts to identify the background correlates of public attitudes have long been an active area of research. Although studies during the height of the Cold War rarely uncovered striking partisan differences on foreign and defense policy, analyses of public opinion during the post-Vietnam era have found that party identification and ideology are consistently correlated to attitudes on these issues.

The chapter by Wittkopf and Hinckley takes the Schlesinger thesis—that the Cold War exhausted the reservoir of internationalist sentiments to the point that the public is ready to "return to the womb"—as the starting point from which they direct their analyses toward assessing hypotheses that identify different sources of attitudes among the general public and elites: the former were posited as reacting primarily to domestic socioeconomic conditions, whereas the latter were more likely to respond to political symbols. They found that both groups are in fact more responsive to political symbols (party and ideology) than to socioeconomic and contextual factors. In explaining their results, Wittkopf and Hinckley point to the possibility that an inability to obtain contextual data from smaller units—these are more sensitive to geographical variations on such factors as crime or unemployment—may have obscured the real impact of the environmental variables. Given the vast socioeconomic differences that may exist even within adjoining areas of a modest-sized city, that explanation may well have merit.

It may also be useful to consider some other reasons for their findings. For example, regional differences have traditionally been cited as a source of attitudes toward foreign affairs; the Midwest was said to be isolationist, the South was the home of free-traders and supporters of martial virtues, and the Northeast was predominantly internationalist. Although these regional differences can help to explain voting patterns in Congress, they may have tended to erode during recent decades, in part because the current generation of Americans is more geographically mobile than their parents, in part because the media, both print and electronic, have become nationalized.[10] Local newspapers and independent television stations have become an endangered species; many are either out of business or have been merged into huge media conglomerates. Most Americans depend on the same sources of information to learn about crime, layoffs arising from outsourcing of jobs to low-cost foreign subsidiaries, and other aspects of the socioeconomic environment. Thus, it would not be surprising if regional and local differences reflected in the statistics that drive the sociotropic model often give way to perceptions that are more sensitive to symbolic politics: party identification, ideological predispositions, and the like.

CONCLUSION

Among the many strengths of the six chapters in Part 2 is that they provide several opportunities for reassessing generalizations that are derived excessively from the United States during the Cold War. Although only two chapters undertake direct and explicit Cold War/post–Cold War comparisons, they all contribute to our understanding of public opinion as we move into the second post–Cold War decade—the first decade of the third millennium.

During the decade following World War II, several distinguished scholars, journalists, and statesmen—including Gabriel Almond, Thomas Bailey, Hans Morgenthau, Walter Lippmann, and George Kennan—feared that a volatile, ignorant, and emotional public would seriously and perhaps even fatally impede the ability of better-informed and more farsighted policymakers to pursue vital national interests in an increasingly dangerous world.[11] However, some of them would later come to have doubts about the proposed remedy of strengthening executive prerogatives vis-à-vis the public and legislatures for conducting foreign affairs.

One of the key themes of these chapters raises a somewhat related question about the conduct of foreign affairs in the post–Cold War era. What are the implications for democratic governance when policymakers attribute considerable potency to public opinion—the nightmare scenario of the observers cited above—yet fail to perceive accurately the actual state of public attitudes and preferences? Most realists would admonish policymakers to follow the advice of the U.S. State Department official who asserted, "To hell with public opinion. . . . We should lead and not follow."[12] Shiraev and Zubok bring up a related point in their conclusion: perhaps it is not always undemocratic for policymakers to decide against public opinion in some cases when some basic human values are at stake. Those who find such prescriptions to be unrealistic in light of political processes in contemporary democratic states, or who are not quite prepared to sever the links between the public and policymakers, would do well to ponder the issue—and possible ways of coping more effectively with it.

III

THE PUBLIC OPINION– FOREIGN POLICY LINKAGE

14

Who Leads and Who Follows?
U.S. Presidents, Public Opinion, and Foreign Policy

Robert Y. Shapiro and Lawrence R. Jacobs

The relationship between public opinion and government policymaking is fundamental to understanding how democracy works, not only in the United States but in liberal democracies worldwide. While some theorists and other writers continue to argue that the existence of free and periodic elections of representatives and leaders ("procedural democracy") is all that "democracy" requires to assure citizens' control of what governments do (e.g., from Schumpeter 1950 to Zaller 1992), others maintain that there should also be identifiable influences of public opinion on some important portion of the policies that governments pursue ("substantive democracy"; see, e.g., Key 1961; Page and Shapiro 1983, 1992; Stimson, MacKuen, and Erikson 1995; Jacobs and Shapiro 1994c). This applies not only to a country's domestic policies but also to a nation's foreign and defense policies.

Foreign and defense policies do not have a privileged place (see Russett 1990; Russett and Graham 1989; Shapiro and Page 1988, 1994). In particular, *The Rational Public* (Page and Shapiro 1992) examined fifty years of trends in Americans' policy preferences and found no strikingly profound differences between foreign and defense issues in the overall nature and quality of public opinion. The main differences that exist are twofold. First, foreign policy issues tend to be less salient. While this in part may be due to their complexity, this can better be attributed to the lower level of visibility of these issues in the mass media—even today on daily television in the United States—*unless* crisis events (such as the war in Serbia and Kosovo) occur in the foreign policy arena. Second, such critical events have tended to unfold or to be sprung on the public through the media more quickly on foreign policy than on domestic issues, so that we find more abrupt shifts in public opinion in response to these occurrences. But by the same token, there is a wide range of domestic issues that is not salient at any moment in time, and domestic crises have occurred that have produced relatively quick movements in public opinion (Page and Shapiro 1992, chap. 2).

Thus, the differences in foreign versus domestic opinions are differences in degree concerning salience and a sense of national urgency that at times may seem large. But when issues are salient in the news media, policymakers, other elites, and the public simultaneously pay a high level of attention to them, so that the public will exert as much influence as it might expect to have on the policymaking process (see Schattschneider 1960). At the same time, the public will respond to new information that becomes available from elites and the media on these issues. We know from accumulated research that once an issue has visibly emerged, public opinion will show considerable stability or respond in sensible and explicable ways to new information, without vacillating randomly or in a volatile way (see the analyses of public opinion offered in other chapters in this volume; Page and Shapiro 1992).

What, then, can be said about the impact of public opinion on American foreign policy? We take as a starting point the general effect of public opinion on policymaking in the United States. Reviewing the growing research literature on this matter, we find a great deal of evidence that government policies in the United States often and substantially reflect what the public wants. While the correspondence or correlation between public opinion and policy (defined in different ways) is apparent, the evidence that these represent genuine causal relationships is far from conclusive (Page 1994).

More precisely, despite decades of research on public attitudes and public policy in the United States, we have only recently begun to understand how and to what extent the public affects the policymaking process on salient domestic issues. We know far less about the effect of public opinion on foreign policy, since such issues have tended to be less salient. While we know much about the volatility, stability, and coherence of public opinion concerning foreign and defense issues through the end of the Cold War, we have limited, if any, systematic knowledge about the causal linkage process that connects public opinion and foreign policy.

This chapter first reviews some of the evidence for the effects of public opinion on foreign and defense policy, including recent research suggesting that important changes may have occurred in American politics. It then takes a closer look at the causal connection over time between public opinion and presidential policymaking and at normative questions about democratic processes. There is evidence that presidents have paid increasing attention to public opinion with the institutionalization of polling and public-opinion analysis in the White House. While this suggests that policymaking has become more responsive to public opinion, recent developments—the winding down of the Cold War and changes in the press's coverage of foreign affairs—have allowed presidents increasing opportunity to lead or manipulate public opinion.

PAST EVIDENCE FOR THE EFFECT OF PUBLIC OPINION ON FOREIGN POLICY

Procedural democracy—the control that voters exert through reward and punishment in elections—provides public opinion with the means to constrain what governments do. Clearly, electoral motivations that lead policymakers to anticipate what voters will do at election time is an important reason to expect government policies not to deviate greatly from what citizens want. V.O. Key's (1960) metaphor of "dikes" constraining the movement of policy is apt, but such structures can be built to channel policy in particular directions, so that public opinion may be more than just a passive constraint on policymaking. We return below to the process by which public opinion affects policy.

The first important empirical question is: How much correspondence, or "congruence," do we find between foreign policy and public opinion? Such correspondence can be defined in many ways, including: the simple matching of policy changes with majority opinion supporting change (or the status quo), to the extent that actual majority preferences can be accurately measured ("majoritarian congruence"; cf. Monroe 1979, Weissberg 1976); the matching of legislative representatives' policy votes with the preferences of their constituents (cf. Miller and Stokes 1963, Weissberg 1976, 1978); comparing changes in public opinion with changes in policy, to see if both move in the same direction ("covariational congruence"; see Weissberg 1976; Page and Shapiro 1983); and, expanding upon the last approach, extensive comparisons over time of trends in public opinion and policy that ideally would involve formal time-series modeling (e.g., Hartley and Russett 1992; Ostrom and Marra 1986; Stimson, MacKuen, and Erikson 1995).

Using these approaches, substantial evidence has shown that foreign and defense policymaking has been, at least in the correlational sense, responsive to majority opinion (Monroe 1979). In addition, as defense issues become salient, legislators' votes in the U.S. Congress have shown responsiveness to constituency preferences (contrast Bartels 1991, findings on defense spending, with Miller and Stokes 1963, results for congressional voting on foreign policy).

Table 14.1 presents summary data on the frequency of "covariational congruence" between changes in public opinion with subsequent changes in policy; that is, a congruent case is one in which opinion changes significantly in a particular direction and *subsequent* policy in the following year shows movement in the same direction. While based on this method we find more frequent congruence for domestic than foreign policy issues (72 percent to 62 percent), there is noticeable variation among foreign policy issues, with congruence occurring most often for what are clearly salient wartime issues. Moreover, the American public ultimately did not constrain the United States from entering World War II or going to war in Vietnam, so clearly the public can push and pull in different directions. The same might be said about the Gulf War in 1991 (cf. Mueller 1994) and perhaps the war in Kosovo, though in these cases—and in the case of foreign policymaking generally—any congruence we find between public opinion and policy might be due to the flexibility that the public allows policymakers. In cases of opinion-policy agreement, the public may be permissively going along with government policies. Indeed, many of the findings in Table 14.1 and in the research cited above may be manifestations of the reverse effect of policy on opinion. Nonetheless, the striking frequency of opinion-

Table 14.1   Congruence Between Changes in Public Opinion and Changes in Policy, 231 Domestic and Foreign Policy Issues

		Percentage Component (N)	
DOMESTIC POLICY			71.6% (109)
Social		78%(55)	
Civil rights and liberties	79% (28)		
Other social and lifestyle	78 (27)		
Economic and Social Welfare		66 (35)	
Social welfare	62 (13)		
Inflation, taxes, other	68 (22)		
Political Reform, Big Govt., Labor		63 (19)	
FOREIGN POLICY			61.5 (122)
World War II		100 (7)	
Vietnam War, Korea, China		71 (17)	
Foreign Aid		65 (26)	
Russia		64 (14)	
National Defense, Draft		53 (19)	
Collective Security		50 (14)	
Other Foreign and Related Policies		52 (25)	

Note: Percentages are based on the *N*s shown in parentheses, which are the total number of congruent plus noncongruent cases.
Source: Shapiro (1982, 70)

policy congruence in Table 14.1 challenges arguments that policymakers have ignored public opinion.

Furthermore, some of the fuller available time-series data and the time-series correlations that have been estimated for them, with time lags for opinion affecting policy, provide even stronger evidence for a causal influence of public opinion. In the case of public opinion and U.S. troop withdrawal from Vietnam, the rate of U.S. troop withdrawal was sensitive to public attitudes toward the war in general and toward the rate of troop withdrawal in particular (see Page and Shapiro 1992; Shapiro and Page 1994). There was an even more impressive correlation between the level of U.S. defense spending and public support for increasing spending (see Shapiro and Page 1994; Hartley and Russett 1992; Ostrom and Marra 1986; Bartels 1991; Wlezien 1995, 1996). The striking interpretation of the public-opinion and spending trends is that the public helped give defense spending a big boost in the early 1980s, peaking after the Iran hostage crisis and the Soviet invasion of Afghanistan. Both the opinion and policy trends subsequently reversed course sharply, with far fewer people thinking we were spending too little on defense and more responding that we were spending too much, with defense spending subsequently cut after the nation entered a deep recession and as the Reagan administration's fiery rhetoric toward the Soviet Union subsided. In this case, public opinion hardly appeared to play a passive role.

Taken together, and given the importance of the specific cases themselves, this evidence for effects of public opinion on policy in the United States, covering the period into the 1980s, is compelling. But it is still rough, and it does not cover the period near the end of and after the Cold War. For one, any simple bivariate analysis of this sort requires that other variables—other explanations—be considered. In addition, as already noted, the causal direction may also be in doubt. Further, persuasive support for a causal effect requires evidence concerning intervening variables and processes that link public opinion to subsequent policy decisions.

Some recent trends have made more compelling and intriguing this need for additional evidence regarding the status and nature of the causal connection between public opinion and policy. There are some data that show that this relationship has varied over time, and that since 1980, government policymaking has been less responsive to public opinion than during the prior period beginning in 1960. As shown in Table 14.2, when the combined data reported in Table 14.1 are compared over time, the 1969–1979 period appears to have been a high point in congruence between changes in public opinion and policies. As noted further below, during this time the Johnson and Nixon administrations began institutionalizing the analysis of public opinion in the White House.

However, Alan Monroe (1998) updated his earlier analysis (1979) of the congruence between majority public support (or opposition) to proposed changes in government policy and subsequent policy, and he found that the consistency between public opinion and policy declined from 1980 to 1993. Table 14.3 summarizes Monroe's findings (Monroe 1998, 14, table 2), which show an overall decline in consistency from 63 percent to 55 percent. Most important, as shown in the table, one of the largest drops occurs in foreign policy issues, from 84 percent to 67 percent. In contrast, defense policy did not exhibit this trend, but moved a bit in the opposite direction. This change in responsiveness to public opinion, particularly in

Table 14.2 Congruence Between Changes in Public Opinion and Changes in Policy: Variations in Congruence Over Time, 1935–1979

Time Period	Percentage Congruent	(N)
1935–1945	67%	(18)
1946–1952	63	(59)
1953–1960	59	(37)
1961–1968	54	(26)
1968–1979	75	(91)

Note: Percentages are based on the *N*s shown in parentheses, which are the total number of congruent plus noncongruent cases.

Source: Shapiro (1982, Table 14, 83)

Table 14.3   Majority Opinion/Policy Consistency by Policy Area: Variations in Consistency, 1960–79, 1981–83

	1960–79		1981–83	
	Consistent (%)	N	Consistent (%)	N
All cases	63	327	55	566
By policy area:				
Social Welfare	63	51	51	45
Economic and labor	67	46	51	156
Defense	52	21	61	49
Foreign policy	84	38	67	150
Civil rights/liberties	59	39	56	61
Energy and environment	72	36	67	27
Political reform	41	34	17	23
Vietnam	71	35	—	—
Miscellaneous	74	27	40	55

Source: Monroe (1998, Table 2, 14)

foreign policymaking, is a puzzle that requires further attention as we examine the causal processes that actually connect public opinion to presidential policymaking.

STUDYING THE CAUSAL CONNECTION

If we stake electoral motivations as the critical driving force behind policymakers responding to public opinion, one point of consensus can be found in the research on the opinion-policy linkage: political parties play a major part in this process.

A number of different studies have shown how party activists, leaders, and government officials convey or magnify the preferences of partisans in the mass public. There is evidence of this in political parties' delegations and platforms in the United States (Monroe 1983; Jacobs 1993; Shapiro and Jacobs 1999); we find this in Congress and in legislative bodies in the American states (Erikson, Wright, and McIver 1993; Page, Shapiro, Gronke, and Rosenberg 1984), as well as in Western Europe (Dalton 1996). While this evidence is also compelling, it has three limitations.

First, it usually does no more (though this might be interpreted as a lot) than add a third variable to our original bivariate analysis, leaving additional work to be done and evidence to be obtained to strengthen any causal inference. Second, it requires that there be party differences on at least some issues of interest; otherwise choices of party allegiance would make no clear difference in conveying preferences into the policymaking process. While there have indeed been such party differences on domestic issues in the United States (on "party cleavage" issues, see Page 1978), in the area of foreign policy there has typically been more consensus than difference (except in evaluating the performance of the president and his party generally, and in the case of defense spending when this issue is framed as a guns-or-butter trade-off that has divided American parties). Parties have not necessary been critical in linking public opinion to foreign policy and security issues. Yet this may be changing, as there has been increasing overall partisan polarization in the U.S. Congress, in which case there could be party differences on foreign policy that could contribute to increasing responsiveness as party control of the Senate and Congress as a whole has changed between 1980 and 1994. Here, however, polarization may prevent consensus-building (especially when supermajority legislative votes are required, as in the case of the ratification of treaties by the Senate) and responsiveness to more centrist public opinion (for a review of the debate on partisan polarization in Congress and its consequences, see Jacobs and Shapiro 2000). Third, even if parties provide a linkage, there may be other political mechanisms at work, which means we must look further for other processes that connect the public to policymaking.

In looking further, the research strategy that needs to be pursued is substantial. We should continue research that looks for *generalizable* patterns and cases of opinion-policy congruence. We should continue to incorporate additional variables that might affect both the public and policymakers or that provide evidence for the role of political parties or other institutional ways of linking the mass public to policymaking (e.g., Risse-Kappen 1994). But the additional work that is now essential is historical and in-depth case-study research. While this analysis may lack the generalizability of research based upon a large number ("N") of cases, it can provide the essential evidence needed to disentangle causal processes and mechanisms. This type of research takes longer to do, requiring archival, interview, secondary analysis, and other ways of gathering evidence that will directly allow us to track how policymakers learn about and respond to public opinion. The case studies that have already been done have helped complement and supplement the research that has already been described. These include, for example, Lawrence Jacobs's (1993) study of health-care policy in Britain and the United States that uncovered a "recoil effect" in which political leaders' efforts to manipulate public opinion led them to track and respond to mass opinion in order to more effectively influence it. Studies of specific foreign policy issues and processes have confirmed that public opinion has mattered notably in U.S.-Chinese relations (Kusnitz 1984), in U.S. policymaking toward the contras in Nicaragua (Sobel 1993), and in foreign policymaking during the Carter (Katz 1998) and Reagan-Bush years (Hinckley 1992). Natalie La Balme (1998) has been engaged in recent research in France that has explored the circumstances under which the French government has been more likely to respond to rather than ignore public opinion in foreign policymaking.

A still better and more important strategy, beyond case studies of individual issues and particular time periods, is one that attempts to synthesize in-depth research in order to unravel historical and current trends in the causal relationship between public opinion and policy. This strategy requires finding trends over time in the extent to which policymakers seek out or otherwise get information on public opinion and respond to or are otherwise affected by this information. Jacobs (1993) did this in the case of health-care policy, and Thomas Graham (1989, 1994), more relevant to this chapter, did the same for nuclear arms control from the beginning of the Cold War to the 1980s. Powlick (1991, 1995), in particular, found that there has been an increase in serious and responsive attention to public opinion in the State Department, representing a change in what Bernard Cohen (1973) had found earlier; but the most recent trend he found was for the Reagan and Clinton administrations to place more institutional emphasis in foreign policymaking on *leading* rather than following public opinion.

In an important book-length treatment of this subject, Douglas Foyle (1999) also emphasizes that, overall, presidents from Truman to Clinton have tended to behave as "realist" (in contrast to Wilsonian "liberal") theorists in international relations: they have tended toward leading and not responding to public opinion in foreign policy. However, this tendency to lead has varied from president to president in ways that show this to be a characteristic of the individual president, not of the office or institution of the presidency. Foyle emphasizes how the extent to which presidents choose to lead or follow public opinion depends on their beliefs about the appropriate role of public opinion in foreign policymaking and the context in which a policy choice has to be made (Foyle 1999, preface). Foyle focused intensively on the Eisenhower administration and provided case studies of crisis issues versus less high pressured and more deliberative policy decisions. While realist decisionmaking occurred in a number of cases, some presidents at certain times—most notably President Clinton in the case of withdrawing American troops from Somalia—were clearly more receptive than others to the public's input into policymaking.

Overall, this in-depth, historically oriented research, focusing on how presidents and others directly used information about public opinion, suggests that there is a reciprocal relationship between public opinion and policymaking: government responds to, as well as leads, public opinion. Clearly, it is necessary to track these processes over time in order to see if particular trends or tendencies have emerged, or if the influences at work hinge on the beliefs and decisionmaking contexts of individual presidents.

We have been engaged in a project along these lines as well, examining, through primary-source research, the increasing institutionalization of public-opinion analysis by American presidents. Our focus has been somewhat different from that of others who have focused on different presidents or different aspects or issues of presidential politics or decisionmaking (see the authors cited above and Heith 1998a, 1998b, 2000; Katz 1998). We started our research with the Kennedy administration and have completed substantial work through the Nixon presidency, followed by Reagan and Clinton. Our two relevant sets of findings for this chapter concern (1) the nature of the linkage process that has evolved; and (2) the particular relationships we have found between public opinion and foreign policymaking by American presidents.

The opinion-policy process that has evolved is one in which presidents have increasingly assembled and analyzed their own information on public opinion. While presidents and politicians have long used unscientific methods to estimate where the public stood on issues, and while scientifically gathered public-opinion data found their way into the White House beginning with Roosevelt, only since Kennedy has the entire process been routinized into the institutional functioning of the presidency.

In brief, the driving force for this is electoral, as presidents once in office strive to be reelected. Presidents started to use their own pollsters and public-opinion consultants or staff during their campaigns, with private polls being paid for by the political parties or other nongovernmental sources (the history of this is described in Jacobs and Shapiro 1995a; Heith 1998a, 1998b, 2000). In these histories, the most important data are the numbers of polls that Johnson, Nixon, and later presidents conducted and, most notably in our judgment (though we have not yet examined all the available data), the figures for Reagan and Clinton during their two terms in office, which show that the level of polling has become substantial indeed. The attention to public opinion during Clinton's 1996 election campaign and continuing into his second term may well put him clearly in the lead.

In addition to the clear electoral objectives of presidents, the other important aspect of the process is that since the Carter administration the scope of the sharing and deliberation over public-opinion information within the administration has expanded (Heith 1998a, 2000). The result is that the White House has become increasingly better positioned than in the past to respond to or to attempt to lead—or manipulate—public opinion.

What patterns, then, have emerged? With respect to the choices faced by Presidents Kennedy through Nixon to lead or follow public opinion, we find striking evidence for cases of government responsiveness to public opinion, cases of opinion leadership, and cases of presidents working against public opinion for particular reasons. Responsiveness occurred on salient issues, especially those that clearly had potential electoral consequences.

As Kennedy ran for the presidency in 1959–1960, his pollster and consultant, Louis Harris, provided public-opinion data that enabled Kennedy's campaign to use issues to heighten Kennedy's image as the candidate who could "get America on the move at home and abroad" (Jacobs and Shapiro 1994b, 531). His emphasis on keeping national defense strong and being vigilant abroad rang true with the American public, but Kennedy did take what he knew to be an unpopular position supporting foreign aid. His purpose was motivated by his need to establish credibility in elite circles and to attempt to educate the public about policies that advanced the nation's interests (Jacobs and Shapiro 1994b, 534).

While Harris did not follow Kennedy to the White House, he continued to provide the president with polling data. Although this was not a formal relationship, it revealed that there was in fact an increased need for this kind of information in a routinized manner in modern politics. Responding to public opinion based on polls early in his administration, as indicated by positions he took in his State of the

Union addresses, Kennedy emphasized his support for the Peace Corps, better relations with allies, strengthening the United Nations, and ameliorating the country's balance of payments (Jacobs and Shapiro 1992).

After Kennedy, White House polling and analysis of public opinion became a regular part of the Johnson and Nixon administrations, with Johnson having available to him information obtained by pollster Oliver Quayle, and Nixon (privately and through the Republican Party) commissioning full polls regarding his public image, support, and policy proposals. During the Johnson administration, the 1964 election provided an important juncture in how the president used information on public opinion. Concerned about being reelected, Johnson at first tended to respond to the public's wishes, emphasizing the popular desire to pursue world disarmament and peace, in sharp contrast to the widely perceived positions of his Republican opponent, Barry Goldwater. Based on his polling reports, Johnson made sure to distinguish himself regarding the use of U.S. military force, including the use of nuclear weapons in Vietnam. But Johnson, like Kennedy, attempted to lead, rather than respond to, the public on the issue of foreign aid. Johnson's apparent strategy of responding to public opinion was particularly pronounced on domestic issues as well. Johnson continued this responsive behavior even after it became clear he would easily defeat Goldwater. He did so to solidify his public support for purposes of leading the public on his racial and social policy agendas after the election (Jacobs and Shapiro 1993).

Our analysis of the relationship between Johnson's policy positions and objectives and his private polling information reveals that beginning after the election, in 1965, Johnson did indeed choose to *lead*, not follow, the public. His forceful leadership on domestic proposals, especially the War on Poverty, had not been demanded by the public, but the public came to change its views and support this effort. In the case of foreign policy, the Vietnam War became an issue of extreme contention, and here Johnson had no intention of letting the public influence his actions. There was a clear break in this opinion-policy relationship between 1964 and 1965–1966, with responsiveness declining and leadership increasing from the first to the second period, with Vietnam being the dominant issue in foreign policy (Jacobs and Shapiro 1993). In the end, however, after 1965–1966, the failure to respond to what Johnson knew to be public opinion on particular aspects of the Vietnam War had increasingly adverse effects on his presidency, which raised normative questions for realist arguments about public opinion and foreign policymaking (Jacobs and Shapiro 1994a). Yet another lesson that could be learned was that while polling could provide important information about the need to respond to public opinion, polling might also provide insights about the best means to move the public in directions presidents might want.

The Nixon administration greatly expanded the institutional organization and sophistication of White House–directed polling and public-opinion analysis. Despite his claims that political leaders should not be influenced by polls, Nixon and his advisers used polling data to avoid taking unpopular positions and to enhance their ability to lead the public on policies that they wanted to pursue, especially in the area of foreign policy (where Nixon clearly wanted to leave his historical mark). The archival evidence shows that Nixon ultimately responded to public opinion in a manner consistent with the trends in public opinion and the withdrawal of troops from Vietnam that we described earlier (for a detailed account of this, see Katz 1998). Clearly, the Vietnam War was regarded as a crucial election issue in 1972, even with a substantial and steady lead by Nixon over his Democratic opponent, George McGovern, in all preelection polling.

While our research on Nixon is not yet complete (see Jacobs and Shapiro 1995a; 1995–1996), we have found that the Nixon administration was persistent in tracking public opinion on a wide range of policy and political concerns (especially approval of the president). Thus, it is not surprising that the general analysis of opinion-policy congruence reported in Table 14.1 and Table 14.2 shows that this kind of responsiveness was higher during the Nixon administration than in previous periods. Indeed, the White House itself not only had a veritable warehouse of its own private polls but also possessed virtually the same publicly available opinion data on which such academic analyses were based (Shapiro 1982; Page and Shapiro 1983). Another impressive case of both opinion responsiveness and leadership in foreign policy concerned the admission of China to the United Nations, paving the way for formal U.S. recognition of China. Our archival evidence clearly shows that Nixon and his advisers had seen the softening of the public's hostility toward China, making it more receptive to efforts to lead it further in a less belligerent direction. The result was Nixon's trip to China and China's admission to the UN, which Nixon and his administration did not finalize until they found further public support for it in their own polling data (cf. Kusnitz 1984). At the same time, Nixon increased the salience of this issue for the public in a way that enhanced his and his party's electoral appeal.

Thus, through the Nixon period we find evidence—at times substantial—for presidential responsiveness to public opinion toward foreign policy. This responsiveness occurred in ways associated with actual or anticipated electoral advantages, during a period in U.S. history in which Cold War foreign policies could become major election-year issues. As the Cold War ended, however, we might have expected this to change: foreign policy issues might no longer arise as potentially make-or-break election issues as the Korean War, Vietnam, and the 1979–1980 Iran and Afghanistan crises had been. While polling, public opinion analysis, and the institutionalization of public-relations activities within the presidency might provide the means for responding to public opinion and gaining the public's favor, these tools and institutions also offered the means to try to direct, not respond to, public opinion.

While we have emphasized the reciprocal relationship between public opinion and presidential policymaking and have cited examples of responsiveness to public opinion, we have increasing reason to believe that the dominant trend is toward less presidential responsiveness and greater efforts at leading or otherwise directing public opinion. We do not think that this has to do with the personal characteristics of presidents, but rather with processes not only institutionalizing the means to track and follow public opinion, but also of learning how to use these means as political resources to lead and manipulate public opinion.

From a theoretical perspective, there are obvious limitations on strong presidential leadership of public opinion (though this may be normatively appealing to many political and foreign policy analysts). Presidents' and their political parties' (who largely pay for such political polling) motivations for election or reelection surely create pressing incentives to be responsive to public opinion, in order to avoid falling too far out of line with the median voter (Downs 1957). Indeed, John Geer's (1996) important book on this subject persuasively contends that these incentives should dominate presidents' use of polling—so much so that leadership should largely occur "by accident." We think that this was very reasonable to expect early in the history of presidents and polling, and clearly this still occurs during election campaign periods; elections are the mechanisms that prevent government policies from deviating too much from public preferences during certain important periods. Consistent with this, and contrary to widespread belief, presidents have tended to keep their campaign promises, although in the case of foreign policy—particularly, most recently, in the case of Bill Clinton—these promises are very often relatively general expressions of policy goals and concerns, for which it is easy to appear to be responsive to public opinion (see Shaw 1998; Jacobs and Shapiro 1995b).

But election periods aside, there is in fact a fairly long period during which presidents have the freedom and opportunity to act without worrying immediately about electoral repercussions from the public. Come the next election, voters' memories may fade concerning government actions that they did not support, especially as other issues supersede and eclipse the not-so-distant past. Presidents may have time to explain, and even claim credit for, actions that the public had not supported, as, for example, Bill Clinton did in the cases of the U.S. invasion of Haiti and in some policies (at least initially) regarding intervention in Bosnia (in which there was ultimately probably supportive but divided public opinion; cf. Sobel 1996b). Further, the electoral incentives for presidents are likely to wane for them, though not for their parties, during their second terms in office. It is true that since Eisenhower only Reagan and Clinton have been second-term presidents, so our evidence regarding such presidents is limited. But the tendency for presidential-opinion leadership between elections is likely to be much more pertinent for future second-term presidents.

To examine trends toward or away from presidential responsiveness to public opinion, the critical starting point is the Carter administration. The Carter administration was the first to have a publicly visible pollster, Patrick Caddell, who was brought in from Carter's successful presidential campaign. Caddell was the institutional successor to the relatively effective polling and public-opinion analysis of the Nixon administration. While the Ford administration has not yet been fully analyzed from this vantage point, it essentially inherited the polling and public-opinion arrangements that Nixon had created through the Republican Party involving pollster-consultant Robert Teeter. But Ford did not benefit, as Nixon and later presidents did, from continuing relationships that began during election campaigns and continued and evolved during presidencies.

To what extent did the Carter presidency try to be responsive to public opinion? Not as much as expected. This is surprising for a president who believed it was desirable for public opinion to have some influence on foreign policy. In terms of his normative beliefs, Carter thought public involvement in open decisionmaking would benefit foreign policymaking by preventing mistakes that might occur if a policy formed in secret (Foyle 1999).

That being said, it is not obvious that Carter would use polling and public-opinion analysis to facilitate this, and the Carter White House clearly did not do the continuous polling of the sort done by later administrations that would have been required for this purpose. The most widely prevalent conclusion about Carter was that he was a "trustee" president more concerned with acting effectively on behalf of the people but not taking direct "delegate"-style guidance from them (see Jones 1988; Hargrove 1988; Shapiro and Jacobs 1999).

As Diane Heith (1998b, for Carter and other presidents) and we (Jacobs and Shapiro 1993, 1994b, for other presidents) have noted elsewhere, polling may affect what issues presidents push to the top of their political agenda, but actual policymaking is a different story. And presidents can independently raise issues that the public will then take up as their own (see Jacobs and Shapiro 1993). Carter was influenced by the actual issues the nation faced and by his own personal assessments of them, and he acted accordingly (cf. Katz 1998; Heith 2000; Foyle 1999). He used polling on foreign policy as a tool for determining how to explain and present his already determined policies to the public. As Katz (1998) argues, however, Carter had difficulty in doing this effectively since he misread the public, whom he thought would be persuaded by arguments that framed positions in terms of liberal-conservative ideology rather than through the more relevant frame of reference of "militant" versus less aggressive or more general activism in foreign affairs. (By contrast, Carter was apparently more effective in responding to and leading public opinion with regard to increasing defense spending in the late 1970s; on his administration, see also Graham 1989, 1994.)

Thus, Carter, in practice, was not especially responsive to public opinion. Furthermore, when it came to using information about public opinion to gain public support in foreign policy, he was ineffective. Later presidents, beginning with Ronald Reagan, picked up where the Nixon administration left off and became better at it. Our working hypothesis is that the Reagan administration's method of analysis and use of information on public opinion are the most informative reference points for future research on public opinion and presidential policymaking.

THE REAGAN ADMINISTRATION

Our analysis of the archival evidence from the Reagan Library is preliminary, and we are doing similar research and reading the work of others based on primary-source evidence for the Bush and Clinton administrations. Our extensive research on domestic policymaking during Clinton's first term in office has revealed that his administration used polling and public-opinion analysis to attempt to direct public opinion to support its health-care reform and related policy efforts from 1993 to 1994; the administration became responsive only in the lead-up period to the 1996 presidential election (Jacobs and Shapiro 2000). If domestic issues were largely treated this way, we do not expect to find foreign policy treated differently (cf. Foyle 1999, containing an analysis of the cases of U.S. intervention in Somalia and Bosnia; but in these cases there was noticeable public opposition early on regarding Bosnia, and in the case of Somalia, public opinion began moving against further intervention *before* American soldiers were killed, wounded, and humiliated in the unsuccessful effort to capture the enemy clan leader there; see Jacobs and Shapiro 1995b, 203–206). But the important point to be made here is that this type of behavior was informed by apparently well orchestrated polling and public-opinion analysis that had not begun with the Clinton administration.

To start, public opinion was regularly monitored in the Reagan White House. Richard Wirthlin and his firm, Decision Making Information (DMI), conducted most of Reagan's public-opinion analysis. We have identified at least 184 privately commissioned surveys in the Reagan archival papers; we believe that more remain buried in papers that have yet to be publicly released. The president's polls were considered a major political resource and were usually controlled by the chief of staff, who would selectively (and carefully) excerpt sections to distribute to the appropriate administration officials.

Several of the surveys were funded, as we have noted, directly by the Republican National Committee, while the rest were apparently funded through the White House. A handwritten memo attached to one of Wirthlin's timely survey reports assured Don Regan, chief of staff, that "most of the . . . questions [in the first part of survey are] coming out of RNC [Republican National Committee] budgets and not ours." This would seem to imply that White House funds were used for surveys. Such use of government funds would represent a significant departure from the practice in past administrations of having the national party foot the bill to avoid accusations that taxpayer money was used for political purposes. In this case, our best judgment is that government funds were not used but rather that the White House used an allocation it had in the RNC's account for surveys.[1]

Reagan's team (primarily through Wirthlin) conducted three distinct forms of public-opinion analysis. First, the White House carefully tracked polls in published materials. It was quite concerned with monitoring how the public and elites were perceiving the state of public opinion.

Second, the White House carefully evaluated the public's reaction to the president's speeches in order to pinpoint the most effective language and presentations. Small groups of fifty adults were regularly assembled to view Reagan speeches and to use handheld devices to record on a five-point scale (from very positive to very negative) their reaction to the president's message, style, and delivery. This "pulseline" analysis was conducted, for instance, on the president's foreign policy speeches related to peace and national security in 1986 and the Venice Summit in June 1987.

The pulseline analysis provided a detailed evaluation of what the audience found appealing or distressing in each section of the president's address. For instance, DMI's analysis of Reagan's nationally televised 1986 address on peace and national security issues reported "negative reaction" to early sections of the speech because of "anticipation that Reagan [was] going to ask for more money for defense" and suspicion that military purchases of new fighters were characterized by "waste and fraud." But the report found that Reagan's claim in his speech that a sustained military buildup would allow the United States to bargain from strength and produce a "secure peace" was favorably received because it offered "hope of real progress."[2] These analyses were apparently incorporated into preparing future presidential addresses.

The third and main aspect of the White House's analysis of public opinion was Wirthlin's "big monthly surveys" on a variety of topics. These were labeled "Flash Results" and typically used identically worded questions to compile trends of attitudes and detect changes or stability in public opinion. Major new issues also received attention and, if they persisted, were added to the pool of questions that were consistently asked. The regular foreign policy topics in Wirthlin's monthly surveys included international trade, the Strategic Defense Initiative, terrorism, and Central America (aid to the Nicaraguan rebels and policies regarding El Salvador and Mexico). For instance, Wirthlin used his analysis to identify a potential weakness in public support for the president's arms-control policy among eighteen- to twenty-four-year-olds; this group was unusually critical of the policy even as it consistently listed foreign policy as its top national concern.[3]

In addition to probing public preferences regarding specific issues, DMI tracked the public's approval or disapproval of Reagan's performance on a range of foreign policy issues, including the Persian Gulf, arms control, Central America, relations with the Soviet Union, terrorism, and international trade.

Two foreign policy issues received particular attention: aid for the Nicaraguan rebels, and the Iran-contra scandal. The White House carefully monitored the public's reaction to the administration's support for Nicaraguan aid. In this case, the administration's policy was largely opposed by the public, and the administration was monitoring the public to see how—and, ultimately, how long—it could maintain a policy at odds with public opinion (see Sobel 1993).

Wirthlin reported in the Spring of 1985 that aiding the Nicaraguan rebels "continues to polarize the nation" and "pose[d] key potential liabilities" to Reagan's job rating, as was evident in the slight decline in public support for the president's handling of foreign policy.[4] By April 1986, Wirthlin wrote Donald Regan, White House chief of staff, that a "majority of Americans continue to disapprove of the way Reagan is handling the situation in Nicaragua" and would prefer to seek a negotiated settlement because of "fear that helping the Contras could lead to another Vietnam." The result was sobering: a "significant majority" approve of the legislative defeat of the administration's request for additional aid, and the public's evaluation of the president's foreign policy performance in April 1986 fell "more sharply in the wake of the Contra aide discussion than at any other time since he assumed office." The administration's policy, Wirthlin explained, was out of step with Americans, who "dislike both the Contras and the Sandinistas and perceive no direct threat."[5] In a subsequent report to Regan, Wirthlin reported that "approval of the President's handling of foreign policy recovered from its plunge in March" but that "much of the recovery can be attributed mainly to the President's handling of the situation in Libya."[6]

The White House also conducted extensive surveys during the Iran-Contra scandal. DMI fielded daily tracking surveys in November and December 1986 and in January 1987. The surveys enabled the president and his senior aides to study over time trends in the public's reaction to the administration's policy toward Iran, the evolving scandal, its impact on the president's job approval, and the public's impression of the media's job in responsibly and accurately reporting the story. The data showed the White House that the public would not be sympathetic to blaming the media; majorities believed the press had been both accurate and responsible.[7]

The White House devoted the time and money to commissioning and analyzing public-opinion research because, according to Wirthlin, the public's evaluations and support represented the president's "most valuable of all political resources."[8] The pollster argued that the president had demonstrated great success in "persuad[ing] a balky legislature" to take action by "amplif[ying] the public's political voice . . . by asking the people to write letters and make telephone calls to Congress."[9] In this instance, presumably and evidently, it was important to identify key policy supporters who might be mobilized visibly to help persuade Congress and the public more broadly.

The White House recognized the political significance of public support but did not accept public opinion as a given. Rather, it attempted to shape it to support the positions the administration already favored. Although further archival research is required, it appears that the White House's extensive public-opinion analysis was used to design the presentation of already decided policies (instead of influencing the actual formulation of these policies).

The White House's use of public-opinion research is strikingly illustrated by Wirthlin's letter to Reagan in April 1985 concerning the administration's Nicaraguan policy: his argument was that the White House ought to consider a new strategy for handling the public rather than change policy. The pollster emphasized that the president's greatest impact on the public occurred when the public was "misinformed" about an issue (the "prime example" was the air-traffic controllers' strike) or when the president already supported the public's position and the president's campaign boosted its press coverage and salience. On Nicaragua, Americans were not significantly misinformed, and they were strongly opposed to the administration's policy. Wirthlin reasoned that "taking the Nicaraguan case directly to the people by . . . giv[ing] major speeches in settings which would dramatize your commitment to this issue" would have the unwanted affect of "raising the political stakes and public saliency" and "squandering" the president's public approval. Instead, Wirthlin recommended a different promotional strategy. He suggested reframing the "aid issue into a 'peace issue,' " deploying "organizational allies" such as the Republican National Committee and administration officials to promote the administration's policy and restricting the president's own supportive statements to "lower profile activities."[10]

The administration and its pollster were confident that the president could sway public opinion under the right conditions. Wirthlin bragged, for instance, that the president's activities and statements during his controversial visit to the Bitburg Cemetery in Germany had favorably turned public opinion.[11]

Public-opinion research was used in two ways to sharpen the presentation of decided policy. First, the research helped to identify the language and words that most appealed to Americans and would be most effective. For instance, one survey ran two questions on the administration's policy of aiding the Nicaraguan rebels; they used identical wording except for the description of the rebels: one question described them as the "Nicaraguan Resistance Fighters," the second as the "Nicaraguan Contras."[12] Wirthlin reported in a separate study that characterizing the administration policy as "humanitarian" made little difference in diminishing public opposition (see Jentleson 1992).[13]

A second use of the research was to identify arguments that might prove persuasive to Americans. For instance, during the president's first term, the White House used polls to identify and test the effectiveness of its arguments for justifying a defense buildup (it turned out, as noted earlier, that public support for spending more on defense was already at its peak). A July 1981 Wirthlin report used the following question: "While both arms control and rebuilding our defense are important components of U.S. policy, which of these three strategies should the U.S. adopt first: (1) rebuild its defenses *before* signing an arms control agreement, (2) rebuild *while* negotiating, or (3) *hold off* on rebuilding to see how negotiations progress." The results found a plurality supporting the administration's policy of building up first and one-third favoring rebuilding while negotiating; only one-fifth favored holding off rebuilding.[14]

We have found little evidence thus far that the Reagan White House's public-opinion research systematically affected responsive decisions on major policy (as opposed to how policy decisions were presented publicly). For instance, Wirthlin repeatedly reported to the White House that aiding the Nicaraguans was consistently unpopular. The pollster's best hope was simply to distance Reagan from a major public campaign that reminded Americans of the president's distance from their views.

INCREASING OPPORTUNITY TO LEAD OR MANIPULATE PUBLIC OPINION

Our analysis of the Reagan administration (in addition to the connection with how the Clinton administration has used polling and public-opinion information) downplays presidents' responsiveness to public opinion. It also makes clear that the use of archival and other historical and in-depth evidence is crucial for untangling what can be a complex relationship between public opinion and policymaking—for foreign and domestic policy issues alike. What we describe, we think, represents a pattern of behavior that will continue. Presidents will continue to use polling and public-opinion analysis to attempt to lead or manipulate public opinion, though the election cycle will provide at least some mechanism for restraining this.

There are other recent developments that point further in this direction. If certain current trends continue, we could find an increasing difference in the observable role of public opinion in domestic versus foreign policy. This pertains to the relevant salience of these types of issues, with foreign policy issues historically much less salient, and this has become increasingly so with the end of the Cold War. The end result may be that presidents will have increasing opportunity to lead rather than respond to public opinion in foreign affairs. This leadership, depending upon how active presidents intend to be in foreign policy, may be facilitated by the fact that since World War II the public has fundamentally had an activist, not isolationist, orientation toward foreign policy and has been favorably disposed toward multilateralism (e.g., given the public's long support for the UN and NATO; Page and Shapiro 1992, chaps. 5 and 6; see Wittkopf 1996; Sobel 1996b).

The end of the Cold War has decreased the visibility of foreign policy in three ways. First, the East-West threat driven by the Soviet Union has disappeared. This has made national security a far less urgent and persistent issue than it had been since the end of World War II. Crises can arise, but they get resolved and disappear, unlike the steady Soviet military and nuclear threat during the Cold War. Second, the end of the bipolar world of the Cold War has made foreign affairs more complex to follow and interpret, which is yet an additional barrier to increasing the public's attention to foreign policy (we will say more about this below). Third, domestic policies have easily filled the gap in the public's attention space.

Moreover, one highly visible domestic issue itself, though under relatively good control at this writing, has been a barrier to the public's automatic attention to ventures in foreign affairs: the federal budget deficit is an automatic barrier to foreign policy initiatives that require additional expenditures. It was especially telling that the congressional Republicans' Contract with America in 1994, which was a set of policy positions that the Republicans hailed as having large majority support, included only one item (of eighteen items listed) that singled out foreign or defense policy: "No troops under UN command and restoration of the essential parts of our national security funding to strengthen our national defense and maintain our credibility around the world." Thus the Contract with America reflected both the meager salience of foreign policy to the American public as well as the enduring elite and public recognition of the need for the United States to be ready to act on the international scene.

The potentially diminishing public attention to foreign policy and support for a strong U.S. presence in world affairs may give presidents and other policymakers greater opportunity than during the Cold War to lead, manipulate, and otherwise control public opinion. This low level of salience, to the extent that it is interrupted by occasional major world events and crises, provides a barrier to public engagement in foreign policy, which in turn makes democratic control of foreign policy more difficult. If, however, crises like the war in Kosovo become frequent and define the nature of international affairs in the twenty-first century, then this could substantially increase the public's attentiveness to foreign policy and alter the nature of the opinion-policy relationship. Whatever happens, however, will not only have short-term consequences but also long-term ones bearing on what young adults learn about foreign affairs and how new generations see the relationship between the public and foreign policymaking. Because of the low salience and high complexity of foreign policy with the end of the Cold War, young adults may come to know less about world affairs than previous generations—and, to be sure, the latter's level of knowledge has not been very great (see Delli Carpini and Keeter 1996; Jennings 1996). Thus, the public's level of engagement in foreign policymaking in the future is an important open question.

Beyond international crises, there are, perhaps, new issues that may enable political leaders to engage the public substantially in foreign affairs (cf. Yankelovich and Immerwahr 1994). These include policy problems that intersect directly with domestic concerns but have strong foreign policy implications: the global economy (though, at this writing, even with recent domestic protest demonstrations against the World Trade Organization, the International Monetary Fund, and the World Bank, it is not clear how concerned the American public is with crises in foreign economies and international financial markets), the global environment, and immigration. The proposal and enactment of the North American Free Trade Agreement (NAFTA) in 1994, which the public belatedly came to support, may be an example of the future ahead. Such issues have the potential of breaking down fully the distinctions between purely domestic and purely foreign policy concerns and of making different policymaking processes equally responsive to public opinion, and thus equally democratic, as a wider range of issues potentially become important in electoral politics in the United States. Of course, NAFTA was a case of presidential leadership—or manipulation—of public opinion, not direct responsiveness to the public's predetermined and strong preferences (cf. Jacobs and Shapiro 1995b). This foreshadows questions about democracy that we will return to at the concluding section.

But with neither the Cold War nor foreign policy crises at issue in American elections, foreign policy remains of relatively little visibility and concern to the American public. Evidence for this is quite apparent and persuasive. For example, even during the period that the press could cite (in January 1997) that a "Crowded, Ambitious Foreign Policy Agenda Awaits President in New Term" (Erlanger 1997), it had also just reported, "Foreign Coverage Less Prominent in News Magazines" (Pogrebin 1996). The data reported in the four graphs shown in Figure 14.1, which are taken from Pippa Norris's (1995) study of the effect of the end of the Cold War on Ameri-

Figure 14.1 Cold War versus Post-Cold War News Coverage

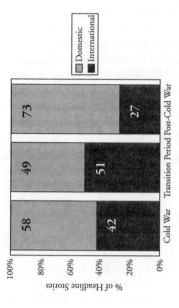

International news, 1973–1975. *Source:* Classified from ABC/CBS news.

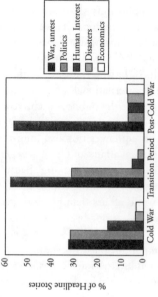

Priority in headline news, 1973–1995. *Source:* Classified from ABC/CBS news.

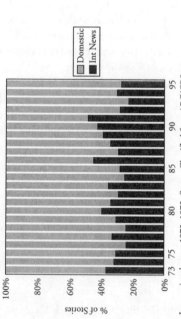

Coverage of the Soviet Union/Russia, 1985–1995. *Source:* Analysis Vanderbilt Abstracts Network News.

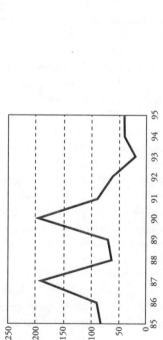

Themes of international stories, 1973–1993.

Source: Pippa Norris, "The Restless Searchlight: Network News Framing of the Post Cold-War." *Political Communication* 12, no. 4 (1995): 363-366.

can news coverage of foreign affairs, show the striking change in television news coverage. The graphs show that international news coverage in general fell off; coverage of the Soviet Union/Russia sharply fell off; after rising during the transition period, lead or headline international news fell off as we entered the post–Cold War world; and while crises such as war and other unrest continued to make the headlines, international news on politics, human interest, disasters, and economics failed to do so.

While this might genuinely reflect the urgency and salience of these issues, Norris persuasively argues and presents evidence showing that because the press could no longer frame foreign-affairs news in terms of what was once the widely understood Cold War, East-West, or communist-anticommunist standard of judgment for evaluating and understanding foreign policy issues, it opted to cover such issues less than it had previously. This, in the long run, could give presidents and policymakers even more of a monopoly over such information relative to the public than they have normally had; thus, they will have a further advantage in their efforts to direct, rather than respond to, public opinion.

Furthermore and perhaps more important, the "Cold War frame" had given the public a way of understanding foreign affairs and thereby at least some vantage point from which it might constrain, if not attempt to influence, the direction of government policy. Without this frame in the post–Cold War world, presidents and other policymakers and political leaders may have greater opportunity to reframe issues for the public and thereby have greater opportunity to direct public opinion in the direction they wish. If there is a dominant new frame that presidents and other political elites come to use on an issue, the mass media may tend to amplify it and thus increase the likely influence of these leaders on public opinion (see Zaller and Chiu 1996; Jacobs and Shapiro 2000). The public will be more dependent than it has ever been on vigorous competition of positions and ideas among elites and the mass media's coverage of them (Zaller 1992), since it will have both less information and fewer predispositions based on relevant frames of reference.

Thus, in addition to improved capacities of presidents to obtain and use information about public opinion in order to lead or manipulate the public, real-world changes in foreign affairs themselves have made it less apparent to presidents that they should be concerned with responding to rather than directing public opinion.

PUBLIC OPINION AND DEMOCRACY

In light of this analysis and discussion, and as we contemplate future research on the effect of public opinion on foreign policy—and on policymaking more generally—it is also important to ask: What will the relationship between public opinion and policy tell us about democracy?

This is not a simple question. If we found that there was no relationship and that the policymakers fully ignored the public, then, according to the standard we posed at the beginning of this chapter, we would conclude that the level of democracy at work does not extend beyond the existence of procedural democracy. In contrast, however, if we found that there was frequent and substantial correspondence between policies and public opinion, and that there was evidence that policymakers waited for public approval before establishing and implementing policies, we would caution against calling this evidence that strong liberal democratic processes are at work. While this would clearly be prima facie evidence for substantive democracy— that is, for the public getting what it wants—we and Benjamin Page have long argued (see Page and Shapiro 1983, 1987, 1992; Jacobs and Shapiro 1994a) that to call this democratic in a fully normative sense requires that we evaluate the quality of the public opinion that is so influential—and that we examine what has influenced this opinion.

At the extreme, if the public was manipulated by political leaders or others through deception or the distortion of information so that the public was led away from preferences that were in its interest, and then government responded to these manipulated preferences, we would not want to call the policies that resulted "democratic" (see also Wheeler 1976; Hilderbrand 1981; Margolis and Mauser 1989; Herbst 1992; Ginsberg 1986). In contrast, democracy does not require that the public form its opinion devoid of any outside influences. In fact, opinion leadership is fundamental to democracy, since the public needs information and interpretations that leaders provide. But what is required is that political leaders or others inform and even persuade the public through accurate and reasonably complete information, so that the public can reach opinions that serve its interests. Thus, to study the causal relationship between public opinion and policy for the purpose of examining the workings of democracy, we must also examine what influences public opinion and the quality of information that the public has received (including, to be sure, information about public opinion itself that is provided through reports and interpretations of opinion-poll results; see Noelle-Neumann 1984; Fried 1997; Jacobs and Shapiro 1995–1996, 1997).

To take this even further, since the quality of public opinion is so central to reaching such normative conclusions about the opinion-policy relationship, we should also not dismiss policymakers' failure to respond to public opinion as undemocratic. There can be cases in which policymakers feel they must make policy decisions that do not have public support, because there is evidence that the public has been misled or manipulated or has not yet fully paid attention to or been informed about the policy at issue. Ideally, such policy decisions should be delayed until the public is more fully engaged in the issues, but even when this delay does not occur, persuading the public after the fact of the merit of a policy need not be dismissed as undemocratic—again, as long as deceit and manipulation have not occurred.

Thus, in order to offer conclusions about democracy, our research strategy requires that we examine additional evidence beyond public support for particular policies, how policymakers have reacted directly or indirectly to this support, and the enacted policies themselves. We must find out what has influenced public opinion and the quality of the information that has led the public to take one position or another. Without knowing this, it is not clear what the implications are for democracy for any decline in presidential responsiveness to public opinion in foreign policymaking.

15

Public Opinion and European Integration
Permissive Consensus or Premature Politicization?

Richard Sinnott

Any account of public opinion on European integration must begin first with a brief examination of the role of public opinion in the integration process and, second, with some discussion of the nature of public opinion itself. The former is needed in order to provide a context within which the significance of public opinion in this area can be interpreted. The latter is required because the analysis of public opinion on European integration raises some complex and difficult questions about the very nature of attitudes. Following introductory sections dealing with these two aspects, the main body of the chapter will examine *evaluations* of European integration, *knowledge* of European Union politics and institutions, and mass political *behavior* in the form of participation in European Parliament elections.[1] A concluding section considers the implications of the evidence presented.

THE ROLE OF PUBLIC OPINION IN THE INTEGRATION PROCESS

Originally, the European integration project was overtly and frankly elitist. As Jean Monnet put it: "I thought it wrong to consult the peoples of Europe about the structure of a community of which they had no practical experience" (quoted in Featherstone 1994, 157). Given the fact that much of the early theory of political integration is largely a gloss on the practice of Jean Monnet and his fellow integrationists, it is not surprising to find that the prevailing academic theory reflected Monnet's view of the role of the mass public. Indeed, one of the grand theorists of European integration argued that, in studying integration, "it is as impracticable as it is unnecessary to have recourse to general public opinion and attitude surveys" (Haas 1958, 15).

In fact, however, researchers did feel the need to pay at least some attention to public opinion. One influential approach was the "permissive consensus" notion put forward by L. Lindberg and S. Scheingold (1970, 41–42); indeed, this became almost a stock phrase, to the point that it may have inhibited rather than encouraged further analysis.[2] Then there was the U-turn on the relevance of public opinion that was executed by the neofunctionalist theorists in their brief but flourishing revisionist phase. In this period, Ernst Haas himself argued for the need to move away from "the stress put on elite loyalties in my own earlier formulations" in order to consider mass attitudes and perceptions (Haas 1971, 26–30). Other contributors to this explicitly revisionist effort elaborated sets of detailed propositions about the role of public opinion that provide a rich vein of ideas and hypotheses (Nye 1971; Schmitter 1971). One particular notion put forward at the time is worth singling out: "politicization," which was identified as one of the four characteristic conditions of the integration process by Joseph Nye, involves a "broadening of the arena of participants" in which "political legitimizing decision-makers and broad political opinion become more heavily involved as integration decisions make heavier incursions upon national sovereignty and the identitive functions of the states." Discussion of the impact of politicization on the prospects for integration leads to the hypothesis that such prospects may be imperiled by premature politicization before supportive attitudes have become intense and structured (Nye 1971, 89).

This is a long way from the views of the original neofunctionalists and also from the permissive-consensus model. Unfortunately, this and many of the other ideas of, if one can put it that way, the "neo-neofunctionalists" disappeared in the retreat from theory that accompanied the doldrums of the integration process. Nye's "premature politicization" may itself have been a premature idea; some twenty years later, it had become much more pertinent and, as suggested below, provides a potentially useful way of interpreting some recent trends in and features of European public opinion on integration.

THE NATURE OF PUBLIC OPINION

The debate about the role of public opinion in the process of European integration matches a more or less contemporaneous debate about the role of public opinion in the foreign policymaking process in the United States.[3] The American debate started with a negative view of the role of public opinion, the argument being that public attitudes to foreign policy lack an adequate knowledge base, are unstructured, are unstable, and have no relevance for policymaking. This interpretation was encapsulated as early as 1950 in Gabriel Almond's view that "foreign policy attitudes among most Americans lack intellectual structure and factual content. Such superficial psychic states are bound to be unstable since they are not anchored in a set of explicit values and means ends calculations or traditional compulsions" (Almond 1950, 69).

This negative view of public opinion, which has been dubbed the "conventional wisdom" by its critics, has been challenged on several fronts. It has been argued that *aggregate* American public opinion on foreign policy is stable (Shapiro and Page 1988, 213) and that public opinion is also structured, provided we look for such structure at a sufficiently abstract and general level rather than at the level of immediate and specific issues (Hurwitz and Peffley 1991, 102–103; Wittkopf 1991, 176). The first of these arguments is persuasive; the second is more debatable, hinging as it does on what one is willing to count as "structure." However, the point about inadequate levels of knowledge is conceded by the revisionists (Holsti 1992, 447) and the fourth point—the question of the relevance of public opinion to foreign policymaking—raises a host of issues, both normative and empirical.

The far-reaching implications of this debate about public attitudes and foreign policy issues is underlined by a brief look at the wider and more fundamental issue: the nature of attitudes as such rather than just the nature of attitudes to foreign policy. Just as the pessimistic view was buttressed by Philip Converse's work on belief systems in mass publics and by his concept of nonattitudes (Converse 1964, 1970), the middle position between the pessimist and revisionist views may be supported by recent reconceptualizations of attitudes that seek to get around the false dichotomy of real attitudes versus nonattitudes. Thus, in examining the nature of the survey response, John Zaller argues that "a sizeable fraction of survey respondents appear to form their opinion during the interview on the basis of the ideas made salient to them by the question, rather than simply revealing pre-existing 'true attitudes.' " He emphasizes, however, that this is not equivalent to the "nonattitudes" position. Indeed, he rejects "the premise of Converse's black-and white nonattitudes model, which is that most response fluctuation is due to essentially random guessing by people who have no meaningful opinions." Individuals have neither "true attitudes" nor "nonattitudes" but "a series of partially independent and often inconsistent ones" (Zaller 1992, 93–94). Survey responses are a function of these and other immediately accessible "considerations." In a similar vein, Michael Delli Carpini and Scott Keeter argue that the stark distinction between real opinions and pseudo-opinions may be inappropriate. Opinions can be constructed on the spot during an interview, but such construction need not be random (Delli Carpini and Keeter 1996, 228).

Rather than delving into the conceptual and methodological issues to which these arguments give rise, this chapter simply notes the main implications. The first implication is that, while individual attitudes are not necessarily well structured or stable, they are not necessarily random, either. These crucial features of any set of attitudes must be investigated case by case, not assumed to be either this or that on an a priori basis. Second, knowledge has a substantial effect on the structure and stability of attitudes, an effect that has been neglected in much public-opinion analysis (Zaller 1992, 18; Delli Carpini and Keeter 1996, 229). The third implication is that the measurement of attitudes is *extremely* sensitive to question wording, format, and context. These points apply to attitudes in any domain. Attention to them is, however, particularly important in the study of public opinion on foreign policy or, in this instance, of public opinion on European integration.

EVALUATIONS OF EUROPEAN INTEGRATION

The sensitivity of the measurement of support for European integration to variations in question wording is immediately evident from Figure 15.1, which charts the performance of four indicators of attitudes to European integration since the early 1970s. The four indicators are customarily labeled "unification," "membership," "benefits," and "dissolution." The level of support for integration elicited by these questions depends both on the stimulus presented in the question and on the response categories, in particular on whether the response categories offer an explicit middle position.

The unification indicator measures support for a very general aspiration ("efforts

Figure 15.1   Attitudes to the European Union on Four Eurobarometer Indicators (unification, membership, benefits and dissolution), 1973–1998

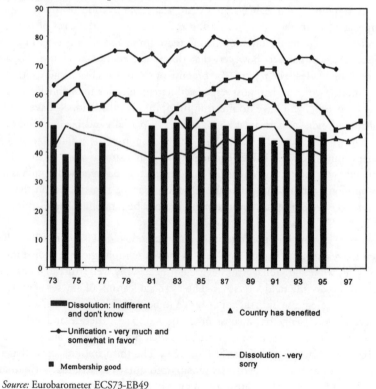

Source: Eurobarometer ECS73-EB49

to unify Western Europe") and does so on a four-point scale ("very much for," "to some extent for," "to some extent against," "very much against") that does not provide an explicit middle or neutral point.[4] The rather vague stimulus and the absence of a middle position combine to produce high levels of support for integration, touching almost 80 percent at the beginning of the 1990s (see Figure 15.1). The membership indicator provides a more concrete stimulus (country X's membership of the European Union) and a three-point scale that includes an explicit middle position ("a good thing," "neither good nor bad," "a bad thing"). As such, it probably provides a more realistic gauge of support for integration that typically runs some 10–20 percentage points behind the unification indicator. The third Eurobarometer indicator asks whether the respondent's country has benefited from membership in the European Union, but, like the unification indicator, it does not provide a middle position (the response categories are "benefited" and "did not benefit"). Because it involves an element of perception as well as evaluation, it is not surprising that the benefits indicator registers a positive response that is slightly lower than that registered by the membership indicator. Indeed, the gap between the two might be greater were it not for the presence of a neutral category in the membership indicator and the absence of such a category in the benefits indicator. Finally, there is the dissolution indicator. This question poses the hypothetical situation of the scrapping of the European Community or European Union, with strong negative and positive options and a middle position ("very sorry," "indifferent," "very relieved").[5] The indicator has been criticized because it is hypothetical; nonetheless, it provides a useful measure of enthusiasm or lack of enthusiasm for European integration, showing, in June–July 1994, for example, a quite modest level of enthusiasm (43 percent) that is actually slightly lower than the level of indifference and don't-know combined (46 percent) (see Figure 15.1).

None of these questions is an ideal indicator of attitudes to integration; nor could it be said that together they form an adequate battery of items. Given the sensitivity of the measurement of public opinion to subtle differences in question wording and question format, one should be cautious in interpreting the evidence and avoid reading too much into the data. In particular, attempts to categorize the indicators in terms of diffuse-affective versus specific-utilitarian dimensions quickly run into difficulties, with, as Niedermayer (1995, 54–55) notes, the only unambiguously utilitarian measure being that based on the benefits question.[6] That having been said, however, these are in many respects the best available data, and provided they are interpreted cautiously, they enable one to make some reasonably valid inferences. Before attempting a summary of the current state of support for European integration as evidenced by these indicators, one must take account of the substantial variation in the indicators over time and across the member states and also examine how the public responds to the integration process as it relates to specific policy sectors.

In terms of changes over time, there was, first of all, a significant falling-off in support for integration between the late 1970s and the early 1980s (see Figure 15.1). This may have been related to the prevailing Eurosclerosis that many commentators on European integration have identified. This was followed, however, by a substantial and sustained rise in support between 1982 and 1991. It is worth noting that this rise predated the arrival of Jacques Delors as president of the European Commission and certainly predated the major initiative of the first Delors presidency, namely, the launch of the Single Market program ("Project 1992"). Yet there can be little doubt that the rise in support for integration was sustained by the activism of the Delors Commission, by the passage of the Single European Act, and by the publicity and promotional efforts that surrounded Project 1992.

In fact, however, the actual arrival of the calendar year 1992 confirmed a general downward trend in support for integration (see Figure 15.1). The period since 1989 is so packed with political and economic developments that it is impossible to attribute this decline to any one factor.[7] Indications that the decline was under way in a number of member states even prior to 1991 (Niedermayer 1995, 67) suggest that it was not simply a response to the signing of the Maastricht Treaty but may also have reflected a negative reaction to the growing intrusiveness of the Single Market program on both the politics and economics of individual states. Another factor was the waning of the euphoria that surrounded the fall of the Berlin Wall and the growth in the realization that that event brought challenges and uncertainties regarding the future shape and role of the EC and was not simply the dawning of a new era of peace and prosperity for all. Whatever its causes, the decline in support for integration that began in the second half of 1991 has shown little or no sign of being reversed.

While overall support for the EU over time has varied by some 20 percentage points, the range in support across countries has been as much as 50 percentage points; in 1997, support as measured by the membership indicator went from 31 percent in Sweden to 83 percent in Ireland. Although any grouping of countries based on definite cutoff points in a distribution such as this is somewhat arbitrary, it is probably useful to think of a group of four countries with high levels of support for EU membership and a group of six with quite low levels. The former comprises Ireland, the Netherlands, Luxembourg, and Italy. The latter is more surprising: predictably, it includes the three most recent entrants to the EU (Sweden, Austria, and Finland) and the United Kingdom; the surprise is that it also includes Germany and Belgium but does not include Denmark. Yet actual opposition to integration is as high in Denmark as in all but one of the low-support countries.

As well as varying over time and between countries, support for European integration varies by policy area. One of the core questions in the integration process is whether decisionmaking competence in relation to particular policy areas should be attributed to the European level or to the national level. Table 15.1 shows the distribution of responses to a series of Eurobarometer items dealing with the Europeanization of issues in European public opinion in December 1995. The range of support for and opposition to Europeanization is quite wide, from the over 75 percent endorsement of European decisionmaking on policy toward the developing world and the fight against drugs to the one-third who accept a European role in health and social welfare, cultural policy, and education. Broadly speaking, one can distinguish three groups of issues based on the level of agreement that the matter should be decided at the European level: issues showing a high level of Europeanization (60 percent or more support for European decisionmaking); issues with moderate Europeanization (at least one-half but less than 60 percent; and issues with low Europeanization (those with less than half saying that policy should be handled at the European level). On the basis of the data in Table 15.1, the first group would run from policy toward the developing world (77 percent for Europeanization) down to and

Table 15.1 **Preference Regarding Attribution of Policy Responsibility to European or National Level 1996**

	Policy should be decided by:		
	European EU	*National Government*	*DK*
High Europeanization			
The fight against drugs	77	19	4
Co-operation with developing countries	77	17	6
Equality for men and women	71	24	5
Trade with countries outside the EU	71	22	7
Scientific and technological research	70	25	5
Foreign policy towards countries outside the EU	70	22	8
Protection of the environment	66	30	4
Currency	62	33	5
Supporting regions with economic difficulties	61	32	7
Competition policy	60	28	12
Moderate Europeanization			
Immigration policy	57	37	6
The fight against unemployment	57	39	4
Fishing policy	56	35	9
Rules for political asylum	55	37	8
Defence	52	44	4
Consumer policy	51	43	6
Agriculture	50	45	5
Rates of VAT	49	42	9
Low Europeanization			
Health and safety of workers	44	52	4
Workers' rights vis-a-vis their employers	42	53	5
Basic rules for broadcasting and press	39	54	7
Health and social welfare	36	59	5
Cultural policy	34	60	6
Education	29	68	3

Source: Eurobarometer 45

including competition policy (60 percent). The moderately Europeanized group of issues extends from immigration policy (57 percent) to agriculture (50 percent) and rates of value-added tax (49 percent), the low group from the health and safety of workers (44 percent) to education (29 percent).[8]

Interstate variation is considerably greater in regard to whether or not some of the issues listed in Table 15.1 should be Europeanized than it is in regard to general support for integration. A pertinent example in the present context is the division between member-state publics regarding the Europeanization of defense, with some countries showing a very high degree of Europeanization and others a very low degree. Ranged on the side of the Europeanization of defense are the Netherlands (76 percent) in first place and, at a somewhat lower level, Belgium, Luxembourg, Italy, and Germany. Sweden and Finland are, on this evidence, overwhelmingly opposed to the Europeanization of decisionmaking in the defense area, Finland being 8 percent for and 90 percent against. On this negative side also, though not as strongly, one finds Ireland, Greece, Denmark, Portugal, and the United Kingdom. However, before drawing any large inferences about the future prospects for a common European defense policy from these data, one should note that the rate of don't-know responses to this item is remarkably—one might say suspiciously—low (an average of 4 percent).

This leads to the hypothesis that some significant proportion of the responses on preferences regarding the Europeanization of defense policy and of the other policies listed in Table 15.1 actually reflects nonattitudes. A Eurobarometer-based research project on turnout in the European Parliament elections of 1994 provided the opportunity to test this hypothesis by using an exploratory question on the overall issue of policy attribution between the national and European levels. The new question, which was inserted in Eurobarometer 41.1, included the specific response category "I haven't really thought about it."[9] This response was chosen by 26 percent of respondents, a proportion that, when combined with the 10 percent who spontaneously offered a don't-know response, means that more than one-third of respondents acknowledge that they do not have any opinion on the basic issue of the appropriate scope of decisionmaking competence of the European and national authorities (Blondel, Sinnott, and Svensson 1998, 65–72). Further evidence from the same study suggests that even those who were willing to express an opinion may not have had a very explicit or well thought out basis for that opinion. Those who did take a view on the question of the overall range of issues decided on by the European Union were asked, "When you say (insert response to previous question), is this a general feeling that you have about the European Union (European Community), or have you specific issues in mind?" This retrospective probe showed that only 17 percent of the sample had specific issues in mind in responding to the original question. This reinforces the view that attitudes in this area may be less than well formed.

This expectation is further confirmed by Eurobarometer data from 1995 on *perceptions* of the allocation of decisionmaking power between national governments and "the European Union level" over a wide range of issues. Among other things, the data show that 38 percent of the European public believes that foreign policy is decided at the EU level, and precisely the same proportion believes that defense matters are decided at the EU level (Eurobarometer 1995, B65). On any reading of the common foreign and security policy, these perceptions are wildly inaccurate. The proportion seeing foreign policy as being "at least to some extent decided at the European Union level" should be much higher, and the proportion seeing the same for defense should be much lower. Lest it be assumed that people are getting it wrong in relation to the common foreign and security policy simply because this is an inherently complex and remote area, one should also note that the proportion perceiving agricultural policy as being *at least to some extent decided at the European Union level* is only 40 percent.

The overall impression can be summarized as follows: There is fairly widespread support for the rather vague notion of "efforts to unify Western Europe"; as a result of a downturn since the second half of 1991, support for membership in the EU is running at only about 50 percent and is matched by an almost equal level of indifference as to whether or not the Union continues to exist; finally, despite initial appearances to the contrary, attitudes to the policy scope of the Union are neither well formed nor well informed. All of this suggests that the permissive consensus, if it ever existed, was a rather fragile creature. One could go further and suggest that the term itself, so much bandied about, was actually misleading in that it glossed over significant flaws in the fabric of public opinion toward integration. Were it not for the prevalence of the permissive-consensus assumption, there might not have been such surprise when, as the integration process began to make greater inroads on the economic and political life of the member-states, support for integration began to wane, a waning that became manifest not only in opinion polls but also in referendums and parliamentary debates in several countries. This is precisely the problem of premature politicization without the building of firm and well-structured public support that Nye warned about in 1970. The warning becomes even more appropriate when one examines European citizens' knowledge of the institutions and politics of the Union.

KNOWLEDGE OF THE EUROPEAN UNION

The Eurobarometer has in recent years provided substantial evidence regarding the public's knowledge of the European Union and of European integration. One of the most comprehensive batteries of knowledge items is contained in Eurobarometer 39 (March–April 1993). These items have a strong institutional bias: they ask about the membership of the Community, the location of the Commission, the name of its president, the names of incumbent commissioners, the Community's most powerful institution (in the sense of having the final say on legislation), and who elects the members of the European Parliament.[10] Despite this institutional orientation, however, these questions can probably be treated as indicative of more general levels of knowledge and understanding.[11] A series of eight questions dealing with knowledge of the above topics can be used to form an index of knowledge of the EU; scores on the index range from 0 to 29. Dividing such a scale into discrete levels is difficult and, inevitably, somewhat arbitrary. On the basis, however, that none of the questions is particularly difficult or abstruse and that taken together they might be regarded as a minimum that a reasonably well informed European citizen ought to know about the Union, the scores can be divided as follows: 0–5: "no knowledge"; 6–11: "very little knowledge"; 12–17: "some but not much knowledge"; 18–23: "moderately well informed"; and 24–29: "very well informed." On this interpretation of the scale, 10 percent of the citizens of the European Union are very well informed, and a further 24 percent are moderately well informed. This means, however, that two-thirds (65 percent) emerge with "some but not much knowledge" *or less* (Sinnott 1996). The inadequately informed two-thirds can be subdivided into three groups: 26 percent with "some but not much knowledge," 24 percent with "very little knowledge," and 15 percent with virtually no knowledge at all.

A simple cross-tabulation shows that levels of support for integration are closely related to levels of knowledge (Sinnott 1996). This relationship is undoubtedly reciprocal: Those who are more positively disposed are more likely to seek out and to retain information about the Union; those who are well informed and feel that they know what is going on are more likely to support the process. It would be difficult to be precise about which of these two causal processes is dominant; one can, however, use these data to estimate the proportions of informed and uninformed support for, and opposition to, European integration. The two variables in question (support and knowledge) can be treated as trichotomies, cross-classification of which yields nine categories of orientation to European integration, ranging from informed support at one end of the main diagonal to ill-informed opposition at the other.[12]

In 1993, only one-fifth of Europeans could have been said to be enthusiastic and at least moderately well informed supporters of the European Union, or European Community as it was then (see Table 15.2). If one adds those who are described here as having "some but not much knowledge," the figure for support with some degree of information rises to almost one-third. From an integrationist perspective, these are not very encouraging figures. Yet it may be some comfort to integrationists to know that only 2 percent fall into the category of well-informed opponents or, indeed, that the lower-right corner (ill-informed opposition) is occupied by only 4 percent. However, given the extent to which indifference and lack of knowledge are major features of public opinion toward European integration, this is small comfort: the most populous cell in the typology, a cell that accounts for one-quarter of European citizens, is that defined by a combination of very little/no knowledge and indifference to the future of the Union (the cell labeled "ill-informed indifference"). Taking account of those who are characterized by at least one of these properties shows that 60 percent of the citizens are either indifferent or ill-informed or both.[13]

While the precise reciprocal influences between support and knowledge are difficult to determine, one can be somewhat more confident about the effect of knowl-

Table 15.2 Typology of Support for and Knowledge of the EU, 1993 (N = 11590)

	Levels of Knowledge		
Response to Hypothetical Dissolution of the EU	*Moderately/ Very Knowledgeable (18–29)*	*Some but not much knowledge (12–17)*	*No/Very little knowledge (0–11)*
Very Sorry	Informed enthusiasm 19%	Somewhat informed enthusiasm 12%	Ill informed enthusiasm 13%
Indifferent	Informed indifference 11%	Somewhat informed indifference 12%	Ill informed indifference 24%
Very Relieved	Informed opposition 2%	Somewhat informed opposition 3%	Ill informed opposition 4%

Source: Eurobarometer 39

edge on the structure of attitudes and, therefore, on the *quality* of support for integration. This effect becomes clear from a detailed analysis of the structure of attitudes to EU policy issues at different levels of knowledge. As well as containing extensive data on knowledge of the European Union, Eurobarometer 39 contains quite a wide range of data on preferences regarding various policy proposals contained in or associated with the Maastricht Treaty and on preferences regarding the attribution of decisionmaking competence between the European and national levels. Given the range of attitude items involved, one would expect to find a fairly clear-cut attitude structure that would differentiate between attitudes toward the development of European economic policies, especially European monetary union, attitudes toward a common foreign and defense policy, attitudes toward the integration of policies on immigration and asylum, and attitudes toward EU cooperation and joint decisionmaking in the fight against drugs and crime. However, one would also hypothesize that the degree to which attitudes are structured would be fundamentally affected by variations in levels of knowledge.

Factor analysis provides a means to test these hypotheses. Generally speaking, the results of the tests confirm the existence of the expected structure among those with the highest level of knowledge of the institutions and politics of the Union. However, the results also demonstrate that the structure of this attitude domain disintegrates as one descends through levels of knowledge and that this disintegration is well under way, even at the second-highest quintile on the knowledge scale. The disintegration is particularly evident in the case of attitudes to the Common Foreign and Security Policy, and the only exception to the disintegrative tendency is attitudes toward European monetary union. Finally, since the two sets of items analyzed come from different parts of the questionnaire, the analysis demonstrates that, at lower levels of knowledge, the "structure" of attitudes comes to depend more on the cues and signals emanating from the immediate context of the items than on real connections between the items based on their substantive content.[14]

In summary: Knowledge of European affairs is low; prevailing attitudes toward the Union are characterized by either indifference or lack of knowledge or a combination of both; and lack of knowledge is particularly important, because any dip below quite a high level of knowledge has a devastating effect on the structure and coherence of attitudes toward integration. These features of the orientations of citizens to the European Union confirm the argument that well-structured, supportive attitudes commensurate with the current stage of integration have not in fact developed. The final section of this chapter examines the implications of all of this for the prospects of developing a European democracy that would involve European citizens in a representative process of supranational governance.[15]

EUROPEAN-LEVEL VOTER PARTICIPATION

At first sight, the prospects of developing a representative political process at the level of the European Union look slim. Turnout in European Parliament elections is low; in some countries it is exceedingly low. Moreover, the prevailing interpretation of European Parliament elections is that they are simply subordinate contests ("second-order elections") that play a minor role in the real power play at the national level; the public's attitudes toward Europe make no difference to its participation in such elections.

Since 1979, direct elections to the European Parliament have taken place at five-year intervals. Over the same period and as a direct result of successive revisions of the EU treaties, the powers of the European Parliament have increased substantially. In contrast to the increasing power and importance of that body, turnout in European Parliament elections has declined, from an average turnout of 65.9 percent in 1979 to 52.4 percent in 1999. In fact, the picture is worse than these figures indicate. Three countries in the European Union (Belgium, Greece, and Luxembourg) have compulsory voting, and Italy had compulsory, or at least quasi-compulsory, voting until 1993. Furthermore, certain countries either regularly or from time to time hold concurrent nationwide elections (national, regional, and local) that artificially boost turnout in the European election. Leaving these countries to one side, turnout in the remaining member-states was 52.9 percent in 1979 and only 39.4 percent in 1999 (see Table 15.3).[16]

Apart from the obvious boost arising from compulsory voting and the concurrence of other elections, turnout in European Parliament elections is affected by the day of voting (Sunday versus weekday).[17] Beyond this, however, there is little agreement as to what causes low turnout in European Parliament elections. The prevailing explanation has been cast in terms of the second-order election model. The es-

Table 15.3 Turnout in Five European Parliament Elections, 1979–99

Country	European elections					Mean turnout in European elections
	1979	*1984*	*1989*	*1994*	*1999*	*1979–99*
Belgium	91.4	92.2	90.7	90.7	90.0	91.0
Luxembourg	88.9*	88.8*	87.4*	88.5*	85.8*	87.9
Italy	84.9	83.4	81.0	74.8	70.8	79.0
Greece	n.a.	77.2	79.9*	71.7	70.2	74.8
Spain	n.a.	n.a.	54.6	59.1	64.4*	59.4
Germany	65.7	56.8	62.3	60.0	45.2	58.0
Ireland	63.6*	47.6	68.3*	44.0	51.0*	54.9
France	60.7	56.7	48.7	52.7	47.0	53.2
Denmark	47.8	52.3	46.2	52.9	50.4	49.9
Austria	n.a.	n.a.	n.a.	n.a.	49.0	49.0
Netherlands	57.8	50.6	47.2	35.6	29.9	44.2
Portugal	n.a.	n.a.	51.2	35.5	40.4	42.4
Sweden	n.a.	n.a.	n.a.	n.a.	38.3	38.3
U.K.	32.3	32.6	36.2	36.4	24.0	32.3
Finland	n.a.	n.a.	n.a.	n.a.	30.1	30.1
Mean—all member states	65.9	63.8	62.8	58.5	52.4	56.3
Mean—states without compulsory voting or concurrent nationwide elections	52.9	49.4	49.5	47.0	39.4	47.6

*European Parliament elections with concurrent nation-wide elections (local, regional, or national)
Source: *European Parliament Election Results.* Strasbourg: The European Parliament, 1999.

sence of this approach is that European Parliament elections, in comparison to national elections, do not affect the distribution of power and that there is therefore less at stake in such elections (Reif and Schmitt 1980; Franklin and van der Eijk 1996). From this starting point, the argument is that turnout will be lower and that those who do turn out to vote will be motivated to do so by national considerations and not by European ones. The problem is that this plausible model receives little or no support when tested against the evidence of voter perceptions, attitudes, and behavior.

The first problem with this analysis is that detailed evidence on perceptions of power and of what is at stake in elections at both levels indicates that electorates by and large do not make the sophisticated calculations about differences between the power of national parliaments and of the European Parliament or about differences in what is at stake between the two kinds of elections that the model requires. Moreover, to the extent that such differential perceptions exist, they have no discernible effect on the propensity to vote (Blondel, Sinnott, and Svensson 1998, 107–163 and 222–236).

The second problem lies in the conclusion that attitudes toward European integration have no significant effect on turnout in European Parliament elections. This counterintuitive finding may have arisen partly because turnout in European Parliament elections has been treated as a simple dichotomy—voted versus did not vote—and partly because of the limited range of attitudes to integration investigated as possible sources of participation and abstention. In fact, abstention in European Parliament elections is a fourfold phenomenon depending on whether it is voluntary or circumstantial and on whether it is accompanied by abstention in national elections or is specific to European elections (Blondel, Sinnott, and Svensson 1998, 40–43). Consequently, there is not one dependent variable but four, and the same explanation does not cover all four cases. The most important dependent variables are voluntary abstention and, especially, voluntary Euro-specific abstention. A logistic-regression analysis using a wide range of contextual and attitudinal variables shows that voluntary Euro-specific abstention is significantly affected by attitudes toward European integration, by attitudes toward the European Parliament, and by attitudes toward the parties and candidates in the election and that it is *not* significantly affected by second-order considerations and calculations (Blondel, Sinnott, and Svensson 1998, 222–236). A vital implication of these findings is that the kinds of attitudes toward European integration considered in this chapter affect the quality of the fledgling European democracy embodied in the European Parliament and in European Parliament elections. This and the other implications of the evidence presented above are considered in the concluding section.

CONCLUSION

Public opinion on European integration certainly escapes the accusation traditionally leveled at public opinion on foreign policy, namely, that it is irrelevant. Events since 1990 have shown that it directly affects the politics of European integration, and theoretical considerations suggest that it can be expected to continue to play a significant role in the integration process. It is considerably less sure that European public opinion escapes some of the other elements of the traditional critique of public opinion on foreign policy, in particular, those touching on the structure of attitudes and on the adequacy of the knowledge base on which such attitudes are built. However, rather than implying that one should abandon the study of European public opinion as something fickle or intangible, this simply means that one should bear in mind that survey responses are constructions that are highly dependent on question wording, question context, and on the knowledge possessed by the respondent; one should take all of this into account in interpreting the available evidence.

Doing so suggests that Europeans' support for integration has declined since late

1991 to what could at best be described as a modest level and that it is now matched by a more or less equal level of indifference. This process illustrates the fragility of what had been too blithely and for too long regarded as the "permissive consensus." The fragility of support for integration is also indicated by evidence that it is not well grounded in knowledge of the institutions and politics of the Union and that low levels of knowledge, indeed, even not-so-low levels of knowledge, radically undermine the structure and coherence of public opinion.

Evidence from the study of participation in European Parliament elections indicates that the culture of democratic representation at the European level is weak and that this weakness adversely affects the response of citizens to the opportunities for democratic participation that are presented to them. At the same time, by showing that the state of European public opinion does affect the takeup of these opportunities, the evidence points to specific ways and means of nurturing the development of a European public opinion in the context of the European-level representative process. All of this is of more than academic interest. If, as in the second-order election model, calculations about relative power and about what is at stake were the main determinants of participation in European Parliament elections, the solution would, in principle, be simple. All that would be needed would be to transform the power of the Parliament by, for example, enabling it to elect the European Commission in the manner in which parliaments elect governments at the national level. Then, the voters, seeing more at stake, would flock to the polls, and a major step forward in the creation of a coherent European public opinion would be taken. The problems with this prescription are manifold. It is at odds with the constitutional nature of the EU. It is simply not practical politics for the foreseeable future. Most important, it distracts attention from the real issues, which are: the parlous state of European public opinion; the extent to which the structure and intensity of supportive attitudes lag behind the politicization of the integration process; and the need to consider interim piecemeal measures to encourage the development and expression of a well-informed and coherent European public opinion.

APPENDIX A: THE MAIN EUROBAROMETER QUESTIONS REFERRED TO IN THE TEXT

The Four Standard Eurobarometer Indicators of Attitudes to European Integration

In general, are you for or against efforts being made to unify Western Europe? Are you . . .?

- For—very much
- For—to some extent
- Against—to some extent

- Against—very much
- DK [Don't know]

Generally speaking, do you think that (our country's) membership in the European union (European Community) is . . .?

- A good thing
- A bad thing
- Neither good nor bad
- DK

Taking everything into consideration, would you say that (our country) has on balance benefited or not from being a member of the European Union (European Community)?

- Benefited
- Not Benefited
- DK

If you were told tomorrow that the European Union (European Community) had been scrapped, would you be very sorry about it, indifferent or very relieved?

- Very sorry
- Indifferent
- Very Relieved
- DK

Standard Eurobarometer Question on Policy Attribution

Some people believe that certain areas of policy should be decided by the [national] government, while other areas should be decided jointly within the European Community/Union. Which of the following areas do you think should be decided by the [national] government, and which should be decided jointly within the European Community/Union?

Policy Attribution Question in Eurobarometer 41.1

There has been a lot of discussion recently about the European Union (European Community). Some people say that too many issues are decided on by the European Union (European Community), others say that more issues should be decided on by the European Union (European Community). Which of the following statements comes closest to your view (show card)

- Too many issues are decided on by the European Union (European Community)
- The number of issues decided on by the European Union (European Community) at present is about right
- More issues should be decided on by the European Union (European Community)
- On some issues there should be more European Union (European Community) decision making and on other issues there should be less (spontaneous)
- I have not really thought about it
- DK

Questions and Response Scores Used to Construct an Index of Knowledge of the European Community (Eurobarometer 39)

Is (our country) a member of the European Community or not?
Yes = 1
No = 0

Here is a map and a list of the countries of Europe as a whole. Please give me the numbers or the names of all countries which are members of the European Community
Twelve correct = 4
Eleven correct = 3
Ten correct = 2
Nine correct = 1
Eight correct or less = 0

How many countries are members of the European Community?
Correct (Twelve) = 4
Incorrect = 0

What is the capital where the European Commission and several other European Community institutions are located?
Correct (Brussels) = 4
Incorrect = 0

What is the name of the President of the European Commission in Brussels?
Correct (Jacques Delors) = 4
Incorrect = 0

Which of the following personalities are, according to you, members of the European Commission?
Five or more correct = 4

Three or four correct = 3
Two correct = 2
One Correct = 1
None correct = 0

Which one of the following institutions of the European Community is, in your opinion, the most powerful, in terms of having the final say on European Community legislation?
Correct
(Council of Ministers) = 4
Incorrect = 0

16

Constraint, Catalyst, or Political Tool?
The French Public and Foreign Policy

Natalie La Balme

In France, there is a recurring debate over the public's influence on foreign policy decisions. It emerges periodically, most notably when decisions are contested or in periods of crisis. As the Kosovo crisis unfolded, the attention granted to the public and its influence on the political will of decisionmakers was revealing. Concomitantly, important questions were raised in the press: How are we to convince the public of the legitimacy of France's participation in NATO operations against Serbia?; Will public opinion prevent the executive from considering France's participation in an eventual ground operation in Kosovo, or will the plight of the ethnic Albanian civilians rather encourage the public to request that the government take action?

Members of the parliament also publicly expressed their views on this issue. Jack Lang, chairman of the Foreign Affairs Committee of the National Assembly, observed that this operation "is not only a military war, it is also a psychological war. We must organize ourselves so that the parliament may be a communication—no, let's say an information—device aimed at the public."[1] Right-wing congressman André Santini stated more specifically that "we must educate the public in order to prevent its swaying from one position to another."[2]

These remarks indicate that elected officials are aware that such military interventions cannot be conducted against the will of the population, or at least without its implicit support. Research on the influence of public opinion on the decisionmaking process in France remains, however, quite scarce. Clearly, therefore, the Kosovo crisis provides a strong impetus for increasing interest in the study of public opinion and foreign policy.

Underlying the comments by the French congressmen are a number of postulates dear to the proponents of the paradigm of minimalism: ignorance, lack of information, and volatility. Public opinion was indeed once considered by American scholars to be an ill-informed, volatile, and mood-driven force (Lippmann 1922; Almond 1950; Converse 1964) that did not matter much to policymakers (Cohen 1973). Yet recent research has revealed that American public opinion is not only rational and stable (Caspary 1970; Page and Shapiro 1988, 1992; Jentleson 1992, 1997) but also an important influence on the U.S. policymaking process. This recent work has consequently cast some doubt on the earlier thesis of the public's impotence. Scholars have not only found substantial congruence between changes in opinion preferences and changes in policies (Page and Shapiro 1983) but have also concluded that the public's beliefs and attitudes guide, or at least significantly constrain, government policy (Sobel 1993). They have suggested several factors that can affect when and how public opinion influences the policy process. These include: (1) the level of public support (Monroe 1979; Page and Shapiro 1983; Graham 1994); (2) the effectiveness of elite leadership efforts and the stage of the policy process (Graham 1994); (3) the type of issue under consideration and the decision context (Russett 1990); and (4) the individual sensitivity of policymakers to public opinion (Powlick 1990; Foyle 1999).

In other democratic countries, however, there is less research on this question. In France, for example, a systematic study of the role of public opinion in the foreign policy process has begun only recently (La Balme 1994, 1998). Our understanding of the linkages between the public and policymaking tends, therefore, to be limited to mere assumptions. The conclusions reached by American scholars cannot simply be generalized across countries, or even liberal democracies, and applied to the French case. As Thomas Risse-Kappen (1991, 1994) has pointed out, the nature of the impact of public opinion on policy is very much context-dependent. For example, whereas the United States has a society-dominated political system allowing for public opinion to strongly impact foreign policy decisions, France, with its comparatively centralized political institutions and a strong national executive, is a state-dominated domestic system where public opinion has a marginal role in policymaking. Accordingly, Risse-Kappen concludes that "in France, . . . decision-makers need not worry too much about mass public opinion" (Risse-Kappen 1994, 255).

Yet while it has been a common assumption that French public opinion has comparatively little effect on foreign policy and that French decisionmakers are insulated from public pressure, some political observers' and the French elite's reactions to the management of the 1999 Kosovo crisis seem to challenge this general assumption. Régis Debray, a leading French intellectual, states that France's foreign policy is today "shaped by television, radio and the press," presumably through actual—or anticipated—public pressure (Debray 1993, 182).

This chapter examines to what extent, on what kinds of issues, and under what circumstances, if any, the French public plays a role in the foreign policymaking process. Specifically, do French policymakers undertake certain courses of action because they believe the public demands some form of action? Do they rule out other actions fearing a lack of support? Do they revise their positions? And how do policymakers perceive and assess public opinion? What indicators do they rely on?

Addressing these issues is more complex than describing the state of, or trends in, public opinion. Research on the causal links between mass opinion and foreign policy decisionmaking has been limited, especially outside the United States. Different methodologies have been used to try to examine this relationship: historical research methods (Graham 1994), statistical associations (Monroe 1979; Page and Shapiro 1983; Russett 1990) and interviews of elites (Cohen 1973; Gowing 1994; Powlick 1990; Strobel 1997). Yet the problem of causal inference remains a challenging one. It is very difficult to disentangle the processes that produce policies and to determine whether it was the public who influenced a policy decision, or vice-versa, or whether other influences were at work.

METHOD AND EVIDENCE

This study has adopted a form of methodological pluralism that mixes interpretative and historical approaches. I first relied on in-depth investigation of public opinion's impact on specific policies as determined through a correlation of polling results and corresponding policy decisions. I also did a thorough analysis of policymakers' memoirs and/or biographies, which provide interesting clues concerning how they perceived public opinion. This preliminary evidence enabled me to shape a number of hypotheses that were then tested through interviews with foreign policy officials. When V.O. Key in 1961 defined public opinion as "those opinions held by private persons which governments find it prudent to heed," he also noted that "if one is to know what opinions governments heed, one must know the inner thoughts of presidents, congressmen, and other officials" (Key 1961, 14). In order to determine how French policymakers perceive public opinion and consider it in evaluating their policy options, I held in-depth, confidential interviews with both civil and military foreign policy decisionmakers.

These interviews, conducted since September 1996, make up the primary source of data for this paper. The subjects consisted of thirty-seven foreign policy officials, including two prime ministers, five foreign secretaries (one of whom later held the position of prime minister), three defense secretaries (one of whom later became a prime minister), six close presidential advisers (secretary general, adjunct secretary general, spokesman, special adviser, etc.), four prime minister advisers, four foreign secretary advisers, ten defense secretary advisers, and five chiefs of staff.[3]

The chapter is divided into two parts. In the first part I describe how French policymakers perceive and assess public opinion. I then explore, through case studies, to what extent policymakers incorporate public preferences into their foreign policy decisions: how they take them into account when selecting a course of action; and how they feel motivated or constrained by these preferences. The case studies cover the foreign military operations during François Mitterrand's presidency. Military operations were chosen for, as Philip Everts states, "whether the consequences are good or bad, and whether we like it or not, the public is always involved in wars, their preparation, conduct or prevention, in one way or another, as participant or observer, and that makes public opinion, what people think and the way they act upon their convictions in the political process; i.e. democracy, a major factor in understanding foreign policy and international politics" (Everts 1998b, 2).

SOURCES OF PUBLIC OPINION

Despite the vast research on the concept of public opinion—one of the most enduring concepts in the social sciences—its definition remains controversial. The difficulty of defining public opinion as an object of empirical study was perhaps best expressed by V.O. Key: "To speak with precision of public opinion is a task not unlike coming to grips with the Holy Ghost" (Key 1961, 8). Yet if public opinion is to be important in the policy process, one must know what policymakers look to in order to evaluate it. What sources of information do they identify as representative of French public opinion?

Several possible sources have been identified by scholars (Cohen 1973; Powlick 1991). These include elites, interest groups, the news media, elected representatives, and the mass public directly as perceived through demonstrations, opinion polls, or other sources. But as a prerequisite to the question of influence, we need to know which of these groups is heard most often by French foreign policy officials. Which "voices" do they listen to?

Consequently, the officials interviewed were asked to discuss how they learned about public opinion concerning foreign policy issues. It was possible for officials to identify more than one source of public opinion. An overwhelming majority (thirty-five out of thirty-seven, or 94 percent) spontaneously answered the news media. As Richard Duqué, former Foreign Ministry spokesman expressed: "On foreign policy questions, public opinion essentially reveals itself through the media. It is very rare for the public to spontaneously express itself. People do not go down in the streets demonstrating against a foreign policy decision as it might be the case for domestic politics."[4] Jean-Louis Chambon, a member of former President François Mitterrand's press service, observed further that "the evening news was for the president a foray into public opinion."[5]

In order to understand why policymakers primarily cited the media, it is important to clearly explain the particularities of the French media and their role within the policymaking apparatus. Indeed, although the French public generally relies on the 8 P.M. televised news or on local or regional newspapers to get information, the policymaking and intellectual communities rely primarily on three widely recognized national newspapers, which follow clearly defined partisan lines: *Le Figaro*, which is center-right, *Liberation*, which is left, and *Le Monde*, which is center-left. A day does not go by without most policymakers reading what is published in *Le Monde*. A provocative article hence immediately becomes the number-one subject of public debate. Take the following illustration of the importance officials concede to this national newspaper: toward the end of his second presidential mandate, in a reprisal against the director of *Le Monde*, with whom he had a tense relationship, François Mitterrand decided to ban the usual distribution of this newspaper within the Elysée Palace (Benamou 1996, 68). Unable to do without this newspaper, most of his advisers secretly slipped out of the palace around 3:00 P.M. (*Le Monde* is an evening paper) to buy it at the closest newsstand. The president himself, although he would not admit it, continued reading it every day.[6]

Only a small number of officials (four out of thirty-seven, or 11 percent) cited elites and intellectuals as a source of public opinion. In fact, the respondents insisted on the shift in the role of elites due to technological advances in the news media. Pierre Messmer, former prime minister during the reign of General Charles de Gaulle, stated: "Today, the role of opinion leaders has shifted from intellectuals to TV journalists. The strength of the new opinion vectors, the television and the radio, is that they are present in every home."[7]

Although these findings differ from those found previously by Cohen (1973) and call into question models of foreign policy linkages that emphasize elites (Almond 1950), they reinforce those found by Powlick in 1991. Indeed, only 12 percent of the officials whom Powlick interviewed cited elites as an operational source of public opinion (Powlick 1995, 433). Hence, in the United States and France, there has been a diminished use of elites as representatives of public opinion. Powlick interprets this evolution as likely resulting from the lessons of Vietnam, but it is asserted here that it can be substantially attributed to the technological evolution in the media. We must nevertheless be cautious in drawing this conclusion about elites, as it is sometimes difficult to distinguish between the media and the intellectual elites themselves, for what the latter say and do is often communicated through the media. During the Bosnian crisis, for example, from 1992 to 1995 and with a peak in 1994, a movement composed of a number of intellectuals—André Glucksmann, Alain Finkielkraut, and Bernard-Henri Lévy, among others—strongly relied on media coverage to defend the cause of the Bosnian Muslims to the point where Hubert Védrine, then secretary-general of the presidency (and current foreign secretary), frequently referred to them as *les intellectuels médiatiques* (intellectuals enjoying prominent media coverage, Védrine 1996, 637).

Regarding other sources of public opinion, strong skepticism was expressed about opinion polls in more than half of these interviews. Whereas policymakers generally agree that there is a heavy reliance on survey data for domestic policymaking, seventeen out of thirty-seven respondents (46 percent) discounted polls as a source of public opinion on foreign policy issues. Very few surveys, with the exception of a yearly barometer on defense issues, are in fact conducted by either the Elysée, the Foreign Ministry, or the Defense Ministry. Yet policymakers' perceptions of opinion polls remain somewhat ambiguous. Although they do not consider polls to be a guide to public opinion (or to correct policymaking), they consider it an error to totally disregard them. In fact, in the months leading up to the Gulf War, Mitterrand was very conscious of French public opinion on this issue, and during January

1991 he ordered two surveys a week to follow the mood of the population.[8] Similarly, a number of government-sponsored surveys were conducted prior to the referendum on the Maastricht Treaty, when Mitterrand and the socialist government realized that there was more opposition toward this treaty than they had expected; they feared that a majority of the public would answer "no" to the referendum. These government-sponsored surveys are often conducted by private institutes and ordered by the Service d'Information du Gouvernement, an administrative service that centralizes and coordinates all government-sponsored surveys. These may have been isolated cases, but it does reveal the policymakers' overall ambivalence toward opinion polls. They may be openly disdainful of opinion polls, but sometimes they rely on them, especially in communications efforts to create consent and bolster support for policies.

Finally, whereas in Philip Powlick's U.S. study a substantial number of those interviewed associate public opinion with the opinion of elected members of Congress, French elected officials are not thought to reflect the views of the public at large. Indeed, only four officials interviewed (11 percent) cited elected members of the parliament as a source of public opinion. This can be explained by the very limited role that the French parliament has with respect to foreign policy. Foreign policy decisions are indeed centralized in the hands of the executive branch. As a former foreign secretary reflects: "Under the Fifth Republic, elected representatives of the parliament play a minimal role with respect to foreign policy questions. When I was foreign secretary, I rarely went in front of parliament. It's not that I do not like the parliament, it's that it has only a very limited role."[9]

Indeed, the Fifth Republic has institutionalized a centralized political system that all presidents have reinforced since General de Gaulle. This is especially true for foreign policy, the *domaine réservé* of the president. The decisionmaking apparatus is in fact even more centralized with respect to foreign policy questions than in any other issue area, and the parliament plays an almost negligible role. Even when presidents are forced into "cohabitation" situations with a government and a parliament of a different political opinion, as has been the case three times in the last ten years, the president retains his prerogatives over foreign policy decisions. This does not mean to suggest that the parliament does not follow foreign policy issues. There is both a foreign affairs and a defense committee within the parliament, which follow these issues and occasionally publish reports on deliberations, but their impact on the decisionmaking process remains marginal.

While these results generally reinforce Bernard Cohen's and Powlick's findings on the importance of the media in linking public opinion to the policy process, it is necessary to be careful in comparing the results of these studies. The current study was conducted with top-level officials in France, whereas Cohen's and Powlick's research focused on lower-level officials, civil servants in the State Department, and, in Powlick's case, the National Security Council staff. Yet it is clear that in both countries the media play a key role in transmitting public opinion to government. Although officials recognize that the media themselves are not the public, the media provide for them a means for gauging attitudes outside of their narrow policy circles to break away from their isolation from the public.

Given this, however, the question remains: To what extent do policymakers in France take public opinion into account when choosing a course of action?

THE PUBLIC'S INFLUENCE ON FOREIGN POLICY DECISIONS

Former UN Secretary General Boutros Boutros-Ghali once stated that "for the past two centuries, it is law that provided the sources of authority for democracy. Today, law seems to be replaced by opinion as the source of authority, and the media serve as the arbiter of public opinion."[10] A report from the Foreign Affairs Committee of the French National Assembly concluded as well that "one must admit the decisive influence of the media on both the decision to launch a military operation and in the way to conduct it."[11] Yet a detailed look at the opinion-policy nexus reveals a far more complex relationship.

Anticipating Public Reactions: The Case of the Gulf War

One aspect of this relationship involves the processes of anticipating public opinion, with policymakers consistently making efforts to gauge public reactions. Powlick's study (1990) reported that 84 percent of the foreign policy officials he interviewed admitted trying to anticipate how the public was going to react (Powlick 1990, 213); at the same time, 91 percent (thirty-four out of thirty-seven) of respondents in the current study reported the same. Hence, policymakers may be quite constrained by their apprehension of the public's possible reactions to a given policy option. Mitterrand's attitude during the Gulf crisis is in fact revealing in this respect. In the Fall of 1990, as the Coalition prepared for Operation Desert Storm, a majority of the French public supported the eventuality of France's participation in the multilateral military operation. Yet Mitterrand felt the need to further mobilize the public. This impulse explains his unprecedented communications effort. Between August and December 1990, at key moments of the crisis (the hostage crisis, the violation of the French residence in Kuwait, etc.), he held six press conferences. His main aim was to "educate" and, according to former Secretary General Hubert Védrine, to "prepare the public for the inescapable consequences of the war-logic initiated by Saddam Hussein" (Védrine 1996, 540). Unsure of how the public would react and in order to prevent a possible uprising, Mitterrand took the lead.[12]

Once Desert Storm was launched, Mitterrand also took the necessary measures to prevent members of his government from publicly debating France's participation in the Gulf War. Indeed, French political elites were divided on this issue. Jean-Pierre Chevènement's position was well known. As defense secretary, he strongly opposed France's participation in the Gulf War and resigned only a few days after the launch of Desert Storm. Many other close advisers and political figures also questioned the reasons for France's participation. Hence, beginning Monday, January 21, 1991, members of the government were able to express themselves on the war only from the Centre Kléber, an international conference center located on Rue Kléber in Paris, and only once did they obtain permission from the Elysée Palace or from Matignon. The aim of this scheme was clear: to prevent any kind of protest and to "unify the public speech."[13]

His decision not to let draftees participate in the war effort was driven by a similar logic. On November 10, 1991, when U.S. Secretary of State James Baker arrived in France to obtain Mitterrand's support for a UN resolution authorizing the use of force, the latter replied: "How will I explain to the French farmers that I threatened the life of their children to restore a millionaire?" (Favier and Martin-Roland 1996, 465). When mothers started to express their fears on televised talk shows, Mitterrand announced during his last press conference prior to Desert Storm that no draftee would take part in the operation on the front or on warships. His closest aides qualified this as a very "personal" and "political" decision that Mitterrand announced without prior notice even to his chief of staff. Senior military officers still question today whether such a decision was justified, especially in light of the logistical difficulties it generated. Yet Mitterrand chose policy options to limit a possible upheaval.

Thus, policymakers can either abstain from or engage in actions by anticipating what they perceive might be an adverse public reaction. Mitterrand felt constrained in this way and therefore took his time to prepare the French for the military operation in the Gulf. As such, the public did have an impact on policy, although it did not divert Mitterrand from his principal objective in this case: to participate in the war's multilateral military operation.

Public Opinion as a Catalyst?

Some observers feel that public opinion can also act as a catalyst in the decision-making process. Régis Debray considers that "the discussion on the judiciousness of a humanitarian military operation, in Africa for example, comes to an end when it is known that 78 percent of the French population approves it" (Debray 1993, 183). A strong majority of the French public supports the idea of UN peacekeeping operations; the French feel they have a moral responsibility to assist suffering people and to allay civilian deaths in countries ravaged by civil war. Since May 1991, between 70 percent and 87 percent of survey respondents agree to the use of force to "intervene, under the auspices of the United Nations, for the respect of international law," "to assist a population in distress (famine, civil war . . .)," or to "contribute to bring peace in a region of the world."[14] Graham's (1994) model of public opinion's impact asserts that a preponderant level of public opinion (70–79 percent) typically causes the political system to act according to its dictates in the United States. Furthermore, it also deters political opposition from challenging the specific decision, and in response to a nearly unanimous opinion (more than 80 percent), decisions appear to be automatic. Yet do policymakers really decide to undertake certain courses of action only because of a belief that the public demands it? Let us look more closely at the decision to participate in the peace operations in Somalia and in Rwanda.

On November 17, 1992, the UN Secretary General's proposal to deploy French troops based in Djibouti to assist in the distribution of humanitarian aid in Somalia was rejected.[15] Members of the French government were divided. The defense secretary at the time, Pierre Joxe, was against any type of humanitarian military operation; Humanitarian Aid Secretary Bernard Kouchner strongly favored such action. In the following days, the French were moved by the haunting images on television of starving people. Across the country, children brought bags of rice to school for the young Somalians. The question of France's participation in the peacekeeping operation was reexamined during a cabinet meeting on December 3 in the president's presence. Mitterrand resolved the dispute, and France was to take part in Operation Restore Hope.

What led him to such a decision? Was it public pressure? Was it political pressure emanating from Francophone African states that wanted to limit U.S. influence on the African continent? Was it political pressure from the United States for France's participation in the peace operation? Pierre Joxe explains that the French president decided to participate in Operation Restore Hope upon receipt of a letter from George Bush. The defense secretary recalls that when he expressed his opposition to the mission, Mitterrand answered: "You're probably right, but we cannot say 'no' to the Americans. They have committed themselves" (Cohen 1998, 426). Yet if Mitterrand first and foremost chose to answer Bush's call, he was also well aware of the public's disposition toward peace operations. In fact, a CSA/La Vie poll taken as the troops arrived in Somalia in December 1992 confirmed 82 percent support for France's participation in the UN-mandated operation.[16] Most of the policymakers whom we interviewed agreed that one of the reasons for France's participation in Operation Restore Hope was to prevent public disapproval had France remained idle. Although public opinion was not the exclusive reason for France's participation in the peace operation, it entered into the decisionmaking process.

The situation in Rwanda was somewhat different. France's first reaction, upon learning of the death of President Juvénal Habyarimana on April 6, 1994, was to evacuate French citizens and not intervene in the conflict. It was only when questions were raised in the media and among humanitarian associations about France's responsibility in the conflict that the French government started to consider a peace operation. Once again, members of government were divided. Foreign Secretary Alain Juppé and the president's personal chief of staff, General Christian Quesnot, were strongly in favor of this operation. Defense Secretary François Léotard and Prime Minister Edouard Balladur were more reluctant. Operation Turquoise was nevertheless decided on June 15.

What led to this decision? "The rise of public opinion pressure as it took the full measure of the massacres that were going on in that country," replied Jean Musitelli, presidential spokesman.[17] The president himself declared that "we could not see the images of what was going on in Rwanda which were brought into all the homes in Europe through the media, and let it be."[18] Policymakers themselves, therefore, admit that public opinion acted as a catalyst to this peace operation. Yet the French public never expressed an outright request for a peace operation. There was no mass mobilization, and the French were actually quite ambivalent toward the operation itself. Questions about the actual intent of Operation Turquoise were in fact raised, due to France's prior support of President Juvénal Habyarimana's regime, accused of massacring hundreds of thousands of Tutsis. Several humanitarian organizations, as well as the press, condemned this operation, although the criticism was not unanimous. Some journalists censured the past acts; other applauded the humanitarian gesture.

The ambiguity of the situation translated itself through the results of a poll taken at the very beginning of Operation Turquoise: 49 percent of the respondents agreed that France, by intervening in Rwanda, "is taking on a role that it should assume"; 35 percent agreed with the opposite, similarly ambiguous, statement that "France is assuming responsibilities that are not hers."[19] Thus, it is quite conceivable, in fact, that what the political leaders feared most was that France be accused of complicity with "genocide" or "ethnic cleansing" at a time when the public was particularly sensitive to such tragedies. One of the aims of Operation Turquoise could very well have been to silence such accusations.

The Somalia and Rwanda cases reveal that the cause-and-effect relationship between public opinion and the decision to participate in peace operations is complex. In both cases, public opinion played a part in decisionmakers' assessments of policy options; yet policymakers did not participate in peace operations only because of a belief that the public demanded some form of action. Public opinion can act as a catalyst, but it does not alone have the power to force governments to launch interventionist military operations. A look at the opinion-policy nexus during the Yugoslavia conflict further reveals that policymakers do not systematically respond to public opinion.

Symbolic Actions to Contain Public Opinion

François Mitterrand realized that the level of public support for France's involvement in the former Yugoslavia had always been strong (survey results showed support of 60–70 percent between 1992 and 1994).[20] He did concede to a number of symbolic gestures in order to contain public opinion. The first example was his call in favor of the opening of a security corridor to Dubrovnik on November 10, 1991. This humanitarian act was led by Humanitarian Aid Secretary Bernard Kouchner on November 20. It occurred "largely under public pressure," admits former Secretary General Hubert Védrine (Védrine 1996, 615), but it remained purely symbolic since no military peace operation was then considered. During the closing press conference of the European Council on June 27, 1992, Mitterrand made a second concession. He admitted that "Serbia is today the aggressor in the Bosnian conflict even if its origin stems from far away." According to Jean Musitelli, a close presidential adviser, Mitterrand regretted having to make what he considered a reduced presentation of the Bosnian situation, but he also wanted to finally silence the criticism that emerged in the press after an interview he gave to *Frankfurter Allgemeine Zeitung* on November 29, 1991, in which he had refused to name the aggressors. Mitterrand's surprise visit to Sarajevo on June 28, 1992, was yet a third symbolic gesture. He admitted the decisive influence of the outspoken intellectual Bernard-Henri Lévy on his decision to go to Sarajevo. Indeed, what prompted his decision was a letter that had been given to him by Bernard-Henri Lévy from President Alija Izetbegovic.[21]

Although Mitterrand did undertake symbolic measures, he did not directly yield to public pressure. He was convinced that the conflict in Bosnia could only be resolved through a political solution. While the atrocities of the ongoing ethnic cleansing drove the public to become increasingly frustrated with the government's performance in Bosnia and to favor the use of force—that is, military violence—to stop the fighting,[22] Mitterrand refused to "engage France—especially alone—in any kind of war in the Balkans" (Védrine 1996, 637). When committed intellectuals criticized his political choices, Mitterrand responded: "What do these personalities want? War? France and its army, alone, in deadly combat? I prefer other ways of doing things."[23] He maintained his political orientation despite this strong intellectual movement and despite survey results that revealed the public's frustration. A survey conducted shortly after General Philippe Morillon's mobilization in Srebrenica reported that 52 percent of respondents thought "the French government is not making a sufficient effort to try to stop the fighting in ex-Yugoslavia," whereas only 31 percent agreed that "the French government is doing everything in its power to stop the fighting."[24] At the time of NATO's ultimatum to the Bosnian Serbs in February 1994, another survey revealed that 52 percent of respondents disapproved of the way that the French president and the French government were handling the crisis.[25] Yet Mitterrand did not yield.

Similarly, despite a lively debate among policymakers on the one hand and outspoken intellectuals and journalists on the other, Mitterrand refused to lift the arms embargo instituted on September 26, 1991, by UN Resolution 713. He strongly opposed the U.S. proposal, upheld by French intellectuals, of "lift and strike" (lift the arms embargo on the Bosnian government and use airpower against the Serbs), and he chose not to budge even when this became an electoral issue during the European elections of 1994.

Hence, this case reveals that policymakers do not systematically respond to public opinion and can in fact choose to confront it when convinced of the judiciousness of their political choices.

THE EXECUTIVE'S MARGIN OF FREEDOM

This is not a comprehensive analysis of the role that public opinion plays in the decision to participate in military operations and in the foreign policy process more generally. It does, however, reveal the possible types of effects public opinion may have on the policy process and illustrate the general conclusion that the public opinion–policy relationship is complex and variable rather than simple and constant. It challenges the assumption of a profound automatic cause-and-effect relationship between public opinion and foreign policy decisionmaking, as well as the total lack of such an effect. It also reveals the leeway for decisions that French policymakers have. While Mitterrand prepared the French for the Gulf War and chose not to let draftees participate in the war effort, the public did not prevent him from engaging France in the multilateral operation. Similarly, in the former Yugoslavia, although Mitterrand consented to symbolic measures in order to contain public pressure and to prevent popular uprising, the public did not drive him to change his policy orientation or allow the French soldiers involved in the peace operation to adopt a more offensive posture. In Somalia, he was pressed to participate in Operation Restore Hope, but he did so very cautiously: French soldiers were deployed in Baïdoa, far from the more troubled zone of Mogadishu, where the American soldiers were stationed.

This opinion-policy nexus is more interactive and reciprocal than unidirectional. Indeed, if the case studies offered here reveal that public opinion is often a constraint that policymakers must figure into policy decisions, there is another dimension to consider. Policymakers can also use public pressure as a political tool to convince their own entourage or international partners. A significant example of this is the mortar attack on the Sarajevo market on February 5,1994, and the subsequent international response. It is often assumed that the public's reactions to the horrific TV images determined the decision to issue the ultimatum to Sarajevo. A close analysis of the decisionmaking process reveals that the reality was quite different.

Long before Sarajevo's massacre, Foreign Secretary Alain Juppé was determined to take firmer action in Bosnia. Even before Christmas 1993, Juppé "had given US Secretary of State Warren Christopher a firm message that either the US must do more to become engaged or the EU would take tougher action alone" (Gowing 1994, 71). British Foreign Secretary Douglas Hurd also "traveled to Washington in the week before the massacre to reinforce the European pressure" (Gowing 1994, 71). Although the United States began to stiffen its position, the Bill Clinton administration still resisted giving more political support to the UN peace efforts. The market massacre then occurred. The emotion raised by the TV images enabled the French government to mobilize all its partners and to demand that the Bosnian Serbs be threatened by air strikes. As White House Communications Director Mark Gearan explained, the market massacre "helped the (French) argument" (Gowing 1994, 71). Assistant U.S. Defense Secretary Graham Allison confirmed that "France was pressing for action. The Sarajevo market massacre crystallized for the Clinton administration that it had to do something; that we could not do nothing. Those who wanted to do something seized on it" (Gowing 1994, 72). Four days later, Clinton backed NATO in issuing an unprecedented ultimatum to the Bosnian Serbs requesting that they withdraw all heavy artillery 20 kilometers from Sarajevo. Alain

Juppé had used the alleged emotions this event caused throughout the public to convince his international partners of the necessity of an ultimatum.[26]

THEORETICAL IMPLICATIONS

The common assumption that French policymakers are insulated from public pressures is thus invalidated. Clearly, public opinion is not irrelevant in the foreign policy process. An attempt has been made to demonstrate that although public opinion is rarely the exclusive factor taken into account when selecting a course of action, decisionmakers can nevertheless be either constrained or motivated by public opinion, and they can also come to use it as a political tool.

At this stage of research, it nevertheless remains difficult to determine theoretical rules that would govern this complex opinion-policy relationship. Yet some empirical rules seem to emerge. According to Hubert Védrine,

> If the public does not have a fixed opinion on a subject, the government can convince it of the judiciousness of its action as long as the media are not opposed to it and that the government has a clear vision of its action. If the public is a priori fixed and the media share the same opinion, the government will not be able to reverse the situation without a sustained effort. If the government does not know what it wants, or does not dare say it, it will suffer from the cumulated weight of the public and of the media, with one following the other, or vice-versa. (Védrine 1996, 65)

Let us note that according to Risse-Kappen (1994) the public's impact in France also depends almost exclusively on the degree to which the top decisionmakers are prepared to take its views into account. Indeed, there are, in France, few institutionalized access points for societal demands on foreign policy issues to reach the political system. Mass public opinion affects policy only if it reaches top decisionmakers, notably the president. It is often he who decides whether to respond to the public's demands. Important determinants of the influence of public opinion on the foreign policy process are thus cognitive factors: policymakers' perceptions about public opinion. In this respect, the media indeed play a decisive role. Although news media are, by definition, primarily transmitters of information, this study reveals that French foreign policy officials are very receptive to them and perceive them to be the main operational source of public opinion—far more than opinion polls, elites, and elected officials. We can conclude, then, that the more media coverage an event receives, the more policymakers are likely to be attentive to the public.

This research also reveals that the public's impact depends on the combination of other variables, such as temporal factors (stage in the policy process, stage in the electoral mandate),[27] variables linked to policymakers' personalities, and the strength of the consensus among the representatives of the executive branch. As an illustration of the importance of this latter variable, in the cases of the Gulf War, Somalia, and Rwanda, the public's impact increased as top decisionmakers (prime minister, foreign secretary, defense secretary) disagreed among themselves on the best action to adopt. A fuller description of these variables is, however, beyond the scope of this chapter. It will thus be the subject of a further writing.[28] To conclude, it can be suggested that French policymakers do retain the power to make policy choices and to lead. Strong will, clear vision, and consensus within the executive branch are nevertheless prerequisites. Public opinion can exert influence on foreign policy, but it largely depends on the government's own assertive position.

17

Where Angels Fear to Tread
Italian Public Opinion and Foreign Policy

Pierangelo Isernia

The NATO air attacks against the Federal Republic of Yugoslavia that started on March 24, 1999, brought to the fore the fundamental problems of Italian foreign policy after the end of the Cold War. On the one hand, no more than a third of the Italian population supported air raids; concomitantly, there was vehement opposition by the Pope and the Vatican state, and the left-wing government coalition was deeply divided on the best way to deal with Slobodan Milosevic. On the other hand, Italy was expected by NATO allies to support the operation as a frontline member of the alliance. Thus, the Italian political leadership was faced with the dilemma of reconciling its desire to be a faithful and reliable ally, its awareness that NATO (i.e., U.S.) policy clashed with several Italian interests and concerns in the region, and the cool attitude of Italian public opinion regarding the war. The Italian government therefore was careful to construct a policy position to deal with these contradictory claims. In stressing its willingness to stand firm beside the allies while encouraging negotiating initiatives from any source, the Italian government was as much attempting to calm internal opposition as it was reflecting the concerns of the majority of its public. In so doing, the Kosovo conflict also pointed to the growing influence of public opinion on Italian foreign policy. The central purpose of this chapter is to describe the nature, long-term evolution, and impact of public opinion on Italian foreign policymaking.

In Italy, it is commonly argued that there is no public opinion on foreign policy: "Italians like movies, soccer and girls. They are not interested in politics and even less in foreign policy" (Kogan 1965, 40). This picture of Italian public opinion depicted in earlier qualitative and quantitative studies remains in place even today (Banfield 1958; Almond and Verba 1983).[1] As the story goes, the lack of interest in and knowledge of international affairs, an outgrowth of the fundamental "backwardness" of Italian society (Schneider 1998), made Italian public opinion so volatile and moody as to defy any serious analysis. Furthermore, the fragmented and decentralized nature of the Italian political system (Hine 1993) makes it very difficult to trace back the role of any single actor in the policymaking process, whereas the existence of strong parties makes them both the natural channel through which the public's demands are articulated and processed and the main interpreters and shapers of the public mood. Clearly, both views have to be reconsidered.

As to the first point, the rich and so far underutilized available survey data shows that Italian public opinion over the long term has not been erratic or volatile in its attitudes on international issues.

As to the second point, with the end of the Cold War and the progression toward supranational integration produced by monetary unification, the context has changed for the opinion-policy relationship in Italy and, probably, for the very role that public opinion in both its organized and unorganized forms plays in the calculations of Italian decisionmakers.

Accordingly, this chapter is organized into two sections. The first describes the nature and evolution of Italian attitudes toward international affairs during the Cold War and spells out the consequences of the post–Cold War international system on those attitudes. The second section examines the relationship between public opinion and foreign policy in the multiparty Italian system, focusing attention on the implications of internal and international changes in the 1990s on the role of public opinion.

ITALIAN PUBLIC OPINION AND FOREIGN POLICY: NATURE AND CONTENT

Cold War Foreign Policy Attitudes

Contrary to the image held by politicians and observers of a moody and volatile public opinion in foreign policy, the available survey data provide a much different picture. At the aggregate level, Italian public opinion is remarkably stable, consistent, and coherent. Examining more than 1,500 questions asked between 1952 and 1993 on Italian foreign policy issues, no more than 56 percent of these questions asked with identical wording at least twice show a change of more than 6 percentage points, a proportion very close to that found in Germany, France, and the United States (Isernia, Juhasz, and Rattinger 1998; Shapiro and Page 1988; Page and Shapiro 1992). Moreover, most of the changes that occur are relatively small: 46 percent of the significant instances of change are less than 10 percentage points, a proportion very close to that reported in the United States (Shapiro and Page 1988, 217). The most dramatic changes (20 percent or more) amount to no more than 9 percent of significant shifts. Changes do not occur frequently in foreign policy, and when they do occur they are not as dramatic as realists like to think.

When changes occur in public opinion in Italy, they are not more abrupt than in other countries. Page and Shapiro (1982, 28–29) classified a change as abrupt "if it occurred at a rate of 10 percentage points or more per year." In the Italian case, 64 percent of significant instances of change were abrupt. Italian public opinion, however, appears to show more frequent fluctuation.[2] Out of 81 questions with enough time points (three or more) to detect these shifts, 58 percent had some fluctuation in Italy, compared to 21 percent in the United States. This amount of change, however, is not dramatic (involving 47 out of 224 questions), and it does not reflect necessarily a capricious or volatile public. It rather reflects the nature of the events and the size and role of Italy in the international arena. Fluctuating opinions were more likely in connection with foreign policy crises (e.g., the Suez crisis in 1956) and other dramatic international events (e.g., the Soviet invasion of Afghanistan in 1979 or the military coup in Poland in 1980), when the public's judgment changed as the situation evolved and the media provided a growing amount of information that helped to frame the issue. In a typical Cold War crisis, the ability of Italian political leaders to influence the events was almost negligible. The fear of "entrapment" (Snyder 1984) in an international crisis in which public opinion senses its own government has nothing to say might well contribute toward increasing the uncertainty and fluctuation of the Italian public.

Thus, the commonly held idea that Italian public opinion is unpredictable and capricious in foreign policy is not supported by the available evidence. Public opinion in Italy does not change more abruptly or more frequently than in the United States, Germany, and France.

Italian public opinion has reacted in sensitive and reasonable ways to events and policies in the foreign realm. So far as attitudes toward the two superpowers were concerned, Italian public opinion came to recognize over time the development and consolidation of an implicit set of "rules of the superpower game" (Gaddis 1986), establishing limits to the acceptable behavior of both sides in order to make the international system more predictable and stable. The improved stability in aggregate public opinion that Isernia, Juhasz, and Rattinger (1998) found moving from the 1950s to the 1980s reflects this process.

There is no doubt that the relationships with the United States and the Soviet Union were, during the Cold War, a crucial component of Italian foreign policy. This was not only an inevitable result of the bipolar system but also a consequence of the competition between the Democratic-Christian Party and the Communist Party. Moreover, it emanated from the powerful attraction the American and Soviet experience exerted at both the mass and elite levels for different political and cultural reasons (D'Attorre 1991). The one important difference was that the pro-Soviet feelings were exclusively concentrated among the communists (and for a short while the socialists), while the popularity of the United States crossed the left-right division, reaching even in the communist constituency.

Between 1954 and 1993, on average no more than 8 percent of the respondents had intense anti-American feelings. Among those with an opinion,[3] on average 89 percent had a very good or somewhat favorable opinion of the United States and only 11 percent a negative one. In contrast, pro-Soviet feelings were spread in no more than an average of 37 percent of the population, with 63 percent having a very or somewhat bad opinion of the Soviet Union. Even at the height of the Cold War, the communists had proportionally more positive feelings toward the United States than the Democratic-Christians did toward the Soviet Union.

These attitudes persisted over the Cold War, with ebbs and flows due to the evolution of the international situation as well as to specific policy issues between Italy and the two superpowers.

However, there was one important attitude change, in that the proportion of those Italians who were indifferent (neither positive nor negative) toward the United States increased. The younger, better-educated generations are much more likely than their less educated elders to be indifferent to the United States. For those born in the 1940s and before, the United States was the country that liberated Italy from fascism and helped its economic recovery. For those born in the 1950s and thereafter, the United States was the imperialist country that invaded Vietnam and obstructed Italian domestic reforms. The proportion of people with "indifferent" attitudes toward the United States increased after the end of the Cold War.

Italian attitudes toward the Soviet Union were less stable and less positive. Negative feelings were highest in the early 1950s (in the first stage of the Cold War) and in the early 1980s (following the Polish crisis and the Afghanistan invasion). Both periods were followed by an improvement in favorable attitudes, namely, during the Nikita Khruschev "thaw period" and the ensuing détente, and again with the arrival of Mikhail Gorbachev and the launching of perestroika. At the verge of the collapse of the Soviet Union, the level of net favor (subtracting the percentage of those with a negative or very negative opinion from the percentage of those with a positive or very positive opinion) toward the country matched that for the United States. Paradoxically, the end of the Soviet Union and the political turmoil accompanying the Russian transition to democracy had a negative effect on the Italian public's attitudes toward the former Soviet Union.

A further confirmation of the Italian public's sensitivity to international events, the importance of the quality of information, and the effects of political manipulation by foreign friends and foes is found in the public's past perceptions of the military balance between the two superpowers. Looking at the indicator of relative military power between the United States and the Soviet Union, it is clear that the Soviet Union never matched the United States in military terms. During the 1970s, the distance between the two leading countries progressively reduced to reach almost military parity, but it grew again in favor of the United States in the 1980s following the military buildup under Ronald Reagan. This trend only partially overlaps with that in Italian public opinion, allowing for some considerations for the role of political manipulation in influencing the public's image.

The American military predominance, especially in nuclear terms, during the 1950s starkly contrasted with Italian perceptions. In that period, only a plurality of Italians considered the United States to be the strongest power, and in November

1957, probably as an effect of the successful launch of Sputnik by the Russians, only 28 percent deemed the United States the strongest military power. This impression prevailed for the last part of the 1950s in a media environment that debated the alleged bomber and missile gaps and American scientific and technological weaknesses. Italian perceptions changed, if only temporarily, with the arrival of President John Kennedy and the demystification of the missile gap (which Kennedy had helped create by skillfully manipulating the issue during his presidential campaign). The Soviet Union became militarily superior again for the rest of the 1960s and 1970s. By the 1980s, the proportion of Italians perceiving the two superpowers as militarily equal constituted a majority.

This shift in the Italian public's perception—from American inferiority to a bipolar parity among the two superpowers—helped to reduce the gap between the perceived and the desired power distribution, a gap ready to be exploited by center-right parties to manipulate the fear of the Soviet threat. Between 1981 and 1988, the proportion of Italians preferring military parity between the United States and the Soviet Union increased from 64 percent to 73 percent. In other words, during the 1980s an increasing majority of Italians came to share the conviction of international relations scholars (e.g., Waltz 1979; Mearsheimer 1994) who considered the bipolar international system as more stable than either the multipolar or unipolar ones.

The 1980s witnessed other attitude changes toward the two superpowers. Between 1981 and 1985, the proportion of Italians believing a Soviet military attack likely in the next five years declined from 20 percent to 7 percent. At the same time, there was a slight decline of the trust in the American government's ability to handle world problems and an increase of trust in the Soviet government's handling of world problems. In December 1982, only 37 percent had trust in the Soviet leadership, whereas 72 percent trusted the U.S. government. By 1987, 89 percent trusted the Soviet Union and 78 percent trusted the United States. However, trust for the Soviet Union declined, probably as a consequence of the domestic turmoil accompanying the country's transition to democracy. In March 1991, only 56 percent trusted the Soviet Union, whereas 72 percent trusted the United States.

In conclusion, at the end of the Cold War the United States was still more liked and trusted than the Soviet Union, but the Italian public was also more critical of American behavior in the international system, more reluctant to trust its ability to handle world problems, and more worried that U.S. behavior might inadvertently cause a war.

THE POST–COLD WAR FOREIGN POLICY ATTITUDES

The events of 1989 and 1990 marked the beginning of a vast and ongoing process of restructuring of the international system. Accordingly, the image of that system prevalent among public opinion in Western European countries and the United

States, nurtured by more than forty years of East-West conflicts and anticommunism, broke apart. To assess the impact of such events on the Italians' image of the international system, one should consider that if stability rather than volatility is the rule, then we should not expect that radical changes in the nature of the international system would immediately affect public attitudes on foreign policy. In other words, attitude change might not be the rapid, sudden process implied by Gabriel Almond's mood theory (1960) and feared by many theorists of democracy but is rather a "tectonic" process taking place at a slow pace.[4] In assessing the impact of the events related to 1989 on public opinion, I shall distinguish between long- and short-term effects.

As to short-term effects, the 1989 events produced a diffuse expectation of immediately benefiting from the so-called peace dividend. For a few months, a strong plurality, if not the majority, of Italians thought it possible to drastically reduce the armed forces and to dismantle the multilateral security arrangements of the past. These opinions, however, lasted no more than a few months. Already in December 1989 and definitely by the end of 1990, it was clear that the NATO alliance and the Italian military establishment had to be put to good use again because of new and often geographically closer sources of instability.

A first short-term impact of communism's collapse is detectable in Italians' attitudes toward military spending. Military expenditures have never been popular in Italy. In the 1980s, an average of about 40 percent of the public was in favor of reducing military spending. In December 1989, this percentage jumped to 62 percent, with only 6 percent supporting an increase in defense expenditures and 27 percent preferring the military budget to stay at the existing level. In January 1992— after the Gulf War and signs of instability in the Balkans—the proportion of those favoring a reduction dropped to 30 percent, the lowest point since 1977. Since then, support for a reduction in defense expenditures has never surpassed 40 percent, while the number of people thinking that expenses should stay at the existing level increased.

A similar pattern is found with respect to attitudes toward the NATO alliance. The Alliance has never been popular in Italy. However, excluding an abrupt short-term fluctuation in NATO support in mid-1989, the overall impact of the Soviet Union's collapse has been an increase in support for NATO. Support for NATO reached one of its lowest levels in May 1989 (when 48 percent of the Italian public considered NATO as "still essential"), but this support increased in June to 59 percent and dropped again abruptly in October to 46 percent (the lowest percentage since this question has been asked), eventually increasing again in December (62 percent). The May-June upswing is probably explained by a NATO meeting on May 30, 1989, in which the Alliance decided to defer the modernization of short-range nuclear forces until 1992. The drop between June and October was a consequence of the upheaval in Eastern Europe, when the Warsaw Pact was falling apart. But these events did not produce a lasting effect. Between October and December, there was a second upswing of 16 percentage points in support for NATO, mostly due to the movement toward NATO of left-wing voters, who would be more likely to see NATO as an outdated institution after the dissolution of Soviet Union. Support for NATO, once it became supported by a majority, stayed at that level among left-wing voters even after 1989, surviving the Kuwait crisis and the Italian decision to join forces in the Gulf War.

However, the collapse of the Soviet Union had more lasting effects as well. The first concerns the depolarization of the East-West cleavage in Italy. The Alliance and the political-military alignment with the West had been for decades a source of continuous friction within the Italian party system. Acceptance of the Alliance was a test to legitimize Italian political parties to govern and was a tool to delegitimize the governmental aspirations of the communists and socialists. Even though the Communist Party gradually moved from a strongly anti-NATO stance to a gradual acceptance of Italy's existing security alignments, communist voters did not buy into such a change of policy (see Figure 17.1). It took more than a decade for the communist constituency to move from an anti- to a pro-NATO stance. Only the physical collapse of the Soviet system moved the majority of the communist constituency (by 1990, the Democratic Left Party) to support the Alliance. By now, NATO membership is a bipartisan choice, able to resist the test of arms, as the Kosovo crisis showed. Asked what was the best way to ensure Italian security, in late April 1999 31 percent answered NATO membership and 35 percent answered a reformed NATO membership with a greater voice for Europeans. Those willing to leave NATO amounted to

Figure 17.1 Attitudes toward NATO by party preference

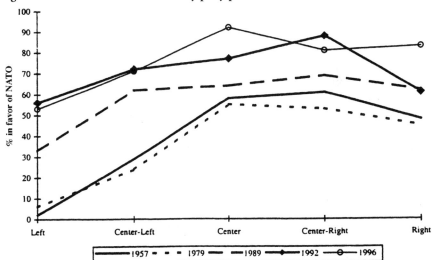

Sources: 1957: Doxa for USIA; 1979: Eurobarometer; 1989: Pragma for USIA; 1992 and 1996: Archivio Disarmo-SWG Difebarometro survey

18 percent, a percentage identical to that in 1995 and in line with five decades of neutralism among one-fifth of the Italian population.

The second long-term effect of the end of the Cold War was a more supportive attitude toward the armed forces, an institution that had never enjoyed an over-whelming degree of enthusiasm among the Italian public in the postwar period. The main implication of this change was a greater propensity to support its use abroad for peacekeeping and even peace-enforcing operations. As a result of the way World War II ended and the poor performance of the military leaders after the armistice of September 8, 1943, the Italian armed forces had been almost "invisible" in Italian society (Battistelli 1996) for more than forty years. Starting in the early 1980s, with the Lebanon multinational force mission, the Italian military came to play a more active role in several peacekeeping operations, culminating in the multinational co-ordination of the Albanian operation in 1997. This helped not only to increase its legitimacy but also to reorient public opinion. As Table 17.1 shows, public support for employing the armed forces in different roles and missions is now quite wide-spread. The use of the military in domestic tasks (such as natural disasters, struggle against Mafia, etc.) is practically unanimous. Peacekeeping missions, especially under the UN banner, are also highly popular. More controversial is the use of Ital-ian armed forces in NATO-led out-of-area missions, as the Kosovo crisis testifies, but still substantial pluralities would support in principle this kind of mission.

However, the Italian public's willingness to support a more active foreign role for Italy rests on domestic political stability, confirming the tight connection between

Table 17.1   Support for Different Tasks of Italian Armed Forces (in percent)

Tasks	11/1992	01/1994	12/1994	01/1996	07/1996
Humanitarian Aid	90	93	NA	NA	NA
Natural Disasters	92	97	94	95	96
Peace-keeping operations under UN	88	85	84	83	79
Domestic Order	77	81	82	83	80
National Defense	70	80	76	79	71
Peace-enforcing operations under UN	55	51	60	63	56
NATO Peace-enforcing operations out of area	39	44	42	47	41
NATO Peace-enforcing operations in Europe	55	62	NA	NA	NA
International terrorism	75	81	NA	NA	NA

Source: Difebarometro survey
NA = Not Asked

Question wording: In thinking about possible tasks for the Italian armed forces in the '90s, could you tell me what tasks do you think Italian armed forces should perform and what they should not perform:
1. Humanitarian aid, etc.

the domestic and international arenas. Internationalism—the desire to see Italy actively involved in international affairs—is closely related to the perceived stability of the Italian internal political system, in particular its executive. If a government is perceived as weak and divided and its life expectancy is low, internationalism dwindles. If a government is perceived as authoritative, enjoys a vast majority, and its life expectancy is long, internationalism grows. Public opinion reacts to international events but at the same time is influenced by the domestic political situation. In other words, Italian public opinion agrees with expert observers and students of Italy that an effective foreign policy rests on a stable and authoritative government (Bellucci 1998).

PUBLIC OPINION AND FOREIGN POLICY: CONNECTIONS AND INFLUENCES

The Opinion-Policy Connection during the Cold War

Moving from foreign policy attitudes and their evolution over time to the analysis of their impact on actual policymaking means a shift to more shaky ground. First, we lack general theories on this connection. Although we have a growing body of comparative evidence that public opinion and public policies are linked (Jacobs and Shapiro 1994), we are not yet able to answer crucial questions as to how, under what circumstances, and by what processes public opinion impacts policy (Page 1994). The traditional alternative between top-down and bottom-up models of elite-masses interaction is not only descriptively inadequate to account for the complex factors involved but also structurally unable to grasp the inherently dynamic nature of the interaction. The impact of opinion on policy is not a static, yes-or-no phenomenon but a dynamic process affected by several factors, each changing over time. Second, the available results are so far centered, with a few exceptions,[5] on the American case (for a recent review of this literature, see Powlick and Katz 1998), a polity that is quite different from European democracies.

Historically, there are three ways through which the European political systems have stabilized the structural relations between the elites and the masses, thereby making it possible for political elites to interpret and, when needed, to manipulate the long-term preferences of their publics. The state machinery was the first instrument used by politicians to establish links between public opinion and the ruling elite. Political parties are the classical link in the era of mass democracy, and the mass media are the most recent development in response to the decline of party strength after World War II.

These three opinion-policy links are characterized by different conceptions of the nature of public opinion, by specific institutional arrangements governing the opinion-policy link, and by different sets of instruments through which political decisionmakers make sense of public attitudes.

Starting with the prevalent image of public opinion in Italy, a useful distinction is that between the sociological and psychological conception of public opinion (Price 1992). According to the sociological conception, the first to be developed on the eve of the French Revolution (Price 1992, 22–23), public opinion is a social product, a collective phenomenon, its fundamental characteristic being its communicative nature. In Blumer's (1953, 46) words the public is "a group of people (a) who are confronted by an issue, (b) who are divided in their ideas as to how to meet the issue, and (c) who engage in discussion over the issue." The psychological conception, a product as much of the scientific development in attitude measurement and sampling during the 1930s (Price 1992, 45) as of the politicization of the mass electorate in the New Deal era, views public opinion as an aggregate of individual attitudes and opinions. Even though the psychological dimension became prevalent, at least in America, this does not necessarily imply that Blumer was wrong (J. Converse 1987). In Italy, there is no doubt that the sociological, more organicist view of public opinion has always been prevalent among the political and cultural elite, explaining, among other things, the profound skepticism toward survey research. The fragmented nature of Italian political culture, vertically dividing the electorate along geographical borders and rigidly encapsulating it in ideologically cohesive political cultures—the "white" Catholic subculture in the northeast and the "red" socialist subculture in the center (La Palombara 1964; Galli 1966)—helped to nurture such an image.

This image of public opinion as socially structured reinforced the role of the parties, the main actor of the political system immediately after the end of World War II. Italy is a case of "dominant party government" (Katz 1986), in which parties are the most important, if not unique, channel of communication for both organized and nonorganized political demands (La Palombara 1964; Hine 1993). In Italy, several factors contributed to strengthening the parties' role not only as the main interpreters of mass opinions but also as the prevalent expressions of those opinions.

The first factor is the weak role the mass media play as an active link between the government and the people (Cohen 1977–1978, 203; 1995). Media in Italy are much less market oriented and more dependent on political and economic support than those in the United States. Italian journalists work under different pressures than their American counterparts. The journalist-politician relationship is highly unbalanced in favor of politicians. Political leaders have a crucial influence on the way issues are defined and on the very attention issues receive from the media. Indeed, the mass media are more a way to communicate among leaders of different parties or even among different factions within the same party than they are a link between the masses and the party elites. Moreover, until a few years ago broadcasting was a state monopoly, tightly controlled by parties and their representatives. Although this changed with the advent of private, for-profit television, Italy still rates quite low among Western democracies in terms of media pluralism. The result of this party influence on the media is not a more consensual press but rather a media that tends to mirror the cultural fragmentation in society.

A second factor is the weak, highly fragmented nature of the state. In Italy, the autonomy of the executive branch is quite low. Governments are a coalition of several, often heterogeneous parties struggling for influence over policies. Several political and institutional actors have a voice in proposing, deciding, and eventually implementing public policies, and veto power is widely dispersed. This is also true in foreign and defense policies, where important roles are played by the prime minister as well as by the defense, foreign, and treasury ministers and the president of the republic. Moreover, the nature of the relationships among them is poorly institutionalized and in a state of continuous flux, depending on the political resources and the personal skills of those occupying these offices. Given these weaknesses, the executive branch has not developed the instruments to systematically and independently monitor and assess public opinion.

Third, the nature of Italian foreign policymaking helps explain the public's sensitivity to international events and its impact on foreign policy. It is commonly argued that the main aim of Italian foreign policy has been to protect the traditional socioeconomic structure from domestic and international threats (Panebianco 1997). For this purpose, the Democratic-Christian Party and its allies saw the alliance with the United States (through NATO) and the economic integration in Europe as the two pillars of their security. Exploiting the "strength of the weak" (Schelling 1980), Italian governments were able to ensure Italian security at low costs both domestically and internationally. This strategy, as much a reflection of domestic cleavages (especially the presence of a strong and deeply rooted Communist Party) as of external requirements, was carried out through a clear-cut separation between two levels of foreign policy.

At the first level, foreign policy was mainly a matter of "belonging" to a bloc (also called a "choice of civilization"), and the parties exploited their bloc's success or the other bloc's threats as weapons to keep and reinforce the attachments of their constituencies. The very symbolic nature of the East-West conflict in a system of nuclear deterrence was a powerful resource for both the governing parties and the oppositions. To limit this state of affairs to the two biggest parties, the Democratic-Christians and the Communists, the former could agitate over the Soviet threat to distract public opinion while delegitimizing Communist Party attempts to affect the government. The communists, in contrast, used foreign issues as an outlet for mobilization to distract the trade unions from demanding radical social reforms in the economy and society in order to allow the party to survive in a period of deep class conflict (Pizzorno 1980).

The conflicts attracted public opinion and media interest, diverting attention from a second, more secret, level of policy: actual policymaking. At this level, decisions were made within small circles of policymakers and bureaucrats without the parties' input to avoid politicization. The fragmented nature of Italian policymaking helped Italian decisionmakers, when they had to act, to make decisions in secrecy and without interference from public opinion. In other words, the opacity of the decisionmaking process acted as a veil of ignorance in order to avoid any influence from public opinion, which was focused on symbolic party politics.

Italian foreign policy is a clear example of the rigid separation between what Lemert (1992) called the electoral and the influence network, with a definite predominance of the latter on the former.[6] There is "an almost systematic independence between the voter's choices and the opinion expressed, that is to say between behavior and attitudes" (Cartocci 1990, 148). This means that the "voting space," as defined by electoral behavior, and the "political space," as defined by the distribution of policy attitudes, do not communicate. What are the implications of this state of affairs? First, issue voting is a negligible determinant of voting vis-à-vis party identification. The common wisdom in Italy is that *voto di opinione* (opinion voting) had no role in structuring the voting intentions (Parisi and Pasquino 1977). Second, parties do not need to worry much about specific policy preferences at the mass level, provided that the electorate is ideologically mobilized and votes along party lines. This is true provided that the electoral space and the opinion space perfectly overlap. When the two do not perfectly match, problems arise. This is particularly so when a party wants to change its policy positions on crucial foreign policy issues. A good example is the enormous difficulties the Communist Party had in convincing its constituency to accept a policy change toward NATO support during the 1970s (Putnam 1977, 1978).

The Italian case, in conclusion, is one in which public opinion had an influence on policymaking mediated through parties. The very reason underlying the two-track conduct of foreign policy was to mirror the distribution of mass opinion at the parliamentary level, since the proportional representation system allowed all nuances of opinion to find their representation in parliament. This hindered the parties' ability to actually control the policymaking process. To overcome the obstacles of such a fragmented system, decisionmaking in foreign policy had to be insulated and managed by bureaucratic actors.

The survival of such a system of opinion–policy relations rested on two interconnected pillars. On the one hand, there was the continuous ability to exploit foreign policy to mobilize public opinion along party lines, an ability crucially dependent on the continuation of the Cold War cleavages. On the other hand, there was the possibility of separating the symbolic and the actual sphere of policy. This possibility rested on the hegemonic role of the Democratic-Christians in the governing coalitions. When both conditions broke down, there was a progressive politicization on the level of actual policies. This is precisely what happened in the Euromissiles affair at the end of the 1970s (Isernia 1996). The Italian decision to deploy the Euromissiles was taken by a small group of people within the government. But the decline of the East-West tension as a consequence of détente and the growing role of the left-wing parties in the government coalition made it impossible to keep the decision out of the political arena. The consequence was a highly controversial decision taken amid furious parliamentary debates and against the will of a vocal opposition widely heard by the public. The end of the Cold War is likely to result in more far-reaching consequences.

THE OPINION-POLICY CONNECTION AFTER THE COLD WAR: THE BOSNIA CASE

The events of 1989 and thereafter changed not only Italian public attitudes on some crucial security issues but the very nature of the Italian party system. The disappearance of the Democratic-Christians, the split of the Communist Party into social-democratic and communist wings, and the dramatic change of party personnel at the parliamentary level (Cotta and Verzichelli 1996) started a process of transition in Italy's political system. These changes affected the opinion-policy links in three ways.

First, there was a weakening of the parties' ability to control policies, at least at the symbolic, manifest level. The crisis of the post–World War II party system brought with it a steady decline in the ability of the parties to control their constituency through the symbolic use of foreign policy and the demarcation between symbolic and actual policy areas.

Second, the collapse of the Soviet Union gave a middle-size power like Italy more room to maneuver and resulted in a more conflict-prone environment close to the country's borders. For the first time since the end of World War II, Italy had to face a more turbulent environment without counting on U.S. support. This made it more likely that foreign policy would intrude on domestic politics.

Third, the weakening of Italian party government, together with the entrance of TV tycoon Silvio Berlusconi into politics and the progressive fluidity of the Italian electorate, changed the way politicians perceived the electorate. The manipulative use of polls by a new breed of politician like Berlusconi increased politicians' attention to public opinion. Although it is too early to tell whether Italy is moving toward an American-style political system (Barnes 1994) or toward a reaffirmation of party politics, we can predict possible changes in the public opinion–mass media–policy relationships by drawing on the Bosnia case (see also Bellucci and Isernia 1998).

In one of the few comparative public-opinion studies exploring European and American attitudes on the intervention in Bosnia, Sobel found, on the one hand, "relatively strong citizen preferences, particularly for multilateral action, with relatively weak governmental policies even about employing allied forces"; and, on the other, that this permissive public mood "contrast[ed] with the impression held by most governments and the media that the American and European publics are unwilling to interfere in the Bosnia conflict" (Sobel 1996b: 145).

The Italian case confirms both conclusions. In the Bosnia crisis there was strong and stable public support for active involvement of Italian troops yet an extreme reluctance on the part of the Italian government to consider and openly discuss such an involvement, even when requested by other countries.[7] Since the data show that

Italian public opinion was strongly in favor of Italian intervention since early 1993, why did the Italian government justify its passivity with an alleged public sentiment that was reluctant to support force and afraid of possible casualties?

As Figure 17.2 shows, support for Italian armed intervention in Bosnia crystallized early and remained high. A majority of Italians were in favor of involvement at the beginning of 1993; the only dip in support, from 69 percent to 57 percent, occurred in 1995, when the media reported critically on the UN's ability to cope with the crisis.

Even more remarkable, as shown in Figure 17.3, public support for armed intervention did not fluctuate in reaction to media attention. Using the volume of reporting on the Bosnia issue in the newspaper *Il Corriere della Sera* as a measure of media attention, Figure 17.3 shows a remarkable contrast between the stability in public support for armed intervention over the 1993–1996 period and the fluctuation in media attention.

Actual public sentiment thus stood in sharp contrast to public opinion as described by Italian Minister of Foreign Affairs Beniamino Andreatta in late 1993 and early 1994. On one occasion, when interviewed by the TV network Telepace on December 23, 1993, Andreatta justified the reluctance of Western countries to get involved in Bosnia by pointing out the public's opposition. The newspaper *La Repubblica*, in an unsigned article entitled *Ma chi vuole l'intervento?* (Who wants the

Figure 17.2   Evolution of support for Italian Armed Intervention in Bosnia

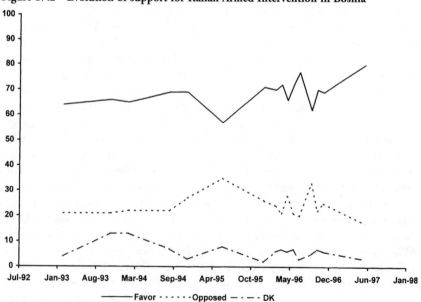

Sources: Euroflash; USIA and Archivio Disarmo-SWG Bosnia Tracking Poll

Figure 17.3   Evolution of Support for Italian Armed Intervention in Bosnia and Media Attention

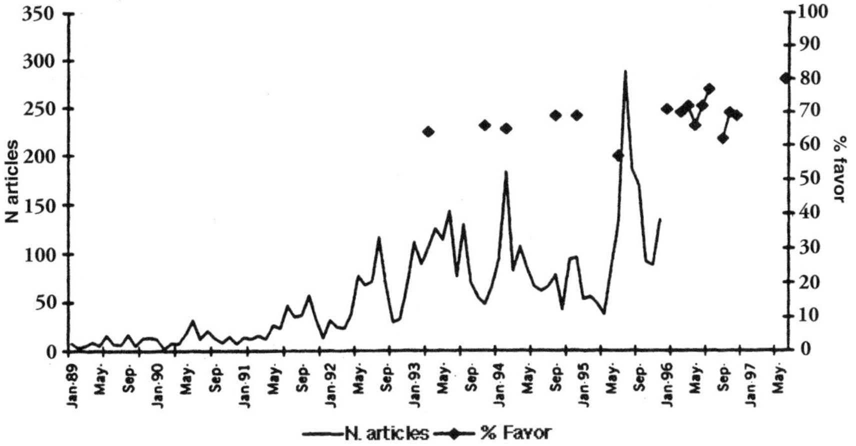

Sources: Euroflash, USIA, and Archivio Disarmo-SWG Bosnia Tracking Poll, Isernia

intervention?), quoted the foreign minister as saying that "our people do not give us—neither in the U.S. nor in Europe—a mandate to use arms to bring justice back." Furthermore, he argued that "many responsibilities for the failures of Western countries in the Balkan issue rest with public opinion."

In this interview Andreatta did not mention survey data to support his argument,[8] but *La Repubblica* backed his statements by citing a survey of eight hundred Italians. The data were said to reveal that "61 per cent of those interviewed do not want 'that in the former Yugoslavia war be added to war' and, therefore, are opposed to any kind of armed intervention" (*La Repubblica*, January 26, 1994). The newspaper did not quote either the date of the survey or the question wording. Both omissions were crucial.[9]

This case reveals interesting facts about the interactions between the media and decisionmakers and about the way decisionmakers use survey results to justify positions. As for the media, this is a typical example of misinterpreting polls. Leaving aside the lack of information about the exact question wording, sample type, confidence intervals, and so forth, it is remarkable that the journalist-editors failed to reveal information they should have known. First, the results were from a survey carried out six months earlier, on August 4, 1993, for a Catholic magazine (*Famiglia Cristiana*). Second, the question wording was biased and made no reference to Italian armed intervention.[10]

More interesting is the question of why Italy's foreign minister cited public opposition as the main obstacle to intervention in Bosnia. Was he misreading the public, manipulating public opinion, or looking at a different survey? In trying to answer this question, one must consider two things. First, the minister knew that important sectors of society and the political establishment were opposed to intervention. The Italian military as well as civilian experts on military affairs opposed intervention on the grounds of technical and political considerations. Italy was already involved in the ill-fated Somalia mission, and Bosnia was considered an even worse bet given the UN's rules of engagement. There was also opposition within the ranks of Andreatta's own party. A survey of members of the Defense and Foreign Affairs Committees in the Chamber of Deputies and the Senate, carried out in the Spring of 1995 by Paolo Bellucci (1998), shows that among the Partito Popolare Italiano members of parliament, 60 percent were opposed to an armed intervention, whereas only 40 percent of the party's constituency expressed the same preference.

Second, equally powerful were the forces in favor of intervention. To mention just the two most important ones: the Vatican and the mass media's editorial writers. The Vatican left no doubt that it considered the use of force justified for humanitarian reasons. As for the media, editorial pages were quick to denounce European passivity and demand that something had to be done right away, even though they were more reluctant to be more specific.

Ultimately, it was the difficult political position of the Italian minister of foreign affairs (and of the Italian government) that explained his misuse of public opinion. Andreatta was caught in the middle of a fight between those who were opposed to intervention and those who were demanding action. Personally probably in favor of intervention, the minister's decision to blame the public was an elegant way to cloak his personal preference and implicate others. The fact that public opinion is an elusive concept, more apt to cloak than to clarify and difficult to test, was helpful to justify the government's position in this particular case. Moreover, the lack of a genuine media interest in understanding public attitudes strengthened the policymakers' case as well.

Eventually, the media mirrored statements coming from decisionmakers, amplifying and confirming them; in so doing, they transformed a dubious political statement into reality.

CONCLUSIONS

This chapter draws four principal conclusions. First, contrary to the common view (that Italian public opinion is fickle and not really in tune with foreign policy events), the data point to an aggregate public much in line with the revisionist school. This was true at the beginning of the Cold War, as it is today. Italian public opinion shows a stability at the aggregate level similar to that found in other Western democracies; when it changes, it does so in eminently reasonable ways. This does not mean that public opinion always has a correct perception of the international system, as the trends in beliefs about the military strengths of the two superpowers showed. But this is more a reflection of the media environment and the effects of propaganda than a clear case of misperception. Yet even when the media messages were realistic and close to the events, as the Bosnia situation showed, Italian public opinion did not show any of the signs of hysteria feared by critics of the role of public opinion in policymaking.

Second, public opinion is not a negligible factor in Italian foreign policy. The problem is that we should be clear about the influence of public opinion and its role in context. Italian foreign policy during the Cold War era reflected and froze public-opinion cleavages. In order to overcome the paralyzing constraints that such cleavages imposed on decisionmakers, Italian foreign policy was characterized by a secretive, insulated decisionmaking process. Its effectiveness crucially depended on conditions that over time progressively weakened, eventually to collapse at the end of the Cold War.

Third, the end of the Cold War produced several significant changes in public opinion. To begin with, the end of the Cold War brought about the end of a domestic cold war as well. The international bones of contention—NATO and the alliance with the United States—dissolved with the collapse of the Soviet Union. Partially in response to this depolarization, the image of the armed forces in Italy became more positive, and support for a less passive foreign policy became more widespread. This twofold change removed two obstacles to a more assertive and autonomous Italian foreign policy, sharpening the contrast between the permissive mood of public opinion and the extreme reluctance of the political elite to exploit the new room for maneuvering.

Fourth, the very nature of the opinion-policy relationship changed with the end of the Cold War. During the post–World War II period, public opinion was mainly shaped by parties and was, above all, defined by parties. In such a highly pluralistic and decentralized political system, almost all nuances of opinion were represented in the Italian party system. Yet the inherently symbolic nature of Italian foreign policy during the Cold War—more a matter of "belonging" than actual policies—helped reinforce the stability of Italian public opinion. The end of the Cold War changed this frame of reference. The Italian political system is exposed to new, more direct challenges and is less able to make the different threads of opinion coexist in the parliamentary system. The growing internationalization imposes an ever bigger price on domestic institutions, making the fragmented decisionmaking system highly dysfunctional. These challenges, together with the transformation of the party system, modify the way the undifferentiated opinions of the masses interact with the decisionmakers. In this context, public opinion, as an aggregate of individual opinions measured by survey, acquires an autonomous weight as it becomes reflected in the more widespread use of survey results in political battles.

The long-term implications are difficult to assess, but they point to a growing role of an individualistic conception of public opinion in foreign policy. Eventually, mass opinion in Italy will tread into the sacred places where only fools rush in.

18

Toward a Comparative Analysis of the Public Opinion–Foreign Policy Connection

Eric Shiraev

Among the many important features of democratic policymaking is the relationship between mass public opinion and foreign policy. What we know today is that policymakers in liberal democracies are aware of public opinion in their countries, although to very different degrees. Moreover, they tend not to undertake actions at odds with an overwhelming public consensus, so that overall there is frequent and substantial correspondence between policy and public opinion (see Risse-Kappen 1991; Chapter 14 in this volume, by Shapiro and Jacobs). Nevertheless, how can one make serious assumptions about the linkages between public opinion and policy when the national cases that have been studied are so dissimilar and the research approaches so diverse? This commentary examines the empirical evidence presented in the previous four chapters and suggests some tactics to help further comparative studies of the opinion-policy connection.

There is a growing body of evidence for the existence of a complex "mediating" variable between public opinion and policymaking. Various studies show that one way or another opinion-poll results reach top decisionmakers. Public opinion itself, however, does not translate automatically into a foreign policy decision. Polling may certainly affect what issue policymakers push to the top of their political agendas, but actual policymaking is played out from a different script (Chapter 14 in this volume, by Shapiro and Jacobs; Wybrow 2000). Just because the public holds a strong and stable opinion about a foreign policy issue, this does not necessarily translate into tangible influence in the policymaking process. In other words, the influence of public opinion on policy is not direct; rather it is conditioned by a mediating "framework" of variables.

Perhaps there is little new in this suggestion. Indeed, many researchers (among them Page and Shapiro 1983; Wittkopf 1990; Bartels 1991; Hinckley 1992; Page and Shapiro 1992; Everts 1996; and Sobel 1998) have already shown that the relationship between opinion and foreign policy can be viewed as mediated by a variety of both stable and contingent conditions. Some suggest at least six mediating factors (Vengroff et al. 2000): the nature of the international problem under consideration; the nature of the proposed policy; the effectiveness of the communication between the elite groups; elites' awareness of the public opinion; the perceived level of public support for a policy; and the structure and timing of decisionmaking. Others refer to at least three factors that mediate the impact of public opinion on policy: the distribution of political preferences among the public; the structure of domestic political institutions; and the bargaining strategies of national decisionmakers at both the national and international levels (see Putnam 1988; Risse-Kappen 1991; and Bellucci and Isernia 2000). There is evidence that public opinion's influence on foreign policy can be mediated by a relatively stable system of values developed over a long period of socialization (Page and Shapiro 1994). Such mediating factors as the structure of the parliamentary system, the views of elected officials, presidential leadership, the effectiveness of elite communication, and elite perception of public opinion are also critical in our understanding opinion-policy linkages (Powlick 1991; Jentleson 1992; Graham 1986).

There are also approaches that put together both international and domestic factors in policymaking (Putnam 1988; Moravcsik 1993). Suggesting the existence of mediating factors between attitudes and policy, Philip Everts refers to a country's general "political context" (Everts 1983). Natalie La Balme (Chapter 16 in this volume), for example, examines the influence of opinion leaders and media coverage as mediating the political climate within which policies are conducted.

When asked about the role public opinion plays in their foreign policy actions, some politicians tell researchers (see La Balme, Chapter 16 in this volume) that political decisions are always made according to the will of the people, while others insist that their choices were based on elites' special expertise regarding what is best for the nation. Perhaps there is very little contradiction in these statements. As La Balme further indicates, the opinion-policy nexus is interactive and reciprocal rather than unidirectional. That is, when expressed opinion precedes policy outputs, then it is said that opinion leads policymakers. If opinion and policy initially diverge, then it is argued that policymakers lead opinion (Yeric and Todd 1996, 163–165).

Various studies show that the nature of the impact of public opinion on policy can be seen as context-dependent (Risse-Kappen 1991). As a step toward further understanding the mediating variables between policy and public opinion usually identified through polling, it is useful to introduce the phrase "policy climate"—a prevailing sentiment among policymakers and other individuals capable of influencing the direction of foreign policy through their roles as security and defense executives, analysts, problem definers, gatekeepers, watchdogs, and experts and commentators (Page and Shapiro 1988, 243; see also Clinton 1975). These political elites constitute the concerned minority, or citizens (Almond and Verba 1963). In parliamentary and public debates, and through statements, televised interviews, printed publications, and other channels, they voice various opinions about international and policy-related events. In short, the policy climate consists of various beliefs about what the country and the government should or should not do on the international level, in the case of international conflict in particular. The media in these circumstances become not only a conductor but also a source of foreign policy attitudes. The policy climate can be salient and nonsalient; it can be assertive or nonassertive; it can become, at times, more susceptible to the influence of the general public and less susceptible when the public cares little about foreign policy. Each country's policy climate at different times can have a different influence on policymaking.

Suppose that the policy climate is empirically measurable. What conclusions can one draw from the chapters in Part 3? To answer this question, let us introduce a frame of reference from which a comparative analysis of opinion-policy linkages can be conducted. The source of each country's particular policy climate is a set of political, ideological, and situational variables. These diverse variables can be examined in terms of several dimensions, or axes (see below). Each axis refers to a different domain of information that may guide the analysis of opinion-policy linkages. The use of this approach can help facilitate a more comprehensive evaluation from a comparative perspective and direct attention to conditions that may be overlooked in a single national case study. This approach will serve well if all the variables are homogeneous; there are clear boundaries among the axes, and the axes are mutually exclusive.

How do these dimensions of the opinion-policy linkage play out in the preceding chapters?

Axis 1

The role that public opinion plays in shaping any country's foreign policy is indispensably related to the political system of that country (Cohen 1977–1978, 196). On this level, we assess how the country's existing political democratic institutions mediate the connection between public opinion and foreign policy. Some political systems—which includes a wide set of actors, like parties, bureaucracies, and pressure groups—may or may not provide for the transmission of opinions into the policy process, so public opinion may or may not act as a catalyst to foreign policy operations. Different governments can have dissimilar traditions of soliciting and considering public opinion in foreign policymaking. For example, compare what Shapiro and Jacobs call the "institutionalization" of polling in the United States with what has occurred in other governments. A comparison of the U.S. system to some democratic transitional systems, for instance, may show how different governmental approaches to polling can be.

Obviously, simply through procedural democracy voters can exert some minimal control over policy through reward and punishment in regularly held elections. However, different types of democracy create different frameworks of relationships between branches of government. For instance, public opinion should influence policy more directly in two-party parliamentary settings than in coalition-based multiparty assemblages. Stronger parties should be stronger conductors of public opinion than weaker ones (Bellucci and Isernia 2000). Also, national systems with consolidated and established channels of communications—involving parties, interest groups, bureaucracies, and the media—will provide better conditions for the expression of public opinion than will systems with fragmented communications.

In the United States, any study of the links between opinion and policy has to take into consideration the presidential political system, with its relatively weak parties and party factions in Congress. In contrast, the role of these actors is much wider in the European context. In parliamentary and presidential systems, where executive power is based on the strength of the parliamentary majority, foreign policy is often influenced and directed by internal political considerations. Typically, the head of the government tries to avoid taking certain policy steps that could undermine the ruling parliamentary majority. In the French system, for instance, a president who lacks a parliamentary majority is forced to appoint a prime minister from an opposing party and then try to find a formula to work together, leading to relative responsiveness to the views of the prime minister and foreign minister. In the Italian political system, the channels of communication between the top foreign policy executives and society are shaped mainly by political parties and the mass media (themselves controlled by political powers).

Thus, foreign policy is perceived as coming from an executive office. In presidential democracies, the highest foreign policy executives appear to be more independent in their activities than are their counterparts in parliamentary systems. It is, therefore, striking when Shapiro and Jacobs suggest that some American presidents have been more susceptive to public opinion at certain times, while at other times they prefer to lead public opinion. One question is whether this behavior is primarily a characteristic of the individual in the Oval Office—personal traits and leadership style—and less that of the institution of the American Presidency. Nevertheless, one should acknowledge that the formal roles inherited by the chief government executives vary from country to country. In the Netherlands, important foreign policy decisions will not be taken by the minister of foreign affairs but by the cabinet as a whole, especially given the fact that the Netherlands is always ruled by often shaky coalitions of two or more political parties. In Great Britain, even when the prime minister enjoys the support of his or her party in parliament, the foreign policy arena will display a historic competition—not unique to Britain—among the Foreign Office, the Joint Intelligence Committee, and the foreign policy advisers to the prime minister. Russian presidents will perhaps preserve a traditional view that any compromises with the opposition or changes in policy under the pressure of public opinion are considered signs of presidential weakness. Further comparative research is needed to clarify certain aspects of how the executive branches function. Are French presidents, for example, more dependent on the nation's intellectuals and other opinion leaders than are American presidents?

Axis 2

At this level, specific political interests mediate the influence of public opinion on foreign policy under definable circumstances. Here, analysts should make direct references to internal political considerations that affect the influence of public opinion, namely, the specific role of parties and interest groups in shaping and mediating specific linkages between mass opinion and foreign policy. On the one hand, foreign policy issues, especially mistakes in foreign policy—picked up by the media and increasingly salient to the public and finally mentioned in opinion polls—are used by the opposition to criticize and denounce the government officials in charge. On the other hand, the government can use specific foreign policy–related issues and potentially successful actions to strengthen its political standing and future electoral prospects.

Certainly, both national and local elections provide some mechanism for determining the ways foreign policy executives pay attention to or manipulate public opinion (see Chapter 14). Perhaps policymakers in democracies are likely to wage wars in which the risks are small and their domestic images weak (Everts 1996). Politicians face severe problems, however, either when success is elusive or when the trade-off between costs (especially in terms of human lives) and interests is seen as unfavorable. If such a mistake is made, it may cost the decisionmaker politically.

The desire to be elected creates pressing incentives for politicians to respond to majority public opinion in order to avoid falling too far out of line with it. Moreover, in the United States and other democracies, foreign policy actions can be linked to other political battles. Parliamentary approval of particular government policies may hinge on yielding to the opposition in some other policy areas. In the case of European unification, a "premature politicization" (see Sinnott, Chapter 15 in this volume) of attitudes toward the issue was perhaps a result of the actions of different national interest groups pursuing distinct political goals. Moreover, European governments could have interpreted public support or opposition to unification in terms of electoral considerations—a kind of motivation that may be hidden from the observer.

It is also important, then, to determine how important a particular election campaign appears to be for the average voter. For example, European parliamentary elections in 1994 had little impact on public opinion about European integration because of the elections' relative insignificance for many European voters. For the same reason, despite the fact that the Bosnia conflict became an issue during the European parliamentary elections, the relative insignificance of the elections could have allowed the French president not to take into account public opinion about the need for military intervention in Bosnia.

Policymakers may try to anticipate public reaction. Expectations of a positive public reaction contribute to a permissive policy climate, whereas anticipation of criticism contributes to a nonpermissive climate. Political opponents would not challenge foreign policy decisions if public support for such actions was overwhelming. In contrast, opposition would be more likely to occur if the public reaction was negative or anticipated to be negative. For example, the actions of the French president to exclude any participation of new draftees in the Gulf War combat operations were designed to appease domestic public opinion. The same considerations perhaps dissuaded the Bill Clinton administration from making any definite commitment to the use of ground troops in Kosovo in the Spring of 1999. Continual references to nationalistic attitudes were made by Russian officials in their rhetoric about NATO expansion and the war in the former Yugoslavia (Shiraev 1999). Avoiding public disapproval was one of the main reasons for France's entry into the military operations in Somalia in 1992 (La Balme, Chapter 16).

Axis 3

From this perspective, the researcher considers the role of values, ideological and religious commitments, and attitudes and ideas shared by and communicated among citizens. For example, humanitarian values shared by opinion leaders and the public may crucially determine public opinion about foreign policy: the Bosnia, Iraq, and Kosovo crises of the 1990s show some evidence for this. Public support for the use of the military in civil and peacekeeping missions has been high among Italians in the 1990s, perhaps because of the idealism inherent in Catholic or socialist ideology (Isernia, Chapter 17).

To take a different example, a person considered a war criminal in American eyes may be perceived by others as a legitimate representative of a struggling people. There might be entire historical periods in which a particular public attitude dominates public opinion on foreign policy. For instance, the public in the United States has oriented toward an activist foreign policy since World War II (Shapiro and Jacobs, Chapter 14). The Vietnam War split American public opinion between isolationism and interventionism (Hinckley 1992). In Russia, the 1999 war in Kosovo put an end to the public's isolationist tendencies of the early and mid-1990s. Some researchers refer to a "culture of opinion"—a set of values shared by a majority of the population—that suggests that rich nations have a moral responsibility to assist suffering people and helpless victims (La Balme, Chapter 16; Isernia, Chapter 17; Vengroff et al. 2000). Others describe a culture of democratic representation in which a popular consensus about national sovereignty and identity influences specific attitudes toward European integration (Sinnott, Chapter 15).

Axis 4

From this point of view, one should pay attention to various contextual and situational factors that determine the quality of information that the public receives (Shapiro and Jacobs, Chapter 14). A special consideration is salience of a particular foreign policy issue and how well the issue is articulated by the government officials or opposition. Framing, priming, and agenda-setting, and the presence or absence of specific media effects, that is, particular media coverage that evokes particular reactions in the public, are also of interest (La Balme, Chapter 16).

For example, the passage of the Single European Act and the activism of the Delors Commission in support of European integration had a promotional effect on public opinion in Europe. Yet the growing intrusiveness of the Single Market program could have produced a decline in support for integration (Sinnott, Chapter 15).

Here, one should not overlook a variety of situational factors that can affect both elite and public perceptions of the linkages between opinion and policy. Among these factors one can examine particular media effects (rally 'round the flag, free-rider, body-bag, innocent-victim, and some others). The massacre at the Sarajevo market during the Bosnia war in 1994 and its extensive coverage by the media may be a good example of how quickly a consensus between governments and the public can be reached about the necessity for action.

Any opinion-policy analysis should also take into consideration the level of consensus or disagreement among the elites, including the media, regarding particular foreign policy issues. Coverage of foreign policy in the media, as Shapiro and Jacobs suggest (see Chapter 14), is crucial for a specific policy climate formation and achievement of a relative agreement between the public and government officials. For example, when the public was asked from the beginning, in the case of European integration, to express opinions about something with which it had no practical experience, government officials could easily infer that they should be responsive to this type of weak public attitude (Sinnott, Chapter 15).

As Sinnott also implies, the wording of the survey questions about European integration, as well as their attachment to a particular policy arena, can influence polling outcomes and the way surveys are interpreted. A fine example is the fact that in 1993 only 19 percent of Europeans could have been called enthusiastic and well-informed supporters of the European Union, even though a less thorough analysis of the poll would have yielded a support base of 44 percent (Sinnott, Chapter 15).

The examination of the opinion-policy nexus should consider the level of unity or disagreement among elites—including the media—regarding particular foreign policy issues. The Italian government was, for instance, divided at a crucial stage of the war in Bosnia: the minister of foreign affairs was in favor of military intervention while the minister of defense was opposed (Isernia, Chapter 17).

Finally, the personal commitment of a leader to a particular decision may also occur. La Balme (Chapter 16) shows how Mitterrand's personal opposition to war made him argue against military involvement in the Balkans and how the U.S. commitment to Operation Restore Hope in Somalia affected his decision to make a commitment in that region. La Balme also demonstrates the importance of a consensus among the governing elites. If the consensus is predetermined by a political alliance among officials, then the policy climate will be strong and relatively stable. In contrast, if government officials are bound by weak party coalitions in the parliament (as in Italy, Israel, Russia, and Germany), then the policy climate will be unstable and malleable.

CONCLUSION

Within this multiaxial approach to the study of the linkages between opinion and policy, we can offer critical assessments and suggestions about future trends in foreign policymaking. As Shapiro and Jacobs argue, the end of the Cold War has decreased public visibility of foreign policy because of the disappearance of the Soviet threat. The ambiguity created by the end of strategic bipolarity has made foreign affairs difficult to interpret and to bring to the public attention, with the exception of a few high-profile cases; the public hence becomes a less visible actor in policymaking. It is important to note that with the disappearance of the Cold War schema in international relations, both policymakers and the media have to frame international news events in new ways. In the absence of a clear ideological consensus about who or what the enemy really is, the public may pay attention to those individuals who can define and explain new international threats to the national interest. Often motivated by political interests and electoral concerns, public officials can exert considerable influence in framing the foreign policy agenda, as they face a public that is more detached from foreign policy issues and has less information and fewer attitudinal predispositions than in the 1980s. Formulating their opinion about foreign policy, members of the public may be more dependent than ever on the outcomes of elite struggles over ideas than on their own stable ideological commitments.

Alternatively, we might argue that the events in Kosovo in 1999 challenged the view that foreign policy would be of relatively little visibility and concern to the American public. Since the Gulf War, no single foreign policy issue has occupied as much time and space in the leading American news media as the war in the former Yugoslavia. NATO's military campaign against Serbia in 1999 both provoked an avalanche of anti-American rhetoric in some world capitals and caused a crisis in U.S.-Russian and U.S.-Chinese relations. A new Cold War era was proclaimed by even moderate Russian officials, and the old ideological clichés were revived (Axis 3) and sold to the Russian public, urging global resistance to American imperialism and expansionism. The paradox is that the old, hostile Cold War perceptions and anti-Western sentiments—often attributed to the influence of a totalitarian state—are being voiced in democratizing countries, where they can be freely expressed in elections and opinion polls and interpreted by local officials as the popular will.

Notes

CHAPTER 1

1. This incident is examined in David Ronfeldt, "Netwar Across the Spectrum of Conflict: An Introductory Comment," *Studies in Conflict and Terrorism* 22 (1999):189–192.

2. Cohen made his suggestion in his provocative essay "A View from the Academy," in *Taken by Storm: The Media, Public Opinion, and U.S. Foreign Policy in the Gulf War,* ed. W. Lance Bennett and David L. Paletz (Chicago: University of Chicago Press, 1994).

CHAPTER 2

1. Assessing the impact of the Cold War's end does not imply that the United States experienced forty-five years of uninterrupted harmony and unity between or among elites, the media, and the public. How best to contain the Soviet Union, whether and how to fight in Korea and Vietnam, what to do about the Middle East—these and many other policy choices provoked disputes. However, with few exceptions, the basic problem definitions were not matters of conflict in mainstream discourse but containing an expansionist Soviet Union and preventing nuclear war. Disagreements centered on solutions and tactics. Since the Cold War, even the problems—perhaps especially the problems—have been matters of heated controversy.

2. Despite significant changes in the media infrastructure during the 1990s, the media of greatest relevance to foreign policy are hypothesized to continue to be the ABC, CBS, and NBC evening-news and Sunday-morning shows as well as *Time, Newsweek, New York Times, Washington Post, Wall Street Journal,* and the Associated Press. The notion that the Cable News Network has a major independent impact—the "CNN effect"—has been undermined by research (Livingston 1997).

3. Just before this chapter went to press, a book assessing similar issues was published (Mermin 1999); its findings could not be incorporated into this chapter.

4. Talbott 1984 and other sources.

5. Aggregating even well-reasoned and priority-ordered mass preferences in some sensible way presents great difficulties. In Riker's (1986) words: "The popular will is defined only as long as the issue dimensions are restricted. Once issue dimensions multiply, the popular will is irresolute. Slight changes in dimensions induce disequilibrium." In other words, typical

invocations of "public opinion" ignore trade-offs. For an influential scholarly solution to such problems, see Page and Shapiro (1992). As the text suggests, it is unfortunately impossible for most journalistic outlets, concerned as they are with the latest controversies and poll results, to apply that solution to improving their coverage of public opinion.

6. The power of visuals is suggested in works by Doris Graber (1990), Brosius (1993), and others, but this remains one of the political communication phenomena most in need of thorough investigation.

7. The Haiti experience could have also betokened a misfiring of democracy. Were it not for President Clinton's decision against perceived public opinion to intervene, an apparent humanitarian success might have not been achieved.

CHAPTER 3

1. Hedley Bull, *The Anarchical Society* (London: Macmillan, 1977).

2. Robert O. Keohane and Joseph S. Nye, *Power and Interdependence: World Politics in Transition* (Boston: Little, Brown, 1977).

3. James N. Rosenau, *Turbulence in World Politics* (Princeton: Princeton University Press, 1990).

4. Robert Falk, *On Humane Governance* (Cambridge: Polity, 1995).

5. Martin Shaw, *Global Society and International Relations* (Cambridge: Polity, 1994).

6. Noam Chomsky and Edward S. Herman, *Manufacturing Consent: The Political Economy of the Mass Media* (New York: Pantheon, 1988).

7. David Mekelberg (unpublished doctoral research, University of Sussex, 1998).

8. Michael Mann, *The Sources of Social Power, Vol. 2* (Cambridge: Cambridge University Press, 1993), p. 76.

9. Anthony Giddens, *The Nation-State and Violence* (Cambridge: Polity, 1985).

10. Justin Rosenberg, "A Non-Realist Theory of Sovereignty?" In Anthony Giddens' *The Nation-State and Violence* (Berkeley: University of California Press, 1987)

11. John B. Thompson, *The Media and Modernity: A Social Theory of the Media* (Cambridge: Polity, 1995), pp. 125–126.

12. Philip M. Taylor, *Global Communications, International Affairs, and the Media since 1945* (London: Routledge, 1997).

13. Martin Shaw, *Civil Society and Media in Global Crises* (London: Cassell, 1996).

14. Martin Shaw, "The State of Globalization," *Review of International Political Economy* 4(3) (1997):497–513.

15. Mary Kaldor, *New and Old Wars: Organized Warfare in the Global Era* (Cambridge: Polity, 1999).

16. Shaw, *Civil Society and Media.*

17. Jean Beaudrillard, "La guerre de Golfe na pas eu lieu," *Libération*, March 29, 1991.

18. Philip M. Taylor, *War and the Media* (Manchester, U.K.: Manchester University Press, 1992).

19. Nik Gowing, *Real-Time Television Coverage of Armed Conflicts and Diplomatic Crises: Does it Pressure or Distort Foreign Policy Decisions?* (Harvard: Shorenstein Center, 1994).

20. Piers Robinson (University of Bristol), paper given at the British International Studies Association, 1998.

21. James N. Rosenau, *Along the Domestic-Foreign Frontier* (Cambridge: Cambridge University Press, 1997).

22. For details see Shaw, *Civil Society and Media*, pp. 79–96.

CHAPTER 4

1. According to Iyengar, "The episodic news frame takes the form of a case study or event-oriented report and depicts public issues in form of concrete instances (for example, the plight of a homeless person or a teenage drug user, the bombing of an airliner, or an attempted murder). The thematic frame, by contrast, places public issues in some more general or abstract context and takes the form of a 'take-out,' or 'backgrounder,' report directed at general outcomes and conditions" (Iyengar 1991, 14). Iyengar's research demonstrates that the episodic frame dominates television news.

2. According to *Washington Post* veteran reporter Walter Pincus, the contemporary news media, including the TV networks, no longer follow the leads of the *New York Times* and the *Washington Post* as they did in the past. Rather, even the most prestigious print-media organizations, such as the *Washington Post*, constantly monitor and are guided by CNN newscasts. Pincus spoke about this reversal in media leadership during a symposium on international terrorism at Lewis and Clark College, Portland, Oregon, in February 1998.

3. We retrieved relevant articles that appeared in the *New York Times* and the *Wall Street Journal* from the LEXIS/NEXIS database, and summaries of the pertinent television programs from the Vanderbilt Television Archive's Abstracts of daily newscasts now available online at http://tvnews.vanderbilt.edu/. The articles on global warming that appeared in the German newspapers were drawn from the archives available on the three news organizations' websites: http://www.welt.de; http://www.handelsblatt.de; and http://www.archiv.berliner-morgenpost.de. Because there is no German equivalent to the Vanderbilt television abstracts, our study does not include an analysis of German television newscasts.

4. The *New York Times* published sixty-five articles during the six months we examined, the *Wall Street Journal* twenty-three, *Die Welt* twenty-six, *Handelsblatt* fourteen, and the *Berliner Morgenpost* fifteen. But the difference between the American and the German press was more pronounced with respect to the length of news stories than the number of articles, in that U.S. newspapers published far more comprehensive and longer pieces. The *New York Times* in particular ran an impressive number of informative articles on global warming from the perspectives of scientists and countries and regions all over the world.

5. Included in these numbers are only sources and actors outside the media. We excluded media-based sources responsible for journalistic descriptions, background information, explanations, and so on that made up the bulk of the global-warming coverage in both the American and the German media.

CHAPTER 5

An earlier version of this paper appeared in *Political Communication* in 1995. The paper grew out of an undergraduate seminar in communication at UCLA and was written while the senior author was a fellow at the Center for Advanced Study in the Behavioral Sciences at Stanford. We also thank Larry Bartels for comments on an earlier draft.

1. The list can be found at Zaller's UCLA website, located at www.sscnet.ucla.edu/polisci/faculty/zaller/.

2. This decision was made without examining media coverage of the terrorist acts.

3. From prior experience, the senior author felt that he could "train" coders to produce significantly higher levels of agreement. Such training, however, often consists of giving coders clear rules for handling certain kinds of inherently ambiguous data. In applying these rules rigidly, coders can boost intercoder reliability without necessarily doing a better job of capturing the actual content; in this way, rigid use of rules can create high reliability at the expense of the actual validity of ratings. For example, the problem alluded to in note 4 below could probably have been avoided through more extensive coder training.

4. The ratings of Coder #1 correlated with those of Coders #2 and #3 at the level of .73 and .75. The ratings of Coders #2 and #3 correlated at the level of .77.

5. The means of the individual coders were .59, .57, and .62; the SDs were .15, .24, and .29. The low SD for Coder #1 reflects his reluctance to assign nonneutral codes in the absence of a strong slant; despite this threshold difference, Coder #1's relative ranking of crises correlated well with rankings of the other coders.

6. The data in this and other tables, along with the SPSS code necessary to reproduce them, are available in a folder called "government's little helper" at Zaller's UCLA website, www.sscnet.ucla.edu/polisci/faculty/zaller/.

7. In designing this study, we considered collecting media data just before and after measurement of congressional opinion so as to establish causal precedence. This, however, did not prove feasible. In some cases, events moved so quickly—as in the start of the Korean War—that it was impossible to measure media content before Congress had reacted. In other cases, the pattern of media and congressional opinion had been stable for so long before we made our measurements—as in, for example, the fall of Saigon in 1974—that it made no sense to pretend that one had actually preceded the other by a significant amount of time. Hence, we abandoned this approach.

8. Although President Reagan withdrew the Marines from Lebanon shortly after their barracks were bombed, his initial response was hawkish.

9. If, incidentally, the media scores of Coders #2 and #3 are combined, congressional and presidential opinion have significant effects (b's of .18 and .14; t-ratios of 1.89 and 1.83, respectively). Coder #1 is the graduate student without coding experience; Coder #3 is an undergraduate (Mark Hunt) who has worked with Zaller on other projects. It is interesting that intercoder reliability statistics, as reported in note 5, contain no hint that findings would differ so strongly by coder.

10. The coefficient for the effect of congressional opinion is .30; given that $.30 \times (1.00 - .16) = .25$, we expect media hawkishness to be .25 units lower. Since the SD of media hawkishness is .21, this amounts to 1.2 SDs.

11. The calculation is $(-.17 - .16 + .03 - (+.07))/.21$, which equals -1.76 SDs.

12. The comparable slope for Coder #3 in the original thirty-five cases was .73.

13. The comparable p-value in the original thirty-five cases was only .30.

14. This is the p-value for equality of variance across the two types of cases, according to Levene's test for equality of variance.

15. This empirical finding can and should be checked in a larger sample of congressional opinion.

16. Technically, our calculation of the association between congressional and media opin-

ion in Figure 5.1 is based on unstandardized coefficients, which are unaffected by the variance of the variables involved.

17. The score was .28 on the measure of media hawkishness. The next lowest score in the 1990s was .43, which was for the start of the Gulf War, over which Congress was divided.

18. *Time*, December 14, 1992, p. 28.

19. *Newsweek*, December 28, 1998, p. 48.

20. *Newsweek*, February 19, 1994, p. 41.

21. Stanley Karnow, *Vietnam: A History* (New York: Penguin, 1997), pp. 386–387.

22. David Halberstam, *The Powers That Be* (New York: Dell, 1979), pp. 619–620.

23. Cited in Bernard Cohen, *The Press and Foreign Policy* (Princeton: Princeton University Press, 1963), p. 85.

CHAPTER 7

1. It may be argued that on balance these changes did not really represent a meaningful trend toward disengagement. However, within the foreign policy discourse, as reflected in the interviews of the policy practitioners discussed herein, it was widely interpreted this way by those who supported the trend as well as those who bewailed it.

2. Powlick's 1995 work, based on his interviews with U.S. State Department and NSC officials, also found news media and elected representatives to be the primary sources of the policymakers' information on public opinion.

CHAPTER 8

For assistance on this chapter, I would like to thank Michael Bocian, Julie Cho, Andrea Cimenti, Joseph Coffey, Cara Jones, Keith Kravitsky, Donald Ferree, Ole Holsti, Larry Hugick, Mary McIntosh, Jerry Mechling, Meinhardt Moschner, Brigitte Nacos, Eric Paras, Rob Persons, Judith Rowe, Ennio Salamon, Robert Shapiro, Eric Shiraev, Richard Ullman, and Robert Wybrow.

1. The U.S. polls were representative national samples of about 1,000 respondents. The European polls commissioned by the European Community (EC) or the United States Information Agency (USIA) were representative samples of about 900–1,000 (see Standard Eurobarometer Technical Specifications, A3 and ORM, 12/17/93, appendix B). The Eurobarometer data were supplied by the Central Archives for Empirical and Social Research at the University of Cologne. The USIA data were taken from Opinion Research Memoranda (ORM) and tables. Most of the U.S. polls used here were found or checked by the Public Opinion Location Library (POLL) of the Roper Center for Public Opinion Research at the University of Connecticut. Tables 8.1, 8.7, and 8.8 question wordings appear at the end of this chapter. Because Tables 8.2–8.6 include items with different related wordings, topics appear in titles and headings, but not the individual question wordings. Those wordings may be checked through the POLL system at the Roper Center or in Sobel (1998).

2. Percentages connected by a short dash (e.g., 31–48 percent) show the percentage, respectively, that approved and disapproved. In this example, 31 percent approved and 48 percent disapproved. Percentages connected by the word "to" and preceded by a range of date

(e.g., 4–7/95, 36 to 40 percent) indicate, for example, several polls during April through July 1995 found from 36 percent to 40 percent in support.

3. Partly because the introductions to the questions provide significant background and the respondents tended toward those with more education, and the results were unweighted, the earlier Program in International Policy Attitudes (PIPA) polls (1993, 1994) typically found higher support for U.S. intervention than did other surveys (see Steven Kull and Clay Ramsay, "US Public Attitudes on US Involvement in Bosnia," Program on International Policy Attitudes, University of Maryland, May 4, 1994). Some of the PIPA questions that distinguish intensity of support also skewed to the more aggressive options. Because most polls besides PIPA and the *Los Angeles Times* did not ask how strongly attitudes are held, it was hard to gauge intensity of opinion; consistently higher overall proportions suggested greater intensity. See also the March 1993 surveys conducted by Market Strategies and Greenberg Research, headed by the president's pollster (Americans Talk Issues, *Global Uncertainties*, #21, Washington, D.C.: ATI Foundation, 1993), for information likely to have reached the White House: e.g., two-thirds preference for the United States and UN to "use military intervention and overwhelming force to defeat the primary aggressors" (3/23/93: 66 percent).

4. The media consistently underreported evidence of U.S. public support for intervention in Bosnia. For instance, in February 1994 ABC's *Nightline* showed a graphic of 18 percent support for U.S. air strikes, without revealing that 57 percent approved of strikes with allies (see ABC 2/7/94). Though a June 4, 1995, *Newsweek* press release noted "a surprisingly large reservoir of public support for U.S. ground troops to aid United Nations forces in Bosnia," the related *Newsweek* article (June 12, 1995, p. 20), located adjacent to a table showing from 61 percent to 78 percent approval for U.S. assistance to UN forces, said that "Bosnia is an unpopular cause; in the latest *Newsweek* Poll, 55 percent of Americans surveyed said Bosnia was not their problem." A *Washington Post National Weekly* column reported a "big [downward] change" in support for U.S. military action from late April but had not reported the April support when it occurred (Morin 1995). Perhaps the assumption that there is no support for U.S. troop involvement or the mistaking of partisan leaders' reaction against deploying U.S. troops for more generally supportive public attitudes drove out the search for an accurate presentation of all the evidence. See also Sobel 1995, 1998; Morin 1998.

5. Early 1993 data cover western Germany alone; later data include the entire country.

6. In late 1994, when Serbs set up antiaircraft artillery around Bihac, the majority of the German public (54 percent), perhaps from historical memory of the German army in Yugoslavia during World War II and general anti-interventionist attitudes, opposed sending Tornado aircraft with the capacity to evade Serbian defenses (*Die Woche*, #50, December 9, 1994). At the same time, 75 percent of Germans thought the international community should not remove their troops (*Stern*, #50, December 8, 1994). By January 1995, a majority (56 percent) supported using the Tornados to protect aid shipments to Bosnia. Between January and June 1995, support for UN "reinforce[ment] of military intervention" grew from 47 percent to 51 percent, but it dropped to 43 percent in July. However, support for employing German soldiers rose from 39 percent to 51 percent between January and July (Politbarometer 1/95, 6/95, 7/95). By October, 55 percent felt German participation in NATO military action was "right" (Politbarometer 9/95).

7. In late July 1995, two-thirds of the British public (65 percent) was dissatisfied with the British government's handling of the Bosnian situation, while a majority (52 percent) supported upgrading the involvement of British troops in Bosnia from peacekeeping to direct participation (MORI 7/21/95).

8. See Risse-Kappen (1991) on the role of domestic structures and coalition-building in the relationship between public opinion and foreign policy, especially in Europe. See also Sobel 1998 and Shiraev and Sobel (forthcoming).

CHAPTER 9

We thank Ole R. Holsti, James N. Rosenau, Andrew Kohut, the Pew Research Center for the Press and the People, and the Inter-University Consortium for Political and Social Research for making available the public opinion data used in this chapter. We also thank Barry Burden and Ole R. Holsti for their helpful comments on an earlier version of the chapter.

1. Four years later, in his report on the seventh of the quadrennial Chicago Council surveys, Rielly (1999, 4) used the term "guarded engagement" to describe "American public and leadership opinion on foreign policy . . . by a largely satisfied superpower."

2. As noted earlier, survey data from 1994 show that the majority of the American people preferred that the United States play an "active role" in world affairs. The 1998 Chicago Council surveys reinforce that viewpoint, showing that 61 percent of respondents supported active global involvement. Furthermore, surveys conducted throughout the 1990s by Ronald H. Hinckley, president of Research/Strategy/Management, Inc., reveal an ebb and flow in Americans' preferences for unilateral versus multilateral responses to global issues, but the portion of isolationists never exceeds 30 percent, which is roughly comparable to the proportion of isolationists in the Chicago Council surveys.

3. The 1998 Chicago Council surveys reveal that the gap between leaders' preferences and those of the general public remain very wide. For example, across a range of twenty questions dealing with domestic concerns, international involvement and vital interests, and economic relations with other countries, the average gap between the preferences of leaders and the general public was a yawning 32 percent. Summarizing these and other data, Rielly (1999, 39) concludes that "the public much more than leaders perceives threats and emphasizes goals related to the domestic impacts of international affairs. . . . Gaps concerning self-interest in foreign policy have appeared in previous surveys but are especially large and prevalent in the middle and late 1990s." Unfortunately, the 1999 Chicago Council surveys were not available at the time the analyses reported in this chapter were completed and thus could not be included.

4. In a broad critique of the Clinton administration's foreign policy performance, Michael Mandelbaum (1996, 26) concluded that "without an overarching principle to guide the nation's foreign relations . . . the promotion of domestic interests is the default strategy of American foreign policy."

5. Some analysts have found it useful to distinguish between "environmental" and "contextual" variables. For our purposes, we treat them interchangeably. See Huckfeldt and Sprague (1995, 9–10).

6. The crimes are murder, manslaughter, forcible rape, robbery, aggravated assault, burglary, larceny-theft, and motor vehicle theft.

7. Although we would prefer to use crime data located more nearly to the communities in which respondents live, Allen and Steffensmeier (1989) show that state-level crime data can be useful.

8. As Holsti and Rosenau (1999b, 36) explain, "Seven questions . . . represent various

dimensions of an MI orientation toward world affairs, including an emphasis on a conflictual world; the expansionist policies of adversaries that constitute a major threat to the United States; the necessity of being prepared to use force, including the CIA, to cope with the threats; the dangerous consequences, as postulated by the 'domino theory,' of failing to meet international challenges; and a zero-sum view of international relations. The seven items on the CI scale emphasize international cooperation and institutions; 'North-South' issues, including global hunger and the standard of living in less developed nations; arms control; foreign aid; and the role of the United Nations."

9. Since 1986, Ronald Hinckley has asked two questions in national surveys that can also be interpreted in the CI/MI framework (see Hinckley 1992). Recent responses indicate that, compared with mid-decade, by the end of the 1990s the American people have moved toward a more internationalist posture, but the movement is away from cooperative internationalism toward militant internationalism.

10. See Wittkopf and McCormick (1998) for an examination of the impact on congressional foreign policy voting of partisanship, ideology, and the interaction of the end of the Cold War and changes in control of the presidency and Congress in the context of other foreign and domestic variables.

11. In terms of the fourfold typology of foreign policy beliefs noted earlier, these results suggest that women are more likely than men to be internationalists, while the latter are more likely to embrace either accommodationist or hard-line foreign policy beliefs.

12. Because the FPLP leader surveys are samples from a population with unknown characteristics, we are cautious in saying that differences in results between 1992 and 1996 reflect changes in the salience opinion leaders attach to their domestic environments. We are particularly sensitive to the impact of California and Washington, D.C., on our empirical results. We should note, however, that differences in the number of respondents from these areas between 1992 and 1996 do not seem to be particularly skewed in one direction or another. In 1992, 7.5 percent of the survey respondents came from California; in 1996, 7.4 percent came from there. In 1992, 3.2 percent came from Maryland, compared with 4 percent in 1996. In 1992, 9.6 percent came from Virginia, compared with 10.1 percent in 1996. The only change that may have some importance is the drop in Washington, D.C., respondents, from 13.2 percent in 1992 to 7.6 percent in 1996. The number of respondents is 2,230 in 1992 and 2,043 in 1996.

13. This may reflect a "California effect," as Asians comprise 15.2 percent of the state's population. Washington, D.C., and New York City follow, with 5.1 and 4.6 percent, respectively.

14. Roughly two-thirds responded affirmative to the question, which is well within the historical range of responses to the half-century-old question. Although the question poses a dichotomy, for which logistic regression is the appropriate analytical technique, we use OLS to make the interpretation of the results in Table 9.4 comparable to those for the CI and MI variables. We note, however, that the substantive interpretation of the results does not change even if logistical regression is used. The same is true for the two other single-item internationalism variables in Table 9.4.

15. The CI and MI scales for the mass sample are not built from single items, as in the FPLP surveys, but through a two-step process in which individual items and scales built from string items are then grouped together using principal components factor analysis. The factor scores are the measures of CI and MI. For details, see Wittkopf (1990).

16. The goal questions in the 1994 Chicago Council surveys are used to create the CI and MI scales. Thus, there is some overlap between our dependent and independent variables. However, empirical testing demonstrates that inclusion/exclusion of any single item in the scale does not affect the scale scores materially.

17. In their 1992 survey, Holsti and Rosenau asked opinion leaders if economic competition from Japan and Europe constituted a threat "to American national security in the remaining years of this century." Fourteen percent responded "extremely serious," another 31 percent "very serious." In 1996, the question was split, with one on Europe and a second on Japan. The response categories also changed, to "very serious" (4 percent yes for Europe, 7 percent yes for Japan) and "moderately serious" (20 percent for Europe, 30 percent for Japan). Due to the skewness of the distributions and the change in question wording, we chose not to include these items in Table 9.3.

18. See also notes 2 and 9 above.

19. Utley (1997, 5–6) put it this way: "The passing of the Cold War era has left many institutions adrift, searching for a new order or definition, and television news is no exception. Without stories from abroad that could be presented as part of an overall threat to American security, newscasts suffered a severe loss in an increasingly competitive medium that thrives—perhaps depends—on drama and conflict to attract and hold an audience's attention. The external threats (say, ICBMs) have been replaced by what many perceive as the threats at home (a mugger on the street corner, drugs, children born out of wedlock)."

CHAPTER 10

1. Between the signing of the Maastricht Treaty in 1991 and the Fall of 1997, average support for integration across Europe plunged by more than 25 percentage points. For a review and analysis of recent trends in public opinion toward integration generally, see Eichenberg and Dalton (1998).

2. The portions of this section on the origins of NATO and the controversies of the early 1980s draw on ibid., 268–270).

3. I say "least" because the Common Foreign and Security Policy preserved unanimous voting in the European Council, while qualified majority voting has been introduced for trade, market, and many other policy issues. The legal provisions of the Maastricht Treaty are interesting, but they go beyond the scope of this chapter.

4. For analysis and sources of data cited in this paragraph, see Eichenberg (1989, esp. 95–97; 132–138).

5. These figures refer to the pooled, Unionwide Eurobarometer sample of Europeans; I present distinct national variations below. These and other figures in this paragraph are taken from Dalton (1978, 18–20) and Dalton and Eichenberg (1998, Table 9.4).

6. The exact question wording is: "Here are a number of present day problems. . . . For each one, would you tell me if it is better that decisions about it be taken by each country acting separately or by the member countries of the European Union acting together?"

7. The discussion in this paragraph is based on surveys in 1979, 1987, and 1989. For these and additional questions using a wider variety of response options, see Eichenberg (1989, 128–129) and Eurobarometer 32 (1989, 41).

8. This section relies heavily on Art's (1996) insightful treatment of intra-European and transatlantic politics as the Cold War came to an end.

9. The sources for Figure 10.3 are Eurobarometer surveys, as listed in Table 10.3.

10. An interesting feature of these surveys is that the increase in support levels through 1995 is unique to external relations; it is *only* in foreign and security policy that support for common Union policies increased. In several other areas (education, social security, Economic and Monetary Union), support for common policies actually declined in reaction to Maastricht. As we note below, the situation in Bosnia appears responsible for this trend, but it seems clear that integration of foreign and defense policy is perceived differently from integration on domestic policies. For surveys on support for integration in all policy areas, see Dalton and Eichenberg (1998, 259).

11. USIA *Opinion Analysis*, M-95–99, June 9, 1999.

12. The wording for the 1985 and 1987 questions in Table 10.3 is not comparable to later questions and the figures are thus listed in italics.

13. This compromise required negotiation of the precise relationship between NATO and the WEU, the latter now the "defense arm" of the European Union. Art (1996, 27–33) describes the details of this negotiation within NATO. Gordon (1997) reviews the same period from the perspective of the EU. The final step in the codification of the European Defense Identity and its relation to NATO came in the June 1996 summit; see "Final Communiqué," Ministerial Meeting of the North Atlantic Council, Berlin, 3 June 1996.

14. The ability of the United States to dominate NATO military missions was dramatically illustrated during the air war against Serbia in 1999. According to Michael Ignatieff's account, General Wesley Clark, the American NATO commander, adapted to the need to maintain NATO solidarity by insulating American forces from the needs of coalition warfare: "Clark kept the coalition from paralyzing the air war by keeping NATO out of missions using American planes. . . . [There] were two completely separate targeting teams, called cells—one for NATO warplanes and the other for EUCOM [American] assets. America was parsimonious in sharing intelligence and targeting information with its allies. Even the British government, America's closest ally, was not always informed of American strike targets and intentions. The United States Air Force kept its key strike aircraft, the B-2 bomber, in Missouri, so that its own allies would not have access to its advanced and highly secret stealth technology." (Ignatieff 1999, 34).

15. The figures in the previous paragraph are from Eurobarometer 34, (Fall 1990); Angus Reid Group (1999); and Eurobarometer 51 (Spring 1999).

16. It is, of course, possible that the responses to this question on defense spending in fact reflect resistance to American domination of NATO. In that case, they paradoxically *confirm* a Europeanist pattern.

17. See Lepgold (1998) on NATO's burden-sharing problems in the post–Cold War era. The war in Kosovo did raise burden-sharing debates in the U.S. Congress, and congressional (as opposed to public) support for the war was tenuous, in part because many legislators considered the problem to be one that Europeans should solve. On these and other disputes that continue to nag U.S.-European relations, see Wallace and Zielonka (1998).

CHAPTER 11

1. I am very grateful to all persons and institutions that over the years have provided me with data and assistance, particularly to Jan van der Meulen and the Stichting Maatschappij en Krijgsmacht.

2. Data from the regular surveys of Stichting Maatschappij en Krijgsmacht since 1963.

3. Publieke opinie-kroniek (9), *Maatschappij en Krijgsmacht* 20 (1998):2.

4. NIPO, Opinieonderzoek Kernwapens, A4121, October 1998.

5. NIPO, Opinieonderzoek Kernwapens, A4121, October 1998; see also *Algemeen Dagblad*, October 22, 1998.

6. Data for 1981 and 1990 come from the European Values Survey (Klingemann and Fuchs 1995). Data for 1997 come from Stichting Maatschappij en Krijgsmacht.

7. In the French case, there is also strong corroborating evidence of increased support for the whole range of possible forms of use of military power, reaching from the traditional to the more modern ones (Cohen 1996, 29, table 3).

8. This was similar to the situation in the Netherlands one year earlier, when humanitarian aid (43 percent) was felt to be the most important present task compared to 23 percent with respect to the classical defense mission. By late 1997, the Netherlands had shifted to the British and French pattern, however.

9. On the question of the support for peacekeeping and humanitarian missions, and the related question of acceptable costs, see also the comparative work of Cohen (1996), which contains case studies of France, the United States, Great Britain, and Germany. The results of that study are in line with the arguments in this paper.

10. See, for instance, the international comparative surveys by Angus Reid group for *The Economist* in the period March 25–April 17, 1999 (N = 500 per country), and CNN, April 22–24, 1999 (www.angusreid.com).

11. NIPO, October 10–11, 1998.

12. NIPO for 2-VandaagTV (April 7, 1999) (N = 251)

13. NIPO.

14. NIPO for SMK; see *Trouw*, April 6, 1999.

15. Poll by NIPO for Stichting Maatschappij en Krijgsmacht (late 1991). See Zonder de Sovjet-Unie, *Maatschappij en Krijgsmacht* 14 (1992):1, 14–18. For more and other data on the Yugoslav conflict, see Everts (1993b, 1994b, and 1996).

16. In the Summer of 1998, new (and some rehashed) facts and allegations concerning neglectful or even criminal behavior of some of the military concerned and efforts of the authorities to cover up unpleasant details in the press led to new debates and new efforts by the then new cabinet to clear up the mess once and for all.

17. The poll was held shortly before the NATO air strikes began August 1995. See also Schennink and Wecke (1995).

CHAPTER 12

1. In contemplating the opinion-policy relationship, it is perhaps necessary to realize that bringing representative government to a people accustomed to autocratic rule requires more than lifting the yoke of repression under which they have lived for centuries.

2. The extreme concentration of power over foreign policy decisionmaking before Gorbachev can be seen in the facts that there were only three general secretaries heading the Politburo from the late 1920s until 1982, and one Politburo member, Andrei Gromyko, held the post of foreign minister for almost thirty years, from 1957 until 1985.

3. See article 86, which says in part: "The president of the Russian Federation exercises leadership of the foreign policy of the Russian Federation."

4. Speaking at a press conference in Paris on April 17, 1991, in the days of early post–Cold War euphoria, Yeltsin said optimistically that Russia could keep this balance, and its relative weakness would not endanger its role as a Great Power. He predicted that Russia would "play a unique role as a bridge between Europe and Asia and that it can contribute toward extending the area of European cooperation, particularly in the economic field, from the Atlantic to the Pacific" (see Sakwa 1993, 294).

5. Russia quickly joined the Coordinating Committee of the London Conference on the Former Yugoslavia. The first Russian battalion of peacekeeping forces was dispatched to the former Yugoslavia on approval by the Russian legislature in March 1992. In 1993, Russia became a member of the five-country contact group on the crisis. Moscow voted for UN Security Council Resolution No. 770 in August 1992, which allowed UN countries to use force to provide humanitarian help to Sarajevo. Moscow supported all key UN resolutions on sanctions, including the 1992 imposition of economic sanctions on Belgrade (*Izvestia*, August 14, 1992, 5). On June 4, 1993, Moscow also voted for UN Security Council Resolution No. 836, which—adopted unanimously by the Security Council's members—authorized "all necessary measures, through the use of air power, in and around the safe areas" in the Republic of Bosnia and Hercegovina to support UNPROFOR in the former Yugoslavia (*The Economist*, "Pax Russiana?" February 19, 1994, 57).

6. Satisfaction with one's life was also low. By Summer of 1995, a ratio between the number of people in Russia satisfied with their life, compared to those who were not satisfied, was 1:8 (*Segodnia*, August 2, 1995). Compared to other European nations, this was a significantly lower level of satisfaction. The Eurobarometer surveys between 1993 and 1995 indicate that Russian respondents repeatedly scored the lowest (with the exception of the 1995 Ukrainian sample) in satisfaction with current events (see also Wyman 1997, 21–23).

7. The secular decline in voter turnouts over time helps to reveal this trend. While 89.8 percent of voters voted in the Soviet Congress of People's Deputies elections of March 1989, only 77 percent of Russian voters voted in the Russian Congress of People's Deputies elections in March 1990. Thereafter, 74.7 percent of Russian voters voted in the Russian Federation's presidential election of June 1991, 54.8 percent voted in the Federal Assembly elections of December 1993, 64.44 percent voted in the December 1995 Duma elections, and 69.81 percent and 68.89 percent voted in the June and July 1996 rounds of the presidential election, respectively. See Sakwa 1996 and White et al. 1997.

8. Russians seem to still act like people who lived under the Soviet system, i.e., they behave in the capacity of what Gabriel Almond and Sidney Verba (1963) termed "subjects"—those who are informed politically but do not actively participate in politics themselves—or "parochials," those who are uninformed and uninvolved politically—and not those of "citizens," who are both informed and active politically.

9. As experts suggest and polls confirm, after the collapse of the Soviet Union ordinary people realized that the real power was far away from ordinary people, as it was twenty or thirty years earlier (as it had been ten or twenty years earlier). In 1982, when the ailing Leonid Brezhnev was still in power, Konstantin Simis wrote about the Russian people's mood of "complete alienation" from the state and "indifference and even hostility" toward the government (Simis 1982, 254).

10. According to the survey, 83 percent of Americans said the same (Wyman 1997, 130).

11. By 1994, opinion polls showed that only 4 percent of Russians fully supported the actions of the Yeltsin government, and 31 percent believed that he should resign. *Ekonomicheskie i Sotsialnye Peremeny: Monitoring Obshchestvennogo Mneniya* #6 (1994):63. In 1995, 60 percent of the respondents favored a change of the country's leaders based on the opinion that they had exhausted their potential. Poll conducted in July by Boris Grushin's Vox Populi service; *Izvestia*, October 13, 1995, 6. The distrust extended to other major Russian institutions. In 1995, the church and army were approved by only 33 and 32 percent of the surveyed people, respectively. Political parties and social movements received a 7 percent approval rating, while the heads of banks had only 6 percent support.

12. In the early stage of Russian democratic parliamentarism, Yevgeny Ambartsumov, chairman of the Joint Committee on International Affairs and Foreign Economic Relations of the Russian parliament, criticized the government for its "duplication" of the U.S. position in all respects. *Izvestia*, June 29, 1992, 3.

13. In June 1992, front-page headlines of the popular *Izvestia*, for example, clearly indicated optimism and high hopes regarding U.S.-Russia partnership: "Russia and USA bury the Cold War and begin an era of partnership" (June 12); "Eleven times U.S. Congress gave Yeltsin standing applause" (June 18).

14. Leonid Abalkin, a renowned economist, suggested that the collapse of the Soviet Union contributed to the disappearance of the country's external enemy. In his opinion, any "enemy search" can be considered as a "healthy" phenomenon that indicates the birth of a new national identity (Abalkin 1995, 41). See also Volkan 1988; Koenigsberg 1992).

15. According to a nationwide survey conducted in July 1995 by Boris Grushin's Vox Populi service, 72 percent believed that Russia should have its own unique path of development, different from other countries. Only 11 percent disagreed with this. Eighty-one percent favored reestablishing Russia's position in the world as a great power, and 70 percent regretted the collapse of the Soviet Union (Kondrashov 1995).

16. In a sample of 230 newspaper articles published between 1991 and 1995 on Russian foreign policy (170 were published by mainstream papers, 60 by procommunist newspapers), the theme of the mistreatment of Russia's interests emerged in 191 publications (quantitative assessment was made by the authors). The Cold War defeat deeply distressed many Russians who profoundly felt the loss of superpower status (*Christian Science Monitor*, "The Eagle and the Bear," September 27, 1995, 20). Nostalgic references to the former Soviet Union policies were made in twenty-one (out of sixty examined) publications in the procommunist *Pravda* and *Sovetskaya Rossiya*.

17. In 230 available analytical publications in the Russian mainstream press between 1991 and 1996, 196 contained information about the U.S. diplomatic and military actions in the Balkan region (all reports about the events in Yugoslavia and other regions can be divided into two categories: journalist reports with no or little comment and so-called analytical publications that resemble editorial columns in major American newspapers). This reveals Russian nervousness about the American presence in the Balkans (Shiraev and Terrio 1999). In the analytical Russian press, the conflict in Bosnia was linked not so much to ethnic cleansing as to the specter of U.S. geopolitical influence in the Balkans.

18. There are many examples of such anti-American rhetoric. For instance, in February 1994 the foreign minister stated that Russia has no intention of listening to lectures on the rules of good behavior from Western politicians (Eggert 1994). During a press conference, President Yeltsin vigorously criticized the United States for its foreign policy course and ac-

cused European countries of allowing themselves to be dictated to from the United States. He also complained that for such a long time the Western countries ignored his international initiatives (press conference with Boris Yeltsin, Official Kremlin International News Broadcast, September 8, 1995). Yeltsin stated on several occasions that he was reluctant to send its troops under American command in Bosnia (see, for example, Yeltsin's interview on French television; see MacKenzie 1995).

19. Analyzing the relationship of public opinion to foreign policy, one can notice how often references to the "popular opposition" were made by Russian politicians. Indeed, both the Yeltsin government and leading policy experts have not been averse to using references to public opposition in speaking about international developments. Quite common were warnings that if the Western help was not substantial enough, the Russian antidemocratic forces would destroy democracy (Arbatov 1992). Speaking in Prague against NATO expansion, the former acting prime minister, Yegor Gaidar, said that expansion would play into the hands of Russian hard-liners and nationalists (*Reuters World Service*, January 16, 1995). Political scientist and deputy to the Duma Yevgeny Ambartsumov (1994) suggested that NATO expansion would provide grist for the mill of the nationalists and radicals in opposition to the Kremlin.

CHAPTER 13

1. Thomas W. Graham, *The Politics of Failure: Strategic Nuclear Arms Control, Public Opinion, and Domestic Politics in the United States—1945–1980*, Ph.D. dissertation, Massachusetts Institute of Technology, 1989; Robert Y. Shapiro and Lawrence R. Jacobs, "The Relationship Between Public Opinion and Public Policy: A Review," in *Political Behavior Annual*, Vol. 2, ed. Samuel Long (Boulder: Westview, 1989), pp. 149–179; Bruce M. Russett, *Controlling the Sword: The Democratic Governance of National Security* (Cambridge: Harvard University Press, 1990); Benjamin I. Page and Robert Y. Shapiro, *The Rational Public: Fifty Years of Trends in Americans' Policy Preferences* (Chicago: University of Chicago Press, 1992); Maxine Isaacs, "The Independent American Public: The Relationship Between Elite and Mass Opinions on American Foreign Policy in the Mass Communications Age," Ph.D. dissertation, University of Maryland, 1994; Ole R. Holsti, *Public Opinion and American Foreign Policy* (Ann Arbor: University of Michigan Press, 1996); and Douglas Foyle, *Counting the Public In: Presidents, Public Opinion, and Foreign Policy* (New York: Columbia University Press, 1999).

2. Arthur M. Schlesinger Jr. "Back to the Womb?" *Foreign Affairs* 74 (July-August 1995):2–8.

3. Kenneth N. Waltz, "The Emerging Structure of International Politics," *International Security* 18 (Fall 1993):76.

4. Lawrence R. Jacobs and Robert Y. Shapiro, "Issues, Candidate Image, and Priming: The Use of Private Polls in Kennedy's 1960 Presidential Campaign," *American Political Science Review* 88 (1994):527–540; Lawrence R. Jacobs and Robert Y. Shapiro, "The Rise of Presidential Polling: The Nixon White House in Historical Perspective," *Public Opinion Quarterly* 59 (1995):163–195; and Foyle, *Counting the Public In.*

5. Bernard C. Cohen, *The Public's Impact on Foreign Policy* (Boston: Little, Brown, 1973).

6. Hadley Cantril, *The Human Dimension: Experiences in Policy Research* (New Brunswick, N.J.: Rutgers University Press, 1967).

7. Arthur H. Vandenberg Jr., *The Private Papers of Senator Vandenberg* (Boston: Houghton Mifflin, 1952).

8. The reader is encouraged to see Steven Kull and I.M. Destler, *Misreading the Public: The Myth of a New Isolationism* (Washington, D.C.: Brookings Institution, 1999).

9. Michael Wines, "Yeltsin Waves Saber at West; His Premier Speaks Softly," *New York Times,* December 11, 1999, A8.

10. Peter Trubowitz, *Defining the National Interest: Conflict and Change in American Foreign Policy* (Chicago: University of Chicago Press, 1998).

11. Gabriel Almond, *The American People and Foreign Policy* (New York: Harcourt Brace, 1950); Thomas A. Bailey, *The Man in the Street: The Impact of American Public Opinion on Foreign Policy* (New York: Macmillan, 1948); Hans J. Morgenthau, *Politics among Nations,* 5th ed. (New York: Knopf, 1978); Walter Lippmann, *Essays in the Public Philosophy* (Boston: Little, Brown, 1955); and George F. Kennan, *American Diplomacy, 1900–1950* (New York: Mentor Books, 1951).

12. Cohen, *The Public's Impact on Foreign Policy,* p. 62.

CHAPTER 14

We thank the Pew Charitable Trusts for research support and Eric Shiraev and especially Ron Hinckley for very helpful comments and corrections. The responsibility for all analysis and interpretations is our own.

1. Reagan Library, PR15, Memo to Regan from Chew, 11/17/86 #448145). Ron Hinckley, who worked at the National Security Council in the Reagan administration, reported to us that according to Tom Griscom, the political liaison at the White House during the last years of the Reagan administration: "At all times these accounts were run through the RNC and not through White House funds." Hinckley's interpretation is that "the RNC had a large budget which had certain allocations for White House and other recipients of the survey results. Each group to add questions to the surveys at a cost from their budget in the RNC account."

2. Reagan Library, PR15, "Analysis of the President's Peace and National Security Address," Decision Making Information (DMI), March 1986, attached to cover note from David Chew to President, 3/4/86.

3. Reagan Library, PR15, "Flash Results, #3084–01," DMI, 4/9–11/85.

4. Reagan Library, PR15, "Flash Results, #3084–01," DMI, 4/9–11/85.

5. Reagan Library, Memo to Regan from Wirthlin, 4/2/86, regarding Nicaragua and aid to the Contras.

6. Reagan Library, Memo to Regan from Wirthlin, 4/8/86.

7. PR15, "American Attitudes toward the Iranian Situation," DMI, 1/14/87 (#459046).

8. Reagan Library, PR15, Letter to President from Wirthlin, 4/10/85.

9. Reagan Library, PR15, Letter to President from Wirthlin, 4/10/85.

10. Reagan Library, PR15, Letter to President from Wirthlin, 4/10/85.

11. Reagan Library, Memo, 5/9/85 (#173361).

12. Reagan Library, PR15, "Flash Results," April 1985.

13. Reagan Library, PR15, "Flash Results, #3084–01," DMI, 4/9–11/85.
14. PR15, "Initial Aggregate Results, Eagle IX," DMI, July 1981.

CHAPTER 15

1. All of the data presented are from the Eurobarometer series of surveys, which have been conducted biannually, on the basis of nationally representative samples, in all the member states of the European Community/Union since the mid-1970s. Details of methodology and fieldwork can be ascertained by consulting Eurobarometer reports.

2. It can be argued that the permissive-consensus model oversimplifies V.O. Key's analysis, from which it derives, and in particular that it obscures the importance of the stratification of opinion that had been Key's central concern (see Sinnott 1995a, 29–30).

3. This and the following paragraphs summarize an analysis of the American debate that is elaborated in greater detail in Sinnott 2000.

4. The wording of this and of the other questions referred to in this chapter is given in Appendix A.

5. The "very" was added to "relieved" in 1993.

6. Eichenberg very sensibly seeks to transcend this not very satisfactory distinction by postulating three components of integration: the cosmopolitan, the utilitarian, and the realist (Eichenberg 1998, 13–15). He is, however, probably being too kind to the unification indicator in treating it as an adequate measure of the cosmopolitan component, and his retention of the utilitarian notion cannot avoid the quagmire of how to categorize the membership indicator (he treats it as utilitarian).

7. There is a substantial and technically highly sophisticated literature on the (mainly economic) determinants of support for integration. Eichenberg (1998) provides an excellent review and extension of this research. From the point of view of the current discussion, the most relevant findings are that "the influence of objective economic circumstances on support for integration was less in the period following Maastricht than it had been before" (Eichenberg 1998, 12) and that the effects vary depending on the indicator of the dependent variable that is used.

8. The Europeanization of issues also depends, of course, on other factors that are more potent than public opinion. There are at least three types of Europeanization (or internationalization) of issues: *attributed* (public opinion), *exogenous* (the claims of European [or international] agencies), and *endogenous* (the nature of the issue). The relationship among these three is explored in Sinnott 1995b.

9. See Appendix B for full question wording.

10. The questions and the scoring assigned to them are discussed in detail in Sinnott 1996.

11. Delli Carpini and Keeter argue that "measures of specific political facts [can be used] as purposive samples of what citizens know" (Delli Carpini and Keeter 1996, 15–16).

12. This analysis uses the dissolution indicator of support for integration and the knowledge scale outlined above, with the latter being in this case divided into three levels (as shown in Table 15.2).

13. Using different data and a different typology, Rattinger reached a somewhat similar conclusion for German public opinion on European integration in 1992: "The share of unmistakable supporters is only half as large as those with relatively indifferent attitudes and low

personal salience of the topic. This latter group makes up well over half our sample" (Rattinger 1994, 539).

14. The hypotheses, data and results are presented in full in Sinnott 2000.

15. It can, of course, be argued that the real democratic foundation of the Union lies in national politics and in the ultimate accountability of governments to their national electorates for the decisions they take in Brussels. In terms of public involvement in a European democratic process, however, this is an indirect and tenuous connection.

16. From an American perspective, it might be argued that these figures are not so bad. Because of different registration procedures, however, there are considerable difficulties involved in comparing turnout in U.S. and European elections. In any event, even allowing for this factor, turnout in the United States is hardly a standard to be emulated.

17. These factors are evident from close inspection of Table 15.3 and are discussed in detail in Blondel, Sinnott, and Svensson 1998, 30–40.

CHAPTER 16

1. Gilles Bresson and Judith Perrignon, "L'opinion publique inquiète les élus," *Libération*, March 31, 1999, 6.

2. Bresson and Perrigon, "L'opinion publique inquiète les élus," 6.

3. In addition, thirty interviews conducted as part of a study on the role of the media in the foreign policy process (fifteen with foreign policy officials and fifteen with foreign policy journalists), as well as thirty-two interviews with elites in a study of public perceptions of humanitarian military operations, also provided background evidence.

4. Interview with Richard Duqué, former State Department spokesman, October 29, 1996.

5. Interview with Jean-Louis Chambon, former member of the Elysée press service, March 21, 1997.

6. This was confirmed in several interviews with the president's advisers.

7. Interview with Pierre Messmer, former prime minister, November 18, 1997.

8. See Elisabeth Dupoirier, "De la crise à la guerre du Golfe: un exemple de mobilisation de l'opinion," in *SOFRES: L'Etat de l'opinion,* ed. Olivier Duhamel and Jérome Jaffré (Paris: Editions du Seuil, 1992).

9. Interview with a former foreign secretary, December 3, 1996.

10. Remarks made at the Freedom Forum Media Studies Center, New York, March 19, 1995. Cited in Warren Strobel, *Late-Breaking Foreign Policy: The News Media's Influence on Peace Operations* (Washington, D.C.: United States Institute of Peace Press, 1997), p. 4.

11. Rapport d'information n°1950 de l'Assemblée Nationale, *La politique d'intervention dans les conflits: éléments de doctrine pour la France,* 1995, p. 21.

12. See also Jacques Gerstlé, "Ralliement et identification au président dans les crises internationales," in *Les individus dans la politique internationale,* ed. Michel Girard (Paris: Economica, 1994), p. 142.

13. Interview with Jean-Louis Chambon, former member of the Elysée press service, April 3, 1997.

14. Baromètre SOFRES/SIRPA, *Les Français et la Défense Nationale.* A thorough study on this subject has been published; see Samy Cohen (ed.), *L'Opinion, l'humanitaire et la guerre:*

une perspective comparative (Paris: Fondation pour les Etudes de Defense/La Documentation française, 1996). Samy Cohen's study reveals that the French have remained, overall, very stable in their attitudes toward peacekeeping operations.

15. Institut des Hautes Etudes de Défense Nationale, Rapport sur *L'intérêt d'un Conseil national de sécurité*, 45ème session, March 1993, p. 22.

16. CSA pour *La Vie, Les Français et l'opération militaire en Somalie et une éventuelle opération à Sarajevo*, December 10, 1992.

17. Interview with Jean Musitelli, former Elysée spokesman, April 1, 1997.

18. Allocution de M. François Mitterrand, Président de la République, à l'occasion de la réception des Ambassadeurs, Palais de L'Elysée, mercredi 31 août 1994 (President Mitterrand's address during the yearly ambassadors' conference, Elysee Palace, Wednesday, August 31, 1994).

19. Sondage TF1/7–7, June 24–25, 1994.

20. Baromètre SOFRES/SIRPA, *Les Français et la Défense Nationale*. See also Natalie La Balme, "The Public's Influence on France's Decision to Use Force," prepared for the workshop "Democracy, Public Opinion, and the Use of Force in a Changing International Environment," ECPR Joint Sessions of Workshops, University of Warwick, March 23–28, 1998.

21. See Bernard Kouchner, *Ce que je crois* (Paris: Grasset, 1995), p. 39.

22. See Cohen, *L'Opinion, l'humanitaire et la guerre.*

23. Vendredi, *Hebdomadaire du Parti Socialiste*, January 21, 1993.

24. IFOP pour *VSD, Les Français et les événements en ex-Yougoslavie*, April 15, 1993.

25. IFOP-GALLUP pour *Le Journal du Dimanche*, GALLUP USA pour *CNN* et *USA Today, L'intervention militaire en Bosnie: l'opinion des Français et des Américains*, February 10, 1994.

26. This was confirmed by Alain Juppé himself during an interview with the author on September 30, 1998.

27. Evidence seems to reveal that public opinion in France has an important impact throughout the policy process (agenda-setting, negotiation of the issue at hand, ratification, and implementation). Yet whereas Thomas Graham (1994) concludes that public opinion in the United States has a direct impact on getting the issues on the agenda and on ratification of agreements but only an indirect effect on negotiations and implementation, our own research reveals that public opinion in France, because of the institutional differences between the two countries (for example, the different role of the French parliament with respect to the U.S. Congress), public opinion in France has more influence on the former two phases than on the latter two. Evidence also reveals that public opinion has more influence during an electoral campaign toward the end of an electoral term rather than at the beginning of a term and during the first rather than the second term.

28. Natalie La Balme, *L'influence de l'opinion publique sur les décisions de politique extérieure en France: une "contrainte permissive."* Doctoral dissertation, Universite de Paris I Pantheon/Sorbonne, 1999.

CHAPTER 17

The title of this chapter is quoted from the following passage from Alexander Pope, *Essay on Criticism* (1711), 622:

No place so sacred from such fops are barred,
Nor is Paul's church more safe than Paul's churchyard;
Nay, fly to altars; there they'll talk to your dead;
For fools rush in where angels fear to tread.

1. Interestingly, American political science has always been inclined to explain the Italian case by making reference to cultural variables, such as amoral familism (Banfield 1958), parochialism (Almond and Verba 1983), and lack of civicness (Putnam 1993); while Italian scholars have preferred to point to structural variables, like the party system (e.g., Sartori 1982). For a recent review of this literature, see Sciolla (1997).

2. A fluctuation "is defined by the number of reversals in direction of significant change within a given time interval" (Page and Shapiro 1982, 28–29).

3. Since question format changed over time, to facilitate the comparison the percentage distributions are calculated excluding those who do not answer or who declared to have a "fair" opinion.

4. The scanty empirical evidence available seems to confirm the "viscosity" of change in public-opinion attitudes. Deutsch and Merritt (1965), studying the impact of different kinds of events on the international images of public opinion at the aggregate level, found that in order to produce a lasting impact events have to be spectacular, cumulative, supported by a substantial governmental effort, and without cross-pressures. If all these conditions were met, no more than 40 percent of the population would change attitude after one or two decades. More recently, Shapiro and Page (1988), in an analysis of aggregate changes in policy preferences (a dimension they claim less open to change than opinions toward political actors) found that "abrupt" changes are quite modest, although more likely in foreign than domestic policy.

5. See Cohen (1977–1978, 1995), Eichenberg (1989), Flynn and Rattinger (1985), Risse-Kappen (1991), and Sinnott and Niedermayer (1995); for a comparative application to another policy area, see Jacobs (1993).

6. Lemert (1992), in studying the opinion-policy link, suggested a distinction between the election network that unites mass and elite, through which politicians get useful information to reach the paramount goal of winning elections, and the influence network, or the set of links that allows policymakers to make sense of the distribution of opinions among the effective public and to figure out the conditions under which latent opinions can become activated.

7. The Italian government was called upon to join UN land forces in Bosnia on several occasions: in September 1992 based on the decision to enlarge UNPROFOR to Bosnia; in January-March 1994 following the United Kingdom's request to involve Italian troops; in December 1994 when assistance in a possible withdrawal of UN troops was discussed; and in July 1995, first in the context of the withdrawal option, and later with respect to the London meeting's decision to organize air strikes. In all cases, the Italian government preferred not to join UN land forces in Bosnia. In July 1995, however, the government did agree to contribute airplanes for tactical air strikes and close air support.

8. This information is based on an interview with the journalist who conducted the TV interview.

9. A few days after the interview I am discussing, Andreatta stressed again that many failures in Bosnia were due to opposition to military intervention by public opinion both in Italy and in other Western countries (including the United States). Later in that year, how-

ever, Andreatta downplayed the influence of public opinion on the Italian foreign policy choices.

10. The question was: "At this point in the Bosnia situation, do you favor or oppose an armed intervention knowing that the peacekeeping forces would suffer human casualties and heavy military expenditures?" Sixty-one percent of the 800 persons interviewed opposed the idea of armed intervention, 28 percent were in favor, and 11 percent did not know.

References

Abalkin, Leonid. *Economic Reform: Zigzags of Fate and Lessons for the Future.* Moscow: Institute of Economics, RAS, 1995.

Alexseev, Mikhail A., and W. Lance Bennett. "For Whom the Gates Open: News Reporting and Government Source Patterns in the United States, Great Britain, and Russia." *Political Communication* 12 (1995): 371–393.

Allen, Emilie, and Daryl Steffensmeier. "Youth Underemployment and Property Crime." *American Sociological Review* 54 (February 1989): 107–123.

Almond, Gabriel. *The American People and Foreign Policy.* New York: Harcourt Brace, 1950.

Almond, Gabriel A. *The American People and Foreign Policy.* New York, Praeger, 1960.

Almond, Gabriel, and Sidney Verba. *The Civic Culture: Political Attitudes and Democracy in Five Nations.* Princeton: Princeton University Press, 1963.

Almond, Gabriel A., and Sidney Verba. *The Civic Culture: Political Attitudes and Democracy in Five Nations.* Newbury Park: Sage, 1983.

Althaus, Scott, Jill Edy, and Patricia Phalen. "The Re-election Motive and Congressional Oversight of U.S. Force Interventions: Debating the Libya Crisis of 1986." Paper delivered at annual meeting of the Midwest Political Science Association (MPSA), Chicago, 1994.

Althaus, Scott, Jill Edy, Robert Entman, and Patricia Phalen. "Revising the Indexing Hypothesis." Paper delivered at annual meeting of the American Political Science Association, New York, 1994.

Althaus, Scott, Jill Edy, Robert Entman, and Patricia Phalen. "Revising the Indexing Hypothesis: Officials, Media, and the Libya Crisis." *Political Communication* 13(4) (1996): 407–422 (original paper delivered at annual meeting of the American Political Science Association, New York, 1994).

Ambartsumov, E. "In the World: Echoes of the Bosnian Bombings." *Moskovskie Novosti,* April 10–17, 1994, A5.

America's Place in the World. Times Mirror Center for the People and the Press. Washington, D.C.: Times-Mirror Co., 1993.

Angus Reid Group. *NATO and the War in Yugoslavia/Kosovo: A Report on International Public Opinion.* URL: http://www.angusreid.com/studies/pr9904222.html, April 23, 1999.

Ansolabehere, Stephen, et al. *The Media Game.* New York: MacMillan, 1993.

Arbatov, Alexei. "Natsionalnaia Ideia i Rossiiskaia Bezopasnost" [National Idea and Russian Security]. *Mirovaia Ekonomika i Mezhdunarodniie Otnosheniia* [MEIMO], no. 5 (1998): 5–13 and no. 6 (1998): 5–19.

Arbatov, G. "Rescue Russia, or Else!" *Newsday,* October 25, 1992.

Art, Robert. "Why Western Europe Needs the United States and NATO." *Political Science Quarterly* 111(1) (1996): 1–39.

Bailey, Thomas A. *The Man in the Street: The Impact of American Public Opinion on Foreign Policy.* New York: Macmillan, 1948.

Baker, James III, with Thomas M. Defrank. *The Politics of Diplomacy: Revolution, War and Peace, 1989–1992.* New York: Putnam, 1995.

Banfield, Edward C. *The Moral Basis of a Backward Society.* Chicago, IL: Free Press, 1958.

Barber, Benjamin. *Strong Democracy: Participatory Politics for a New Age.* Berkeley: University of California Press, 1984.

Barner-Berry, Carol. "Nation Building and the Russian Federation." In *The Russian Transformation,* edited by Betty Glad and Eric Shiraev. New York: St. Martin's Press, 1999.

Barnes, Samuel H. *L'elettorato italiano e la teoria della democratizzazione,* In *L'Italia fra crisi e transizione,* edited by M. Caciagli, F. Cazzola, L. Morlino and S. Passigli. Bari: Laterza, 1994.

Bartels, Larry M. "Constituency Opinion and Congressional Policy Making: The Reagan Defense Buildup." *American Political Science Review* 85 (1991): 457–474.

Battistelli, Fabrizio. *Soldati. Sociologia dei militari italiani nellera del peacekeeping.* Milan: Angeli, 1996.

Baturin, Andrei, and Sergei Gryzunov. "Dance with a Broom, as Performed by Zhirinovsky." *Russian News Agency Novosti, special to Izvestia,* 1 February 1994, 4.

Bausin, Alexei. "Who Should Decide Europe's Future?" *Vek,* no. 46, 1995, p. 4.

Beal, Richard, and Hinckley, Richard. "Presidential Decision-making and Opinion Polls." *Annals of the American Academy of Social Science* 472 (March 1984): 72–84.

Beaudrillard, Jean. "La guerre de Golfe n'a pas eu lieu." *Libration,* March 1991.

Bellucci, Paolo. *Difesa, politica e societ. La politica militare italiana tra obiezione di coscienza e professionalizzazione delle Forze Armate.* Milan: Angeli, 1998.

Bellucci, Paolo, and Pierangelo Isernia. "Massacring in Front of a Blind Audience? Italian Public Opinion and Bosnia." *Centro Interdipartimentale di Ricerca sul Cambiamento Politico Occasional Papers,* n.2, 1998.

Bellucci, Paolo, and Pierangelo Isernia. "Massacring in Front of a Blind Audience? Italian Public Opinion and Bosnia." In *International Public Opinion and the Bosnia Crisis,* edited by R. Sobel and E. Shiraev. Penn State University Press, forthcoming 2000.

Benamou, Georges-Marc. *Le Dernier Mitterrand.* Paris: Plon, 1996.

Bennett, W. Lance. "Marginalizing the Majority: Conditioning the Public to Accept Managerial Democracy." In *Manipulating Public Opinion,* edited by M. Margolis and G. Mauser. Pacific Grove, Ca.: Brooks/Cole, 1989.

Bennett, W. Lance. "Toward a Theory of Press-State Relations." *Journal of Communication* 40(2) (1990): 103–125.

Bennett, W. Lance. "The Media and the Foreign Policy Process." In *The New Politics of American Foreign Policy,* edited by David Deese. New York: St. Martin's Press, 1994a.

Bennett, W. Lance. "The News about Foreign Policy." In *Taken by Storm: The Media, Public Opinion, and U.S. Foreign Policy in the Gulf War,* edited by W. Lance Bennett and David L. Paletz. Chicago: University of Chicago Press, 1994b.

Bennett, W. Lance. "An Introduction to Journalism Norms and Representations of Politics." *Political Communication* 13(4) (1996): 373–384.

Bennett, W. Lance, and David L. Paletz, eds. *Taken by Storm: The Media, Public Opinion, and U.S. Foreign Policy in the Gulf War.* Chicago: University of Chicago Press, 1994.

Blondel, Jean, Richard Sinnott, and Palle Svensson. *People and Parliament in the EU; Partici-pation, Democracy and Legitimacy.* Oxford: Oxford University Press, 1998.

Blumer, Herbert. "The Mass, the Public, and Public Opinion." In *Reader in Public Opinion and Communication*, edited by Bernard Berelson and Morris Janowitz. New York: The Free Press of Glencoe, 1953.

Bogaturov, Alexei. "Russia-U.S.: Politics of Selective Resistance." *International Affairs* (Moscow) 44(4) (1998): 29–39.

Bolshakov, Vladimir. "Yugoslavia: Trevozhnoe Ozhidanie" [Tense Waiting]. *Pravda*, February 22, 1994, p. 3.

Braestrum, Peter. *Big Story.* New Haven: Yale University Press, 1979.

Bresson, Gilles, and Judith Perrignon. "L'opinion publique inquiète les élus." *Libération*, March 31, 1999.

Brody, Richard. *Assessing the President: The Media, Elite Opinion, and Public Support.* Stanford, Ca.: Stanford University Press, 1991.

Brosius, Hans-Bernd. "The Effects of Emotional Pictures in Television News." *Communication Research* 20 (1993): 105–24.

Brown, Archie. *The Gorbachev Factor.* New York: Oxford University Press, 1996.

Bull, Hedley. *The Anarchical Society.* London: Macmillan, 1977.

Bull, Hedley. "European Self-Reliance and the Reform of NATO." *Foreign Affairs* 61(4) (1983): 874–92.

Busuyev, Vitaly. *Rossiyskaya Gazeta*, May 28, 1992, p. 7.

Cameron, David. "The 1992 Initiative: Causes and Consequences." In *Europolitics*, edited by Alberta Sbragia. Washington, D.C.: Brookings Institution, 1992.

Cantril, Hadley. *The Human Dimension: Experiences in Policy Research.* New Brunswick, N.J.: Rutgers University Press, 1967.

Cappella, Joseph N., and Kathleen Hall Jamieson. *Spiral of Cynicism.* New York: Oxford University Press, 1997.

Carr, E.H. *Socialism in One Country.* Vol. 1. London: Macmillan and Co, 1958.

Cartocci, Roberto. *Elettori in Italia. Riflessioni sulle vicende elettorali negli anni Ottanta.* Bologna: Il Mulino, 1990.

Caspary, William. "The Mood Theory: A Study of Public Opinion and Foreign Policy." *American Political Science Review* 64 (June 1970): 536–47.

Chomsky, Noam, and Edward S. Herman. *Manufacturing Consent: The Political Economy of the Mass Media.* Pantheon Books, 1988.

Citrin, Jack, Beth Reingold, and Donald P. Green. "American Identity and the Politics of Ethnic Change." *Journal of Politics* 52 (November 1990): 1124–1154.

Citrin, Jack, Ernst B. Haas, Christopher Muste, and Beth Reingold. "Is American Nationalism Changing: Implications for Foreign Policy." *International Studies Quarterly* 38 (March 1994): 1–31.

Clinton, Richard. "Politics and Survival." *World Affairs* 138(2) (Fall 1975): 108–127.

Cohen, Bernard C. *The Press and Foreign Policy.* New Jersey: Princeton University Press, 1963.

Cohen, Bernard C. *The Public's Impact on Foreign Policy.* Boston: Little, Brown, 1973.

Cohen, Bernard C. "Political Systems, Public Opinion, and Foreign Policy: The United States and the Netherlands." *International Journal* 33(1) (1977–1978): 195–216.

Cohen, Bernard C. *Democracies and Foreign Policy: Public Participation in the United States and the Netherlands.* Madison: University of Wisconsin Press, 1995.

Cohen, Samy, ed. *L'Opinion, l'humanitaire et la guerre: Une perspective comparative.* Paris: Fondation pour les Etudes de Defense, La Documentation française, 1996.

Cohen, Samy, ed. *Mitterrand et la sortie de la guerre froide.* Paris: PUF, 1998.

Converse, Jean M. *Survey Research in the United States: Roots and Emergence, 1890–1960.* Berkeley: University of California Press, 1987.

Converse, Philip E. "The Nature of Belief Systems among Mass Publics." In *Ideology and Discontent,* edited by D.A. Apter. New York, Free Press, 1964.

Converse, Philip, E. "Attitudes and Non-attitudes: Continuation of a Dialogue." In *Quantitative Analysis of Social Problems,* edited by E.R. Tufte. Reading: Addison Wesley, 1970.

Converse, Philip E. Public Opinion and the Political Process. *Public Opinion Quarterly,* 51 (1987): S12–S24.

Cook, Timothy E. "Domesticating a Crisis." In *Taken by Storm: The Media, Public Opinion, and U.S. Foreign Policy in the Gulf War,* edited by W. Lance Bennett and David L. Paletz. Chicago: University of Chicago Press, 1994.

Cotta, Maurizio, and Luca Verzichelli. "La classe politica: cronaca di una morte annunciata." In *Il Gigante dai piedi dargilla. La crisi del regime partitocratico in Italia,* edited by Maurizio Cotta and Pierangelo Isernia. Bologna: Il Mulino, 1996.

Cutler, Lloyd N. "Foreign Policy on Deadline." *Foreign Policy* 56 (1984).

Dahl, Robert A. *Democracy and Its Critics.* New Haven: Yale University Press, 1989.

Dalton, Russell. "The Uncertain Future of European Integration." Paper presented at the annual meeting of the American Political Science Association, New York, 1978.

Dalton, Russell J. *Citizen Politics: Public Opinion and Political Parties in Advanced Western Democracies.* Chatham, N.J.: Chatham House Publishers, Inc., 1996.

Dalton, Russell, and Richard Eichenberg. "A People's Europe: Citizen Support for the 1992 Market and Beyond." In *The 1992 Project and the Future of Integration in Europe,* edited by James Ray and Dale Smith. New York: M.E. Sharpe, 1993.

Dalton, Russell, and Richard Eichenberg. "Citizen Support for Policy Integration in the European Union." Paper presented to the convention of the International Studies Association, San Diego, 1996.

Dalton, Russell, and Richard Eichenberg. "Citizen Support for Policy Integration." In *European Integration and Supranational Governance,* edited by Wayne Sandholtz and Alec Stone Sweet. New York: Oxford University Press, 1998.

Dankert, Peter. "U.S.-European Relations: Defense Policy and the Euro-Missiles." In *Drifting Together or Apart?* edited by Richard Eichenberg. Lanham, Md.: University Press of America, 1986.

D'Attorre, Pier Paolo. "Sogno americano e mito sovietico nellItalia contemporanea." In *Nemici per la pelle. Sogno americano e mito sovietico nellItalia contemporanea,* edited by Pier Paolo D'Attorre. Milan: Angeli, 1991.

David, Paul A. "Clio and the Economics of QWERTY." *American Economic Review* 75 (1985): 332–37.

Davis, Stephen. "The Role of Communication and Symbolism in Interest Group Competition: The Case of the Siskiyou National Forest, 1983–1992." *Political Communication* 12 (1995): 27–42.

Davison, W.P. "The Third-Person Effect in Communication." *Public Opinion Quarterly* 47 (1983): 1–15.

de Boode, S. "Meningen in de media: Het debat over militair ingrijpen in Bosni/Joegoslavi." *Transaktie* 22(4) (1993): 362–368.

de Boode, S. "Het debat na Srebrenica." *Transaktie* 24(4) (1995): 509–515.

de Tocqueville, Alexis. *Democracy in America*. New York: Doubleday, 1969.

Debray, Régis. *L'Etat seducteur*. Paris: Gallimard, 1993.

Deese, David, ed. *The New Politics of American Foreign Policy*. New York: St. Martin's Press, 1994.

Deese, David A., ed. "Making American Foreign Policy in the 1990s." In *The New Politics of American Foreign Policy*, edited by David A. Deese. New York: St. Martin's Press, 1994.

Delli Carpini, Michael, and Scott Keeter. *What Americans Know about Politics and Why It Matters*. New Haven: Yale University Press, 1996.

DePorte, Anton. *Europe Between the Superpowers*. New Haven: Yale University Press, 1986.

Destler, I.M. "Foreign Policy and the Public: Will Leaders Catch the Full Message?" *The Brown Journal of World Affairs III* (Winter/Spring 1996): 265–270.

Deutsch, Karl W., and Richard L. Merritt. "Effects of Events on National and International Images." In *International Behavior: A Social-Psychological Analysis*, edited by Herbert C. Kelman. New York: Holt, Rinehart, and Winston, 1965.

Dobrynin Anatoly. *Sugubo Doveritelno* [Very Confidentially]. Avtor: Moscow, 1997.

Donsbach, Wolfgang. "Motivations for Exposure Towards Political News: The Role of the Media in Knowledge and Opinions Toward the European Currency." Paper presented at the conference on Public Opinion, the Mass Media, and European and American Foreign Policy, New York, N.Y., November 19–29, 1998.

Dorman, William A., and Steven Livingston. "News and Historical Content: The Establishing Phase of the Persian Gulf Policy Debate." In *Taken by Storm: The News Media, U.S. Foreign Policy, and the Gulf War*, edited by W. Lance Bennett and David L. Paletz. Chicago: University of Chicago Press, 1994.

Downs, Anthony. "An Economic Theory of Democracy." New York: Harper and Row, 1957.

Edinger, Lewis J., and Brigitte L. Nacos. *From Bonn to Berlin: German Politics in Transition*. New York: Columbia University Press, 1998.

Efron, Sonni. "Russia Moves to Encircle Capital of Rebel State." *Los Angeles Times*, December 12, 1994, A1.

Eggert, Konstantin. "Defeat in Bosnia, United Russia, and the West." *Izvestia*, April 3, 1994, p. 3.

Eggert, Konstantin. "A 'Great-Power' Foreign Policy Is Too Expensive." *Izvestia*, December 16, 1995, p. 3.

Eichenberg, Richard. *Public Opinion and National Security in Western Europe*. London: MacMillan (Ithaca: Cornell University Press, 1989).

Eichenberg, Richard. "Measurement Matter: Cumulation in the study of public opinion and European integration." Paper presented at the annual meeting of the American Political Science Association, Boston, 1998.

Eichenberg, Richard, and Russell Dalton. "Europeans and the European Union: The Dynamics of Public Support for European Integration." *International Organization* 47 (1993) 507–534.

Eichenberg, Richard, and Russell Dalton. "Post-Maastricht Blues: Do Political Economy Models Still Explain Citizen Support for European Integration?" Paper presented to a seminar of the Center for West European Studies, University of Pittsburgh, 1998.

Eisinger, Robert. "Pollster and Public Relations Advisor: Hadley Cantril and the Birth of

Presidential Polling." Paper presented at the annual meeting of the American Political Science Association (1994a).

Eisinger, Robert. "Presidential Polling in the 1950s and Beyond. Pollster and Public Relations Advisor: Hadley Cantril and the Birth of Presidential Polling." Paper presented at the annual meeting of the American Association of Public Opinion Research (1994b).

Entman, Robert M. *Democracy Without Citizens: Media and the Decay of American Politics.* New York: Oxford University Press, 1989.

Entman, Robert M. "Framing U.S. Coverage of International News: Contrasts in Narratives of the KAL and Iran Air Incidents." *Journal of Communication* 41(4) (1991): 6–27.

Entman, Robert M. "Framing: Toward Clarification of a Fractured Paradigm." *Journal of Communication* 43 (1993).

Entman, Robert M. "Reporting Environmental Policy Debate: The Real Media Biases." *Press/Politics* 1(3) (1996): 77–92.

Entman, Robert M., and Susan Herbst. "Reframing Public Opinion as We Have Known It." In *Mediated Politics: Communication in the Future of Democracy,* edited by W. Lance Bennett and Robert M. Entman. New York: Cambridge University Press, forthcoming 2000.

Entman, Robert M., and Benjamin I. Page. "The News before the Storm: The Iraq War Debate and the Limits to Media Independence." In *Taken by Storm: The News Media, U.S. Foreign Policy, and the Gulf War,* edited by W. Lance Bennett and David L. Paletz. Chicago: University of Chicago Press, 1994.

Entman, Robert M., and David L. Paletz. "Media and the Conservative Myth." *Journal of Communication* 30(3) (1980): 154–165.

Entman, Robert M., and Andrew Rojecki. "Freezing Out the Public: Elite and Media Framing in the U.S. Anti-Nuclear Movement." *Political Communication* 10 (1993): 155–173.

Erikson, Robert S. "Constituency Opinion and Congressional Behavior: A Reexamination of the Miller-Stokes Data." *American Journal of Political Science* 22 (1978): 511–535.

Erikson, Robert S., Gerald C. Wright, and John P. McIver. *Statehouse Democracy: Public Opinion and Policy in the American States.* New York: Cambridge University Press, 1993.

Erlanger, Steven. "Crowded, Ambitious Foreign Policy Agenda Awaits President in New Term." *The New York Times,* 19 January 1997, p.L21.

Eurobarometer, *Report on Standard Eurobarometer 43.* European Commission Directorate General X, Autumn, 1995.

European Commission. *Top Decision Makers Survey: Summary Report.* Brussels: European Commission, 1996.

Everts, Philip P. "Public Opinion, the Churches, and Foreign Policy: Studies of Domestic Factors in the Foreign Policy of the Netherlands." Leiden: Institute for International Studies, 1983.

Everts, Philip P., ed. *Controversies at Home. Domestic Factors in the Foreign Policy of the Netherlands.* Dordrecht: Martinus Nijhoff, 1985.

Everts, Philip P. "Inleiding." In *Nederland in een veranderende wereld,* edited by Philip P. Everts. Assen: van Gorcum, 1991.

Everts, Philip P. *Wat denken de mensen in het land? Ontwikkelingen in de publieke opinie over problemen van buitenlandse en defensiepolitiek, 1983–1992.* Nijmegen: Studiecentrum Vredesvraagstukken, 1992.

Everts, Philip P. "Support for War: Public Opinion on the Gulf War, 1990–1991." In *Peace Research for the 1990s,* edited by J. Balazs and H. Wiberg. Budapest: Akadmiai Kiad, 1993a.

Everts, Philip P. "Ontwikkelingen in de publieke openie." *Jaarboek Vrede en Veligheid 1993.* Nijmegen: Studiecentrum Vredesvraagstukken, 1993b, 186–197.

Everts, Philip P. "What Do the Dutch Think about the Germans? Some Reflections on Public Opinion among Neighbours." Paper presented at the conference entitled "The Future of Security and Stability in Europe and the Role of Germany Therein," Rijksuniversiteit Groningen, November 24, 1994a.

Everts, Philip P. "Ontwikkelingen in de publieke openie." *Jaarboek Vrede en Veligheid 1994.* Nijmegen: Studiecentrum Vredesvraagstukken, 1994b, 205–223.

Everts, Philip P. "NATO, the European Community and the United Nations." In *Public Opinion and Internationalized Governance,* edited by O. Niedermayer and R. Sinnott. Oxford: Oxford University Press, 1995.

Everts, Philip P. *Laat dat maar aan ons over! Democratie, Buitenlands beleid en Vrede.* Leiden: DSWO Press, 1996a.

Everts, Philip P. "The 'Bodybag Hypothesis' as an Alibi: Public Support for UN Military Operations in the Netherlands—The Case Of Bosnia Herzegovina." *Politics, Groups, and the Individual* 6(1) (1996b): 75–84.

Everts, Philip P. "Public Opinion and Decisions on the Use of Military Force in Democratic Societies." Paper prepared for presentation in the workshop "Democracy, Public Opinion, and the Use of Force in a Changing International Environment," Joint Sessions of the European Consortium for Political Research, University of Warwick, March 23–28, 1998a, revised version.

Everts, Philip P. "The Casualty Hypothesis: Contradictory Evidence." Paper prepared for the annual meeting of the American Political Science Association, Boston Marriott Copley Place and Sheraton Boston Hotel and Towers, September 3–6, 1998b.

Everts, Philip P. "Blijft de publieke opinie de navo-acties tegen Servi steunen?" *Transaktie* 28(2) (1999): 237–259.

Everts, Philip. "Innocence Lost: The Netherlands and the Yugoslav Conflict." In *International Public Opinion and the Bosnia Crisis,* edited by R. Sobel and E. Shiraev. Penn State University Press, forthcoming 2000.

Falk, Robert. *On Humane Governance.* Cambridge: Polity, 1995.

Fallows, James. *Breaking the News: How the Media Undermine American Democracy.* New York: Pantheon, 1996.

Favier, Pierre, and Michel Martin-Roland. "La décennie Mitterrand" 1: *Les ruptures, 1981–1984.* Paris: Seuil, 1990.

Favier, Pierre, and Michel Martin-Roland. "La décennie. Mitterrand" 2: *Les preuves, 1984–1988.* Paris: Seuil, 1995.

Favier, Pierre, and Michel Martin-Roland. "La décennie Mitterrand" 3: *Les défis, 1988–1991.* Paris: Seuil, 1996.

Featherstone, "K. Jean Monnet and the Democratic Deficit in the EU." *Journal of Common Market Studies* 32/2 (1994): 149–70.

Ferguson, G. "Parties and Politics in Russia." *The Public Perspective,* 1996, 2: 44.

Ferguson, Thomas, and Joel Rogers. *Right Turn: The Decline of the Democrats and the Future of American Politics.* New York: Hill and Wang, 1986.

Fields, James M., and Howard Schuman. "Public Beliefs About the Beliefs of the Public." *Public Opinion Quarterly,* 40 (1976): 427–448.

Fiske, Susan T., and Shelley E. Taylor. *Social Cognition.* New York: McGraw-Hill, 1991.

Flynn, G., and H. Rattinger, eds. *The Public and Atlantic Defence.* Totowa, N.J.: Rowman and Allanheld, 1985.

Foyle, Douglas. *Counting the Public In: Presidents, Public Opinion, and Foreign Policy.* New York: Columbia University Press, 1999.

Franklin, Mark, and Cees van der Eijk, eds. *Choosing Europe? The EU and National Politics in the Face of EU.* Ann Arbor: University of Michigan Press, 1996.

Fried, Amy. "Muffled Echoes: Oliver North and the Politics of Public Opinion." New York: Columbia University Press, 1997.

Gabel, Matthew. "Public Opinion and European Integration: Citizen Politics in the European Union." Ann Arbor: University of Michigan Press, 1997.

Gaddis, John L. "The Long Peace." *International Security* 10(4) (Spring 1986).

Galli, Giorgio. *Il Bipartitismo imperfetto. Comunisti e Democristiani in Italia.* Bologna: Il Mulino, 1966.

Gans, Herbert. *Deciding What's News.* New York: Vintage, 1980.

Goldberg, Ronald Allen. "The Senate and Vietnam: A Study of Acquiescence." Ph.D. diss., University of Georgia, 1974.

Gardner, Richard N. "The Comeback of Liberal Internationalism." *Washington Quarterly* 13 (Summer 1990): 23–39.

Geer, John G. *From Tea Leaves to Opinion Polls: A Theory of Democratic Leadership.* New York: Columbia University Press, 1996.

Gergen, David. R. "Diplomacy in a Television Age: The Dangers of a Teledemocracy." In *The Media and Foreign Policy,* edited by Simon Serfaty. New York: St. Martin's Press, 1991.

Gerstlé, Jacques. "Ralliement et identification au president dans les crises internationales." In *Les individus dans la politique internationale,* edited by Michel Girard. Paris: Economica, 1994.

Giddens, Anthony. *The Nation-State and Violence.* Cambridge: Polity, 1985.

Giles, Michael W., and Arthur S. Evans. "External Threat, Perceived Threat, and Group Identity." *Social Science Quarterly* 66 (March 1985): 50–66.

Giles, Michael W., and Melanie A. Buckner. "David Duke and Black Threat: An Old Hypothesis Revised," *Journal of Politics* 55 (August 1993): 702–713.

Ginsberg, Benjamin. *The Captive Public: How Mass Opinion Promotes State Power.* New York: Basic Books, 1986.

Ginsberg, Roy. *The Foreign Policy Actions of the European Union.* Boulder: Lynne Rienner Press, 1989.

Gitlin, Todd. *The Whole World Is Watching.* Berkeley: University of California Press, 1980.

Glad, Betty, and Eric Shiraev, eds. *The Russian Transformation.* New York: St. Martin's Press, 1999.

Goble, Paul. "Dangerous Liaisons: Mocsow, the Former Yugoslavia, and the West." In *The World and Yugoslavia Wars,* edited by R. Ullman. Washington, D.C.: The Council on Foreign Relations, 1996.

Goethals, G. R. "Fabricating and Ignoring Social Reality: Self-serving Estimates of Consensus." In *Relative Deprivation and Social Comparison: The Ontario Symposium on Social Cognition,* Vol. 4, edited by C. P. Herman and M. P. Zanna. Hillsdale, N.J.: Lawrence Earlbaum Associates, 1986.

Goldberg, Ronald Allen. "The Senate and Vietnam: A Study of Acquiescence." Ph.D. diss., University of Georgia, 1974.

Gorbachev, Mikhail. "Opasno Kogda s Rossiei Obrashaiutsa Kak s Mladshim Partnerom" [It is dangerous when Russia is treated as a junior partner]. *Nezavisimaya Gazeta*, February 22, 1994, p. 2.

Gordon, Philip H. "Europe's Uncommon Foreign Policy." *International Security* 22 (1997): 74–100.

Gorma, Hubert J. "The Discovery of Pluralistic Ignorance." *Journal of the History of the Behavioral Sciences*, 22 (1986): 333–347.

Gornovstaev, Dmitry. "Two Bears before 1996." *Nezavisimaya Gazeta*, November 10, 1994, p. 1.

Gowing, Nik. *Real-Time Television Coverage of Armed Conflicts and Diplomatic Crises: Does it Pressure or Distort Foreign Policy Decisions?* Harvard: Shorenstein Center, 1994.

Graber, Doris A. "Seeing Is Remembering: How Visuals Contribute to Learning from Television News." *Journal of Communication* 40(3) (1990): 134–155.

Graber, Doris A. *Processing the News: How People Tame the Information Tide*. Washington, D.C.: Congressional Quarterly Press, 1988.

Graber, Doris. A. *Mass Media and American Politics*. Washington, D.C.: Congressional Quarterly Press, 1997.

Graham, Thomas W. *The Politics of Failure: Strategic Nuclear Arms Control, Public Opinion, and Domestic Politics in the United States: 1945–1980*. Ph.D. diss., MIT, 1989.

Graham, Thomas W. *Public Attitudes toward Active Defense: ABM and Star Wars, 1945–1985*. Cambridge: Center for International Studies, MIT, 1986.

Graham, Thomas W. "Public Opinion and U.S. Foreign Policy Decision-Making." In *The New Politics of American Foreign Policy*, edited by David E. Apter. New York: St. Martin's Press, 1994.

Graziano, Luigi. *La Politica Estera Italiana nel Dopoguerra*. Milan: Marsilio, 1968.

Grosser, Alfred. *The Western Alliance*. New York: Vintage Books, 1982.

Haas, Ernst B. *The Uniting of Europe*. Stanford: Stanford University Press, 1958.

Haas, Ernst B. "The Study of Regional Integration: Reflections on the Joy and Anguish of Pretheorizing." In *Regional Integration: Theory and Research*, edited by L.N. Lindberg and S.A. Scheingold. Cambridge: Harvard University Press, 1971.

Hafner, Donald L. "Presidential Leadership and the Foreign Policy Bureaucracy." In *The New Politics of American Foreign Policy*, edited by David A. Deese. St. Martin's Press, 1994.

Halberstam, David. *The Powers That Be*. New York: Dell, 1979.

Hallin, Dan. "Vietnam and the Myth of the Oppositional Media." *Journal of Politics* 46(1) (1984): 2–24.

Hallin, Daniel C. *The Uncensored War*. New York: Oxford University Press, 1986.

Hallin, Daniel C. "Hegemony: The American News Media from Vietnam to El Salvador: A Study of Ideological Change and Its Limits." In *Political Communication Research*, edited by David L. Paletz. Norwood, N.J.: Ablex, 1987.

Hanson, Elizabeth C. "Guest Editor's Introduction: International News After the Cold War: Continuity or Change?" *Political Communication* 12 (1995): 351–355.

Hargrove, Erwin. *Jimmy Carter as President: Leadership and the Politics of the Public Good*. Baton Rouge: Louisiana State University Press, 1988.

Hartley, Thomas, and Bruce Russett. "Public Opinion and the Common Defense: Who Governs Military Spending in the United States?" *American Political Science Review* 86 (December 1992): 905–915.

Hartley, Thomas, Murray Shoon, and Bruce Russett. "The End of the Cold War, Attitude Change, and the Politics of Defense Spending." *Political Science and Politics* 27 (March 1994): 17–21.

Hearst, David. "Bear's Sore Heart." *The Guardian* 14 (London) September 17, 1995.

Heith, Diane J. "Staffing the White House Public Opinion Apparatus, 1969–1988." *Public Opinion Quarterly* 62 (Spring 1998a): 165–189.

Heith, Diane J. *The Public Opinion Apparatus and the Presidential Agenda.* Paper presented at the annual meeting of the American Political Science Association, Boston, September 3–6, 1998b.

Heith, Diane J. "Presidential Polling and the Potential for Leadership." In *Presidential Power: Forging the Presidency for the 21st Century,* edited by Robert Y. Shapiro, Martha J. Kumar, and Lawrence R. Jacobs. New York: Columbia University Press, forthcoming 2000.

Herbst, Susan. *Numbered Voices: How Opinion Polling has Shaped American Politics.* Chicago: University of Chicago Press, 1992.

Herbst, Susan. *Reading Public Opinion.* Chicago: University of Chicago Press, 1998.

Herman, Edward S., and Noam Chomsky. *Manufacturing Consent.* New York: Pantheon, 1988.

Hickey, Neil. "Money Lust: How Pressure for Profit Is Perverting Journalism." *Columbia Journalism Review.* July/August 1998.

Hilderbrand, Robert. *Power and the People: Executive Management of Public Opinion in Foreign Affairs, 1897–1921.* Chapel Hill: University of North Carolina Press, 1981.

Hinckley, Ronald H. *People, Polls and Policymakers: American Public Opinion and National Security.* New York: Lexington Books, 1992.

Hine, David. *Governing Italy. The Politics of Bargained Pluralism.* Oxford: Oxford University Press, 1993.

Hoffmann, Stanley. "Obstinate or Obsolete: The Fate of the Nation-state and the Case of Western Europe." *Daedalus* 95 (1966): 862–915.

Hoffmann, Stanley. "Cries and Whimpers: Thoughts on West European Relations in the 1980s." *Daedalus* 113 (1984): 221–252.

Hoffman, Stanley. "Yugoslavia: Implications for Europe and for European Institutions." In *The World and Yugoslavia's War,* edited by Richard Ullman. New York: Council on Foreign Relations, 1996, 98.

Holsti, Ole R. "Public Opinion and Foreign Policy: Challenges to the Almond Lippmann Consensus." *International Studies Quarterly* 4(36) (1992): 439–466.

Holsti, Ole R. *Public Opinion and American Foreign Policy.* Ann Arbor: University of Michigan Press, 1996a.

Holsti, Ole. *Foreign Policy Leadership Project* (sponsored by Duke University and George Washington University, March 1996b).

Holsti, Ole R., and J.N. Rosenau. *American Leadership in World Affairs.* Boston: Allen and Unwin, 1984.

Holsti, Ole R., and J.N. Rosenau. "The Structure of Foreign Policy Attitudes: American Leaders, 1976–1984." *Journal of Politics* 52 (February 1990): 94–125.

Holsti, Ole R., and J.N. Rosenau. "Internationalism: Intact or In Trouble?" In *The Future of American Foreign Policy,* 3d ed., edited by Eugene R. Wittkopf and Christopher M. Jones. New York: St. Martin's, 1999a.

Holsti, Ole R., and J.N. Rosenau. "The Political Foundations of Elite's Domestic and Foreign-Policy Beliefs." In *The Domestic Sources of American Foreign Policy: Insights and Evidence*, edited by Eugene R. Wittkopf and James M. McCormick. Lanham, Md.: Rowman and Littlefield, 1999b.

Hood, M.V., and Irwin L. Morris. "Amigo o Enemigo? Context, Attitudes, and Anglo Public Opinion toward Immigration." *Social Science Quarterly* 78 (June 1997): 309–323.

Hosking, Geoffrey. *Russia: People and Empire, 1952–1917.* Cambridge: Harvard University Press, 1997.

Huckfeldt, Robert, and Carol W. Kohfeld. *Race and the Decline of Class in American Politics.* Urbana: University of Illinois Press, 1989.

Huckfeldt, Robert, and John Spague. *Citizens, Politics, and Social Communication: Information and Influence in an Election Campaign.* New York: Cambridge University Press, 1995.

Huntington, Samuel P. "The Erosion of American National Interests." *Foreign Affairs* 76(5) (1997).

Hurwitz, Jon, and Mark Peffley. "American Images of the Soviet EU and National Security Issues." In *Debating National Security: The Public Dimension*, edited by Don Munton and Hans Rattinger. Frankfurt: Verlag Peter Lang, 1991.

Ignatieff, Michael. "The Virtual Commander: How NATO Invented a New Kind of War." *The New Yorker* 75 (1999): 30–36.

Isaacs, Maxine. *The Independent American Public: The Relationship Between Elite and Mass Opinions on American Foreign Policy in the Mass Communications Age.* Ph.D. diss., University of Maryland, 1994.

Isernia, Pierangelo. *Dove gli Angeli non mettono piede. Opinione pubblica e politica di sicurezza in Italia*, Milano: Angeli, 1996.

Isernia, Pierangelo. "Opinione pubblica e politica di difesa in Italia." In *L'Elmo di Scipio. Il Nuovo modello di difesa*, edited by Carlo Maria Santoro. Bologna: Il Mulino, 1992.

Isernia, Pierangelo, and P. Bellucci. "Italian Public Opinion and the Support for the Use of force: The Case of Bosnia." Paper prepared for presentation in the workshop "Democracy, Public Opinion, and the Use of Force in a Changing International Environment," Joint Sessions of the European Consortium for Political Research, University of Warwick, March 23–28, 1998.

Isernia, Pierangelo, Zoltan Juhasz, and Hans Rattinger. *Foreign Policy and the Rational Public in Comparative Perspective.* Paper presented at the annual meeting of the American Political Science Association, Boston, September 3–6, 1998.

Iyengar, Shanto, and Donald R. Kinder. *News That Matters.* Chicago: University of Chicago Press, 1987.

Iyengar, Shanto. *Is Anyone Responsible?* Chicago: University of Chicago Press, 1991.

Jacobs, Lawrence, R. "The Recoil Effect: Public Opinion and Policy Making in the U.S. and Britain." *Comparative Politics* 24 (January 1992): 199–217.

Jacobs, Lawrence R. *The Health of Nations: Public Opinion and the Making of American and British Health Policy.* Ithaca: Cornell University Press, 1993.

Jacobs, Lawrence R., and Robert Y. Shapiro. "Public Decisions, Private Polls." Paper prepared for delivery at the annual meeting of Midwest Political Science Association, Chicago, 1992.

Jacobs, Lawrence R., and Robert Y. Shapiro. "The Public Presidency, Private Polls, and Policymaking: Lyndon Johnson." Presented at the annual meeting of the American Political Science Association, Washington, D.C., September 2–5, 1993.

Jacobs, Lawrence R., and Robert Y. Shapiro. "Lyndon Johnson, Vietnam, and Public Opinion: Rethinking Realist Theory of Leadership." Presented at the annual meeting of the Midwest Political Science Association, Chicago, 1994a.

Jacobs, Lawrence R., and Robert Y. Shapiro. "Issues, Candidate Image, and Priming: The Use of Private Polls in Kennedy's 1960 Presidential Campaign." *American Political Science Review* 88 (1994b): 527–540.

Jacobs, Lawrence R., and Robert Y. Shapiro. "Studying Substantive Democracy." *PS: Political Science and Politics* (March 1994c): 9–17.

Jacobs, Lawrence R., and Robert Y. Shapiro. "The Rise of Presidential Polling: The Nixon White House in Historical Perspective." *Public Opinion Quarterly* 59 (1995a): 163–195.

Jacobs, Lawrence R., and Robert Y. Shapiro. "Public Opinion and President Clinton's First Year: Leadership and Responsiveness." In *The Clinton Presidency: Campaigning, Governing, and the Psychology of Leadership*. Edited by Stanley A. Renshon. Boulder: Westview Press, 1995b.

Jacobs, Lawrence R., and Robert Y. Shapiro. "Presidential Manipulation of Polls and Public Opinion: The Nixon Administration and the Pollsters." *Political Science Quarterly* 110 (Winter 1995–1996): 519–538.

Jacobs, Lawrence R., and Robert Y. Shapiro. "Pollwatch: The Media's Reporting and Distorting of Public Opinion Toward Entitlements." Presented for discussion at the annual meeting of the American Political Science Association, Washington, D.C., September 1997.

Jacobs, Lawrence R., and Robert Y. Shapiro. *Politicians Don't Pander: Political Manipulation and the Loss of Democratic Responsiveness.* Chicago: University of Chicago Press, 2000.

Jacobson, Gary. *The Politics of Congressional Elections*, 3d ed. New York: HarperCollins, 1993.

James, Patrick, and John R. O'Neal. "The Influence of Domestic and International Politics on the President's Use of Force." *Journal of Conflict Resolution* 35 (June 1991): 307–332.

Janis, Irving. *Groupthink: Psychological Studies of Policy Decisions and Fiascoes.* Boston: Houghton-Mifflin, 1982.

Jennings, M. Kent. "Political Knowledge Over Time and Across Generations." *Public Opinion Quarterly* 60 (Summer 1996): 228–252.

Jentleson, Bruce. "The Pretty Prudent Public: Post-Vietnam American Opinion on the Use of Military Force." *International Studies Quarterly* 36 (1992): 49–73.

Jentleson, Bruce, and Rebecca Britton. *Still Pretty Prudent: Post-Cold War American Public Opinion on the Use of Military Force.* Paper presented at the American Political Science Association Conference, Washington, D.C., August 1997.

Jervis, Robert. *Perception and Misperception in International Politics.* Princeton: Princeton University Press, 1976.

Jones, Charles O. *The Trusteeship Presidency.* Baton Rouge: Louisiana State University Press, 1988.

Kaase, M., and K. Newton. *Beliefs in Government.* Oxford: Oxford University Press, 1995.

Kagarlitsky, B. A. Transcript of Presentation. "Piat let posle Belovezhia (Five years after the Belovezh Agreement)." Moscow: Aprel-85, 1997, 52–57.

Kaldor, Mary. *New and Old Wars: Organized Warfare in the Global Era.* Cambridge: Polity, 1999.

Kamen, Al. "A World of Advice: Don't Quit." *Washington Post*, August 12, 1998, p. A13.

Katz, Andrew Z. "Public Opinion and Foreign Policy: The Nixon Administration and the Pursuit of Peace with Honor in Vietnam." *Presidential Studies Quarterly* 28 (Summer 1997): 496–513.

Katz, Andrew Z. *Public Opinion and the Contradictions of President Carter's Foreign Policy.* Unpublished paper. Denison University, 1998.

Katz, Richard S. "Party Government: A Rationalistic Conception." In *Vision and Realities of Party Government,* edited by F. G. Castles and R. Wildenmann. New York: de Gruyter, 1986.

Keating, Tom, and Nicholas Gammer. "The New Look in Canada's Foreign Policy." *International Journal* 48 (1993): 720–748.

Kelley, Jack. "Clinton's Moscow Welcome Uncertain; Frustrated Russians Cool to the USA." *USA Today,* January 12, 1994, 1A.

Kellner, Douglas. *The Persian Gulf TV War.* Boulder: Westview Press, 1992.

Kennamer, J. D. "Self-serving Biases in Perceiving the Opinions of Others: Implications for the Spiral of Silence." *Communications Research* 17(3) (1990): 393–404.

Kennan, George F. *American Diplomacy, 1900–1950.* New York: Mentor Books, 1951.

Kennedy, Paul. *The Rise and Fall of the Great Powers.* New York: Random House, 1987.

Kennedy, Paul. "A Declining Empire Goes to War." In *The Future of American Foreign Policy,* edited by Charles W. Kegley Jr. and Eugene R. Wittkopf. New York: St. Martin's, 1992.

Keohane, Robert O., and Nye, Joseph S. *Power and Interdependence: World Politics in Transition.* Boston: Little, Brown, 1977.

Kern, Montague, Patricia Levering, and Ralph Levering. *The Kennedy Crises.* Chapel Hill, University of North Carolina Press, 1983.

Kernell, Samuel. *Going Public: New Strategies of Presidential Leadership.* 2d ed. Washington, D.C.: Congressional Quarterly Press, 1993.

Key, V.O. *Southern Politics in State and Nation.* New York: Alfred A. Knopf, 1949.

Key, V.O. Jr. *Public Opinion and American Democracy.* New York: Alfred A. Knopf, 1961.

Kinder, Donald R., and D. Roderick Kiewiet. "Sociotropic Politics: The American Case." *British Journal of Political Science* 11 (April 1981): 129–161.

Kissinger, Henry. *Diplomacy.* New York: Simon and Schuster, 1994.

Kliamkin, I., and V. Lapkin. "Sotsialno-Politicheskaya Ritorika v Postsovetskom Obshchestve" [Social-political rhetoric in the post-Soviet society]. *Polis* 1: 99–115, 1996.

Klingeman, H.-D, and D. Fuchs. *Citizens and the State.* Oxford: Oxford University Press, 1995.

Koenigsberg, R. *Hitler's Ideology.* New York: Library of Social Science, 1992.

Kogan, Norman. *La politica estera italiana.* Milan: Lerici, 1965.

Kohut, Andrew. "Washington Leaders Wary of Public Opinion." Washington, D.C.: Pew Center for People and the Press, April 17, 1998.

Kohut, Andrew, and Robert Toth. "A World of Difference: The Public and Opinion Leaders Are Poles Apart on the U.S. Role in Global Affairs." *Washington Post National Weekly Edition,* January 5, 1998, 22.

Kondrashov, Stanislav. "Who Are Russian Voters More Dissatisfied with—Clinton or Yeltsin?" *Izvestia,* 13 October 1995, 6.

Kondrashov, Stanislav. "Who Was Forced to do Something Against His Own Interests in Gorazde and How Did It Happen?" *Izvestia,* April 20, 1994, 3.

Kortunov, Sergei. " 'Imperskoe' i natsionalnoe v rossiiskom soznanie" ['Imperial' and national motives in Russian mentality]. *Mezhdunarodnaia Zhizn* 5 (1998): 15–27.

Kouchner, Bernard. *Ce que je crois.* Paris: Bernard Grasset, 1995.

Krauthammer, Charles. "The Unipolar Moment." *Foreign Affairs* 70(1) (1991): 23–33.

Kremenyuk, Viktor. "Deputy Director of the Russian Academy of Sciences' Institute of the USA and Canada Comments on President Bill Clinton's Visit to Moscow." *Novaya Yezhednevnaya Gazeta*, 15 January 1994, 2.

Kull, Steven. *Answers on Bosnia: A Study of U.S. Public Attitudes*. Program in International Policy Attitudes (PIPA), University of Maryland, May 16, 1995.

Kull, Steven. *Seeking a New Balance: A Study of American and European Public Attitudes on Transatlantic Issues*. Washington, D.C.: Program on International Policy Attitudes, 1998.

Kull, Steven, and I.M. Destler. *Misreading the Public: The Myth of a New Isolationism*. Washington, D.C.: Brookings Institution, 1999.

Kull, Steven, I.M. Destler, and Clay Ramsay. *The Foreign Policy Gap: How Policymakers Misread the Public*. College Park, Md.: The Center for International Security Studies at the University of Maryland, 1997.

Kull, Steven, and Clay Ramsay. *U.S. Public Attitudes on U.S. Involvement in Bosnia*. Program in International Policy Attitudes (PIPA), University of Maryland, 4 May 1994.

Kusnitz, Leonard A. *Public Opinion and Foreign Policy: America's China Policy, 1949–1979*. Westport, Conn.: Greenwood Press, 1984.

La Balme, Natalie. *L'influence des médias sur les décisions de politique étrangére en France. Mémoire de DEA sous la direction de Samy Cohen*, Université de Paris I Panthon/Sorbonne, 1994.

La Balme, Natalie. "Entre déclaration d'intention et engagement sur le terrain: l'ambivalence de l'opinion publique américaine." In *L'Opinion, l'humanitaire et la guerre: une perspective comparative*, edited by Samy Cohen. Paris: Fondation pour les Etudes de Défense, La Documentation française, 1996.

La Balme, Natalie. "L'influence de l'opinion dans la gestion des crises." In *Mitterrand et la sortie de la guerre froide*, edited by Samy Cohen. Paris: PUF, 1998.

La Balme, Natalie. "The Public's Influence on France's Decision to Use Force." Paper ECPR joint sessions of workshops, Warwick, March 23–28, 1998.

La Balme, Natalie. "The Public's Influence on France's Foreign Policy Decisions." Paper presented at the annual meeting of the American Political Science Association, Boston, September 3–6, 1998.

La Palombara, Joseph. *Interest groups in Italian politics*. Princeton: Princeton University Press, 1964.

Lacorne, Denis. "Le rang de la France: Mitterrand et la guerre du Golfe." In *Mitterrand et la sortie de la guerre froide*, edited by Samy Cohen. Paris: PUF, 1998.

Lakoff, George. *Moral Politics: What Conservatives Know That Liberals Don't*. Chicago: University of Chicago Press, 1996.

Lantis, Jeffrey S. *Domestic Contraints and the Breakdown of International Agreements*. Westport: Praeger, 1997.

Lapitsky, Vladimir. "Bayonets and Placards?" *Rossiiskaya Gazeta*, 27 March 1999.

Lawrence, Regina G. *Politicians, Public, and the Game of Politics: How the News Covered the Welfare Reform Debate*. Paper delivered at the 1998 annual meeting of the American Science Association, Boston, Sept. 3–9, 1998.

Lebed, Alexander. Press Conference. Moscow, May 13, 1996.

Lemert, James B. "Effective Public Opinion." In *Public Opinion, the Press, and Public Policy*, edited by David J. Kennamer. Westport: Praeger, 1992.

Lepgold, Joseph. "NATO's Post–Cold War Collective Action Problem." *International Security* 23 (1998): 78–106.

Lerner, Daniel, and Morton Gorden. *Euratlantica*. Cambridge: MIT Press, 1969.

Levesque, Jacques. *The Enigma of 1988: The USSR and the Liberation of Eastern Europe*. Berkeley: University of California Press, 1997.

Lichter, Robert S., Stanley Rothman, and Linda S. Lichter. *The Media Elite*. Bethesda: Adler and Adler, 1986.

Lindberg, L.N., and S.A. Scheingold, eds. *Europe's Would-Be Polity: Patterns of Change in the European Community*. Englewood Cliffs, N.J.: Prentice-Hall, 1970.

Lippmann, Walter. *Public Opinion*. New York: Macmillan, 1922.

Lippmann, Walter. *Essays in the Public Philosophy*. Boston: Little, Brown, 1949.

Livingston, Steven. *The CNN Effect Revisited*. Harvard/Shorenstein Center for Press, Politics, and Public Affairs, 1997.

Lloyd, John. "East-West: New Cold War in the Making." *Financial Times*, April 12, 1991, 1.

Lukas, Richard C. *The Strange Allies—United States and Poland, 1941–1945*. Knoxville: University of Tennessee Press, 1978.

Luttwak, Edward N. *The Endangered American Dream: How to Stop the United States from Becoming a Third World Country and How to Win the Geo-Economic Struggle for Economic Supremacy*. New York: Simon and Schuster, 1993.

MacArthur, John R. *Second Front: Censorship and Propaganda in the Gulf War*. Berkeley: University of California Press, 1992.

MacKenzie, Jean. "High-Profile President Looks Like a Candidate." *The Moscow Times*, 20 October 1995.

Madigan, Charles. "Polls: Public Support for War Slipping." *Chicago Tribune*, May 28, 1991, 1.

Mandelbaum, Michael. "Foreign Policy as Social Work." *Foreign Affairs* 75 (January/February 1996): 16–32.

Manigart, Philip, ed. *The Future of Security in Europe: A Comparative Analysis of European Public Opinion*. Brussels: Royal Military School, 1992.

Mann, Michael. *The Sources of Social Power*, Vol. 2. Cambridge: Cambridge University Press, 1993.

Margolis, Michael, and Gary Mauser, eds. *Manipulating Public Opinion*. Chicago: Dorsey Press, 1989.

Matza, D. *Delinquency and Drift*. New York: Wiley, 1964.

Mearsheimer, John. "Back to the Future: Instability in Europe After the Cold War." *International Security* 15 (1990): 5–56.

Mearsheimer, John J. "Back to the Future: Instability in Europe after the Cold War." In *The Cold War and After: Prospects for Peace*, edited by Sean M. Lynn-Jones and Steven E. Miller. Cambridge: MIT Press, 1994.

Media Monitor. "The Great Greenhouse Debate: Media Coverage and Expert Opinion on Global Warming." December 1992.

Melville, Andrei. "Russia's Open-Ended Transition: Toward an Integrated Research Model." In *The Russian Transformation*, edited by Betty Glad and Eric Shiraev. New York: St. Martin's Press, 1999.

Mermin, Jonathan. *Debating War and Peace*. Princeton: Princeton University Press, 1999.

Meyn, Herman. *Massenmedien in der Bundesrepublik Deutschland*. Berlin: Edition Colloquium, 1996.

Mifflin, Laurie. "Big Three Networks Forced to Revise News-Gathering Methods," *New York Times*, October 12, 1998, C1, 2.

Mikulski, K.I., ed. *Elita Rossii o nastoyashem i budushem strany* (Russian elite about the country's present and future). Moscow: Vekhi, 1995.

Miller A., V. Hesli, and W. Reisinger. "Understanding Political Change in Post-Soviet Societies: A Further Commentary on Finifter and Mickiwicz." *American Political Science Review* 90 (March 1996): 153–156.

Miller, Warren E., and Donald E. Stokes. "Constituency Influence in Congress." *American Political Science Review* 57 (March 1963): 45–56.

Mlechin, Leonid. "Moscow Is Making a Mistake by Shunning Joint Actions with the West in Bosnia." *Izvestia*, April 23, 1994, 1, 3.

Monroe, Alan D. "Consistency Between Public Preferences and National Policy Decisions." *American Politics Quarterly* 7 (January 1979): 3–19.

Monroe, Alan D. "American Party Platforms and Public Opinion." *American Journal of Political Science* 27 (February 1983): 27–42.

Monroe, Alan D. "Public Opinion and Public Policy, 1980–1993," *Public Opinion Quarterly* 62 (March 1998): 6–28.

Moravcsik, A. "Introduction: Integrating International and Domestic Theories of International Bargaining." In *Double-edged Diplomacy: International Bargaining and Domestic Politics*, edited by P.B. Evans, H.K. Jacobson, and R.D. Putnam. Berkeley: University of California Press, 1993.

Moravcsik, Andrew. "Negotiating the Single Act." *International Organization* 45 (1989): 19–56.

Morgenthau, Hans J. *Politics among Nations*. 5th ed. New York: Knopf, 1978.

Morin, Richard. "Toning Down Tough Talk on Bosnia." *Washington Post National Weekly Edition*, June 12–18, 1995, 35.

Morin, Richard. "How Do People Really Feel about Bosnia?" *Washington Post National Weekly Edition*, December 4–10, 1995, 34.

Morin, Richard. "Missing the Story on Bosnia: A Researcher Finds That the Media Are Underreporting Public Support for NATO Peacekeeping." *Washington Post National Weekly Edition*, April 27, 1998, 35.

Mueller, John. *War, Presidents, and Public Opinion*. New York: Wiley, 1973.

Mueller, John. *Policy and Opinion in the Gulf War*. Chicago: University of Chicago Press, 1994.

Mueller, John. *Quiet Cataclysm: Reflections on the Recent Transformation of World Politics*. Reading, Mass.: Addison-Wesley, 1995.

Nacos, Brigitte L. *The Press, Presidents, and Crises*. New York: Columbia University Press, 1990.

Nacos, Brigitte L. *Terrorism and the Media: From the Iran Hostage Crisis to the Oklahoma City Bombing*. New York: Columbia University Press, 1996a.

Nacos, Brigitte L. "After the Cold War: Terrorism Looms Large as a Weapon of Dissent and Warfare." Current World Leaders 39 (4) (1996b): 11–26.

Neumann, Russel W., et al. *Common Knowledge*. Chicago: University of Chicago Press, 1992.

Neustadt, Richard E., and Ernest R. May. *Thinking in Time: The Uses of History for Decision Makers*. New York: Free Press, 1998.

Niedermayer, Oskar, *Trends and Contrasts In Public Opinion and Internationalized Gover-

nance, edited by Oskar Niedermayer and Richard Sinnott. Oxford: Oxford University Press, 1995.

Niedermayer, Oskar, and Richard Sinnott, eds. *Public Opinion and Internationalized Governance.* Oxford: Oxford University Press, 1995.

Nikonov, Vadim. Transcript of Presentation. "Round Table: Five Years after the Belovezh Agreement" (Piat Let Posle Belovezhia). Moscow: Aprel-85, 1996, 49–51.

Nincic, Miroslav. "A Sensible Public: New Perspectives on Popular Opinion and Foreign Policy." *Journal of Conflict Resolution* 36 (December 1992): 772–789.

Nincic, Miroslav. *Democracy and Foreign Policy: The Fallacy of Political Realism.* New York: Columbia University Press, 1992.

Noelle-Neumann, Elisabeth. *The Spiral of Silence: Public Opinion and Our Social Skin.* Chicago: University of Chicago Press, 1984.

Noelle-Neumann, Elisabeth. *The Spiral of Silence: Public Opinion—Our Social Skin.* 2nd ed. Chicago: University of Chicago Press, 1993.

Norris, Pippa. "The Restless Searchlight: Network News Framing of the Post–Cold War World." *Political Communication* 12 (1995): 357–370.

Norris, Pippa. "News of the World." In *Politics and the Press: The News Media and Their Influences,* edited by Pippa Norris. Boulder: Lynne Reinner, 1997.

Nunn, Sam, and Pete Domenici. *The CSIS Strengthening of America Commission.* Washington, D.C.: Center for Strategic and International Studies, 1992.

Nye, Joseph S. *Peace in Parts: Integration and Conflict in Regional Organization.* Boston: Little, Brown, 1971.

O'Neill, Thomas P. *Man of the House.* New York: Random House, 1987.

Oldendick, R.W., and B.A. Bardes. "Mass and Elite Foreign Policy Opinions." *Public Opinion Quarterly* 46 (1982): 368–382.

Openkin, L. "I reka vremeni vspiat ne techet" [And a river of time doesn't flow backwards]. *Rossiiskaya Gazeta,* June 7, 1996, 3.

Oreglia, S. "L'opinione pubblica e la politica estera: UN analisi del pubblico francese in prospettiva comparata." Master's thesis, University of Siena, 1997.

Ostrom, Charles W., and Brian Job. "The President and the Political Use of Force." *American Political Science Review* 80 (1986): 541–566.

Ostrom, Charles W. Jr., and Robin F. Marra. "U.S. Defense Spending and the Soviet Estimate." *American Political Science Review* 80 (1986): 819–842.

Page, Benjamin I. *Choices and Echoes in Presidential Elections: Rational Man and Electoral Democracy.* Chicago: University of Chicago Press, 1978.

Page, Benjamin I. "Democratic Responsiveness? Untangling the Links Between Public Opinion and Policy." *PS: Political Science and Politics* (March 1994): 25–29.

Page, Benjamin I. *Who Deliberates? Mass Media in Modern Democracy.* Chicago: University of Chicago Press, 1996.

Page, Benjamin I., Paul W. Gronke, and Robert M. Rosenberg. "Constituency, Party, and Representation in Congress." *Public Opinion Quarterly* 48 (Winter 1984): 741–756.

Page, Benjamin I., and Robert Y. Shapiro. "Changes in Americans' Policy Preferences, 1935–1979." *Public Opinion Quarterly* 46 (Spring 1982): 24–42.

Page, Benjamin I., and Robert Y. Shapiro. "Effects of Public Opinion on Policy." *American Political Science Review* 77 (March 1983): 175–190.

Page, Benjamin I., and Robert Y. Shapiro. *The Rational Public: Fifty Years of Trends in Americans' Policy Preferences.* Chicago: University of Chicago Press, 1992.

Page, Benjamin I., and Robert Y. Shapiro. "Democratic Responsiveness? Untangling the Links Between Public Opinion and Policy." *PS: Political Science and Politics* 27 (1994): 25–28.

Paletz, David. *The Media in American Politics.* New York: Longman, 1999.

Panebianco, Angelo. *Guerrieri democratici. Le democrazie e la politica di potenza.* Bologna: Il Mulino, 1997.

Parenti, Michael. *Inventing Reality, the Politics of the Mass Media.* 2nd ed. New York: St. Martin's Press, 1993.

Parisi, Arturo, and Gianfranco Pasquino. "Relazioni partiti-elettori e tipi di voto." In *Continuit e mutamento elettorale in Italia,* edited by Arturo Parisi and Gianfranco Paquino. Bologna: Il Mulino, 1977.

Parker, Richard. "The Future of Global Television News: An Economic Perspective." *Political Communication* 12 (1995): 431–446.

Patterson, Thomas E. *Out of Order: How the Decline of Political Parties and the Growing Power of the News Media Undermine the American Way of Electing Presidents.* New York: Knopf, 1993.

Patterson, Thomas E., and Wolfgang Donsbach. "News Decisions: Journalists as Partisan Actors." *Political Communication* 13 (1996): 455–468.

Peresvet, Alexander. "Peacekeeper in the Helmet." *Ogonyok* No. 31 (July 1995).

Pew Research Center for the People and the Press. *America's Place in the World II.* Pew Research Center, 1997.

Pew Research Center for the People and the Press. "Public Appetite for Government Misjudged: WASHINGTON LEADERS WARY OF PUBLIC OPINION." URL: http://www.people-press.org/leadrpt.htm, April 17, 1998.

Pijpers, A.E. *Kanonnen en Boter. Beschouwingen over oorlog en integratie in Europa.* Amsterdam: Jan Mets, 1996.

Pinkerton, James P. "Environmanticism: The Poetry of Nature as Political Force." *Foreign Affairs* 76(3): 2–7.

Pizzorno, Alessandro. *I soggetti del pluralismo. Classi, partiti, sindacati.* Bologna: Il Mulino, 1980.

Pogrebin, Robin. "Foreign Coverage Less Prominent in News Magazines." *New York Times,* September 23, 1996, D2.

Political Science and Politics. "Symposium: Public Opinion, Institutions, and Policy Making." *PS: Political Science and Politics.* (March 1994): 9–38.

Powlick, Philip. "The American Foreign Policy Process and the Public." Ph.D. diss., University of Pittsburgh, 1990.

Powlick, Philip. "The Attitudinal Bases for Responsiveness to Public Opinion among American Foreign Policy Officials." *Journal of Conflict Resolution* 35 (December 1991): 611–641.

Powlick, Philip. "Public Opinion in the Foreign Policy Process: An Attitudinal and Institutional Comparison of the Reagan and Clinton Administrations." Paper presented at the 1995 annual meeting of the American Political Science Association, Washington, D.C., September 1–4, 1995.

Powlick, Philip. "The Sources of Public Opinion for American Foreign Policy Officials." *International Studies Quarterly* 39 (December 1995): 427–451.

Powlick, Philip J., and Andrew Z. Katz. "Defining the American Public Opinion/Foreign Policy Nexus." *Mershon International Studies Review* 42 (1998): 29–61.

Price, Vincent. *Public Opinion.* Newbury Park: Sage, 1992.

Pushkov, Alexei. "Russia and America: The Honeymoon's Over." Part Three. Moscow News, January 10, 1994.

Putnam, Robert D. "Diplomacy and Domestic Politics: The Logic of Two-Level Games." *International Organization* 42(3) (1988): 427–460.

Putnam, Robert D. "Italian Foreign Policy: The Emergent Consensus." In *Italy at the Polls: The Parliamentary Elections in 1976,* edited by H.R. Penniman. Washington, D.C.: American Enterprise Institute, 1977.

Putnam, Robert D. "Interdependence and the Italian Communists International Organization." 32(2) (1978): 301–349.

Putnam, Robert D. *Making Democracy Work.* Princeton: Princeton University Press, 1993.

Putnam, Robert D. 1995. "Bowling Alone." *The Journal of Democracy* (January 1997).

Rachlin, Allan. *News as Hegemonic Reality.* New York: Praeger, 1988.

Rattinger, Hans. "Public Attitudes to European Integration in Germany after Maastricht: Inventory and Typology." *Journal of Common Market Studies* 32(4) (December 1994).

Rattinger, H. "Causal Models of German Public Attitudes on Foreign Policy and Security after Unification." Paper presented at the annual meeting of the International Studies Association, Acapulco, Mexico, 1996.

Reif, Karl-Heinz, and Hermann Schmitt. "Nine Second-Order Elections: A Conceptual Framework for the Analysis Of European Elections Results." *European Journal of Political Research* 8 (1980): 3–4.

Richman, Alvin. "The Polls—Trends: American Support for International Involvement: General and Specific Components of Post–Cold War Changes." *Public Opinion Quarterly* 60 (Summer 1996): 305–321.

Rielly, John E., ed. *American Public Opinion and U.S. Foreign Policy 1995.* Chicago: Chicago Council on Foreign Relations, 1995.

Rielly, John E. ed. *American Public Opinion and U.S. Foreign Policy 1999.* Chicago: Chicago Council on Foreign Relations, 1999.

Riker, William H. *The Art of Political Manipulation.* New Haven: Yale University Press, 1986.

Risse-Kappen, Thomas. "Public Opinion, Domestic Structures, and Foreign Policy in Liberal Democracies." *World Politics* 43 (July 1991): 479–512.

Risse-Kappen, Thomas. "Masses and Leaders: Public Opinion, Domestic Structures, and Foreign Policy." In *The New Politics of American Foreign Policy,* edited by David A. Deese. New York: St. Martin's Press, 1994.

Rockman, Bert A. "Presidents, Opinion, and Institutional Leadership." In *The New Politics of American Foreign Policy,* edited by David A. Deese. New York: St. Martin's Press, 1994.

Rodin, Ivan. "Foreign Ministry Doesn't Like Three Factions' Draft." *Nezavisimaya Gazeta,* January 22, 1993, 2.

Rohde, David W. "Partisanship, Leadership and Congressional Assertiveness in Foreign and Defense Policy." In *The New Politics of Foreign Policy.* Edited by David A. Deese. New York: St. Martin's Press, 1994.

Rosenau, James N. *Turbulence in World Politics.* Princeton: Princeton University Press, 1990.

Rosenau, James N. *Along the Domestic-Foreign Frontier.* Cambridge: Cambridge University Press, 1997.

Rosenberg, Justin. "A Non-Realist Theory of Sovereignty?" In Anthony Giddens, *The Nation-State and Violence.* Berkeley: University of California Press, 1987.

Rubtsov, V. "Nakazanie svobodoi" (Punishment by Freedom). *Polis* 6 (1995).

Russell, Dick. "The Media and the Environment: Redefining National Security." *Extra* 1(8) (1988): 8–10.

Russett, Bruce. "Democracy, Public Opinion, and Nuclear Weapons." In *Behavior, Society, and Nuclear War*, Vol. 1, edited by Philip E. Tetlock, Jo L. Husbands, Robert Jervis, Paul C. Stern, and Charles Tilly. New York: Oxford University Press, 1989.

Russett, Bruce M. *Controlling the Sword: The Democratic Governance of National Security.* Cambridge: Harvard University Press, 1990.

Russett, Bruce. *Grasping the Democratic Peace. Principles for a Post–Cold War World.* Princeton: Princeton University Press, 1993.

Russett, Bruce, and Thomas W. Graham. "Public Opinion and National Security Policy: Relationships and Impacts." In *Handbook of War Studies*, edited by Manus Midlarsky. London: Allen and Unwin, 1989.

Russett, Bruce, Thomas Hartley, and Shoon Murray. "The End of the Cold War, Attitude Change, and the Politics of Defense Spending." *PS: Political Science and Politics* (March 1994): 17–21.

Sakwa, R. *Russian Politics and Society.* London: Routledge, 1993.

Sandholtz, Wayne, and John Zysman. "1992: Recasting the European Bargain." *World Politics* 42 (1989): 1–30.

Sarnow, Stanley. *Vietnam: A History.* Paperback, New York: Penguin, 1997.

Sartori, Giovanni. *Teoria dei partiti e caso italiano.* Milano: SugarCo., 1982.

Schattschneider, E.E. *The Semi-Sovereign People.* Hinsdale, Ill.: Dryden Press, 1960.

Schelling, Thomas C. *The Strategy of Conflict.* Cambridge: Harvard University Press, 1980.

Schennink, B., and L. Wecke. "Draagvlak voor de VN vredesoperaties en de vn na Sebrenica." Paper for the Conference Vijftig jaar vn-vredesoperaties, Nijmegen, October 23, 1995.

Schlesinger, Arthur Jr. "Back to the Womb? Isolationism's Renewed Threat." *Foreign Affairs* 74 (July/August 1995): 2–8.

Schmidt, Helmut. "Europa Muss Jetzt Handeln." *Die Zeit*, January 11, 1985, 1.

Schmitter, Philippe C. "A Revised Theory of Regional Integration." In *Regional Integration: Theory and Research*, edited by L.N. Lindberg and S.A. Scheingold. Cambridge: Harvard University Press, 1971.

Schneider, Jane, ed. *Italy's Southern Question.* Oxford: Berg, 1998.

Schneider, William. "Introduction: From Foreign Policy to Politics as Usual." In *The New Politics of American Foreign Policy*, edited by David A. Deese. New York: St. Martin's Press, 1994.

Schneider, William. "The New Isolationism." In *Eagle Adrift: American Foreign Policy at the End of the Century*, edited by Robert J. Lieber. New York: Longman, 1997.

Schumpeter, Joseph A. *Capitalism, Socialism, and Democracy.* New York: Harper, 1950.

Sciolino, Ellen. "Nunn Says He Wants Exit Strategy if U.S. Troops Are Sent to Bosnia." *New York Times*, September 2, 1993.

Sciolla, Loredana. *Italiani. Stereotipi di casa nostra.* Bologna: Il Mulino, 1997.

Sears, David O., Richard R. Lau, Tom R. Tyler, and Harris M. Allen Jr. "Self-Interest vs. Symbolic Politics in Policy Attitudes and Presidential Voting." *American Political Science Review* 74 (September 1980): 670–684.

Serfaty, Simon, ed. *The Media and Foreign Policy.* New York: St. Martin's, 1991.

Shami, Jacob, and Michael Shamir. "Pluralistic Ignorance Across Issues and Time: Information Cues and Biases." *Public Opinion Quarterly* 61 (1997): 227–260.

Shapiro, Robert Y. *The Dynamics of Public Opinion and Public Policy.* Ph.D. diss., University of Chicago, 1982.

Shapiro, Robert Y. and Benjamin I. Page. "Foreign Policy and the Rational Public." *Journal of Conflict Resolution* 32(3) (June 1988): 211–247.

Shapiro, Robert Y., and Benjamin I. Page. "Foreign Policy and Public." In *The New Politics of American Foreign Policy*, edited by David A. Deese. New York: St. Martin's Press, 1994.

Shapiro, Robert Y., and Lawrence R. Jacobs. "The Relationship Between Public Opinion and Public Policy: A Review." In *Political Behavior Annual*, Vol. 2, edited by Samuel Long. Boulder: Westview Press, 1989.

Shapiro, Robert Y., and Lawrence R. Jacobs. "Public Opinion and Policymaking." In *Public Opinion*, Carroll J. Glynn, Susan Herbst, Garrett J. O'Keefe, and Robert Y. Shapiro. Boulder: Westview Press, 1999.

Shaw, Carolyn M. "President Clinton's First Term: Matching Campaign Promises and Presidential Performance." *Congress and the Presidency* 25 (Spring 1998): 43–65.

Shaw, Martin. *Global Society and International Relations.* Cambridge: Polity, 1994.

Shaw, Martin. *Civil Society and Media in Global Crises.* London: Pinter, 1996.

Shaw, Martin. "The State of Globalization." *Review of International Political Economy* 4 (1997): 497–513.

Sherman, Peter. "Russian Policy toward the United States." In *Russian Foreign Policy Since 1990*, edited by Peter Sherman. Boulder: Westview Press, 1995.

Shiraev, Eric, and Deone Terrio. "Russian Decision-making Regarding Bosnia: Indifferent Public and Feuding Elites." In *International Public Opinion and the Bosnia Crisis*, edited by R. Sobel and E. Shiraev. Penn State University Press, forthcoming 2000.

Shiraev, Eric. "Attitudinal Changes During the Transition." In *The Russian Transformation*, edited by Betty Glad and Eric Shiraev. New York: St. Martin's Press, 1999.

Shiraev, Eric. "The Post Soviet Orientations toward the United States and the West." In *The Russian Transformation*, edited by Betty Glad and Eric Shiraev. New York: St. Martin's Press, 1999.

Shlapentokh, Vladimir. "The Changeable Soviet Image of America." In *Anti-Americanism: The Annals of the American Academy of Political and Social Science*, Vol. 497, edited by T. Thornton. Newbury Park: Sage Publications, 1988.

Sidorov, Sergei. "Russia's Position Is Clear: No NATO Air Strikes Against the Bosnian Serbs." *Krasnaya Zvezda*, February 19, 1994, 1.

Sigal, Leon. *Reporters and Officials.* Lexington, Mass.: D.C. Heath, 1973.

Sigelman, Lee, and Eric Shiraev. "The Rational Attacker in Russia?" Paper delivered at the annual meeting of the International Society of Political Psychology, Montreal, Canada, 1998.

Simes, Dimitri. "The Imperial Consensus: From Czars to Reformers, Why Russia Keeps Returning to the Dream of Empire." *Washington Post*, December 25, 1994.

Simis, K. *USSR: The Corrupt Society.* New York: Simon and Schuster, 1982.

Sinnott, Richard. "Bringing Public Opinion Back In." In *Public Opinion and Internationalized Governance*, edited by Oskar Niedermayer and Richard Sinnott. Oxford: Oxford University Press, 1995a.

Sinnott, Richard. "Policy, Subsidiarity and Legitimacy." In *Public Opinion and International-*

ized Governance, edited by Oskar Niedermayer and Richard Sinnott. Oxford: Oxford University Press, 1995b.

Sinnott, Richard. "European Public Opinion and the EU: The Knowledge Gap." Institut di Ciencies Politiques i Socials Working Papers, 105/96, Universita Autonoma, Barcelona, 1996.

Sinnott, Richard. "Knowledge and the Position of Attitudes to a European Common Foreign and Security Policy on the Real-to-Random Continuum." Paper presented at the annual meeting of the American Political Science Association, Boston, 1998.

Sinnott, Richard, and Oskar Niedermayer, eds. *Public Opinion and Internationalized Governance*. Oxford: Oxford University Press, 1995.

Smirnov, Andrei. "Paradoxes of Post-Soviet Perceptions." *Segodnya*, September 20, 1997, 1, 4.

Smith, Raymond. *Negotiating with the Soviets*. Bloomington: Indiana University Press, 1989.

Snyder, Glenn H. "Security Dilemma in Alliance Politics." *World Politics* 36(4) (1984): 461–495.

Sobel, Richard. "Public Opinion about United States Intervention in El Salvador and Nicaragua." *Public Opinion Quarterly* 53 (Spring 1989): 114–128.

Sobel, Richard. "Staying Power in the Mideast." *Dallas Morning News*, October 10, 1990.

Sobel, Richard. *Public Opinion in U.S. Foreign Policy: The Controversy over Contra Aid.* Lanham, Md.: Rowman and Littlefield, 1993.

Sobel, Richard. "What People Really Say About Bosnia." *New York Times*, November 22, 1995, A23.

Sobel, Richard. "Polling in Foreign Policy Crises." *Public Perspective* 7(2) (February 1996a).

Sobel, Richard. "U.S. and European Attitudes toward Intervention in the Former Yugoslavia: Mourir pour la Bosnie." In *The World and Yugoslavia's Wars*, edited by Richard Ullman. New York: Council on Foreign Relations, 1996b.

Sobel, Richard. "Portraying American Public Opinion toward the Bosnia Crisis." *Harvard Journal of Press/Politics* 3(2) (1998): 16–33.

Sobel, Richard, and Eric Shiraev, eds. *International Public Opinion and the Bosnia Crisis*. University Park: Pennsylvania State University Press, forthcoming.

Spanier, John. *American Foreign Policy Since World War II*. Washington, D.C: Congressional Quarterly Press, 1992.

Steel, Ronald. "The Domestic Core of Foreign Policy." In *The Domestic Sources of American Foreign Policy: Insights and Evidence*, edited by Eugene R. Wittkopf and James M. McCormick. Lanham, Md.: Rowman and Littlefield, 1999.

Stimson, James. *Public Opinion in America: Moods, Cycles, and Swings*. Boulder: Westview Press, 1991.

Stimson, James A., Michael B. MacKuen, and Robert S. Erikson. "Dynamic Representation." *American Political Science Review* 89 (September 1995): 543–565.

Strobel, Warren P. *Late-Breaking Foreign Policy: The News Media's Influence on Peace Operations*. Washington, D.C.: United States Institute of Peace Press, 1997.

Surikov, A. "Pruning of Missiles in Exchange for Handouts." *Pravda*, September 19, 1997, 4.

Szabo, Stephen. *West European Perceptions of Security Issues*. Washington, D.C.: Office of Research, United States Information Agency, 1988.

Talbott, Strobe. *Deadly Gambits*. New York: Knopf, 1984.

Taylor, Philip M. *War and the Media*. Manchester: Manchester University Press, 1992.

Taylor, Philip M. *Global Communications*, International Affairs and the Media since 1945. London: Routledge, 1997.

Thompson, John B. *The Media and Modernity: A Social Theory of the Media*. Cambridge: Polity, 1995.

Thornton, T., ed. *Anti-Americanism. The Annals of the American Academy of Political and Social Science*, Vol. 497. Newbury Park: Sage Publications, 1998.

Thornton, Thomas. "Preface." In *Anti-Americanism: The Annals of the American Academy of Political and Social Science*. Vol. 497. Edited by T. Thornton. Newbury Park: Sage Publications, 1988.

Times Mirror Center for the People and the Press. *America's Place in the World: An Investigation of the Attitudes of American Opinion Leaders and the American Public About International Affairs*. Times Mirror Center, 1993.

Trubowitz, Peter. *Defining the National Interest: Conflict and Change in American Foreign Policy*. Chicago: University of Chicago Press, 1998.

Umbach, F. "The Role and Influence of the Military Establishment in Russia's Foreign and Security Policies in the Yeltsin Era." *Journal of Slavic Military Studies* 3 (1996): 467–500.

USIA (United States Information Agency). *The New European Security Architecture*, Vol. 2. Washington, D.C.: Office of Research and Media Reaction, 1996.

USIA (United States Information Agency). "West European Publics Are Confident in NATO, but Unclear about Its Potential New Missions." *Opinion Analysis* M-75–78. Washington, D.C.: Office of Research and Media Reaction, 1998.

Utley, Garrick. "The Shrinking of Foreign News." *Foreign Affairs* 76 (March/April 1997): 2–10.

van der Meulen, J. "Publieke opinies over de krijgsmacht." *Maatschappij en Krijgsmacht* 17(1) (1995): 3–8.

van der Meulen, J. "Publieke opinie-kroniek (10)." *Maatschappij en Krijgsmacht* 20 (1998): 63–69.

van der Meulen, J., and M. de Konink. "Zero-Dead? Testing the Casualty Hypothesis: Dutch Public Opinion and Peacekeeping in Bosnia." Paper ECPR joint sessions of workshops, Warwick, 1998.

Vandenberg, Arthur H. Jr. *The Private Papers of Senator Vandenberg*. Boston: Houghton Mifflin, 1952.

Védrine, Hubert. *Les Mondes de François Mitterrand*. Paris: Fayard, 1996.

Vengroff, Richard, Erin Carriere, and Marc O'Reilly. "In the Service of Peace: Reflexive Multilateralism and the Canadian Experience in Bosnia." In *International Public Opinion and the Bosnia Crisis*, edited by R. Sobel and E. Shiraev. Penn State University Press, forthcoming 2000.

Volkan, Vamik. *The Need to Have Enemies and Allies*. New Jersey: Jason Aronson, 1988.

Volkov, Dmitry. "Russia's Attitude Toward NATO Cools." *Segodnya*, February 26, 1994, 1.

Voss, D. Stephen. "Beyond Racial Threat: Failure of an Old Hypothesis in the New South." *Journal of Politics* 58 (November 1996): 1156–1170.

Wallace, William. "European Defence Cooperation: The Re-opening Debate." *Survival* 26 (1984): 251–262.

Wallace, William, and Jan Zielonka. "Misunderstanding Europe." *Foreign Affairs* 77 (1998): 65–79.

Waltz, Kenneth N. *Theory of International Politics.* New York: Random House, 1979.

Waltz, Kenneth N. "The Emerging Structure of International Politics." *International Security* 18 (Fall 1993): 76.

Weir, Fred. Interview with the *Hindustan Times.* April 8, 1999, p. 1.

Weissberg, Robert. *Public Opinion and Popular Government.* Englewood Cliffs, N.J.: Prentice-Hall, 1976.

Weissberg, Robert. "Collective vs. Dyadic Representation in Congress." *American Political Science Review* 72 (1978): 535–547.

Wertman, Douglas A. "Italian Attitudes on Foreign Policy Issues: Are There Generational Differences?" In *The Successor Generation: International Perspectives of Postwar Europeans,* edited by Stephen F. Szabo. London: Butterworths, 1983.

Wheeler, Michael. *Lies, Damn Lies, and Statistics: The Manipulation of Public Opinion in America.* New York: Liberight, 1976.

White, S., R. Rose, and I. McAllister. *How Russia Votes.* Chatham: Chatham House Publishers, 1997.

Whitney, Craig R. "Europe Has Few Doubts on Bosnia Force." *New York Times,* December 5, 1992, 9.

Wittkopf, Eugene R. *Faces of Internationalism: Public Opinion and American Foreign Policy.* Durham, N.C.: Duke University Press, 1990.

Wittkopf, Eugene R. "Public Attitudes Toward American Foreign and National Security Policies since Vietnam." In *Debating National Security: The Public Dimension,* edited by Don Munton and Hans Rattinger. Frankfurt: Verlag Peter Lang, 1991.

Wittkopf, Eugene R. "What Americans Really Think About Foreign Policy." *Washington Quarterly* 19 (Summer 1996): 91–106.

Wittkopf, Eugene R., and James M. McCormick. "Congress, the President, and the End of the Cold War: Has Anything Changed?" *Journal of Conflict Resolution* 42 (August 1998): 440–466.

Wlezien, Christopher. "The Public as Thermostat: Dynamics of Preferences for Spending." *American Journal of Political Science* 39 (November 1995): 981–1000.

Wlezien, Christopher. "Dynamics of Representation: The Case of U.S. Spending on Defence." *British Journal of Political Science* 26 (1996): 81–103.

Wood, David, and Birol Yesilada. *The Emerging European Union.* White Plains: Longman, 1996.

Wright, Gerald C. "Contextual Models of Electoral Behavior: The Southern Wallace Vote." *American Political Science Review* 71 (June 1977): 497–508.

Wybrow, Robert. "British Attitudes towards the Bosnian Situation." In *International Public Opinion and the Bosnia Crisis,* edited by R. Sobel and E. Shiraev. Penn State University Press, forthcoming 2000.

Wyman, M. *Public Opinion in Postcommunist Russia.* London: Macmillan Press, 1997.

Yankelovich, Daniel, and I.M. Destler, eds. *Beyond the Beltway: Engaging the Public in U.S. Foreign Policy.* New York: Norton, 1994.

Yankelovich, Daniel, and John Immerwahr. "The Rules of Public Engagement." In *Beyond the Beltway: Engaging the Public in U.S. Foreign Policy,* edited by Daniel Yankelovich and I.M. Destler. New York: Norton, 1994.

Yemma, John. "On Past, Future: No Shortage of Surprises for the Scholars." *Boston Globe,* April 11, 1999, A24.

Yeric, Jerry, and John Todd. *Public Opinion: The Visible Politics*. Itasca, Ill.: F.E. Peacock Publishers, 1996.

Yushin, Maxim. "Moskva Zovet k Sderzhannosti" [Moscow is calling for a restraint]. *Izvestia*, February 8, 1994, 1, 3.

Zaller, John R. *The Nature and Origins of Mass Opinion*. Cambridge: Cambridge University Press, 1992.

Zaller, John. "Strategic Politicians, Public Opinion, and the Gulf War." In *Taken by Storm: The News Media, U.S. Foreign Policy, and the Gulf War*, edited by Lance Bennett and David Paletz. Chicago: University of Chicago Press, 1994.

Zaller, John, and Dennis Chiu. "Government's Little Helpers: U.S. Press Coverage of Foreign Policy Crises, 1945–1991." *Political Communication* 13 (1996): 385–405.

Zaller, John. *A Theory of Media Politics: How the Interests of Politicians, Journalists, and Citizens Shape the News*. University of Chicago Press, forthcoming.

Zhirinovsky, Vladimir. Ostankino radio Mayak (Moscow), June 16, 1996.

Zubok, Vlad, and Konstantinne Pleshakov. *Inside The Kremlin's Cold War*. Cambridge: Harvard University Press, 1996.

Zyuganov, G. "Interview." *Russia TV channel*, Moscow, May 17, 1996.

Index

About the Editors and Contributors

Bruce Chadwick is a recent Ph.D. graduate of Columbia University.

Dennis Chiu, a graduate of UCLA and Santa Clara University School of Law, is an attorney with Murphy, Pearson, Bradley, and Feeney in San Jose, California, specializing in civil litigation and political law.

Richard C. Eichenberg is associate professor of political science and former director of the International Relations Program at Tufts University. He has published numerous articles and chapters on public opinion, foreign policy, and European integration and is the author of *Public Opinion and National Security in Western Europe* (1989).

Robert M. Entman is a professor and heads the department of communication at North Carolina State University. His most recent books are *The Black Image in the White Mind* (2000, with Andrew Rojecki) and *Mediated Politics: Communications in the Future Democracy* (2000, edited with W. Lance Bennett).

Philip Everts is director of the Institute for International Studies, Leiden University. He serves in the government's Advisory Council on International Questions. His latest book is *Laat dat maar aans ons over! Democratie, buitenlandse politick en vrede [Leave it to us! Democracy, foreign policy, and peace]* (1996).

Ronald Hinckley, Ph.D., is president of Research/Strategy/ Management, Inc., and former director of the Office of Research, United States Information Agency. He is the author of *People, Polls, and Policymakers: American Public Opinion and National Security* (1992), as well as numerous chapters and articles on public opinion.

Ole R. Holsti is the George V. Allen Professor of Political Science at Duke University. In 1999 he received the Lifetime Achievement Award from the American Political Science Association. He is the author of *Public Opinion and American Foreign Policy* (1996).

Natasha Hritzuk is a recent Ph.D. graduate of Columbia University.

Pierangelo Isernia is associate professor of political science at the University of Siena. His main research interests are public opinion and foreign policy in comparative perspective, international relations, and political methodology.

Lawrence R. Jacobs is professor of political science at the University of Minnesota. He is the author of *The Health of Nations* (1993) and *Politicians Don't Pander: Political Manipulation and the Loss of Democratic Responsiveness* (2000, with Robert Shapiro).

Steven Kull, a political psychologist, is director of the Program on International Policy Attitudes, a joint program of the Center on Policy Attitudes and the Center for International Security Studies at the University of Maryland. He is the author of *Misreading the Public: The Myth of a New Isolationism* (1999, with I. M. Destler).

Natalie La Balme is a research fellow at the Fondation pour la Recherche Stratégique in Paris and a lecturer in political science at the Institut d'Etudes Politiques de Paris.

Brigitte L. Nacos is adjunct associate professor of political science at Columbia University and serves as U.S. correspondent for several publications in Germany. She is the author of *Terrorism and the Media* (1996) and *From Bonn to Berlin: German Politics in Transition* (1998, with Lewis J. Edinger).

Benjamin I. Page is the Gordon Scott Fulcher Professor of Decision Making at Northwestern University. He has authored a number of books and articles on American politics, including *Who Deliberates? Mass Media in Modern Democracy* (1996) and *The Rational Public: Fifty Years of Trends in Americans' Policy Preferences* (1992, with Robert Shapiro).

Clay Ramsay is research director of the Center on Policy Attitudes in Washington D.C.

Robert Y. Shapiro is professor of political science at Columbia University and is the author of *The Rational Public: Fifty Years of Trends in Americans' Policy Preferences* (1992, with Benjamin Page) and *Politicians Don't Pander: Political Manipulation and the Loss of Democratic Responsiveness* (2000, with Lawrence Jacobs).

Martin Shaw is professor of international relations and politics and the director of the graduate program in contemporary war and peace studies at the University of Sussex. A sociologist, his most recent book is *Civil Society and Media in Global Crises: Representing Distant Violence* (1996).

Eric Shiraev is research associate at the Institute for European, Russian, and Eurasian Studies at George Washington University. He is coeditor of *The Russian Transformation* (1999) and *Russian Anti-Americanism* (2000).

Richard Sinnott is associate professor of politics at University College Dublin, National University of Ireland. He is the author of *Irish Voters Decide: Voting Behaviour in Elections and Referendums since 1918* (1995) and *People and Parliament in the European Union: Participation, Democracy, and Legitimacy* (1998, with Jean Blondel and Palle Svensson).

Richard Sobel is a lecturer in government at Harvard University and a senior research associate at the Roper Center for Public Opinion Research at the University of Connecticut. He is the editor of *Public Opinion in U.S. Foreign Policy: The Controversy over Contra Aid* (1993) and the author of *Public Opinion in American Foreign Policy: From Vietnam to the Nineties* (forthcoming).

Eugene R. Wittkopf is the R. Downs Poindexter Distinguished Professor of Political Science at Louisiana State University. He is the author of *Faces of Internationalism: Public Opinion and American Foreign Policy* (1990) and the coauthor of *American Foreign Policy: Pattern and Process*, 5th ed. (1996, with Charles W. Kegley, Jr.).

John Zaller is professor of political science at UCLA. His fields of research are public opinion, elections, and the mass media.

Vlad Zubok is a research fellow at the National Security Archives in Washington, D.C. He is the author of *Inside the Kremlin's Cold War* (1996).